Battered WOMEN

A PSYCHOSOCIOLOGICAL STUDY OF DOMESTIC VIOLENCE

Battered WOMEN

A PSYCHOSOCIOLOGICAL STUDY OF DOMESTIC VIOLENCE

EDITED BY

MARIA ROY

Founder and Executive Director of
ABUSED WOMEN'S AID IN CRISIS, INC.

VNR VAN NOSTRAND REINHOLD COMPANY

NEW YORK   CINCINNATI   ATLANTA   DALLAS   SAN FRANCISCO
LONDON   TORONTO   MELBOURNE

Van Nostrand Reinhold Company Regional Offices:
New York Cincinnati Atlanta Dallas San Francisco

Van Nostrand Reinhold Company International Offices:
London Toronto Melbourne

Library of Congress Catalog Card Number: 77-8697
ISBN: 0-442-27201-4

Manufactured in the United States of America

Published by Van Nostrand Reinhold Company
450 West 33rd Street, New York, N.Y. 10001

Published simultaneously in Canada by Van Nostrand Reinhold Ltd.

15 14 13 12 11 10 9 8 7 6 5 4 3 2 1

Library of Congress Cataloging in Publication Data
Main entry under title:

Battered women.

   Includes index.
   1. Wife beating—Addresses, essays, lectures.
I. Roy, Maria.
HV6626.B35   362.8'2   77-8697
ISBN 0-442-27201-4

To my father, who was the gentlest of men.
To my husband, who is the gentlest of men.
To a future world with true love and respect between men,
women, and their offspring.

No lions rage against the lioness:
The tiger to the tigress is not fierce:
No eagles do their fellow birds oppress:
The hawk does not the hawk with talons
pierce:
   All couples live in love by nature's law,
Why should not man and wife do this and more?

HEALE, WILLIAM, 1609

William Heale (1581?–1627), English clergyman, published "An Apologie for Women, or An Opposition to Mr. Dr. G. his assertion, who held in the Act at Oxforde Anno 1608 that it was lawfull for husbands to beat their wives," in 1609. Selected passages from Heale's work, translated into modern English by Quandra Prettyman Stadler, are found at the beginning of each chapter. She is an Associate in English at Barnard College in New York. Her most recent publication was *Out of Our Lives; A Selection of Contemporary Black Fiction.*

Preface

The problem of battered women is not a new one. What is new is that it is just beginning to be recognized as an important social problem. Brutal husbands exist at many levels of society; they are not confined to the poor or working class. Rather, they are usually supporting their families, their wives financially dependent on them. According to a recent Harris Poll, 20% of all Americans approve of hitting a spouse on appropriate occasions; but among the college educated, this percentage rises to 25%. There are no simple answers to complex questions about causes and solutions. Why does a man become violent, harming, and in some instances, murdering a person once loved by him? What makes a woman stay in the situation for years? What is the correlation between wife beating and crime in the streets? The answers are intricate.

The primary intent of this book is to explore the many aspects of the problem, and to demonstrate that a broader understanding of the dynamics involved must be achieved before practical and long lasting solutions can be employed. In order to accomplish this, I have included original articles, and some previously published material, written by experts in the fields of psychiatry, psychology, neurology, sociology, law enforcement, arbitration, legislation, and service programming. Each contribution represents a very specialized point of view. No one claims to have all the answers. The book provides an all-encompassing perspective that includes historical, present day, and future implications. Endeavoring to understand the past and its effects on the present may help to prevent wifebeating in the future. Research and direct services for battered women are limited at the present time. For this reason, there is a paucity of statistics on the subject, which explains why many of the authors must rely on the same sources. Hopefully, this book will inspire more research and encourage new service programs. The term "wifebeating" as it is referred to in this book, is extended to include all those women assuming the role of wife in household relationships. The women need not be legally married.

In addition, this book demonstrates that wifebeating is a phenomenon that is cyclic—that is passed on from one generation to another and could be prevented through a gestalt approach representing societal, educational, legislative, and programmatic changes and improvements. Furthermore, this book ascertains that in a violent society, all members are capable of violence against one another; men can injure women and children; women can harm children. In a society where violence is condoned and victims are blamed, accused of provocation, all members tolerating the violence are potential perpetrators. Since men are usually taller, heavier, and stronger than women, they can do the most harm. Both men and women must admit that men, women, and children learn that physical aggression can be a very useful tool, and that given the right set of circumstances, everyone can be violent.

Finally, and most importantly, the book stands as a documentation of the problem—proof that must somehow be translated into actual services for the families involved. City, state, and federal government; organized religion; and the media must all be held accountable and must respond to the problem with new programs, new laws, new interpretations of the marriage contract, and new and responsible television and radio programming. Violence as a way of life that begins in the home and extends to the streets, affects all of us. Let us begin to reduce the violence around us by emphasizing that wifebeating is its root cause—and must be eradicated.

MARIA ROY

But oh, unmanlike men, and stain of your sex! Is this a point of your manhood, or any ornament of your valor, to busy yourselves for the disgrace of women, whom nature hath disarmed of corporal strength, and education disabled of mental courage for revenge? Is this the thankful tribute you repay into the author of your being? Is this the sweet embracement you bestow upon the paps that give you suck? Is this the grateful allowance you afford them for their sorrow and pains at your birth, for their care and diligence in your youth, for their love and carefulness throughout your life? All such courtesies (me seems) should not be so ungratefully forgotten, much less injuriously remembered. But why talk I with these men of gratitude the greatest of virtues, who never were acquainted with any virtue at all? And therefore had it been the highest of women's misfortune, to have been traduced by this infamous crew, they might easily have smiled it out counting no dishonor to be evil-spoken of by them who never learned to speak well of any. But now this bad cause hath got better patron; especially when in the university, in open debate in public disputation their names are called into question, their capacity throught unfit for learning, themselves adjudged worthy of blows. To let pass the rest; what more strange and prodigious paradox? What opinion more unnatural and uncivil than this of theirs, <u>That it is lawful for a husband to beat his wife?</u>

Most impure heart which did first conceive, and more that barbarous tongue, which did afterward bring forth such a monster of opinion. Had I but one word to speak (save only my orisons) but one only line to write, I would both speak and write them in defiance thereof.

HEALE, WILLIAM, 1609

Acknowledgments

This book is an outgrowth of my work as founder and director of Abused Women's Aid in Crisis, Inc. (AWAIC), an organization offering help to battered women since 1975. Establishing this organization could not have been possible without the cooperation of Joanne Milano, administrative director of the Cardinal Spellman Headstart Center in New York City. Without her genuine concern for battered women, the first New York State conference on the subject and the initial groundwork for the formation of AWAIC could never have been accomplished. Her continuing involvement and moral support are most cherished.

Carolyn Chrisman, AWAIC's Training Director and my dear friend and colleague, who has continued to work selflessly and with unending tenacity even under the most trying conditions, has contributed greatly to this effort. I am indebted to her for her help in conducting and recording many of the interviews for the survey reported in Chapter 2 of this book.

Nancy Castleman, an exemplary board member, has contributed invaluable advice and technical assistance for the AWAIC project. I am indebted to her.

Special thanks to Miriam Friedlander of the New York City Council for making the city government work for battered women; to Councilman Robert Steingut for his help, advice, and support; and to Candice Butcher of New York City's Human Resources Administration for her efforts in developing the Henry Street/AWAIC pilot shelter program for battered women.

I am grateful to the Fund for the City of New York, the Ms. Foundation, The New York Foundation, the New York Community Trust, and The Eastman Foundation for their grants, which supported AWAIC during its genesis, and to Bertram Beck of The Henry Street Settlement for harboring our offices in borrowed space during a time of great financial need. In addition, I would like to thank Daytop Village in New York City for providing free meeting room space for AWAIC's monthly evening meetings. I would also like to thank The Joint Foundation Support for recommending three grants to AWAIC.

This book would not have been possible without the cooperation of the AWAIC staff, its volunteers, and its clients. Special thanks to Josephine Soucy and Anita Black, AWAIC volunteers, for their help with typing parts of the manuscript.

Finally, and with extra special thanks, I am truly indebted to my husband for his patience and his expertise in research and development. His hours of valuable work in helping to interpret the statistical data for Chapter 2 represent his true love and affection.

Contents

6. The Law and Law Enforcement / 137

7. Future Trends and Prevention / 193

Appendices / 299

Index / 331

1 An Historical Perspective

Indeed some ancient ages of barbarism (before either civility was fully embraced or Christianity firmly established) seemed to draw from nature the practice of some such tyranny. Africanus reports of the Scythians, Tacitus of the Germans, Gellius of the Romans, Caesar of the French: with whom it was a received custom to dispose of their wives both life and liberty according to their pleasure. And hence it was that Mr. Doctor William Gager seemed to allege his history Publius Sepronius who divorced his wife for seeing a play. Of Ignatious Mecennius who beat his wife for being found in his cellar. Of Faunus who killed his wife for drinking a cup of wine. Fit proofs for confirmation of such a truth. Recount the time, it was in a paganistic and barbarous age. Observe the persons, they lived as mirrors of rigor and cruelty and are registered as monuments of murder and tyranny. Weigh the reasons that moved them thereunto; they will sooner call you into laughter than persuade you of imitation. Lastly judge of all and all is but as though a physician should go into an apothecary shop where is a variety of wholesome medicines, yet prescribes he some poison some drug to strength his sick patient.

HEALE, WILLIAM, 1609

WIFEBEATING: A RECURRING PHENOMENON THROUGHOUT HISTORY

Terry Davidson, Journalist and author of the forthcoming book: *Conjugal Crime—*
Hawthorne Books.

In 1869, the British philosopher John Stuart Mill wrote: "From the earliest twilight of human society, every woman . . . was found in a state of bondage to some man . . . How vast is the number of men, in any great country, who are little higher than brutes, and . . . this never prevents them from being able, through the laws of marriage, to obtain a victim. . . . The vilest malefactor has some wretched woman tied to him, against whom he can commit any atrocity except killing her—and even that he can do without too much danger of legal penalty."[1]

Five years later, an American state, one of the 13 original British colonies, ruled against wife-whipping. Its courts refused, however, to hear all complaints from battered wives. "If no permanent injury has been inflicted, nor malice nor dangerous violence shown by the husband, it is better to draw the curtain, shut out the public gaze, and leave the parties to forget and forgive."[2]

One hundred and one years after that, in 1975, a judge in a nearby state had a wifebeating case before him. A high-salaried trade association executive, living next door to a United States senator, had broken three bones in his wife's face. The husband had a history of wifebeating. Until her latest injuries, his wife had been afraid of the consequences of reporting him. A hearing had been scheduled, but instead, the Superior Court judge held an "informal settlement discussion" behind closed doors. Afterward, the judge told an inquiring reporter: "This is the best way to handle this type of situation. This is a family matter. They can settle this without airing a lot of dirty linen."[3]

One of the greatest blocks to dealing with the widespread problem of wifebeating is the tacit acceptance and covering up of the crime. Down through the ages, someone has always been "settling" the matter by drawing the curtain, shutting out the public gaze, and deciding not to air a lot of dirty linen. Wifebeating has a history which has been deliberately denied documentation. The law has been condoning violence to wives for centuries. Why this is so is a matter for conjecture and evolving theories.*

---

*The sociological researchers Suzanne K. Steinmetz and Murray A. Straus, in their preface to the excellent collection of articles on various forms of family violence up

A visit to a large library recently showed that there is no volume on the *history of wifebeating in the western world.* There was no category called "Wifebeating" in the card catalogue (nor, until very recently, in *Readers Guide*). Every librarian, anthropologist, and historian I turned to for reference help remarked on the "almost impossible job" I had ahead of me.

Other researchers have noticed this lack of literature on the subject of wifebeating. Steinmetz and Straus noted, ". . . The literature on violence and the family is nowhere well covered." In studying a recommended bibliography of over 400 items, they did not find suitable material on husband-wife violence.[6]

In Straus' introduction to Richard J. Gelles' book, *The Violent Home*, he characterized the lack of research as "selective inattention." In clinical studies of battered wives, "husband-wife violence is seen as a relatively rare type of behavior traceable to individual pathology. Until very recently, sociologists and psychologists . . . have almost completely ignored husband-wife violence."[7]

A University of Michigan Law School study found wifebeating statistics hidden under other designations in police and hospital emergency room records.[8]

Social caseworker Beverly Nichols, writing in the journal *Social Casework*, stated she "could find no articles in professional journals that dealt with abuse in marriage." And yet she also found that family agency files are filled with complaints of wifebeating.[9]

Despite the lack of documentation, there is a history. And when the history is uncovered, it comes as a culture shock. Some of the nations we most respect as representing the highest civilization, and some of the institutions we most revere as representing the highest spirituality come under indictment.

---

to 1974, addressed themselves to this point. They observed that after checking on about 20 likely novels, they found no material on "fights, slappings, or throwing things between husband and wife," although there were novels depicting husband-wife murder. They commented: "We think that says something about the extent to which husband-wife violence is unconsciously repressed by novelists.

"Even anthropologists seem to avoid material on husband-wife violence. As Paul Bohannan wrote to our colleague Amnon Orent: 'There are two reasons for this, it seems to me. One is that the middle-class anthropologists . . . share the middle-class horror of violence. . . . A second point [is that] . . . the people in colonial situations do not misbehave in the anthropologist's presence; they are even shy of telling about violent episodes for fear they will be considerd misbehaving."[4]

Two novels were later located by sociologist Richard J. Gelles: *The Godfather* and *Gone With The Wind*. In each book, a husband battered his pregnant wife—a phenomenon paralleling many actual case studies.[5]

When we consider our own nation's 200 years of growth and progress, it is a shock to read laws from the 1800s which regulated wifebeating: not criminalized it, but permitted it. Expected it. Accepted
it. Before 1871, a husband was able to go unpunished for "beating
[his wife] with a stick, pulling her hair, choking her, spitting in her
face, kicking her about the floor."[9] Marital violence was his "privilege." It was, in fact, an "ancient" privilege which would be long
honored. The first case decided in a United States court acknowledging the husband's right of "chastisement" occurred in 1824 in the
Supreme Court of Mississippi.[10] And the law, in this new democracy,
would not allow the battered wife to "vex or discredit or shame" the
family name by seeking legal protection or relief. Such was the status
of married women in the fledgling democracy, founded "under God."

The "privilege" of wifebeating is ancient indeed. In order to find a
time in history when wifebeaters did not enjoy having custom and
the law on their side, it is necessary to go back more than 2000 years
to pre-Christian times; even further than that, to pre-Biblical times.

In pre-Biblical times, the lands which became Europe had no gods.
The deity was female. Neolithic*Europe—as well as Syria and Libya—
had a homogeneous system of religious ideas, based on worship of
the many-titled Mother-goddess. The various creation myths revolved
around a goddess who was powerful but not unloving. The Mother-
deity was not interested in punishing her creations. Punishment and
eternal revenge, however, became themes of the later patriarchal
creation story told in the Bible.

When women were sovereign in religious matters—and indeed in
all matters—men were not battered by women. Women did not treat
men as though a battered-battering relationship was destined and
correct. There is no evidence that men were denied fields in which
they might act without female supervision. It is possible that they
"adopted many of the 'weaker-sex' characteristics hitherto thought
functionally peculiar to man," according to Robert Graves. Men
"could be trusted to hunt, fish, gather certain food, mind flocks and

---

*The Neolithic period, or New Stone Age, is the period in all human cultures when
people used stone, rather than metal tools. It began about 7000 B.C., and ended in
Mesopotamia and Egypt about 3000 B.C. when people began to use Bronze. However,
many other peoples, in remote parts of the earth, were still in the Stone Age when
Europeans began their voyages of exploration and discovery in the A.D. 1400s.
Most American Indians were among them.

herds, and help defend the tribal territory against intruders so long as they did not transgress matriarchal law."

At that time in history, men were not understood to have a role in procreation. Men were lovers. Men were for women's pleasure. They were not fathers. For procreation, it was believed that somehow ancestral spirits, carried by wind or river, resulted in the tribe's next generation, born of the women who had that magic ability to bear children. The men of the tribe "feared, adored and obeyed the matriarch; the hearth which she tended in a cave or hut being the earliest social centre, and motherhood their prize mystery."[11]

Once man realized the significance of his participation in coitus, however, man's religious status gradually changed as woman's status gradually became debased. As man became the Patriarch, society did an about-face toward a repressive mode of living.

Among the swings in attitudes as society descended from the matrist to patrist modes was a change from a politically democratic to a politically authoritarian way of life, according to G. Rattray Taylor.[12] From an attitude of trust in research, society shifted to skepticism and suspicion of research and inquiry. Society moved from permissive to restrictive attitudes toward sex. Values changed. Whereas human well-being had been considered more treasured than chastity, the opposite became the rule. From enjoying hedonism and welcoming pleasure, society came to prefer aceticism and a fear of pleasure; spontaneity and exhibition were replaced by inhibition and fearing spontaneity. Gender differences had been minimized by clothing; clothes came to be used to maximize sexual identity. A deep fear of incest gave way to a deep fear of homosexuality. Overall, general oppressiveness accompanied the change from Mother-religion to Father-religion.

Early Greek mythology tells of the changing relations between the procreating Queen and her lovers, and ends when the *Iliad** was composed and kings boasted, "We are far better than our fathers!" The period ends, according to Graves, with woman's "eclipse by an unlimited male monarchy."

---

*Homer's epic poem about war and its effect on love and family life was composed orally in a traditional style. Homer used materials handed down by generations of poet-singers. It was probably written in the 800s or 700s B.C. In contrast is a legend from another culture, already well-entrenched in patriarchy and woman's eclipse. The Adam and Eve story in *Genesis*, although finalized much later, was taken from various stories told as early as the ninth century.

In order to better understand the Biblical attitudes toward women—reflecting the harsh culture of the times—it is helpful to understand the myths which pre-dated the Old Testament. It is unsettling—and may shock many readers—to note that the creation story of the Bible was to become the rationale for the long history of legalized mistreatment of women. The Bible itself records it, and modern history has continued the atrocities in the name of the Bible.

Two creation myths—American Indian and Greek—from the Stone Age, provide an interesting contrast.

The Mission Indians of California have a non-violent, non-punitive story of The Origin of the World. It includes a separation story which is in no way the result of a curse:

The Earth, Tamaiawot, was a woman, the mother of all people. She was a person (atakh). Her feet pointed north, her head south. Her younger brother, the Sky, Dupash, was a man. All things and all people were born from Tamaiawot's belly. At first all the people traveled together, led by the eagle (aswut), going to the end of the world and then westward in a single long row. When they stopped to sleep, they all crowded together in a pile, without enough room. They discovered that some people did not like others, so they separated and formed different languages.[13]

A very early Greek creation myth portrays quite a different culture. Some of that culture had an influence on the storytellers who would give input to the Biblical creation story. In this case, the "Goddess of All Things" was a woman, Eurynome. She arose from Chaos and decided to begin a work of creation. Catching hold of the North Wind, she rubbed it between her hands, and it became the great serpent Ophion. She danced more and more wildly until the snake was "moved to couple with her." She laid the Universal Egg and bade the snake hatch it for her. "Out tumbled all things that exist."

The snake god, in this case, represents the father, not the Tempter. This father, however, is quite the opposite of the Old Testament concept of father. He's not very important. He has very little power. While the couple is at home on Mount Olympus, Ophion annoys Eurynome so much by his constant claiming to be the author of the Universe that she bruises "his head with her heel" and banishes him to the dark caves below the earth.[14]

Many centuries later, the Hebrew writers would fashion their own creation myth, which would also incorporate a snake as a significant figure. In their culture, the creator diety would become the stern Jehovah, who will also punish a snake, saying (Gen. 3:15): "And I will put enmity between thee and the woman, and between thy seed and her seed; it shall bruise thy head and thou shalt bruise his heel."

The woman, of course, was Eve. The stern deity also had a punishment in store for her (Gen. 3:16): "I will greatly multiply thy sorrow and thy conception: in sorrow thou shalt bring forth children; and thy desire shall be to thy husband, and he shall rule over thee."

And then the writers of this dialogue, as if to make certain that husbands would henceforth know the Fall of Man was the fault of the wife, added extra blame to the lines punishing Adam (Gen. 3:17): "Because thou hast harkened unto the voice of thy wife, and hast eaten of the tree, of which I commanded thee, saying, 'Thou shalt not eat of it': cursed is the ground for thy sake. . . ."

The Adam and Eve story, as we shall see, has been twisted into the rationalization for much of the Christian world's mistreatment of wives. It has aided and abetted the view of woman as inherently evil. It caused early Christian church authorities—in the few instances of documentation of wifebeating—to recommend marital violence. The first Christian emperor tortured his wife to death. To this day, while his name is celebrated, his deed is virtually unknown in Christian history. Although these eminent figures may have neglected to be scrupulous about honoring the Ten Commandments, they lived as if they were obeying a mandate from God in their belief in extreme physical abuse to wives.

Sociologists Steinmetz and Straus observed this unfortunate impact of the Adam and Eve story, stating, "The curse placed by God on all women when Eve sinned is only the earliest example in our culture of the sexually restrictive ethic, the placing of the 'blame' for sex on women, and the resulting negative definition of women—all of which tend to make women culturally legitimate objects of antagonism."[15]

The attitude that women are culturally legitimate objects of antagonism is clear throughout the Old Testament. In the book of Deuteronomy (25:11, 12), among the "divers laws and ordinances," there is one punishing with mutilation a wife if, in coming to the rescue of her husband in a fight with another man, she touches the opponent's genitals: "When men strive together one with another, and the wife of the one draweth near for to deliver her husband out of the hand of him that smiteth him, and putteth forth her hand, and taketh him by the secrets:

"Then thou shalt cut off her hand, thine eyes shall not pity her."

In another passage (22:13–21) there is a law regarding the disposal of a wife unable to prove her virginity: "Then they shall bring out the damsel to the door of her father's house, and the men of her city shall stone her with stones that she die . . . so shalt thou put evil away from among you."

Despite the life-and-death emphasis on virginity, there was a father in the book of Judges (Chapters 19 and 20) who casually offered up his virgin daughter to save "a certain Levite," a stranger who was enjoying his hospitality. And the guest offered his concubine/wife to a gang of sodomists who raped her all night until she died:

"Now as they were making their hearts merry, behold, the men of the city . . . beset the house round about and beat at the door . . . saying, Bring forth the man that came into thine house, that we may know him.

"And the . . . master of the house went out unto them and said . . . Nay, my brethren . . . do not so wickedly . . . Behold, here is my daughter a maiden, and his concubine; them I will bring out now, and humble ye them, and do with them what seemeth good unto you: but unto this man do not so vile a thing. . . .

"But the men would not . . . So the man took his concubine, and brought her forth unto them, and they knew her, and abused her all the night until morning: and when the day began to spring, they let her go.

"Then came the woman in the dawning of the day, and fell down at the door of the man's house where her lord was . . . and her hands were upon the threshold."

The Levite happened to stumble on her on his way out. All he said was, "Up, and let us be going." But she was dead.

"And the Levite, the husband of the woman that was slain" dismembered her body into twelve parts, sending them "into all the coasts of Israel." He wanted revenge. There is no mention of any feeling of compassion for the woman or punishment for the husband for pushing her to her torturous death, and there is no criticism of the host for offering his very young daughter the same fate.

And yet the Adam and Eve story—that rationale for so much

violent mistreatment of women thereafter—might easily have appeared in another version.

There are two versions in Genesis itself, as the scholar Vern Bullough[16] points out. The first mentioned* (Gen. 1:27, 28) has God creating the first couple together: "male and female created he them." It is generally agreed by Biblical scholars that this account was created later, following the Babylonian exile. However, as the Bible editors and compilers finalized the Book,the Adam and Eve version, though written in more primitive times, appears later, in Genesis 2:18.

The misogynist Apostle Paul—whose own philosophy would influence billions of husbands and Christian church leaders and lawmakers thereafter—made sure to emphasize that "the man is not of the woman; but the woman of the man. Neither was the man created for the woman; but the woman for the man" (I Cor. 11:8, 9).

The history of how the Old Testament was written would take volumes in itself. However, the influences on the Adam and Eve story can be traced briefly as follows:

The pastoral-nomadic tribes of the Children of Israel drew cultural influence from their stays in the more sophisticated Egyptian and Canaanite civilizations. The Babylonian captivity also left its influence. It was during this period, in the sixth century B.C., that the Old Testament, "based on Sumerian-Babylonian history and legend, was conceived and partially written, but not without great distortion and bowdlerizing." As the new religion came into being, the patriarchs dethroned the ancient Mother-goddess—whom they themselves had once worshiped, as did their neighboring nations—and enthroned "male strife in the form of Yahweh" (Jehovah).[18]

In the most ancient civilization of Sumeria, the Goddess of All Things is Tiamat, according to the oldest known creation myth, *Enuma Elish.* During their Babylonian captivity, the people of the Bible heard this legend and "decided to include this myth in their national literature, with the one difference that Tiamat must become

---

*The Bible itself was written over many centuries, from about 750 B.C. to 150 A.D. The Bible was not written consecutively. Genesis was not the first book written; it was put together about the fourth century B.C. from material from various sources. The Adam and Eve story contains elements dating back to the ninth century. It is called, by one Biblical scholar, "thoroughly primitive, naive, and anthropomorphic in its conceptions."[17]

a god and their own ancient goddess, Iahu, or Anat,* must be completely abolished."

On their return from Babylon, they began the bowdlerizing which would result in the new creation story: "They took the lines of the *Enuma Elish:* "In the beginning Tiamat brought forth the heaven and the earth . . . Tiamat, the mother of the gods, creator of all . . . , and worked them over in their patriarchal minds and came out with: 'In the beginning God created the heavens and the earth,' etc., a close paraphrase of the original . . ." (A further translation can be found in "The Enuma Elish," translated by William Muss-Arnolt, in *Assyrian and Babylonian Literature.* New York: Appleton, 1900, pp. 282–283.)

In trying to understand the Adam and Eve story, Robert Graves suggests that the reader must be aware that when its writers "decided to disown their own old Goddess-religion and adopt male monotheism, they were obliged to recast all the popular myths concerned with the Goddess—which was no light task."[20]

It may have been no light task, but the early Christian church authorities chose to accept the recasting and use it against women. Although Jesus Himself was egalitarian in His teachings, and Imperial Rome of His time practiced a certain amount of emancipation for women, the men around Jesus were "not, however, metropolitan Romans but provincials whose thinking reflected their own social milieux," and with it, the Old Testament attitudes about women. "Texts from the Roman law, many obsolete, were used to justify the Greco-Jewish bent for keeping women away from public functions (e.g., the priesthood) and subordinate to the male."[21]

St. Paul was known for such statements as ". . . Adam was not deceived, but the woman being deceived was in the transgression. . . ." (I Timothy 2). And ". . . Wives, submit yourselves unto your own husbands, as unto the Lord. For the husband is the head of the wife. . . ." (Ephesians 5)—a phrasing used in some marriage ceremonies today.

Paul's interpretations had an influence on St. Augustine (354–

---

*Anat or Anath: Canaanite goddess, sister of Baal. A somewhat vengeful and violent deity, but loyal to her brother Baal. She has some characteristics in common with the Greek goddess Artemis. The golden calf which Aaron's people worshiped while Moses was away receiving the Ten Commandments was a form of Baal worship (EX:32).[19]

430), who tried to explain, on *On the Holy Trinity*, that man was created in the image of God, not woman. However, she *together* with her husband might be considered so, although not separately.

The early Christian church, like all growing organizations, had many factions and splinter groups. In 325 A.D., a council was called (in what would be northwest Turkey today) to sort things out and to allow the strongest bishops of the Roman empire to condem as heresy those prevailing beliefs they did not approve. The surviving beliefs were then systematized into the *Nicene Creed*, which is still in use today. The council was presided over by Constantine I The Great, called by history the first Christian emperor of Rome, because he was baptized on his deathbed. According to theologian Paul Tillich, "Constantine in Byzantium was the Christ for the whole Christian church."[22]

A fact of Constantine's life which is seldom mentioned in history, however, is that he had his wife, Fausta, killed. "The *Catholic Encyclopedia* fails to mention the fact that Constantine scalded his young wife to death in a cauldron of water brought to a slow boil over a wood fire . . ." Instead it gives an explanation for Constantine's conversion: "In deciding for Cristianity, Constantine was no doubt influenced by reasons resulting from the impression made on every unprejudiced person by the moral force of Christianity."[23]

It had been through marriage to Fausta, Maximian's infant daughter, whom Constantine had married in 298 by proxy, that Constantine had secured the empire. He executed her when she became an adult, of no further use to him.

This precedent set the pattern for the next 14 centuries. Thirteen centuries later, the Abbé de Brantôme was to deplore the freedom with which "our Christian lords and princes murder their wives. To think that the pagans of old, who did not know Christ, were so gentle and kind to their wives; and that the majority of our lords should be so cruel to them."[24]

A thousand or so years after the gentle, egalitarian Jesus, the problem of the status of wives was resolved once and for all by Gratian, a jurist from Bologna, who wrote the first enduring systematization of church law, the *Decretum* (c. 1140). "Women should be subject to their men . . . The image of God is in man and it is one. Women were drawn from man, who has God's jurisdiction as if he were God's vicar . . . Therefore woman is not made in God's image . . . Adam was beguiled by Eve, not she by him. It is right that he whom woman led into wrongdoing should have her under his direction, so that he may not fail a second time through female levity."[25]

The Catholic church rulers ignored the fact that Jesus Himself did not teach some of the attitudes they were teaching. "The nature of the human hand in the formulation of Christian attitudes toward women is evident when it is emphasized that Jesus, who is regarded by Christians as the messiah, was never reported by any writer of the canonical Gospels as having derogatory attitudes toward women." There is no warning from Him about them, no intentional labeling of them as inferior. Many of His important followers were women—yet the Bible writers left them anonymous. "In His dealing with women, Jesus refused to be bound by the shackles of petty convention." Women emerge as persons, because they were treated by Jesus as persons. Before the women-hating/fearing authoritarian men took over, women "played an important part in the emerging Christian church. They were among the earliest and most faithful converts (Acts 16:14, 15; 17:4, 12, 34). They displayed charismatic gifts (Acts 21:9). They devoted themselves to charity (Acts 9:36–42), dispensed hospitality (Acts 12:12; 16:15, 40; Romans 16:2), labored in the tasks of evangelism (Romans 16:1, 3–4, 6, 12; Philippians 4:2–3), and imparted instruction in the faith (Acts 18:26).[26]

Nevertheless, Jesus' spirit of love gradually became re-interpreted as it was in the *Decretum*. The *Decretum*'s influence, in fact, grew to become a reference for Christianity's actually extolling wifebeating. "In a medieval theological manual, now in the British museum, under the word *castigare*," the historian G. G. Coulton reports, "the example for its use is given as 'a man must castigate his wife and beat her for her correction, for the Lord must punish his own as is written in Gratian's *Decretum*.' "[27]

With the established church apparently endorsing and encouraging wifebeating, the people of the Middle Ages had formed norms concerning the correctness of the victim/victimizer relationship. In the question of who-beats-whom, any instance of the wife being the beater (instead of the beaten) was an occasion for ribaldry.

I discovered an outstanding example of this attitude in a British journal reporting on a sixteenth century French custom. It seems that throughout the countryside, French communities would include a group of players, or carnival actors, whose ribaldries mocked any of the populace who had deviated from local norms. They were called charivaris. The entire community would turn out to poke fun at the butt of the extended practical joke. In a French marriage, the norm, where beating was concerned, was husband-beats-wife, not vice versa. A typical charivari stunt would be dressing up a "battered husband" and parading him through town, "ridden through festive crowds sitting backwards on an ass, or drawn on a cart, pulled with kitchen paraphernalia and punched and kicked in the genitals.[28,29]

If anyone were to suffer at the hands of man, it had to be woman. On at least one notable occasion, the norm caused history to be recast.

Gilles de Rais was a French nobleman and soldier who served with Joan of Arc. Later in life, however, he "indulged a fondness for small boys to extravagant proportions. He abducted, raped and murdered between forty and one hundred . . . peasant youths in his Brittany castle."[30] He was the original Bluebeard.

Bluebeard/de Rais confessed in 1440 that he was influenced by reading about Caligula, the Caesar who had "sported with children and took singular pleasure in martyring them."

The true story of Bluebeard has "metamorphosed from a terrifying account of a sex-murderer of small boys to a glorified fantasy of a devilish rake" who killed six wives for unlocking the door to the murder room. "It is almost as if the *truth* of Bluebeard's atrocities was too frightening to men to survive in the popular imagination. . . ."[30] But the familiar figure of the physically abused wife was the norm, and that is how Charles Perrault, the creator of the Mother Goose fairy tales, re-told the story in 1697.

In subsequent versions, Bluebeard became less and less of a villain. Jacques Offenbach's 1866 operetta, *Barbe-Bleue*, is a "rollicking burlesque, based only loosely on the Bluebeard theme." The theme appears in a minor 1901 work of Maeterlinck, *Ariane et Barbe-Bleue*. In Bela Bartok's 1911 opera, *Duke Bluebeard's Castle*, "the horrific elements of wife-murder and minimized, and Bluebeard is presented as a discontented, searching philosopher."[31]

In early history, the men who wrote down the events of their times, the "historians," often reflected their own biases or those of their patrons. Perhaps, then, it is not so astonishing how little of the history of wifebeating, particularly the churchly compliance with it, is known to today's clergymen and church scholars. When I contacted several of these authorities for suggested references, the response was a sincere doubt that the established church played the role it did.

Martin Luther, who started the Protestant Reformation in 1517, "has been called the most influential German who ever lived . . . Every aspect of Luther's life has been examined by both friends and foes."[32] There is no evidence that he supported the rampant anti-woman attitudes of the Middle Ages. In fact, in many ways he "looked upon the opposite sex as a kind of friendly rival and he lacked the fear of some of his clerical predecessors." He was opposed to the practice of ridiculing women in public. He taught that men, "no matter how antagonized they might be by the female, should always keep in mind that women are also God's creation." He even felt "called upon to upbraid the Archbishop of Mainz, who had been quoted as condemning the 'stinking, putrid, private parts of women.'"[33]

Yet even *he* casually admitted to a mild form of physical abuse to his wife, the former nun Katherine—and clearly without any sense of guilt. In fact, he was praising his happy marriage! "I am rich, God has given me my nun and three children; what care I if I am in debt, Katie pays the bills. . . . George Kark has taken a rich wife and sold his freedom. I am luckier, for when Katie gets saucy, she gets nothing but a box on the ear."[34]

One of the most colorful Frenchmen was Napoleon Bonaparte. His influence was vast because of the Civil Code he formalized (1800–1804). Although the laws in the Code were a breakthrough into freedom for many disenfranchised groups (such as homosexuals and Jews), they marked a demise of the rights and safety of women, especially married women.

A feminist pamphlet has referred to an old saying, attributed to Napoleon and his Code: "Women, like walnut trees, should be beaten every day." A check with the Cultural Division of the French Embassy for a verification and translation in context revealed that the quote was not to be found in the Code. It was thought, however, to have been an accepted saying of the time, reflecting Napoleon's attitudes about wives as fickle, defenseless, mindless beings, tending toward Eve-like evil.

The British Common Law influenced American law. The Napoleonic Civil Code had a very widespread influence. It is still the law of France—with certain modifications, including some recent statutes on the rights of women. It is "still the law of Belgium and Luxemburg," according to Vincent Cronin's 1972 biography of Napoleon; "It was the law of the Rhine district of Germany until the end of the nineteenth century; it has left an enduring mark on the civil laws of Holland,

Switzerland, Italy and Germany; it has been carried overseas to leave its imprint of political equality and *a strong family* on countries as diverse as Bolivia and Japan."[35] (Italics mine.)

Consider that phrase: "a strong family." It sounds so *good.* But it bodes very little good for a wife. A useful clue in reading history is an understanding of what "a strong family" actually implies. It implies legalized ownership and dominance of men over women, but it is seldom so boldly acknowledged in print.

Under the old aristocracy, wives had enjoyed a large measure of freedom and an influential place in society. The law gave them separate property rights. The French Revolution (1789–1799) had broadened their rights even more. When Napoleon came to power, he imposed his views that women must be legal minors their entire lives. They were "owned" by their fathers first, and later, by their husbands.

Napoleon is remembered for his declaration to the Council of State: "The husband must possess the absolute power and right to say to his wife: 'Madam, you shall not go out, you shall not go to the theatre, you shall not receive such and such a person; for the children you bear shall be mine.' "[36]

Napoleon wanted only three valid grounds for divorce: attempted murder, adultery, and impotence. Wifebeating was not a legal ground—unless it could be proved attempted murder, or the husband also wanted the divorce. Napoleon's *"strong family feeling* (italics mine) leads him to add that maltreatment, perversion, and adultery should be concealed beneath the formula of mutual desire," according to biographer Emil Ludwig. ". . . His social sense is so strong that he maintains it would be necessary to punish an adulterous woman by criminal procedure unless she were punished by being divorced."[37]

The little Emperor was very big on punishing women. The only time he legalized any sense of equality between husband and wife was when the husband was the wrongdoer in a crime against society. Take, for example, Napoleon's attitude on bankruptcy:

"Bankruptcies take away men's fortunes without destroying their honour; and that is what it is important to destroy," he declared. In order to humiliate the bankrupt man, "prison would do it, even if it were but for an hour. It was also desirable that in every case the woman should share the misfortune of her husband."[38]

Napoleon's reasoning for believing it was just that a wife share her husband's imprisonment is classic: ". . . For how can we forbid a woman to do so when she is convinced of her husband's innocence? Or is this conviction of hers to deprive her of her rights as a married woman; is she to lose the title of wife, and to become the man's concubine? Many men have become criminals owing to their wives. Are we to forbid those who have been the cause of the misfortune from sharing that misfortune?"

What gave this lawmaker his notions of right and wrong in marriage? Genesis again. When one of his councillors questioned him about the severity, he brushed it aside, saying, "Do you not know that the angel told Eve to obey her husband. . . ?"

In Britain, the situation was just as bad, but British women had a champion in the enlightenment philosopher John Stuart Mill (1806–1873). He petitioned Parliament on behalf of women's rights. He wrote a controversial essay which is still much quoted today. His *The Subjection of Women* caused much fury among the men of his time, but it may have been the first significant document to spark the raising of public consciousness about the plight of battered wives.

"From the very earliest twilight of human society, every woman . . . was found in a state of bondage to some man," he wrote. The marital bondage of his enlightened age was the "single relic of an old world of thought and practice. . . ." Mill argued eloquently that the trend of his times was toward freedom and away from old bondage—except in the customs and laws against women. "Human beings are no longer . . . chained down by an inexorable bond to the place they are born to, but are free to employ their faculties, and such favorable chances as offer, to achieve the lot which may appear to them most desirable." In Mill's eyes, therefore, the lack of rights for wives "stands out an isolated fact in modern social institutions."

He pleaded that, with the current laws on the books, husbands had the legal power, as well as the power of opinion and custom, to physically abuse wives, and wives had no recourse to law:

". . . Men are not required as a preliminary in marriage to prove that they are fit to be trusted with absolute power over another human being . . . The vilest malefactor has some wretched woman tied to him, against whom he can commit any atrocity except killing her—and even that he can do without too much danger of legal penalty.

"And how many thousands are there in every country, who, without being in a legal sense malefactors in any other respect, because in every other quarter their aggressions meet with resistance, indulge in the utmost habitual excesses of bodily violence towards the unhappy wife, who alone, at least of grown persons, can neither repel or escape from their brutality; and towards whom the excess of dependence inspires their mean and savage natures, not with a generous forbearance, and a point of honour to behave well to one whose lot in life is trusted entirely to their kindness, but on the contrary with a notion that the law has delivered her to them as their thing, to be used at their pleasure, and that they are not expected to practice the consideration towards her which is required from them towards everybody else."[39]

Mill's essay sparked the discussion and controversy he hoped it would. In 1874, a report showing statistics about the suffering of women and children was brought to the attention of Parliament. For a while it seemed as if some reform legislation might result, but nothing came of it.

In 1878, *The Contemporary Review* published a paper by an upper-class British woman, Frances Power Cobbe, who was happily married and wanted to help her less fortunate sisters. She reported on a section of Liverpool where husbands' brutality had become so oppressive that the area was referred to as the notorious "kicking district."

"There are also various degrees of wife-beating in the different localities," Cobbe wrote in "Wife Torture in England." In London it seldom "goes beyond a severe 'thrashing' with the fists—a sufficiently dreadful punishment, it is true, when inflicted by a strong man on a woman; but mild in comparison of the kickings and tramplings and 'purrings' with hob-nailed shoes and clogs . . . Nowhere is the ill-usage of woman so systematic as in Liverpool and so little hindered by the strong arm of the law; making the lot of a married woman whose locality is the 'kicking district' of Liverpool simply a duration of suffering and subjection to injury and savage treatment, far worse than that to which the wives of mere savages are used. . . . The condition of the women [might] be most accurately matched by that of the negroes on a Southern plantation before the war struck off their fetters."

Just as under the French Civil Code, a woman under British law was punished more severely than a man would be for the same offense. ". . . Not only is an offense against a wife condoned as of inferior guilt, but any offense of the wife against her husband is regarded as a sort of *Petty Treason*. . . .

"Should she be guilty of 'nagging' or 'scolding,' or of being a slattern, or of getting intoxicated, she finds usually a short shrift . . . and even humane persons talk of her offense as constituting if not a justification for her murder, yet an explanation of it. She is, in short, liable to capital punishment without judge and jury for transgressions which in the case of a man would never be punished at all, or be expiated by a fine of five shillings."[40]

This unequal treatment for husbands and wives had existed throughout history. The judicial inequity still survives today, in cases summarized by recent law journals.

One of the reasons nineteenth century British wives were dealt with so harshly by their husbands and by their legal system was the "rule of thumb." Included in the British Common Law was a section regulating wifebeating. The law was created as an example of compassionate reform when it modified the weapons a husband could legally use in "chastising" his wife. The old law had authorized a husband to "chastise his wife with any reasonable instrument." The new law stipulated that the reasonable instrument be only "a rod not thicker than his thumb." In other words, wifebeating was legal.

And what of the land of the free across the ocean? Could American wives look forward to emancipation from legalized wifebeating? In 1776, as John Adams was working on the drafting of the Declaration of Independence, Abagail Adams wrote her husband a plea that women might fare better in the newly created nation than they had in England: ". . . In the new code of laws I suppose it will be necessary for you to make, I desire you would remember the ladies and be more generous and favorable to them than your ancestors."

The man who would become the second president of the United States (1797–1801) refused. "Depend on it," John Adams replied, "we know better than to repeal our masculine systems."

American law was founded on British Common Law. Common Law reflects the customs of the people of a nation. The early British judges based their decisions on what the community seemed to feel was correct. Women had no voice in these matters. After a number of courts had made similar rulings, the first decision then would become the precedent, and what was once custom now became law.

Sir William Blackstone wrote the *Commentaries of the Laws of England* (1765–1769) which "had great influence in the American colonies, where it provided the colonists with their chief source of information about English law."[41]

Blackstone saw nothing unreasonable about the wifebeating law. In fact, he believed it to be quite moderate. He wrote, "For, as [the husband] is to answer for her misbehavior, the law thought it reasonable to intrust him with this power of chastisement, in the same moderation that a man is allowed to correct his apprentices or children . . ."[42]

With Blackstone as a guide, America's first states formed their wifebeating laws. In 1824, Mississippi held that some "moderate chastisement . . . would be allowed in order to enforce the salutory restraint of domestic discipline." The court further sought to protect the husband from his wife's attempts for justice: "Perhaps the husband should still be permitted to exercise the right to moderate chastisement, in cases of great emergency and to use salutary restraint in every case of misbehavior, without subjecting himself to vexatious prosecutions, resulting in the discredit and shame of all parties."[43]

In 1874, North Carolina withdrew the husband's "right to beat his wife—but at the same time exempted him from appearing in court in case he *did* beat his wife after all! "We may assume that the old doctrine that a husband had a right to whip his wife, provided he used a switch no bigger than his thumb, is not the law in North Carolina. Indeed, the courts have advanced from that barbarism until they have reached the position that the husband has no right to chastise his wife under any circumstances."

The court then added that it did not, however, intend to hear every case of wifebeating: "If no permanent injury has been inflicted, nor malice nor dangerous violence shown by the husband, it is better to draw the curtain, shut out the public gaze, and leave the parties to forget and forgive."[44]

In 1886, Pennsylvania also almost passed an anti-wifebeating bill. The proposed bill suggested making wifebeating punishable by 30 lashes to "any male person [who] shall wilfully beat, bruise or mutilate his wife."[45]

The proposed bill, however, did not pass.

Two states are on record as rescinding the "ancient privilege" of wifebeating in 1871. Both Alabama and Massachusetts agreed that the "privilege, ancient though it be, to beat her with a stick, to pull her hair, choke her, spit in her face, or kick her about the floor, or to inflict upon her like indignities is not now acknowledged by our law."[46]

Most states, however, did not rescind the old laws; they merely tended to ignore them in recent years. Sometimes. As Robert Calvert comments in the "Criminal and Civil Liability in Husband-Wife Assaults" section of the Steinmetz and Straus compilation, "There is no enlightened period in history that can be designated as the time the woman's right was elevated . . . Nevertheless, despite the ambiguity of the law on this matter, it seems as though the right of husbands to use physical punishment is no longer present. But husbands have lost this right by change in customary useage more than by legal change."[47]

Today, the law has ceased forbidding a wife to bring action against her violent husband. However, the law grants her much less protection than if that same violence had been inflicted on her by someone else. A 1971 law journal summarizes a California wifebeating law, for example: ". . . It would appear that the harm required is greater than simple assault but less than aggravated assault. Cases indicate that visible bruises and injuries must be present."[48]

Another law review found that some courts have "allowed the husband to defend on the ground that he was provoked by his wife. . . ." (That is the same complaint voiced in "Wife Torture in England," written in 1878 and noted above.)

Further, for a husband today to be "guilty of the battery of his wife something more than an unpermitted touching or even minor injury is required. One court has stated several times that either 'permanent injury' must have been inflicted or the husband's conduct must have been prompted by a 'malicious and wrongful spirit.'"[49] (The precedents date back to some of the early North Carolina decisions already here quoted.)

Is it possible that public consciousness might be raised, despite the ancient laws and the Biblical injunctions? Yes, there is reason for hope. The child abuse laws broke through similar barriers once the public became aware of the extent of the problem. And just recently, a major church body reviewed the traditional patriarchal, Biblical attitudes toward women. The churchmen looked at St. Paul's utterances in a new light.

An Episcopal newsletter reported that a commission of the Lutheran Bishops' Conference of Norway has resolved that women can no longer be asked "to be submissive" to their men. "The Apostle Paul's admonition merely reflected the mores of his time and . . . is not eternally binding for the church, the bishops declared. . . . With the advent of the women's liberation movement, the patriarchal social order is more and more being questioned by an ethical consciousness in accord with the Christian understanding of the value and the rights of all mankind. Today the Christian Church must realize this basic view by working towards woman's liberation to the best of its Christian understanding."[50]

REFERENCES

1. Mill, John Stuart, *The Subjection of Women* (1869). Introduction by Wendell Robert Carr. Cambridge, Mass.: M.I.T. Press, 1970.
2. *State* v. *Oliver*, 70 N.C. 60, 61., 1874 (Criminal Liability).
3. Peterson, Bill, "Battered Wife Syndrome: Shame, Fear Keep Most Women Silent," *Washington Post* (September 13, 1975).
4. Steinmetz, Suzanne K and Straus, Murray A. (eds.), *Violence in the Family*. Toronto: Dodd, Mead, and Co., 1974.
5. Gelles, Richard J., *The Violent Home: A Study of Physical Aggression Between Husbands and Wives*. Beverly Hills: Sage Publications, 1974.
6. Steinmetz and Straus, *Violence in the Family*.
7. Gelles, *Violent Home*.
8. Nichols, Beverly B., "The Abused Wife Problem," *Social Casework* **57**, *No. 1*: 27–32 (January 1976).
9. Eisenberg, Sue E. and Micklow, Patricia A., *The Assaulted Wife: "Catch 22" Revisited (An Exploratory Legal Study of Wifebeating in Michigan)*. Ann Arbor: University of Michigan Law School, copyright 1974, unpublished.
10. Ibid.
11. Graves, Robert, *The Greek Myths: 1*. Baltimore: Penguin, 1955.
12. Taylor, G. Rattray, *Sex in History*. New York: Vanguard Press, 1954.
13. Burrows, David J., Lapides, Frederick R., and Shawcross, John T. (eds.), *Myths and Motifs in Literature*. New York: The Free Press, 1973.
14. Graves, *Greek Myths*.
15. Steinmetz and Straus, *Violence in the Family*.
16. Bullough, Vern L., *The Subordinate Sex*. Urbana: University of Illinois Press, 1973.
17. Bates, Ernest Sutherland (ed.), *The Bible Designed to be Read as Living Literature*. New York: Touchstone (Simon & Schuster), 1936.
18. Davis, Elizabeth Gould, *The First Sex*. Baltimore: Penguin, 1973.
19. Bénet, William Rose (ed.), *The Reader's Encyclopedia*. New York: Thomas Y. Crowell, 1965.
20. Graves, Robert, *Adam's Rib*. New York: Yoseloff, 1958.
21. O'Faolain, Julia and Martines, Laura (eds.), *Not in God's Image*. New York: Harper & Row, 1973.

22. Tillich, Paul, *A History of Christian Thought* Carl E. Braaten (ed.). New York: Touchstone (Simon & Schuster), 1972.
23. Charles G. Hergerman (ed.), *Catholic Encyclopedia*, **IV**. New York: Appleton, 1912, pp. 295–301. In Davis, *First Sex*.
24. Pierre de Bourdeille, Abbé de Brantôme, *The Lives of Gallant Ladies*. London: Elek Books, 1961, p. 21. In Davis, *First Sex*.
25. *Corpus Iuris Canonici*, A. Friedberg (ed.), 2 vols., Leipzig, 1879–1881, Vol. I., Pt. II, C. 33, q. 5, c. 12, 13, 17, 18. in O'Faolain and Martines, *Not in God's Image*.
26. Bullough, *Subordinate Sex*.
27. G. G. Coulton (ed.), *Life in the Middle Ages* **III**. New York: Macmillan, 1910, p. 119. In Davis, *First Sex*.
*28. Thane, Pat, "Cruel Kicks," *New Society:* 627, London (September 18, 1975).
*29. Davis, Natalie Zemon, "The Reasons of Misrule: Youth Groups and Charivaris in Sixteenth Century France," *Past and Present*, Oxford, England, (February 1971).
30. Brownmiller, Susan, *Against Our Will: Men, Women and Rape*. New York: Simon & Schuster, 1975.
31. Bénet, William Rose, *Reader's Encyclopedia*.
32. Zeleny, Robert C. (ed.), *World Book Encyclopedia*. Chicago: Field Enterprises Educational Corp., 1972.
33. Bullough, *Subordinate Sex*.
34. Quoted in *Sex and the Church*, Oscar E. Feucht and other members of the Family Life Committee of the Lutheran Church (eds.). St Louis: Concordia Publishing House, 1961, p. 84. In Bullough, *Subordinate Sex*.
35. Cronin, Vincent, *Napoleon Bonaparte, An Intimate Biography*. New York: Morrow, 1972.
36. Herold, Christopher, *The Age of Napoleon*. New York: American Heritage Publishing Co., 1963.
37. Ludwig, Emil, *Napoleon*. New York: Boni & Liveright, 1926.
38. Ward, A. W. (ed.), *The Cambridge Modern History* **X**, "Napoleon." New York: The Macmillan Co., 1906.
39. Mill, *Subjection of Women*.
*40. Cobbe, Frances Power, "Wife Torture in England," *The Contemporary Review*, London (1878).
41. Zeleny, *World Book Encyclopedia*.
42. Blackstone, Sir William, I, *Commentaries on the Laws of England*, 444, 1765.
43. *Bradley* v. *State*, Walker, 156, Miss.
44. *State* v. *Oliver*.
45. Adams, C., *Wife Beating as a Crime and Its Relation to Taxation*. Philadelphia: Philadelphia Social Science Association, 1886, pp. 3, 17.
46. *Fulgham* v. *State*, 46 Ala. 143, 1871; *Commonwealth* v. *McAfee*, 108 Mass. 458, 1871.

---

*I am indebted to two British correspondents, Paul Barker, editor of *New Society*, and social historian Pat Thane, for References 28, 29, and 40.

47. Steinmetz and Straus, *Violence in the Family.*
48. Truninger, Elizabeth, "Martial Violence: The Legal Solutions," *The Hastings Law Journal* (November 1971).
49. "Rape and Battery Between Husband and Wife," *Stanford Law Review* (July 1954).
50. "Norway's Bishops Say Women Are Equal," *Trinity Parish Newsletter* (74 Trinity Place, New York 10006), (March–April 1976).

2 A Research Project Probing A Cross-Section of Battered Women

First, if a husband may lawfully beat his wife, then is the wife legally bound to endure his beating. . . . In answer whereof that shift will not serve, to say the law authorizes a man to beat his wife but lightly, and not in such sort as may cause her departure. This is too coarse a salve for such a sore. For a little beating to some women is more than much to others; and therefore in them it will breed the same or worse effects and how little soever it be they are not bound to take it.

HEALE, WILLIAM, 1609

A CURRENT SURVEY OF 150 CASES*

Maria Roy, Founder and Executive Director of Abused Women's Aid In Crisis, Inc.

The following survey of women/victims represents a sample of 150 American women who were strongly motivated to find solutions to their problems, who had endeavored to extricate themselves from their violent homes numerous times, and who were unable to find viable alternatives to their home life situations. This study provides an analysis of the dynamics of the observed violent relationships, the victims' probing attempts to secure help, the nucleating and maintaining factors, and cross-correlations of the various components of the problem. Wifebeating has no simple solutions or single cause. This premise serves as the foundation for the design of the study which demonstrates that no one factor in isolation creates and nurtures wifebeating; rather, several factors occurring together in combination make its growth and maintenance inevitable.

Methodology

Data on the following study of wife abuse (including women in common-law type household relationships) were derived within a period of one year from the AWAIC (Abused Women's Aid in Crisis)[1] Hotline intake questionnaire followed by on-site, in-depth interviews with the women calling the organization for help and information. The data, 150 cases selected at random from among 1000 of AWAIC's case samples probes the personal histories of each woman; her individual interaction with public and private outside agencies, i.e., law enforcement, court system, social services, marriage counselors, and family and friends; the effects of external variables such as drugs and alcohol; and the histories of parental violence which serve as contributing and maintaining factors in the growth and perpetuation of a violent home situation.

Because of the exploratory nature of the project and the small sample size (somewhat biased), this study's findings must be seen as somewhat tentative. Yet the following factors seem the key to understanding wifebeating.

a. Type of relationship

---

*I am grateful to Pradip K. Roy for his help with interpreting statistical data and with helping to write parts of this article. I am also grateful to Nancy Castleman for her comments and suggestions.

b. Duration of relationship
c. Type of violence
d. Onset of violence
e. Frequency of violence
f. History of parental violence
g. Effects of violence on the children
h. Help sought from outside sources
    1. police
    2. Family Court
    3. family or friends
    4. marriage counselor
    5. protective shelters
i. Drug addiction and/or alcohol related problems

In addition, in spite of the small, biased sample size, the study probes a population reflecting a cross-section of socio-economic groups (lower, middle, and upper); length of relationships (ranging from a few days to 25 years or more); and parental histories ranging from unremarkable to those presenting child abuse and neglect. Other factors investigated indicate the frequency of beating (from once in three months to twice daily); the time of onset (from before marriage to after 20 years of marriage with no previous history of violence); and the degree of violence (from verbal abuse to assault with a deadly weapon).

Not all of the respondents reported every aspect of the violent confrontations, and some completely or partially avoided answering queries of their personal histories (in part, because not all of the 150 cases could be followed in depth). Thus, there are varying numbers reporting information about different aspects of the violent home life. However, most of the correlations of the factors stated above and their cross correlations are based on $N = 150$.

Study Part I: Exposition
Type and Duration of Relationship

Figure 1 indicates quite clearly that the most common type of relationship is the legal marriage. Figure 2 indicates the duration of the relationships; according to a fine scale interpretation, the first peak occurs between 2.5 years and 5.0 years of cohabitation. (The second peak occurs between 7.5 years and 15 years, then decreases gradually after 15 years.) A broad scale reading indicates that all degrees of abuse occur most often between 2.5 and 15 years of cohabitation.

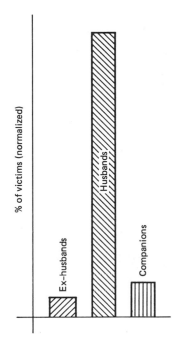

Fig. 1. Type of relationship.

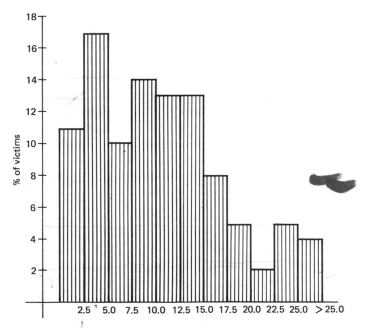

Fig. 2. Time (duration) of relationship (in number of years).

Types of Violence

The types of violence (Fig. 3) described include the following: SA/sexual abuse (forcible rape); VA/verbal abuse (obscenities and personal attacks on character); PA/physical abuse (black eyes, biting, broken ribs, choking); and PAW/physical abuse with a weapon (knife, gun, baseball bat).

Onset of Violence

Onset of violence (Fig. 4) is characterized in the histogram below into four broad time segments:

1. Immediate: occurring between 0–1/10 the duration of the relationship
2. Early: occurring between 1/10–1/3 the duration of the relationship
3. Middle: occurring between 1/3–2/3 the duration of the relationship
4. Later: occurring between 2/3 of the relationship and the time when the interview was conducted

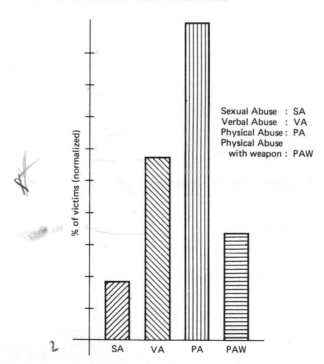

Fig. 3. Types of violence.

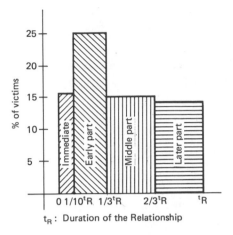

t_R : Duration of the Relationship

Fig. 4. Onset of violence.

An important, explanatory cross-correlation is that most of the population in the "immediate" and "early" categories are those whose relationship is under seven years duration. Most of the population in the "later" category reported relationships enduring for thirteen years or more.

Frequency of Violence

The frequency of violence (Fig. 5) correlation describes frequency on a scale in ascending order from LO/less often (violent episodes occurring less than once a month) to VVO/very very often (occur-

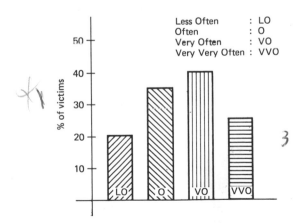

Fig. 5. Frequency of violence.

ring between 1–3 times per *week*). An important cross correlation is that VVO frequently includes physical abuse with a weapon and sexual abuse (forcible rape). Of those couples living together and not legally married, a very high percentage fall into the sexual abuse and physical abuse with a weapon categories.

Parental Violence

Data on parental violence (Fig. 6) are based on each woman's reconstruction and recollection of the events of her own childhood. Information obtained concerning the history of violence in the husband's childhood was not elicited first hand from the husbands, but rather from the information reported by the wives sampled. Most of the wives based their information on what their husbands told them over the years, and on the information garnered from their mothers or fathers-in-law. Since it was not possible to interview the men concerned, the next best approach was the one described above. In spite of these shortcomings, the results obtained prove to be very interesting and significant for the following reasons:

History of Violence

a. Evidence that husbands who beat their wives most often come from homes in which they themselves were beaten or where they

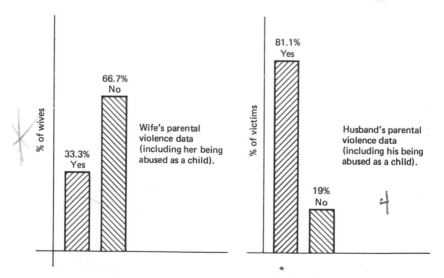

Fig. 6. Parental violence.

had witnessed their own fathers beating their mothers has been firmly established in the literature; our responses corroborate these findings.

b. This sample indicates that a less significant percentage of the battered women as compared to their husbands, were beaten as children or remember seeing their mothers beaten by their fathers. A large proportion of the women remembered a happy home life and have found their own husbands' acts of violence confusing and perplexing. These findings do not corroborate many of the already existing studies linking early patterns of violence in childhood to acceptance of violence in adult life. It is easy to understand why a woman brought up in an atmosphere of violence assumes the role of victim in her own family as an adult; it is likely that these women would not appear in this study since they would be less likely to seek help (see Gelles, R., "Experience with Violence as a Child," in this book). Even taking this into consideration, it is difficult to understand why so many of the subjects interviewed recall their childhood as secure and non-violent. Keeping this in mind, how

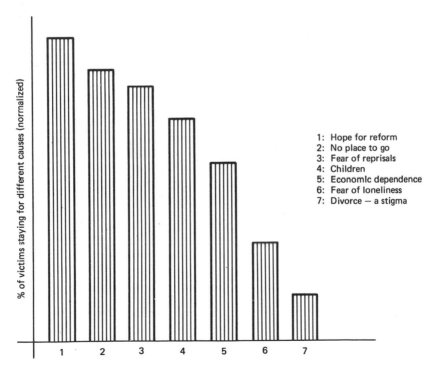

1: Hope for reform
2: No place to go
3: Fear of reprisals
4: Children
5: Economic dependence
6: Fear of loneliness
7: Divorce — a stigma

y-axis: % of victims staying for different causes (normalized)

Fig. 7. Factors causing the victims to stay.

can we explain why so many of these women remained in the relationships for as long as they did. (Refer to Fig. 7 for a tentative explanation.)

Reasons for Staying

The two main reasons women gave for staying were a. hope that their husbands would reform, and b. no place to go. It stands to reason that using their own fathers (reported as nonviolent) as role models for husbands would serve to encourage the women to hope that someday their own husbands would "give up" being violent and start behaving as husbands "should."

Help Sought

Many women reported that they were completely confused by their husband's violence and that they tried to get help very soon after the incidents occurred. Figures 8 and 9 show that over 90% of the women thought of leaving and would have done so had the resources been available to them. This seems to comfirm that social organization

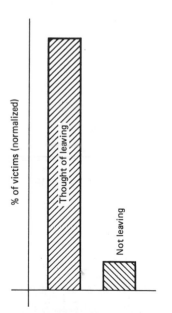

Fig. 8. Leaving home—an alternative.

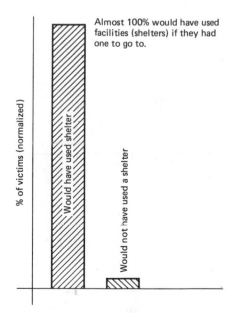

Fig. 9. Shelter facility—an alternative.

based on sexism is highly responsible for condemning women/victims to live in life and death situations in the home, and that for those women who grew up in the absence of violence—who had high expectations for happy marriages and who sought help but found nothing available—there were simply no viable alternatives to their violent home situations.

What is most significant is that in those cases where the woman has had a non-violent childhood, she is—despite her positive and assertive attempts—unable to get help, because society does not provide the resources.

Effects on Children

All of the women interviewed indicated that their children were affected in some negative way by the beatings (Fig. 10). About 45% of the assaults on the women were accompanied by similar physical assaults on at least one child in the household. The remaining 55% were situations in which the children were not assaulted, but were witnesses to the attacks on their mothers. *Ninety-five percent of the victim/mothers did not report their husband to the authorities for child abuse.*

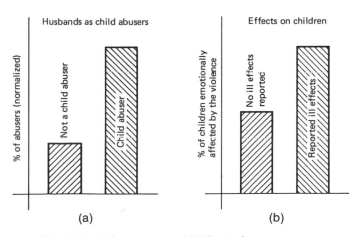

Fig. 10. (a) Concurrent child battering.
(b) Wifebeating—ill effects on children.

Sources of Help

Fear of reprisals and counter charges by the husband against the wife were reasons most often given by the women for failure to lodge complaints. However, many attempted to secure help for themselves from the police, the Family Court, family, friends, or marriage counselors. The following histograms (Figs. 11–15) demonstrate the percentage of women who sought the above kinds of intervention.

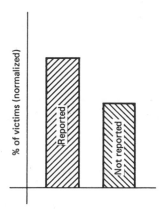

Fig. 11. Reporting to police.

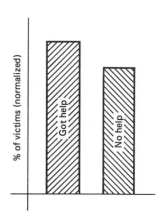

Fig. 12. Family Court.

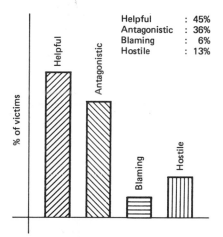

Helpful   : 45%
Antagonistic : 36%
Blaming   : 6%
Hostile   : 13%

Fig. 13. Attitudes of probation officers at Family Court as reported by victims.

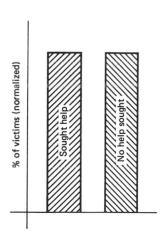

Fig. 14. Sought help from family or friends.

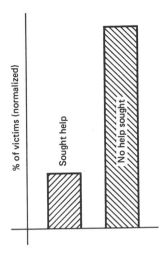

Fig. 15. Sought help from marriage counselor.

Police

Ninety percent of the 2/3 of the population seeking police help (Fig. 12) reported that the police clearly avoided arrest and did not inform the victims of the citizens arrest alternative, again confirming existing studies. The remaining 1/3 who did not summon help from the police failed to do so for the following reasons, in descending order of frequency:

1. Fear of reprisals from husband on themselves or next of kin
2. Fear of social disgrace
3. Lack of faith in the police system's response
4. To prevent the children from witnessing their fathers being apprehended by the police

Figure 16 reflects the response of the victims to the attitudes of the police who were summoned to the home, and the legal remedy options utilized by the victims. About 70% of the respondants did not find the police helpful; almost all of those (A) who found the police helpful pointed to referrals to the Family Court for an Order of Protection or a temporary removal of the husband from the premises, and/or asking the victims if they preferred to press charges. A small fraction of those police who were considered helpful (G) removed the

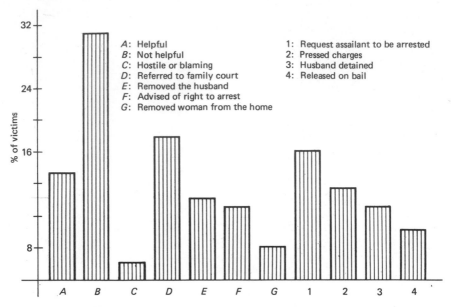

Fig. 16. Police attitudes as reported by victims.

women and children to a safer place (usually a neighbor's apartment). Some police, characterized as not helpful, also referred the women to the Family Court. In addition, a small fraction (*B*) were considered hostile or blaming (*C*). Approximately 75% of *A* and 25% of *B* requested that the husband be arrested; out of which, 70% actually did press charges.

Family Court

In New York, the Family Court System can afford help in the form of an Order of Protection. Most of the women who were able to secure an Order of Protection felt it really did not offer the protection they so badly needed. The Order is issued for a limited time, usually for up to one year, and cannot be renewed. Upon expiration, the woman must go down to the Court again and start from the beginning. She may be denied another Order because her husband may not have violated the terms of the original Order (leaving the Court to conclude that the husband has spontaneously rehabilitated himself). What the Court system fails to recognize is that in some cases, the very Order of Protection successfully *deters* those husbands who have respect for authority from committing further violence.

Paradoxically, the Court will deny a request for a subsequent Order without reviewing the efficacy argument.

In no case when the husband has clearly violated the terms specified, was he adequately reprimanded by the Court. Warrants for arrest are very infrequently issued for violations. Most women indicated that the system offered no real protection. In many cases, women who went to the Court desperate for help were diverted from the Court by the Department of Probation, whose functions are tied to post-adjudicatory services. Currently, the Department has been involved in pre-adjudicatory services as they relate to Family Court, commonly referred to as Intake and Preliminary Probation Procedures. Expansion of the pre-adjudicatory services in the late 1960s and early 1970s provided for expansion programming which "focuses upon the development of alternatives to judicial processing of individuals who do not present a serious threat to others. It is 'an opportunity, and not a solution' which enables probation to cooperate with community agencies in obtaining and/or reallocating resources to meet needs of those diverted."*

Forty-five percent of the victims responding to the questions concerning the attitudes of the Family Court Probation Department (Fig. 13) felt that the staff was helpful; 36% indicated antagonism; and 13% indicated a definite hostility. Thus, some suggestions for improving the Family Court System are necessary.

SUGGESTED RECOMMENDATIONS FOR THE COURTS

1. Increase the number of legal options available to the victim by giving the victim the authority to transfer the case from the Family Court to Criminal Court. Rarely employed, transfer, is left totally to the discretion of the justice presiding. (Refer to City Council Resolution #491-A in the appendix of this book for information on specific directives made by the New York City Council to its municipal agencies.)

2. Mandate that the husband secure professional help, either through binding arbitration (Refer to Dellapa, F., in this book) or family counseling.

3. Review progress periodically.

---

*Manual of Probation Goals and Standards, Issued by New York State Division of Probation. Albany, New York, January 1975.

4. Mandate arbitration, counseling, or treatment as an alternative to fines, imprisonment, or an order out of the home.

5. Disseminate information on Court procedure for police and social agencies. Often, expectations based on misinformation are unrealistic. People then demand what the Court cannot possibly deliver. Frustrations mount and valuable time is wasted. (Refer to Roy and Goodman in Chapter 5 of this book.) The Court system is not a panacea for wifebeating—people must be made aware of the Court's functions in order to make the best possible use of it. The Family Court, historically, is intent on reconciliation and the preservation of the family unit. What the court fails to recognize is the dissolution of the family unit in the presence of wifebeating.

6. Designate the battered wife as a probation officer of the court in those cases when a wife does not want a divorce, legal separation, or her husband jailed. The wife, then, would act as an officer of the court . . . assault on her would also be an assault upon an officer of the court. Violation of the probation, reported by the wife/probation officer reported to the judge, would insure the immediate arrest of the husband by the police. Penalties, in terms of jail sentences, might be served on weekends or at night, thus enabling the husband to continue to work and support the family. In conjunction with the appointment of the wife as a probation officer, mandatory counseling could be ordered—failure to attend would result in revocation of probation. Such an innovative approach has been in operation since the spring of 1976 by Judge Jack F. Crawford, City Court Judge in Hammond, Indiana.

Family or Friends

Seeking help from the wife's family or friends (Fig. 14) could be a source of danger to them since husbands may threaten or harm them as well. For this reason, a majority of the women who had access to families in a position to help, chose not to involve them. Fear of reprisals directed at their relatives or friends was a strong deterrent.

Counseling

More than 75% of the women reported that they did not seek the professional help of a marriage counselor (Fig. 15) because of social, familial, and economic pressures. A large contributing factor was unwillingness on the part of husbands to accompany their wives for marriage counseling (90% of the cases). The women who actually did consult a marriage counselor did not return for continued help after the second visit, since their husbands refused to accompany them.

Drugs

As each interview was conducted, it became evident that drug related problems were monumental. No attempt was made to analyze the root causes of the drug problem; the mere presence of drugs in so many cases was significant. One could speculate that drugs could act as catalysts to violence—contributing and maintaining the level of violence in the relationship. The most common drug used by the husbands was alcohol.

Ninety percent of the men involved in relationships exceeding seven years duration were reported to have alcoholic and not other drug problems. Possibly, the men on hard drugs—their participation in street life and crimes of violence outside the home, and in some cases, apprehension on charges of drug possession, often leading to arrests and convictions with jail terms—may be responsible for curtailing the length of these relationships.

About 85% of the violent husbands had either an alcoholic and/or other drug problems. These men were inclined to beat their wives at a higher frequency, either when under the influence of drugs (including alcohol) or when sober; and their violence was usually characterized by physical assault with or without a weapon, usually leading to serious injuries, and including sexual assault. Husbands in this group did not have to be drunk or on other drugs when committing a violent act; very often, the assaults came during sobriety or when the effects of hard drugs had worn off.

More than 80% of the men who drank occasionally were inclined to beat their wives only when under the influence of alcohol.

In relationships of less than 3½ years duration, a very high percentage of concurrent alcohol and hard drug use was reported, usually leading to constant violence. Included under Fig. 4 (Onset of violence), in relationships of eight years or more with no prior violence, is a high percentage of husbands who developed a drug problem because of frustrations caused by the following reported triggering mechanisms:

1. Money problems
2. Jealousy and fear of wife's infidelity
3. Conflicts over children
4. Sexual incompatibility

Drinking seemed to act as a catalyst for violence in these cases.

Study Part II: Causation

Nucleating and Contributing Factors. Based on previous research in this field, the following nine factors were investigated as possible agents for the eruption of violence. They were: 1) arguments over money, 2) jealousy, 3) sexual problems, 4) husband's drinking or taking other drugs, 5) conflicts over the children, 6) husband's unemployment, 7) wife's desire to work outside the home, 8) pregnancy, and 9) wife's drinking or taking other drugs. The respondents were instructed to check off those factors from the above list which most often lead to violent confrontation. (Refer to Fig. 17.)

1. *Arguments over money.* Of those reporting arguments over money as a factor, some indicated that lack of money due to the husband's unemployment was the basis of many arguments resulting in physical violence. Others reported that the husbands controlled all of the earned income by keeping tight reins on the budget. The wives were given just enough money to buy groceries for the family. They almost always needed to ask for spending money for their own personal items—clothes, perfumes, etc. This was the case in middle and upper middle class homes.

2. *Jealousy.* Of those reporting jealousy as a factor, most cited that sexual problems such as impotency, frigidity, denial, excessive demands, led to arguments in the bedroom that resulted in physical violence. In such instances, the husband usually doubted his own virility and questioned his wife's fidelity. He would therefore, discourage her from participating in activities outside the home. In extreme cases, some of the husbands even questioned the paternity of one or more of the children. A small percentage of those citing

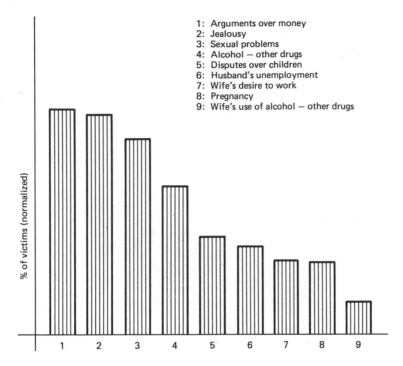

1: Arguments over money
2: Jealousy
3: Sexual problems
4: Alcohol — other drugs
5: Disputes over children
6: Husband's unemployment
7: Wife's desire to work
8: Pregnancy
9: Wife's use of alcohol — other drugs

% of victims (normalized)

Fig. 17. Nucleating and contributing factors.

jealousy as a factor indicated that they felt threatened when their wives went back to school.

3. *Sexual problems.* Of those citing sexual problems as a cause of violence, most reported that the problems began very early in the relationship (during the honeymoon period, if not sooner). The husbands' acts of brutality often caused the wives to withdraw both physically and emotionally. The women expressed a feeling of alienation from their husbands—a feeling of worthlessness. This low self-esteem resulting from the violent acts made sexual intimacy for the women very difficult. In addition, many women related that their husbands constantly accused them of infidelity and adultery. A smaller percentage reported that their husbands had problems with sexual identity, having had previous or concurrent sexual relationships with men.

4. *Alcohol.* Of those citing alcohol-other drugs as a precipitant to violence, a large proportion indicated that their husbands beat them when drunk. Very often drinking was used by the husband to "numb" the anger. Paradoxically, alcohol as a depressant of function breaks down inhibitions and thereby increases rather than decreases the anger or the mechanism for controlling it.

A small proportion reported that their husbands were drug addicts—using heroin, cocaine, or barbiturates.

5. *Disputes over children.* Of those citing arguments over the children, most indicated that their husbands resented parental responsibilities, both emotional and financial. They usually had arguments over disciplining the children—often when the husband would beat one of the children. The wives felt that their husbands regarded children as a threat to the relationship because the children would "rob" them of their wives' affections.

6. *Husband's unemployment.* Of those citing unemployment as a precipitant to violence, many indicated that this added stress to a relationship that had already gone awry. The lack of employment increased already existing feelings of insecurity about the husband's virility, self-worth and productivity.

7. *Wife's desire to work outside the home.* Of those citing a wish to secure work, as a precipitant to violence, many reported that this was a problem when the husband rated his occupational and/or educational status as lower than his wife's. Others stated that their husbands refused to permit them to seek employment, because "a wife's place is in the home, and a husband's responsibility is as the breadwinner of the family."

8. *Pregnancy.* Of those citing pregnancy as a precipitant to violence, many reported that an unplanned pregnancy put a great strain on the relationship. Many indicated that the husbands were jealous toward the unborn newcomer and resented the intrusion. Pregnancy, occurring in a relationship already troubled by sexual problems, unemployment and deep-rooted personal problems, caused additional frustration and resulted in explosive bursts of anger and physical abuse.

9. *Wife's use of alcohol—other drugs.* Of those citing alcohol

or other drugs as a precipitant to violence, many indicated that their husbands beat them to keep them in line and to make them stop drinking.

Maintaining Factors. At the conclusion of the interview, each woman was requested to check off, in order of primary importance, those factors which prevented her from leaving (Fig. 7). The results were as follows:

1. Hope that husband would reform
2. No place to go
3. Fear of reprisals from husband
4. Children made it very difficult to find an alternative place to stay
5. Financial problems based on unemployment and lack of money
6. Afraid of living alone
7. Divorce is a shameful state—a stigma

Conclusions

This study corroborates the original premise that wifebeating as a social problem is generated and compounded by many combustible factors. Some outstanding factors that occur in great frequency are the existence of alcohol or other drug problems, jealousy, sexual problems, and financial problems. Most important is the presence of violence in the parental history of an overwhelming number of the husbands—a factor which should be weighed very heavily when considering preventive measures for future generations.

In addition, the study points up the need for the creation of alternative solutions to the problem. It offers convincing proof that violent husbands do not reform spontaneously and that violence does not attenuate with time. In order for the vicious cycle of violence to be broken, society needs to recognize its obligation to find solutions, to offer help and immediate protection for all the women and children who actively seek it, and to help provide guidance and assistance to the men who need to explore non-violent modes for the expression of conflict.

References

1. AWAIC, INC.,* 1976, National clearinghouse for information and referrals.
2. Goode, William J., "Force and Violence in the Family," *Journal of Marriage and the Family* 33 (November 1971). 624–636 (Also reprinted in Steinmetz and Straus, 1976).
3. Heale, William, "An apologie for women: that it was lawful for husbands to beat their wives," 1609.
4. Pizzey, E., *Scream Quietly or the Neighbors Will Hear.* Harmondsworth: Penguin, 1974.
5. Pogrebin, Letty C. "Do Women Make Men Violent?" *Ms. Magazine* (November, 1974).
6. Truninger, E., "Marital Violence: The Legal Solutions," *Hastings Law Journal* **23,** *259* (November, 1971).
7. Wonberg, Kenneth W. and Horn, John L. "Alcoholism Symptom Patterns of Men and Women," *Quarterly Journal of Studies on Alcoholism* (March, 1970).

*AWAIC, Inc. was founded in 1975 to offer specialized services to battered women and their families. Located in New York City (GPO Box 1699, New York, N.Y. 10001), AWAIC provides the following services: 1) telephone counseling; 2) supportive counseling; 3) nationwide clearinghouse function for referrals and information; 4) training and consulting to outside agencies; 5) community out-reach programs.

3 Social Aspects

If the adultery of a wife be a wrong unto the husband, why not the adultery of an husband an injury unto the wife? Or if suspicion only may discharge a man of his wife, who is more happy than the jealous husband, who as often as his mind changes may therewithal change his wife? Or if all the luster and glory of wedlock descend only from the husband unto the wife, and none reflects again from the wife unto the husband, it is hard to be conceived how there can be a true society, or a fit match?

HEALE, WILLIAM, 1609

NO PLACE TO GO: THE SOCIAL DYNAMICS OF MARITAL VIOLENCE*

Richard J. Gelles, Ph.D., Department of Sociology, University of Rhode Island

Violent confrontations between family members are categorically different from acts of violence between individuals who are not related. First, family violence tends to take place in the privacy of the home, while most other violence takes place in public settings (bars, street corners, etc.). Secondly, when violence occurs in public places, there are often bystanders or "seconds" present to intervene and either break up the fight or aid one of the participants. Violence at home is a private affair with no bystanders (other than children) and no "seconds" to help out the combatants. Thirdly, when violence occurs in a public setting, like a tavern, someone may call the police before or during the affair to break up the battle. In instances of family violence, the police are either called by a neighbor who lives close by (in the next apartment) or by a family member after the battle is over. Even if the police are called into a home, their response is likely to be quite different from their response to public violence. This chapter focuses on the violent confrontation between husbands and wives. The individual factors which "cause" men to beat their wives and wives to become victims have been discussed in other selections in this book, and the social and cultural factors associated with family violence have been discussed in my previous work.[7,9] The purpose of this chapter is to examine the social dynamics of family violence by analyzing the violent situation—where, when, and under what conditions family violence occurs; the interaction which precipitates family violence; and the aftermath of family violence. By providing insight into the dynamics, we hope we can help people understand the situation of marital violence, why violence between husbands and wives can be so devastating, and why the victims of family violence are often deprived by reasonable solutions to opt for in trying to solve the problem of violence.

---

*Part of this chapter is synthesized from Chapters 3 and 5 of *The Violent Home: A Study of Physical Aggression Between Husbands and Wives*, by Richard J. Gelles © 1974 by Sage Publications, Inc. This material appears here by permission of the Publisher. This research was supported by NIMH grants MH 15521 and MH 24002.

Methodology

Data on family violence were derived from in-depth, unstructured interviews with members of 80 families. Twenty families suspected of using violence were chosen from the files of a private social service agency. Another 20 families were selected by examining a police "blotter" to locate families where the police had been called in to break up a violent dispute. An additional 40 families were interviewed by selecting one neighboring family for each "agency" or "police" family.*

The interviews were carried out in two cities in New Hampshire. The procedure used for selecting families enhanced the likelihood of locating families where violence had occurred, but it also meant that this sample was not representative of any larger population.

Major limitations of this study are that it was exploratory in nature, the sample was small, and the representativeness of the sample was unknown. These problems all impinge on the generalizability of findings generated by this research.

There are, however major strengths in the research which tend to offset the limitations. First, this is a unique study. The area of spousal violence has long suffered from "selective inattention"[4] on the part of society and the research community. While some data have been gathered on the topic of family violence, most of the studies focus on one type of population—petitioners for divorce,[15] patients of psychiatrists,[20] patients of physicians,[5] or college students.[21,23] This study is one of the few which examines not only those in special circumstances (agency clients, or those calling the police for help), but also an equal number of families who had no contact with agencies of social service or control (Reference 22 is another study which looks at families who are not part of special populations).

A second strength of the methodology is that it yielded a population without a working class, middle class, or lower class bias. The respondents ranged from those at the lowest regions of the social ladder to middle class individuals who had graduated college and earned salaries exceeding $25,000. (For a complete discussion

---

*For a complete discussion of the methodology, including an evaluation of the sampling procedure and instrument, see Reference 7, pp. 36–43.

of the social characteristics of the respondents and their families, see Reference 7, pp. 205–15.)`

The interviews with the 80 respondents located 44 families where violence between spouses had occurred in the marriage. Because the interview technique was unstructured, not all the respondents could remember every aspect of the violent confrontation; thus, there are varying numbers of respondents who report information about different aspects of the violent situation.

Violence in the Home: Spatial Location

We have stated that the family predominates in acts of violence ranging from pushing and shoving to homicide and torture.[25] When acts of violence take place between family members, they typically take place in the home. The home is the likely setting for violence for a number of reasons, including the fact that the nuclear family household structure, which is typical of urban-industrial societal structure, insulates families from social control and assistance in coping with intra-family conflict.[14] Other factors which lead to violence in the home are the intensity of involvement of family members in interactions and activities at home, the fact that individual activities in the home frequently impinge on one another, and the general acceptance that violence between family members is often justifiable.[24]

Thirty of the 44 respondents who had experienced spousal violence discussed where the violence took place. All 30 respondents said that violence occurred at home, while only 4 respondents said that some incidents took place outside the house or apartment.

Our research revealed that the typical location of marital violence was the kitchen. The bedroom and living room are the next most likely scenes of violence. Some respondents were unable to pinpoint exact locations because their battles began in one room and progressed throughout the house. The only room in the house where there was no violence was the bathroom.

Our research contrasts with the analysis of spacial locations of intra-family homicides. The research on lethal family violence found that the bedroom was the deadliest room in the house.[18,27] Marvin E. Wolfgang reports that 20% of *all* victims of criminal homicide

TABLE 1. SPATIAL LOCATIONS OF CONJUGAL VIOLENCE MENTIONED BY RESPONDENTS.

PLACE	% RESPONDENTS MENTIONING LOCATION ($N = 30$)
Kitchen	63
Bedroom	27
Living room	27
TV room	3
Dining room	3
Hall	7
Front steps	3
All over house	17
Out of house (movie, bar, street, etc.)	7
Car	7

were killed in the bedroom. In addition, the bedroom is the room where a female is most likely to be killed (35% of female victims were killed in the bedroom). The next deadliest place in the home is the kitchen. Women are the usual offenders in the kitchen, 29% of female offenders committed their murders in this room.[27]

Spatial Dynamics of Spousal Violence. Why is the home or apartment the arena for spousal combat, and why are certain spatial locations in the home frequently battlegrounds? We have addressed this question briefly in the introduction of this article and will investigate the spatial dynamics of family violence in more detail in this section.

The household seems to be the locale of family violence for a number of reasons. First, it is where the majority of family life and family interaction takes place. Secondly, the home is the "backstage" region of family behavior.[10] Protected by the privacy of one's own walls, there is no need to maintain the presentation of family life as harmonious, loving and conflict-free. Thirdly, because the home is where family members reside, keep their clothing, their checkbooks, their money, their children, etc., the household is the *home territory* for both combatants. It is difficult and often undesirable for one participant in a family conflict to suddenly get up and leave the house or apartment. Even if the husband or wife can flee the scene of a festering conflict, he or she must eventually return home.

Within the home, the kitchen is the typical location of non-lethal violence and the most common scene of lethal violence carried out by the wife. The kitchen, because it is where family members routinely congregate, is the location where most family interaction takes place. The kitchen is where family news is exchanged over dinner, children are asked to report on their day at school, the wife relives her day, and the husband may discuss what happened at work.[3] Because of the high level of interaction in the kitchen and the variety of topics discussed, there is a great potential for family arguments and conflict. In addition, family members are somewhat constrained to stay in the kitchen until dinner is complete. One of our respondents discussed why most of her family's arguments took place in the kitchen:

> I guess the worst place in the house is the dinner table. I think it is terrible. A man comes home to eat his dinner and somebody's, I don't mean every night, but if anything . . . see, I'm alone every day, all day, and if there's something that might be worrying me, I can't quote anything off hand, it builds up in me all day. All I got to do is think. And by the time he gets home I'm just ready to pop off and it's typically at the dinner table.

Even during non-eating hours, the kitchen is the focal point of much family interaction. A secretary who had been repeatedly beaten by her husband discussed the location:

> Most of the incidents took place when he was drinking . . . they took place in the kitchen, the kitchen has more activity than any room in the house.

The second most common location for spousal violence is the living room. Like the kitchen, the living room is a setting for a wide range of family activities. The television, typically situated in the living room, often becomes the focal point of family conflict. One wife talked about her husband striking her because she got in the way of the television:

> Once, when I was pregnant. I wanted to talk with him about something. He had come home from work. I don't remember what it was. He had the TV on and he didn't want to listen to me. We had a big fight. He pushed me. He must have wanted to push me out of the way. I wouldn't move so he pushed me.

The most lethal room in the house, the bedroom, is also a scene of conflict and stress. The majority of the conflicts which occur in this room revolve around sex and intimacy. Arguments about the wife's "frigidity" or the husband's "impotence" were discussed by respondents who related incidents of marital violence in the bedroom. A major reason why the bedroom is a scene of deadly or serious violence is that it is a difficult room to escape from. While a husband or wife can bolt from the kitchen table or leave the living room, escaping from an argument in the bedroom is extremely difficult, considering that one must get up and get dressed. Furthermore, bedroom conflicts typically take place late at night and there is *no place to go.*

The demilitarized zone of the home is the bathroom. No respondents reported any conjugal violence in this room. The bathroom, typically the room in the house that *always* has a lock, is often used as a refuge for family members to hide in to avoid violence.

Time and Violence

Evening was the time of day when spouses were most likely to engage in physical violence; from after dinner (8:00 PM) until bedtime (11:30 PM). The next most likely time period for marital violence was during or around dinner time (5:00 PM to 8:00 PM). Late evening (11:30 PM until 7:00 AM) was the third most violence-prone time of day.

Our data on time of day and marital violence are quite similar to the temporal patterns of murder found by students of criminal homicide. Wolfgang reports that 50% of all criminal homicides occur between 8:00 PM and 2:00 AM. Fifty-five percent of our respondents mentioned violence occurring in this time period. The second deadliest time of day was from 2:00 PM to 8:00 PM.[27]

Temporal Dynamics of Violence: Time of Day. We found that there were characteristic types of violence and causes of violence depending on the time of day.

Morning and Afternoon. Marital violence which erupts in the morning or afternoon typically happens on a day when neither the husband nor wife works, or when they work the night shift and are home in the morning. Morning incidents of violence often are caused

TABLE 2. TIME OF DAY OF CONJUGAL VIOLENCE MENTIONED BY RESPONDENTS.

TIME OF DAY*	% RESPONDENTS MENTIONING TIME OF DAY ($N = 27$)
Morning (7:00 AM to noon)	7
Afternoon (noon to 5:00 PM)	15
Early evening (5:00 PM to 8:00 PM)	22
Evening (8:00 PM to 11:30 PM)	37
Late night (11:30 PM to 7:00 AM)	19
Anytime	11

*The hours given are approximations derived from the discussions of violence in the interview. Respondents were not asked, nor did they give, *exact* times when violence took place.

by residual conflict from the night before. A housewife discussed one instance of morning violence.

He grabbed me and put me against the wall and choked me and the minute he let go I just hit him. He had been drunk the night before and he was going out (in the morning). I asked him not to go out because there were a few things that needed to be done. And he said no. Well, I think I grabbed him before he hit me, before he grabbed my throat. I think I grabbed him and told him that he was going to have to stay home . . . and then he let go of me. I hit him and he hit me and I hit him back.

The groundwork for this battle had been laid the night before when the husband was drunk. When he began to go out in the morning, the wife felt this was adding insult to injury and either precipitated the attack or started it herself.

Other morning or afternoon violence occurs when the husband works the "graveyard" shift, from 11:00 PM until 7:00 AM. In these instances, conflict may arise when the wife is aggravated by the husband being under foot or when the husband is disturbed by the wife's interference with his sleep or relaxation time. A housewife whose husband works evenings described one of their morning fights:

It was Saturday. He had worked all night and I had to take his uniform to the cleaners and run to the post office and dragging the baby with me. I was tired of taking care of the baby and he wanted his dinner. The girl across the street—her husband is overseas—she's got 2 kids and it was the first time she ever asked me if she could use my washer. I have a tendency to let people take advantage of me. Instead of telling me why he got mad he picked up his lunch and the tray and threw it across the room. I started laughing and he got mad. The fight went all the way up the stairs and he ended up putting a hole in the baby's wall.

We got the impression from our interviews with family members that most morning or afternoon violence results from a spill-over of conflict from the previous evening. In addition, violence tended to grow out of colliding time schedules or obligations which arose when both partners were home during the day.

Evening. Evening violence typically takes place in the kitchen during dinnertime or when one partner desires to be fed. One factor contributing to dinnertime violence is the accumulation of frustration by the end of the day. This frustration is supposed to be alleviated by the tranquility and harmony of the family; however, the opposite often occurs—the frustration builds to a crescendo during dinnertime as the wife complains about her day, the husband complains about his day, and the children yell, cry, spill or throw their food, and generally disrupt the dinner.

Late Night. Studies of criminal homicide indicate that early morning (2:00 AM to 7:59 AM) is the time when homicides in the home clearly outnumber homicides outside the home.[27]

Late evening violence typically involves arguments about sex or alcohol or both. Sometimes, late evening violence will commence in the kitchen when an inebriated spouse comes home and demands dinner. The sequence of events related by a respondent who was a regular victim of marital violence was similar to situations we found in numerous other families.

> . . . but when he was drinking, well I couldn't very well greet him with open arms. He'd be gone a day and a half and of course he was bombed when he did come home. He expected to be welcomed home and I was irritated and mad about him spending the money in the first place and he'd hit me . . . how he got up those four flights of stairs I'll never know. He made it to the door, managed to unlock it and he slipped . . . Well, I used to greet him . . . like how many times he's come home hungry, he hasn't eaten all day, no lunch, no supper. And he'd pop in and take a leftover and start frying himself something. When I was in bed . . . I figured let him be . . . he'll go to bed or he'd fall asleep. Many times it was burnt to a crisp. He fell asleep in a plate of spaghetti, face and all, and yet he was breathing. I got to the point where I got so disgusted, so angry with him . . . I could have just sunk his face in the plate more!

TABLE 3. DAY OF THE WEEK OF CONJUGAL VIOLENCE MENTIONED BY RESPONDENTS.

DAY OF THE WEEK	% RESPONDENTS MENTIONING DAY OF WEEK ($N = 13$)
Sunday	23
Saturday	8
Weekend (no day mentioned)	38
Weekend (combined total)	69
Weekday	15
Other: (pay day, husband's day off, when husband home when working 11–7 shift)	23

Day of the Week. Only 13 of our respondents could remember what day of the week violence took place. Of those who did remember, 38% said marital violence took place on a weekend, 23% said Sunday, and 8% said Saturday. Thus, 69% of the respondents indicated spousal violence happened on a weekend.

The data on marital violence are consistent with research on assault and homicide. Pittman and Handy found that 55% of assaults happened on weekends.[17] Pokorny stated that homicides are high on weekends with the peak on Saturday.[18] Wolfgang's data on homicide in Philadelphia revealed high rates on Saturdays.[27]

Temporal Dynamics of Violence: Day of Week. Obviously, violence between husband and wife is most likely to occur during days when both are home. There were other factors related to what day marital violence erupted. A number of wives reported that alcohol related violence took place predominantly on weekends, because this was when their husbands drank the most.

There are other stressful days of the week; pay day may be one day when arguments arise over how to divide and spend money. If a husband is off from work on a weekday, and his wife is at home, this also might produce a violence prone day of the week.

Time of Year. There was little recall concerning what time of year violence typically took place. When respondents did remember incidents, they were typically distributed throughout the year. Some respondents did remember fights near or around birthdays or anniversaries. One pattern which *did emerge*, however, was that six respondents cited Christmas or New Year's Eve as times when particularly severe incidents of violence exploded. Two women who were beaten recalled when it happened.

> He hit me two days before New Year's. Oh, it was awful. I just felt worse—it was the worst time of the year I ever spent. He brought me here and I was bleeding bad, you know.

> One time, we were going to Manchester and it was around Christmas time, and I was pregnant then. We had a fight. This was going on down Main Street. And he said, "You can get right out here!" I had to call my father to come pick me up.

It is possible that people recall violence which occurred in the holiday season because they are able to associate the incident with special circumstances (Christmas trees, parties, etc.) and the events stand out because of these associations and not because that time of year led to violence. However, it could be that certain times of the year *are* related to violence in the family.

There may be a number of factors which contribute to the likelihood of marital violence occurring at Christmas and New Year's. First, this is a time of year that places great financial burdens on the family. Secondly, if the family cannot afford to buy presents and gifts, this can be extremely frustrating. Families with financial problems may look around at their neighbors' Christmas trees, lighting displays, and piles of gifts, and see their own economic shortcomings in sharp contrast with their neighbors' status. The holiday season presents families with the yearly opportunity to compare themselves with their neighbors and friends in terms of financial resources. Thirdly, Christmas and New Year's Eve are festive occasions where the image of family harmony, love, and togetherness is fostered by songs, advertisements, and television specials. Families with on-going conflict or who are isolated from friends, neighbors, and relations may see this in bold relief compared to the idealized image of the family which is presented during the Christmas season. These factors and others may contribute to the holiday season being one of great family stress and vulnerability to violence.

Other People

A consistent pattern in the social dynamics of marital violence is that the incidents generally occur when there are no non-nuclear family members present. None of our respondents reported an incident of violence where anyone other than the husband, wife, or children were in the house. In fact, we were informed that many husbands waited until no one was present to beat their wives.

> He's never hit me in front of anyone . . . he's too smart for that . . . people come over to protect me if they know he's around.

There are a number of reasons why marital violence happens when no one other than the combatants is present. First, violence between husband and wife is considered deviant by the wider society (even though it is condoned by virtue of the fact that most people will not get involved in other people's marital affairs). Husbands do not want to be publically labeled "wifebeaters" and wives do not want to be embarrassed by other people seeing their husbands hit them. Moreover, wives feel that if it is known that they are being beaten and do not leave, people will think they are masochists. In an attempt to maintain the conventional image of peace and harmony in the family, husbands postpone beating their wives and wives are reluctant to admit they are being beaten.

A second reason why outside members are not present in episodes of family violence is that neighbors or friends of violent couples do not want to get involved. A neighbor of a battered wife stated:

> Well, next door, I met a girl and she invited me over one night and asked me to stay with her because her husband had come home the previous night and put his fist through the glass—he was drunk, very drunk. She called me because she thought her husband wouldn't come in if I was there—it didn't work—he came in and I immediately took off. If they were going to beat each other I wasn't going to be there.

Another woman stated that she feared being beaten by her neighbor's husband if she got involved.

> I hear her screaming . . . it sounds like he's throwing her against the wall. I don't want to go over or call the police on him because he might just come over and beat me up. That's why we haven't become good friends. I just don't want to be part of that at all.

Thus, violent families isolate themselves by attempting to keep up an image of harmony and gentleness while their neighbors, all too aware of the violence, try to avoid getting involved. This isolation contributes to the incidents of violence and to the escalation of violence because it cuts off violent families from sources of social support, social resources, and social control.

We noted one interesting aspect of marital violence. In some families where violence was clearly predicted by a combination of factors, the respondent reported no incidents of violence ever occurring. One thing that these families had in common was the presence of a non-nuclear family member in the household. Families had foster children, fathers, in-laws, or boarders living in on a full time basis. It would seem that the presence of these people served to mitigate against the likelihood of violence taking place. It is possible that husbands are afraid to hit their wives if the wife's brother is in the home, or it might be that the additional people provide additional resources (baby-sitters, rent payers) who strengthen what otherwise might be a violent marriage.

Precipitating Violence

Violence in a marriage can occur as a consequence of a number of different events. Husbands may beat their wives if they were fired from a job; wives have hit husbands to get them to become more "active" sexually. A number of our respondents reported that incidents of marital violence arose out of one partner's attempt to intervene in the punishment of children. Arguments over drinking or sex were cited by families as leading to violence.

The list of events which precipitate marital violence in a family is perhaps as long as the list of events which take place in families. There did appear to be patterns of events which produced violent reactions. The patterns that emerged in our interviews were in terms of the role the victim played in bringing about violence and the reaction of the offender to the victim's behavior.

Role of the Victim. Victims of marital violence, whether they were men or women, were not simply "whipping boys" or "hostility sponges" for violent partners. Rather, the victim tended to play an active role in his or her own victimization.[12,16,19,27] (See Lion, J. R., in Chapter 5 of this book, for an analysis of victim precipitation.)

A consistent pattern in the interactions which led to marital violence was that verbal aggression led to physical aggression. Husbands or wives who verbally assaulted their spouses frequently provoked violent reactions. In fact, the more aggressive the verbal attack, the higher the likelihood of a violent response.

This pattern of verbal aggression leading to physical aggression has been discussed in the work of Straus[23] and stands in sharp contrast to the theory that if couples get out their pent-up hostilities they will reduce the potential for violence in their marriage.[1,2,13] The notion of verbal aggression being cathartic and a "violence insulator" led to the development of a number of marital counseling techniques, including the sale of foam rubber bats to be used by couples to vent their aggression. If our data from the 80 interviews are correct and Straus' research accurate, then couples who use verbal aggression to solve problems are *more prone* to have their arguments end in violence than couples who use a more "civil" and rational approach to family problem solving.[23]

Reaction of the Offender. If verbal assaults tend to produce violent responses from spouses, then we need to answer two important questions: 1) Why are verbal assaults so devastating to a spouse? and 2) What particular types of verbal assaults are most likely to produce violent reactions?

The first question is answered by proposing that prolonged interaction, intimacy, emotional closeness, and the intense investment of self in family life exposes the vulnerability of both partners and strips away the facades that might have been created to shield personal weaknesses of husbands and wives. As a result, couples become experts in attacking each other's weaknesses and are able to hurt each other effectively and efficiently.[11] Moreover, in the family, as opposed to other social groups or institutional settings, it is difficult to turn off verbal abuse by the most common method—ignoring the person.

The answer to the second question posits that certain individuals have experienced self-devaluating events, and thus, their self-evaluations are vulnerable. Given this vulnerability, one reaction to an attack or perceived attack on an aspect of self-concept is violence towards the attacker.

In conclusion, we find that through the intensity and duration of interaction in marriage, partners become experts on each other's vulnerability. Each soon knows how to go for their partner's "jugular." (Refer to Shainess, N. in Chapter 5 of this book.) However, in marriage as in other social situations, both spouses are not equally armed verbally. Thus, the partner who has less verbal skill will often tend to compensate for a verbal attack by using physical force as a resource.

Aftermath: Why do they Stay?

Our interviews with 80 family members revealed 44 marriages where violence had occurred at least once in the marriage. In almost half (21) of the marriages where violence had occurred at least once, marital violence was a regular event, taking place at least monthly and as often as daily. The unusual thing about the finding that violence was a regular and patterned aspect of family relations in almost 20% of the 80 families we talked to, was that people would remain in violent marriages knowing that their partner was violent and knowing that they stood a good chance of being hit at least once a month. We interviewed too few men who were victims of violence to discuss their situation, but we did talk to enough women victims (41) to draw conclusions about why battered wives stay with violent husbands.

The conventional wisdom suggests that a woman who is beaten by her husband and stays with him is a masochist or mentally ill. This "wisdom" is based on the assumption that any reasonable person, having been beaten, would avoid being hit again. This section summarizes our findings on what factors influence the decision to either stay or leave an assaultive husband.* Three major factors appeared to influence the actions of abused wives: The extent of the violence they experienced, their experience with violence as a child, and social and economic resources. In addition, the response of the police or courts influenced abused wives' actions.

Severity and Frequency. The more severe and frequent the violence a wife experienced, the more she tried to leave her husband by getting a divorce or professional intervention in the form of police or social worker assistance. Of the eight women who were either shot at, stabbed, choked, or hit with a hard object, five had obtained divorces after the incident, two had called the police, and one had visited a social service agency. At the other end of the violent continuum, of the nine women whose severest violent experience was a push or shove

---

*The complete analysis of the question, "Why do wives stay with abusive husbands?" can be found in Gelles.[8]

or had objects thrown at them, one got a divorce, one called the police, and seven sought no assistance at all.

The frequency of violence also influenced women's actions. Only 42% of the women who had been struck once in their marriage sought intervention or tried to leave their husbands, while 100% of the women who were hit once a month and 83% of the women struck once a week had either obtained a divorce or separation, called the police, or visited a social service agency for help.

Experience with Violence as a Child. Women who had observed conjugal violence in their families of orientation were likely to be victims of marital violence in their families of procreation. Of the 54 women (in our sample of 80 families) who never saw their parents physically fight, 46% were victims of violence in their own marriage, while 66% of the 12 women who observed their parents hit one another were later victims of violence by their own husbands. In addition, the more frequently a woman was struck by her parents, the more vulnerable she was to grow up and be the victim of marital violence.

Not only does experience with and exposure to violence as a child influence whether a woman is likely to be hit by her husband, experience and exposure to violence affect what a woman does after she has been hit. Although being a victim of parental violence played no part in determining a wife's actions after a beating, those women who observed marital violence in their parents' marriages were slightly *more likely* to seek intervention if their husbands struck them. It appears that exposure to conjugal violence makes women *less tolerant* of family violence and more desirous of ending a violent marriage.

Resources. The fewer alternatives a woman has to her marriage, the fewer resources she possesses in terms of formal education or job skills, the more "entrapped" she is in her marriage and the less likely she is to seek help or get a divorce after being beaten by her husband. We found that women who were unemployed, had not completed high school, had fewer children, and had younger children, were less likely to seek a divorce or outside assistance after being beaten.

External Constraint. Even if a woman attempts to get help after being beaten by her husband, her chances of getting effective assistance are minimal. Police, courts, and many social service agencies are currently unable or unwilling to provide much help for the battered woman. In fact, women are not only *not encouraged* to seek help, they are often actively discouraged. Truninger[26] and Field and Field[6] document how the procedures and attitudes of police officers and courts create a situation where, unless the wife is killed, she gets minimal legal assistance. As Field and Field note, there is often an official acceptance of violence between "consenting" adults.[6]

Even if a woman wants to get help and protection from her husband, she all too frequently finds out that agents and agencies she calls are ineffective or incapable of providing meaningful assistance. Thus, the attitudes and actions of official agencies of social control often serve to keep women with their violent husbands.

Summary: No Place to Go

Our situational analysis of violence between family members and our examination of the aftermath of violent incidents in the family leads to the inescapable conclusion that the picture of the abused wife is quite grim. She is typically beaten in a location, at a time of day, on a day of the week, and at a time of the year when there are few places she can escape to. In addition, she is struck when no one is present to protect her (aside from her children). Granted, that same situation exists for men who are victims of violence in marriages; but men are typically bigger and stronger than their wives and often possess more material and social resources. Women are typically less educated, hold less prestigious jobs, earn less money, and are delegated more responsibility for their children than are men. Thus, in a violent confrontation where the first reaction might be to flee, women realize that they have few places to flee to and few resources to aid in their flight. Moreover, if a woman leaves without her children, she is stigmatized as a neglectful mother (the same is not true for men who leave their families—they are simply "deserters").

Even if a woman leaves, she soon confronts police department "stitch rules," which prescribe that a woman must have received a certain number of stitches from a violent attack to be able to file an assault charge against her husband.[6] Of course, if a beaten wife stays with her husband (because she does not want to or cannot leave) she is labeled a masochist by society.

Temporary shelters and counseling for battered women are two initial steps which ease the burden of beatings, but in the long run, changes of a broader scope are needed. We should not expect beaten women to solve their problems for themselves, since, as we have seen in this chapter and the rest of this book, violence between spouses is a complicated and multifaceted phenomenon. Changes in legal statutes, police training, and social attitudes towards violence between family members are important and difficult steps which must be taken if individuals are to be protected from their violent spouses.

REFERENCES

1. Bach, George R., "Therapeutic Aggression" (set of 10 cassettes). Chicago: The Human Development Institute, 1973.
2. Bach, George R. and Wyden, Peter, *The Intimate Enemy*. New York: Avon Books, 1968.
3. Bossard, James H. S. and Boll, Eleanor Stoker, *The Sociology of Child Development*. New York: Harper and Row, 1966.
4. Dexter, Louis A., "A Note on Selective Inattention in Social Science," *Social Problems* **6**: 176–182 (Fall 1958).
5. Faulk, M., "Sexual Factors in Marital Violence," *Medical Aspects of Human Sexuality*, 1976.
6. Field, Martha H. and Field, Henry F., "Marital Violence and the Criminal Process: Neither Justice nor Peace," *Social Service Review:* **47**(2): 221–240 (1973).
7. Gelles, Richard J., *The Violent Home: A Study of Physical Aggression Between Husbands and Wives*. Beverly Hills: Sage Publications, 1974.
8. Gelles, Richard J., "Abused Wives: Why Do They Stay?" *Journal of Marriage and the Family* **38** (November 1976).
9. Gelles, Richard J. and Straus, Murray A., "Determinants of Violence in the Family: Toward a Theoretical Integration." In *Contemporary Theories About the Family*, W. Burr, R. Hill, F. I. Nye, and I. Reiss (eds.) New York: Free Press, 1977.
10. Goffman, Erving, *The Presentation of Self in Everyday Life*. Garden City, New York: Anchor Books, 1959.
11. Goode, William J., "Force and Violence in the Family." *Journal of Marriage and the Family* **33**: 624–636 (November 1971).
12. Hentig, Hans von, *The Criminal and His Victim: Studies in the Sociobiology of Crime*. New Haven: Yale University Press, 1948.
13. Howard, Jane, *Please Touch: A Guided Tour of the Human Potential Movement*. New York: Delta Books, 1970.
14. Laslett, Barbara, "The Family as a Public and Private Institution: An Historical Perspective," *Journal of Marriage and the Family* **35**: 480–492 (August 1973).
15. Levinger, George, "Sources of Marital Dissatisfaction Among Applicants for Divorce," *American Journal of Orthopsychiatry* **26**: 803–807 (October 1966). Pp. 126–132 as reprinted in Paul H. Glasser and Louis N. Glasser (eds.), *Families in Crisis*. New York: Harper & Row.
16. Palmer, Stuart, *The Violent Society*. New Haven: College and University Press, 1972.

17. Pittman, David J. and Handy, William, "Patterns in Criminal Aggravated Assault," *Journal of Criminal Law, Criminology and Police Science* 55(4): 462–470 (1964).
18. Pokorny, Alex D., "Human Violence: A Comparison of Homicide, Aggravated Assault, Suicide, and Attempted Suicide," *Journal of Criminal Law, Criminology and Police Science* 56: 488–497 (December 1965).
19. Schafer, Stephen, *The Victim and His Criminal: A Study in Functional Responsibility.* New York: Random House, 1968.
20. Snell, John E., Rosenwald, Richard J. and Robey, Ames, "The Wifebeater's Wife: A Study of Family Interaction," *Archives of General Psychiatry* 11: 107–113 (August 1964).
21. Steinmetz, Suzanne K., "Occupational Environment in Relation to Physical Punishment and Dogmatism," pp. 166–172 in *Violence in the Family*, S. Steinmetz and M. Straus (eds.). New York: Harper & Row, 1974.
22. Steinmetz, Suzanne K., "Intra-Familial Patterns of Conflict Resolution: Husband/Wife; Parent/Child; Sibling/Sibling," unpublished Ph.D. dissertation, Case Western Reserve University, 1975.
23. Straus, Murray A., "Leveling, Civility, and Violence in the Family," *Journal of Marriage and the Family* 36: 13–30 (February 1974).
24. Straus, Murray A., "Sexual Inequality, Cultural Norms, and Wife Beating," paper presented at the International Institute on Victimology, Bellagio, Italy, 1975.
25. Straus, Murray A., Gelles, Richard J. and Steinmetz, Suzanne K., "Violence in the Family: An Assessment of Knowledge and Research Needs," paper presented to the annual meetings of the American Association for the Advancement of Science. Boston, February 23, 1976.
26. Truninger, Elizabeth, "Marital Violence: The Legal Solutions," *The Hastings Law Journal* 23: 259–276 (November 1971).
27. Wolfgang, Marvin E., *Patterns in Criminal Homicide.* New York: John Wiley & Sons, 1958.

WIFEBEATING, HUSBANDBEATING—A COMPARISON OF THE USE OF PHYSICAL VIOLENCE BETWEEN SPOUSES TO RESOLVE MARITAL FIGHTS

Suzanne K. Steinmetz, University of Delaware

While there has been an apparent growth of awareness of marital violence, there is a tendency to view this form of aberrant behavior as one resulting from the "macho" ideology, which supports the male's use of physical force to maintain his dominance over his mate. Upheld by both tradition and the law, macho ideology fosters the brutal beating of wives by their spouses and denies these wives access to social structural mechanisms which might protect them from further abuse.

While no one would deny that this treatment of women—in fact, this treatment of any human being—is reprehensible, a closer examination of the battered spouse phenomenon is needed, with an emphasis on investigating male and female differences in the use of physical violence to resolve marital conflicts. While understanding the mechanisms which might facilitate these acts of violence does not justify such behavior, it is important, at least, to recognize the existence of circumstances in which a class of perpetrators (husbands) might, in some families, be victims.

Dimensions of Husband-Wife Physical Violence

We have learned from Margaret Mead's classic study, *Sex and Temperament* that aggressive interaction is essentially learned behavior and that it may be defined as a male or female characteristic, depending on the society.[13] While aggression may have instinctual roots in human development,[1,2,12] the arousal of this aggression, as well as the method by which this aggressiveness is displayed, appears to be learned behavior.[4,9] Thus, we must look to the socialization processes, the structural characteristics of the society, as well as to individual differences between spouses, for the explanation of this phenomenon.

Unfortunately, while the horrors of wifebeating are paraded across the media and crisis lines and centers are being established, the other side of this coin—husbandbeating—is still hidden under a cloak of secrecy. This is certainly easy to understand. In a society which tends to view men as strong, physically dominant, and aggressive, while women are viewed as weak, physically submissive, and vulnerable, no male wants to admit that his wife is physically abusing him. Furthermore, the "mating gradient,"[10] in which the male is expected to be taller, stronger, physically dominant, older, and more experienced than his mate, is considered desirable and tends to reinforce male/female differences.

Estimates on the Frequency of Marital Abuse

Because of the personal guilt felt by women who experience beatings, the inability to safely report the incident, and the lack of protection offered the women who do seek police and legal methods to end the abuse, this type of family violence is grossly under-reported. In a random sample of New Castle County (Delaware) families, 4 cases of severe and repetitive beatings occurred out of the 57 intact families interviewed. The number of intact families in this county was estimated to be 94,000 in 1975. During 1975, however, only 26 cases of serious family assault were reported to the police. This represents about 0.0003% of the families experiencing spousebeating; or, to use the usual census designation, 28 per 100,000 families. Of the total number of serious family assaults, wives were the victims in 24 instances (or 26/100,000). However, in the random sample of New Castle County families, 0.07% of the wives suffered severe abuse, or 7,016 per 100,000. This magnitude of under-reporting (the difference between 26/100,000 reported abuse and 7,016/100,000 estimated) suggests that only about 1 out of 270 incidents of wife-beating are ever reported to the authorities.

Although there were no husbands as victims of serious assault among the study population, in two of the cases reported to the police, the victim was the husband. If the same degree of under-reporting was present for husbands, then one could suspect that 540 incidents (574/100,000) occurred in New Castle County during 1975. Since it is far less likely that a man would report his wife's abusive behavior, this is probably an extremely conservative estimation. In fact, in both incidents of husbandbeating, a neighbor, not the husband, reported the abuse. Unfortunately, little empirical data exists on husbands who have experienced physical batterings from their wives. Evidence of this phenomena is located in a few isolated studies of divorce applicants or an occasional newspaper article.*

We do know that over 3% of 600 husbands in mandatory conciliation interviews listed physical abuse by their wife as a reason for the divorce action.[11] While this is far lower than the nearly 37% of wives who mentioned physical abuse, there are several factors besides lower actual rates which should be noted. First, Levinger's study showed that women had nearly twice the number of total complaints than did men. Therefore, unless one is willing to assume that it is the husband's fault when a marriage fails, it appears that women might be more comfortable voicing their complaints. A second and related factor is that the traditional role of husbands in a divorce action is to take the blame for the failure. Thus, even if the husband desires

---

*One minister who does extensive marital counseling estimates that about 20% of his cases involve husbands beaten by their wives (Marvin Hummel, personal communication).

the divorce, etiquette demands that he allow his wife to initiate the action. Extending this to a conciliatory interview, it is reasonable to expect that a husband might be less ready to expose his wife's faults. Some support is provided for this position by examining the types of complaints commonly made by husbands, i.e., sexual incompatibility and in-laws, both traditionally accepted, male-oriented complaints. A final consideration is that males in our society suffer considerable psychological pressure to maintain their dominant position over females.[3,20] Thus, given the psychological stress of recognizing the wife's physical dominance, it is unlikely that many men would be willing to admit their physical weakness to a third party. However, regardless of the factors which might operate to differentially effect reporting rates, it is obvious that the phenomena of husband "beating" does exist. The question which needs to be addressed is to what degree husbands and wives differ in their use of physical violence to resolve marital conflict.

Method

The data reported is from a larger study investigating family configurations of conflict resolution.[22] Fifty-seven families were randomly selected fitting the criteria of being intact and containing two or more children between the ages of 3–18 residing at home. Although there were no Black families in the study, there was a wide range of ethnic, religious, and social class representation. The research design consisted of a semi-structured, in-depth interview with a parent; a questionnaire administered to a parent and a child; and diaries in which all family conflicts, the participants involved, and the method of resolution were recorded for a period of a week. This provided data from two parents and a child in 35% of the families and one parent and a child in the remaining families in the sample, thus counteracting the effect of the "wife's view" of families.[16,21] The data reported in this paper is primarily from the interview and questionnaire parts of the research.

Results

Over 60% of all families participating in this study experienced some form of marital violence during their marriage. As noted in Table 1, the types of physically violent acts covered a wide range.

TYPE 1.   TYPES OF PHYSICALLY AGGRESSIVE ACTS USED TO RESOLVE MARITAL CONFLICTS.

PERCENT OF FAMILIES*		TYPE OF PHYSICAL AGGRESSION
51	(N = 25)	Throwing things
31	(N = 15)	Pushing, shoving, grabbing
22	(N = 11)	Hitting the spouse with their hand
12	(N = 6)	Hitting spouse with something hard

*Forty-nine families participated in the questionnaire part of the study

Some families had engaged in all of the above forms of physical aggression, while others had used only one form. In some families, the wife committed the physically aggressive act; in other families, the husband was the aggressor; while in many families, reciprocal physical violence was displayed.

Frequency of Specific Acts of Marital Violence. Although wives and husbands may use similar acts of physical violence to resolve marital conflict, one can posit that perhaps spouses differ in the frequency to which they resort to a specific method. The violent act may be a single occurrence, as one wife noted:

... I had kept it in for so long. He had gone to bed this one night and I forgot just why it was, but I went up and hit him on the back. It wasn't the best thing in the world and I couldn't get away with it a second time.

Or, as another respondent noted when asked if she had ever been slapped:

Yes, once . . . I lost my temper. I think I asked for it, really. I threw something.

However, for some spouses, the use of physical violence to resolve conflict is the rule rather than the exception, as noted by the following description of the "typical" fight between one couple:

Mrs. A: . . . We would get into a big argument and I would just keep needling and pushing until he would slap me to shut me up.

Interviewer: Did you shut up?

Mrs. A: No, I would hit him back. It just ended up in a bigger argument.

Using the data from the questionnaire part of the study, the fre-

TABLE 2. PERCENT OF HUSBANDS AND WIVES WHO SELECT PHYSICALLY VIOLENT METHODS FOR RESOLVING MARITAL CONFLICTS.

| | FREQUENCY OF ACT | | | | | |
| | A FEW TIMES | | SOMETIMES | | ALMOST ALWAYS | |
TYPE OF PHYSICAL VIOLENCE USED	HUSBAND %	WIFE %	HUSBAND %	WIFE %	HUSBAND %	WIFE %
Throwing things	20 (N = 10)	27 (N = 13)	18 (N = 9)	10 (N = 5)	0	0
Pushing, shoving, grabbing	20 (N = 10)	12 (N = 6)	6 (N = 3)	6 (N = 3)	4 (N = 2)	4 (N = 2)
Hit with hand	14 (N = 7)	14 (N = 7)	6 (N = 3)	4 (N = 2)	0	2 (N = 1)
Hit with something hard	6 (N = 3)	6 (N = 3)	4 (N = 2)	4 (N = 2)	0	0

quency of each type of physically violent act was computed separately for husbands and wives. These data, in Table 2, suggest considerable similarity between the frequency of methods used by males and females to resolve marital conflict.

Who Did More Damage? The data from the interview part of the survey, and supported by reports of wifebeating, suggests that men do more damage. There are several possible reasons for this:

1. Because of socialization, women are taught better impulse control; they stop aggressive behavior before any damage occurs.
2. Because women are more verbal than men, men resort to physical means to support their dominant position.
3. Because men are physically stronger, they are capable of causing more physical damage to their wives than wives are capable of causing to husbands.

The myth of women receiving socialization for greater impulse control appears to have little support in reality—at least as far as marital fights are concerned. The data provided on Tables 1 and 2, plus insights gained from the in-depth interviews, suggest that women are as likely to select physical violence to resolve marital conflicts as are the men. Furthermore, child abusers are more likely to be women, and women throughout history have been the prime perpetrators of infanticide.[24] While it is recognized that women spend more time with children and are usually the parent in a single parent home (which is prone to stress and strains resulting in child abuse), and that fathers in similar situations might abuse their children more, these findings do indicate that women have the potential to commit acts of violence and, under certain circumstances, to carry out these acts.

The second point is also questionable. Although the myth of the verbally abusing, nagging women is perpetuated in the media—mainly in comic form—the data to support this myth is lacking. There appeared to be small random differences in the use of verbal violence in the families studied. Furthermore, Levinger, in his study of divorce applicants, found that wives were three times more likely to complain of verbal abuse than their husbands.[11]

It appears that the last reason is more plausible. The data reported suggests that at least the intention of both men and women towards using physical violence in marital conflicts is equal. Identical percentages of men and women reported hitting or hitting with an object. Furthermore, data on homicide between spouses suggests that an almost equal number of wives kill their husbands as husbands kill wives.[27] Thus it appears that men and women might have equal potential towards violent marital interaction; initiate similar acts of violence; and, when differences of physical strength are equalized by weapons, commit similar amounts of spousal homicide. The major difference appears to be the male's ability to do more physical damage during non-homicidal marital physical fights. When the wife slaps her husband, her lack of physical strength, plus his ability to restrain her, reduces the physical damage to a minimum. When the husband slaps his wife, however, his strength, plus her inability to restrain him, results in considerably more damage.

Support for this position is provided by the following account in a newspaper article describing the beating a physically weaker husband had received from his wife. This article noted that a wealthy, elderly New York banker had won a separation from his second wife, who was 31 years his junior. During the 14 year marriage, the husband had been bullied, according to the judge, by "hysteria, screaming tantrums, and . . . vicious physical violence practiced on a man . . . ill-equipped for fistfights with a shrieking woman." The judge noted that the husband wore constant scars and bruises. Once his wife shredded his ear with her teeth, another time she blackened both his eyes, and on still another occasion, injured one of his eyes so badly that doctors feared it might be lost.[26]

Discussion

The data presented suggests several possibilities for reducing spouse abuse—especially wifebeating, since the physical damage far exceeds that which occurs in husbandbeating. One could attempt to remove those conditions which appear to result in wifebattering. Based on O'Brien's findings, this would require that men be able to adequately fulfill the male role of major economic provider via full employment, increased wages, adequate education, and job skill training. Implementation of this, as O'Brien notes, runs counter to the goals of the Women's Liberation Movement, as well as civil rights legislation.[14] Another solution might be to train women in the martial arts so they are more equally matched in the marital arena. One cannot help but wonder about the existence of repeated attempts of wifebeating, if the husband were decked by the "little woman." While information on husbands' reaction to this form of interpersonal interaction is lacking, there is evidence that battered and abused women reach a point at which they can no longer tolerate this behavior, and often they turn to weapons to equalize their spouses' greater physical strength. Therefore, while defending oneself may avoid a battering, the long term result might be homicidal.

This suggests that the solution lies in a two-pronged attack on the problem, an immediate as well as long term solution. First, there needs to be a mechanism which will provide protection from further physical abuse by the battering spouse. Second, the long term solution requires the re-education of family members, starting with young children.

There is ample evidence to suggest that family interaction patterns are transmitted to succeeding generations. We know that abusing parents were often abused children.[25,28] Furthermore, clinical studies have shown that individuals who commit acts of violence often have family backgrounds steeped in violence, not only by experiences of abuse as children, but often witnessing acts of physical violence between their parents.[6,7,8,17,18] Patterns of intra-family interaction were found to exist in which parents used similar methods to discipline children as they used to resolve marital conflict, and their children imitated these methods when dealing with siblings.[23] Furthermore, these patterns were found to exist over three generations.[22] Thus, it would appear that long-term solutions to the problem of spousebattering would require a restructuring of all family interaction patterns with an emphasis on the use of non-violent methods of resolving problems.

REFERENCES

1. Ardrey, R., *The Territorial Imperative*. New York: Atheneum, 1967.
2. Bach, G. R. and Goldberg, H., *Creative Aggression*. New York: Avon, 1975.
3. Balswick, J. O. and Peek, C., "The Inexpressive Male: A Tragedy of American Society," *Family Coordinator* **20**: 363–368 (1971).
4. Bandura, A., *Aggression—A Social Learning Analysis*. Englewood Cliffs, New Jersey: Prentice-Hall, 1973.
5. Bard, M., "The Study and Modification of Intra-Familial Violence," in J. Singer (ed.) *The Control of Aggression and Violence*. New York: Academic Press, 1971.
6. Duncan, J. W. and Duncan, G. M., "Murder in the Family: A Study of Some Homicidal Adolescents," *American Journal of Psychiatry* **127**: 1498–1502 (May 1971).
7. Duncan, G. M., Frazier, S. H., Lintin, E. M., Johnson, A. M., Barron, A. J., "Etiological Factors in First Degree Murder," *Journal of American Medical Association* **168**: 1755–1758 (1958).
8. Easson, W. M. and Steinhilber, R. N., "Murderous Aggression by Children and Adolescents," *Archives of General Psychiatry* **4**: 47–55 (January 1961).
9. Eron, L. D., Walder, L. O., Lefkowitz, M. M., *Learning of Aggression in Children*. 1971. Boston: Little Brown.
10. Leslie, G. R., *The Family in Social Context*. New York: Oxford Press, 1967.
11. Levinger, G., "Sources of Marital Dissatisfaction Among Applicants for Divorce," *American Journal of Orthopsychiatry* **36**: 803–807 (October 1966).
12. Lorenz, K., *On Aggression*. New York: Harcourt Brace, 1966.
13. Mead, M. *Sex and Temperament in Three Primitive Societies*. New York: William Morrow, 1935.
14. O'Brien, J. E., "Violence in Divorce-Prone Families," *Journal of Marriage and the Family* **33**: 692–698 (1971).
15. Parnas, R., "The Police Response to Domestic Disturbances," *Wisconsin Law Review:* 914–960 (fall 1967).
16. Safilios-Rothschild, C., "Family Sociology of Wives' Family Sociology? A Cross-Cultural Examination of Decision-Making," *Journal of Marriage and the Family* **31**: 190–301 (1969).
17. Satten, J., Meninger, K., and Rosen, I., "Murder Without Apparent Motive: A Study in Personality Disorganization," *American Journal of Psychiatry* **117**: 48–53 (1960).

18. Silver, L. B., Dublin, C. C. and Lourie, R. S., "Does Violence Breed Violence? Contributions From a Study of Child Abuse Syndrome," *American Journal of Psychiatry* **126**: 404–407 (September 1969).

19. Stark, R. and McEvoy, J. III, "Middle Class Violence," *Psychology Today* **4**: 52–65 (November 1970).

20. Steinmetz, S. K., "Male Liberation—Destroying the Stereotypes," in E. Powers and M. Lees (eds.) *Process in Relationship*. New York: West Publishing Co., 1974.

21. Steinmetz, S. K., "The Sexual Context of Social Research," *The American Sociologist* **9**: 111–116 (August 1974).

27. Steinmetz, S. K., "Intra-Familial Patterns of Conflict Resolution: Husband/Wife: Parent/Child; and Sib/Sib." Unpublished Ph.D. thesis. Case Western Reserve University, 1975.

23. Steinmetz, S. K., "The Use of Force for Resolving Family Conflict: The Training Ground for Abuse," *Family Coordinator* (1977).

24. Straus, Murray A., Gelles, R., and Steinmetz, S. K., "Theories, Methods and Controversies in the Study of Violence Between Family Members," seminar presented to the annual meetings of the American Sociological Association, New York. 1973.

25. Wasserman, S., "The Abused Parent of the Abused Child," *Children* **14**: 175–179 (September–October 1967).

26. *Wilmington Evening Journal* (Delaware): 2 (April 21, 1976).

27. Wolfgang, M., *Patterns in Criminal Homicide*. New York: John Wiley & Sons, Inc., 1958.

28. Zalba, S. R., "Treatment of Child Abuse," *Social Work* **11**, *No. 4:* 8–16 (1966).

BATTERED WOMEN: A SOCIAL PSYCHOLOGICAL PERSPECTIVE*

Suzanne Prescott Governors State University
Carolyn Letko College of St. Francis

The Problem of Marital Violence

While statistics reveal that in New York State in 1973, there were almost 5000 rapes reported, almost three times that number of wife-abuse complaints went to Family Court! *Unreported* cases could perhaps double or triple that number. Undetected and hidden for the most part, statistics and estimates are most difficult to retrieve, since most women will not make public the conflict in their marriages.

As is true of much of women's history, the stories of battered

*This research was supported by a mini-grant from Governors State University, resources made available from the College of Human Learning and Development, at Governors State University, Park Forest South, Ill. 60466.

women are singularly absent in literature. While many women do not confide their stories to others, those that do—and increasing numbers do—have created limited understanding of the causes and effects of violence on women, their marriages, and their families. We do not know what resources have ultimately been contacted by women caught up in violent relationships. The current study was undertaken in order to permit battered women to tell their stories and to provide part of the crucial missing perspective.

Failure in the past of research and literature to provide detailed accounts of women who are beaten in marriage has helped to lend support to popular, though untrue, stereotypes of violence in marriage. And, as with rape, denial to women of opportunities to expose marital violence has permitted the persistence of explanations which too often justify the husband's behavior and blame the victims. An earlier study, and one of the first to examine battered women and their husbands, reports about studies of the wives of alcoholics and suggests that their studies ". . . do make clear the concept that a husband's behavior may serve to fill a wife's needs even though she protests it," and that ". . . this type of family equilibrium may be a more or less effective solution to mutual needs, although vulnerable to specific kinds of stress."[9]

Similar justifications of male behavior have plagued the efforts of women who have been working on the problem of rape. They have found repeatedly that many men and social agencies, including police and the courts, have suggested that women entice their rapists in order to fulfill their own needs. Similarly, the remarks of Snell suggests that wife beating is solicited by wives, that violence is an acceptable form of the status quo, and that violence constitutes an acceptable solution to marital disagreement.

The authors also offer a character description of beaten wives, describing the wife's "aggressiveness, masculinity, frigidity, and masochism."[9] Clearly the above descriptions demonstrate the need for women's perspectives to be presented. As women's stories so often indicate, what men describe as aggressiveness in females, women see as asserting their personal integrity; what men automatically see as masculinity in females, women sense as their own competence. What some men may see as frigidity, appears to women to be a natural lack of sexual responsiveness to their violent husbands. And what men see as masochism, women report as the sense of being trapped inside their marriages.

The limited history of research into marital violence has gone through two significant periods. Early studies took an approach which can be characterized as "blaming the victim." In these studies, causes of marital violence were assumed to stem from personal or internal forces, rather than external social forces. These studies did little to disconfirm prevailing stereotypes concerning marital violence. A second wave of research initially focused on evaluating available evidence and exploding myths surrounding home conflict.[10,13] Myths were replaced by theoretical models which discounted unicausal explanations of violence. The new models[2,10] highlight the *multicausal* nature of marital violence and the dynamic interaction of psychological and wider social variables.

The use of physical force, either to control women's behavior or as an emotional outburst, is condoned by major social institutions, including the legal system. Sexual relations are frequently considered part of wives' duties to their husbands. It might be expected that women who experience violence and discord may not enjoy sexual relations or desire to have sex with their husbands as a result. A respondent to the current study asked, "How can you enjoy sex and feel loving toward a man who treats you like an animal?" State laws do not provide women with the right to refuse sex under these conditions.

For men, employment opportunities and lack of work satisfaction may lead to frustration, insecurity, and a sense of failure. In the home, and inside the marriage, economic and work related experiences may affect spouse relations.[2] The contributions of employment to marital discord may reflect the husband's fear of, or anger at, failure to live up to personal or family expectations for the family's economic support. In addition, men who feel declining ability to control their careers may see the marriage as the main area of control which they must maintain—the one area where they can continue, through the exercise of physical force, to maintain their authority. A wife's employment and ambitions may contribute to the lessening of economic hardship, but may actually contribute to her spouse's sense of failure and lack of control. If both spouses have accepted the traditional role division of husband as the economic provider and wife as bearer of responsibility for the home, husbands may see wives' employment as a breach of their traditional sex role. Women who have accepted traditional responsibility for the success of their marriage may experience a sense of guilt when their marriage leads to violence. Restrictions and limitations stemming from state laws, and the world of work, may help to create conditions which couples are unprepared to deal with successfully. Women reported on family financial conditions and their husbands' employment status.

On the community level, support systems are inadequate to meet the needs of couples in conflict. The help and support which might be expected from police, lawyers, clergy, and relatives are insufficient to meet the needs of women. Women in the current study were asked which community agencies they had contacted, and they reported their subsequent experiences. Negative experiences with police, lawyers, and clergy were more often reported than the helping experience women sought. Persons in these agencies are for the most part men, who share beliefs in traditional marital roles, and who may themselves condone the use of force as a means of control. For some of these men, undoubtedly, the women who seek their intervention serve to remind them of conditions in their own marriages. Each of these occupational roles, and the authority vested in these roles, may provide men with the opportunity to exercise control over women, just as they seek to control their own wives. Lack of supporting resources from these groups in the community can contribute to a woman's sense of being trapped, isolated, and feeling helpless in marriage.

The direct effects of marital violence on women, their marriages, and their children have received the least attention in previous studies. While divorce or homicide may be notable and obvious outcomes of conflict, many effects on women go unnoticed. From womens' reports, violence may be expected to affect self concept, pleasure derived from sexual relations in marriage, desire to bear children, and may affect children themselves. Though positive effects of marital violence could hardly be expected, women report becoming more independent and learning to establish new relationships and other sources of support. Still, the level of violence sustained by these women and the lack of readily available support systems highlights the need for extending our understanding and, more important, extending resources to couples in conflict. Marital violence may be one expression of couples' marital dissatisfaction, and when it leads to divorce, it may be one of the few solutions available. But as one woman described her violent marriage and subsequent divorce, "It's a hard way to get out of a bad relationship."

While an understanding of marital violence requires looking at the contributions of social institutions and community resource patterns, a close examination of the marital relationship itself is essential. Marriage brings together individuals who have adopted aspects of traditional male and female sex roles. Through social learning and their personal histories, gradually behaviors thought to be appropriate or inappropriate to each sex are sorted out. Individuals learn not only what is appropriate to their own roles, but adopt expectations about the appropriate behavior of the opposite sex. Many of these beliefs, values, and behaviors regarding sex roles are expressed in the course of marriage. In this way, for example, men may adopt the role of provider while expecting women to be responsible for the home, child rearing, and even the success of the marriage itself. Women may accept the roles of mother and homemaker, while expecting financial security from their mates. When these and other expectations are not met in marriage, conflict may and often does arise.

Aspects of roles were of particular interest in the current study. Each partner possesses expectations concerning the use of physical force and how conflicts should be handled. We also examined the role of communication in marital relations. When traditional sex roles emphasize male authority, men may not only expect to influence important areas of family decision making, but may also expect that the final word in disagreements is theirs, and that physical force is justified in maintaining their authority. Should strain arise over lack of ability or desire to meet either explicit or implicit expectations, conflict may be settled through the arbitrary use of authority by the male head of household.

Expectations concerning communication in marriage have received little study. While modern expectations place stress on intimacy and openness in communications, couples adopt informal and often not explicit expectations, concerning what are appropriate and what are taboo topics for discussion. A crucial aspect of communication as it relates to violence in marriage is the role of communication in settling disagreements. Unfortunately, most couples come to marriage with insufficient communication skills for resolving their conflicts. There is currently concern over whether the popular media display realistic models of conflict resolution and whether our own family histories are particularly effective examples of how to resolve disagreements. As one respondent indicated, "I grew up in the era of 'Ozzie and Harriet' and 'Leave It To Beaver' and I had no idea what marriage would really be like." Violence does not seem to be a successful way to end marital disputes, yet our culture does not provide many obvious prescriptions for settling disputes otherwise. Many couples prefer to argue away from their children. Thus, when couples can discuss or settle disagreements without physical force, children are not often observers.

The lack of available cultural models reflecting realistic conflict resolution, and the presence of immediate role strains such as conflict over financial matters, do not appear to account for the severe violence experienced in marriage. Specific instances reported by women indicate that many conflicts arise over seemingly trivial disagreements. The explosive psychodynamics which may characterize marital violence suggests that early experience plays a role insofar as patterns of childhood intimacy and early social learning may serve to condition couples responses later in their own marriages.

Oftentimes, the crucial role of early experience has appeared in research as the attempt to show that wifebatterers or child abusers were beaten as children. Like other single-cause explanations, history of family violence does not guarantee that individuals will be violent as adults. What is suggested, however, is that some aspects of early relationships and some early forms of social learning may further be reinforced by traditional sex role upbringing, and may facilitate the expression of violence in marriage. In the current data, it is possible to examine this question in two ways. First, by looking at the family backgrounds described by abused women, we can look to whether there is a relationship between early childhood trauma and later marital discord. Data that relies on memories of early experiences, however, may not be as reliable as reports of current situations. Thus, the second and more important source of information is the women's reports of the effects of violence in their own marriage on their children. It is possible by examining these responses to understand what specific early experiences can affect children and how these early experiences may establish expectations regarding the use of violence and the role of communication in marriage.

The Women's Movement at its core represents expanding opportunities for women. For many women, this has meant rising expectations for marital satisfaction and personal growth. Often, however, men experience the Women's Movement as a threat to their own opportunities and sphere of influence. As couples enter marriage and go through their adult years, they encounter the often incompatible desires to more firmly rely on old values and early expectations in the face of changing social values and the lack of social consensus concerning current sex roles. At the same time, they may find that their marriage is a testing ground for trying out new behaviors, developing new expectations, and changing sex roles. The need for security of old traditions and the need for new growth may lead couples to face new frustrations and may lead to conflict in marriage.

Understanding marital violence involves a broad perspective which can demonstrate the ways in which formal social institutions, as well as cultural beliefs, communities, sex roles, and personal histories serve to reinforce maladaptive behaviors in marriage. The subsequent results examine the role of employment and income on marital disagreements, the effects of violence on women and their children, the relationship of early childhood experience to subsequent marital discord, and the experience of women with community groups that were contacted for support.

Methods

Major difficulties are encountered by researchers who study taboo topics such as marital violence or rape. Because such studies are not done on samples representative of the whole American population, it is difficult to estimate the number of couples who experience marital violence. However, predictions which place estimates as high as 50–70% have been made by Gelles[2] and Straus.[15] Other studies indirectly estimate the degree to which violence is condoned in marriage. Investigators have successfully used limited populations in order to study marital violence. Researchers admit the difficulties of obtaining data, as well as using data to generalize to a larger population. These limitations have undoubtedly limited exploration of marital violence. Ironically, marital violence may be the most frequently unreported American crime. Despite difficulties, increasing general interest, especially among women's groups and renewed interest on the part of researchers, is producing an expanding body of exploratory studies of marital violence.

The current study is based on the reports of 40 women who responded to a survey containing 53 questions concerning marital violence, employment, age, education, and family background. The surveys were developed following pilot interviews with battered women and a pilot survey. Extensive pretesting helped to insure that questions on the current survey were ones to which women could provide meaningful answers, and which disclosed effects of violence which had not previously been discussed. One example to be discussed later is the reported effect of marital violence on the children of battered women.

In order to obtain respondents to our survey, an ad was placed in the classified section of *Ms.* magazine in the summer of 1975. Women were asked to share their information on marital violence with the senior author. All replies were guaranteed confidentiality. A total of 66 survey requests were received, and 43 surveys (65%) were returned. Two were completed by women who had not experienced physical violence, one was returned "addressee unknown," and two were returned too late to be included in the analysis. Thirty-eight were used in the statistical analysis, and 40 were used for analysis of the open-ended response items.

The respondents were likely to share characteristics of *Ms.* readership in general, and therefore were more likely to be supportive of women's issues, relatively young, more liberal, more educated, more frequently employed than women in general. Respondents to surveys are by definition more cooperative than non-respondents. In addition, respondents were self-identified "battered women." Women who may experience violence but do not consider themselves battered women, victims, or participants in marital violence did not respond. It should be noted that not all women against whom physical force has been used consider themselves abused women. Women who are forced to have sexual relations with their husbands against their will may not consider themselves battered wives, although this experience has been described by some as sexual assault.

When characteristics of the actual respondents were checked, our expectations were borne out. From the pilot data, it was concluded that respondents were supportive of a variety of women's issues. Respondents to the earlier pilot study supported, on the average, seven out of ten women's issues (including such issues as equal pay and abortion). Nearly half (46%) of the respondents to the current survey were between ages 30–39 (an age span often implicated in marital violence), 30% were younger than this age group, and 20% were older. Eighty-two percent of the women (compared to 73% of the men either had some college, completed college, or had an advanced degree. Three-fourths (76%) of the women were employed at the time of the survey. A high proportion (56%) of the respondents were employed in professional or managerial occupations. In comparison, women's reports indicate that although 90% of their male partners were employed, only 30% of them were employed in a similar professional or managerial capacity.

It should be noted that employment levels and employment satisfaction have been implicated in previous marital violence research as potential contributors to marital violence. In the current sample, two differences in important social status characteristics were noted. Women, on the average, were better educated; and in a number of cases, they held better jobs than American women on the whole.

Nearly half of the respondents were divorced (49%). Forty-six percent were still married, and two respondents reported violence in relationships with their lovers. Eighty-three percent of the women had children (with an average of 2.9 children per couple with children).

The structure of the survey provided both open-ended response items and multiple choice items. In addition to the data obtained to the open-ended replies, women also were free to add comments. Although Gelles[3] had not cited the survey method as a useful tool for examining marital violence, the current response rate and data appear to lend credibility to its usefulness and suggest that such a technique might continue to be used.

For the present report, the data proved useful in three ways. Responses from women were often detailed enough to add a qualitative dimension lacking in many previous reports. All identifying information, such as names and places, have been removed and, in some cases, quotations have been slightly paraphrased to protect respondents. Portions of these women's narratives provide substantiation for and clarification of observed frequencies reported in the Tables. Secondly, as a characteristic of exploratory research, although the sample is not random and cannot be generalized to a specific population, the observed sample characteristics do not suggest that the respondents are a particularly deviant group. Thus, it is possible to note whether observations are in accord with conclusions provided by previous research. Perhaps most important, the responses raise new hypotheses for subsequent exploration.

The Violent Experience

Women respondents indicated the nature of the violence they had experienced. Nearly all of the respondents had received verbal abuse (N = 36), and pushing/slapping (N = 35), and large numbers of women had experienced more serious physical abuse. Twenty-four women (63%) had been punched or kicked, 12 women had been sexually abused (32%), a weapon had been used against 9 women (24%), and 8 women (21%) had experienced some other type of abuse, like strangulation or choking. Forty-three percent of the respondents indicated that they had some small or large scars resulting from the use of physical force by their partners.

Thirteen women (43%) of the 30 women who had children indicated that their partners' physical violence had also been extended to their children. These women indicated that one particular child was more likely to be the recipient of violence, and most often (N = 8) this turned out to be the oldest male child. One surprising result was the proportion of women, over one-third, who indicated that their husbands' violence had made them hesitant to have more children. The issue of birth control has received much more consideration over the last 20 years, and has led women to consider more carefully whether they wish to bear children. Violence and marital discord may be factors in family planning, although drops in fertility rates have not been linked to marital violence. Several considerations may make women hesitant to have more children. Gelles, in a previous study,[3] has noted that pregnant women experience an unusually high level of violence. The actual expectation or threat of this violence may be a deterrant to having more children. In addition, women may anticipate the financial responsibility of additional children, and a woman who is contemplating divorce may be especially hesitant about incurring further responsibilities when she faces a future in which her children may have to rely upon her exclusively for care and support.

Women were asked to describe in detail the most recent occasion of physical abuse and their participation in the conflicts. Over half the women (57%) reported that they had participated physically in at least one argument, though two-thirds of the participating women indicated that they participated rarely. Nearly all women who did not participate expressed fear of retaliation. "My husband hits a lot harder than I can . . . he is much bigger and stronger and fear stops me," was the type of comment made by several women. However, many women's responses indicated that they had not been socialized to expect to participate in violence. "I grew up in a sheltered and non-violent home," one woman reported; "Females are not taught or conditioned to use violence," replied another woman.

Many women did not tend to see disputes as exclusively the fault of their husbands. Eighty percent of the women felt that the blame was shared, and described their participation in the conflict. When women report the causes of violence, each spouse's failure to meet the expectations of the other was most frequently cited. Lack of agreement over the appropriate role of spouse was identified by 43% (16) of the respondents. Other women, however, could not pinpoint areas of conflict over specific aspects of sex roles. Some women simply identified the lack of communication skills as a precursor to violence (11%). A higher proportion of women (20%) indicated that emotional disturbance or upset seemed to lead to the immediate conflict. The rising expectations of women for personal growth and achievement may mean that traditional sex role prescriptions are inadequate to meet personal needs. Changing economic conditions may make it increasingly difficult for each partner to live up to the expectations of his or her partner, especially when a woman works and is also responsible for home and child care. Lack of agreement over expectations for each others' behavior in other crucial areas of marriage was mentioned. One respondent reported:

> I went to bed but my husband was still up. After a short time he came in and said he wanted sex. As I was nearly asleep I mumbled something and tried to go back to sleep. He then went to the kitchen, filled a pitcher with cold water, and came back to my bed and poured cold water over me. He did this a number of times.

Another woman reported reprisal in a child-rearing dispute.

"I smacked my daughter's hand, and my husband took my arm and repeatedly hit my hand against the edge of the table."

Two women reported discord as a result of their recent employment, or their husbands' financial responsibilities.

> It was concerning my recent promotion to a high level job. My husband appeared to be happy for my opportunity but since I began the job and got some publicity locally . . . he is sick of hearing about my damn job!

Another women reported that the most recent violent incident of her marriage was caused by "reminding him of responsibilities. i.e., bills to pay, time to mow the lawn, go to work, etc."

While disagreements over specific behavior expectations is important, the role of verbal communication skills in marriage is underscored by respondents. Nearly half the respondents (47%) said they did not feel free to talk to their husbands about their husbands' violence. Women reported that either their own inability to communicate or, more often, their husbands' inability to engage in discussion contributed to the most recent incident of abuse. Thirty-one (84%) women reported that violence in their relationship was accompanied by a decrease in the quality of communication in their marriage. When husbands find that violence is a successful means of ending dispute, and when wives find that they cannot discuss the unpleasant effects of their spouses' violence, the options for women in their marriages are seriously restricted. A development of generally more satisfactory solutions to marital discord may mean not only placing more restrictions on the use of physical force in marriage, but increasing the general level of communication skills in marriage.

Violence in relationships, besides its immediate and obvious effects on physical well-being, can have serious and lasting effects inside the marriage. The impact of the violence on women and their children has not received attention. Whether physical abuse or force is a method of settling immediate disputes, or accompanies a husband's emotional outburst in reaction to disagreement, a woman's fear, and lack of physical strength in comparison with her spouse, may make the use of force a means by which the spouse can end disputes in the short run, and most women (82%) reported being fearful on the most recent occasions of physical abuse. Yet, in the long run, the use of physical force as a continuing pattern in marital discord may build up resentment. Virtually all respondents (90%) reported anger resulting from the most recent occasion.

Men's enhanced ability to use this form of control in order to win in the short run may be expected to cause resentment in wives who do not possess this means of control.

Husbands' violence affects women in a variety of other ways. Nearly three-fourths of the women report being depressed. Nearly as many report feeling trapped (68%) or helpless (55%). These feelings may further help in understanding what contributes to the tendency of women to remain in marriage. Depression is accompanied by low emotional energy at a time when women may need this resource in order to deal with violence in their marriages. Depression can affect how frequently or how persistantly women seek help directly from community agencies or other helping groups. In addition, for women with children, with low education, and without marketable job skills, there are few alternatives to ending the violence in their marriages.

Following the most recent violent experience, one-third of the women reported feelings of humiliation, and one-fourth (26%) reported feeling guilty. Women may feel guilty because they assume that violence in their marriages indicates their own shortcomings in meeting their husbands' expectations. As the Women's Movement has led to the questioning of women's total responsibility for marital success, women who have married more recently may experience these feelings less often, especially when they can identify the source of dispute as stemming from wider social conflicts instead of their own inadequacy. Still, many women report that conflict affects their self-esteem. One-fourth of the respondents report feeling either "inadequate," "unworthy," or "unattractive" as a result of marital violence.

As marital violence can be expected to have an impact on a woman's psychological state of well-being, it may also be expected to affect satisfaction with the marital relationship in a number of ways. Not only do women report a decrease in quality of communication with their spouses, but nearly three-fourths (73%) report a decrease in the quality of their sexual relationships. Nearly three-fourths indicated that the violence had a range of other negative effects, including a general distrust of men and fear of remarriage.

While violence in marriage could be expected to have few positive effects, most women (84%) could pinpoint at least one positive outcome. They reported that violence had helped them to become more independent. Many indicated that they were able to establish new relationships by reaching out or seeking others. As one woman described it, "I was able to find new sources of approval. He had been pretty much my sole source of self-esteem, but I learned that others could be important sources of support." Traditional women's roles have confined sources of self-respect to appropriate performance of traditional sex role prescriptions and have placed heavy emphasis on the husband as the exclusive source of approval and reward. Changing sex roles, which bring women into the employment world and into contact with a broader range of persons, may lessen the burden on husbands as the sole source of their wives' satisfaction, while also lessening wives' willingness to remain in violent marriages in order to maintain approval, status in the community, and the increasingly limited rewards of their violent marriages.

While there has been an increase of interest in protection and the rights of children, similar protection and concern has not been extended to wives, and studies have not explored the reaction of children to their parents' marital violence. Yet violence between spouses may cause extreme emotional reactions in children, and may establish in early childhood a response to conflict which could persist into adulthood.

There was little evidence in the current data that fighting or beating in the women's own family backgrounds and their partners' backgrounds were related to current marital conflicts. Only four women reported that they had been beaten as children, while eleven women reported that their husbands had been beaten as children. This was particularly interesting since these women reported that in their current marriages, violence was also more likely to be directed toward sons. However, 24 women reported fighting between their parents when they were growing up. Women who reported this fighting were more likely to report that their own husbands acted violently toward their children. They were also more likely to report that their husbands were dissatisfied with their jobs. If there had been fighting between the parents of these women's husbands, the women were more likely to report conflicts in their own marriages over specific violations of sex role expectations. Fourteen women, however, did not know whether their husbands had been beaten. More accurate data might uncover the relation between violence in family backgrounds and current levels of violence.

In the current reports, 23 women indicated that their children had observed marital disputes on one or more occasions. Most typically (13 of 30 mothers, or 43%) reported that their children reacted with fear or crying, and 7 mothers reported that their children withdrew from conflicts. While some children ($N = 4$) reacted to the immediate situation by siding with one parent or the other, two children actually responded with violence of their own toward their father. One respondent indicated that her children had learned not to bring up topics which were likely to arouse her spouse, and others indicated that their children were confused or disturbed by the violence ($N = 3$). The response of one mother indicates the range of effects that violence may have on children.

> The youngest girl screams and cries hysterically, yelling at her father to let me alone. The boy acts disgusted and retreats into himself. Lately, he's asked questions about why we married. My daughter says she won't ever marry. My oldest child screamed and became extremely fearful. I put him is psychotherapy where he was advised to walk away, as the fights were not his fault or his business. He is less frightened now.

Thirteen of the 30 mothers (43%) indicated that the violence may have affected their children's attitude toward marriage. These same women reported that their daughters expressed fear of marriage or general distrust of men and intimate relationships. One woman reports, "Although young at the time of the divorce, my daughter recalls that 'Daddy used to hit you.' This was never talked about in front of her after we separated. Her remarks are based on memory." Another woman said, "At ten my daughter vehemently stated she never wants to marry or have children."

Children are normally expected to be affected by the quality of their relationship with their parents, and women's reports suggest that children form attitudes about marriage and sex roles by observing their parents. The reports of these women also suggest that children begin to develop behaviors or typical responses to marital violence which could form the basis of their response to disputes later in their own marriages.

There may be some concern over what children learn from their parents' physical violence. Both sexes may learn that violence is one way of settling disagreements. Children themselves may tacitly come to expect that the use of physical force in marriage is a legitimate expression of authority. More specifically, boys and girls can learn that physical abuse is a form of control exercised by men over women, and unfortunately, for their own marriages later on, they may receive the impression that violence is a way to "win" a disagreement. If these impressions are carried over into adulthood, they could be detrimental to marital problem-solving ability.

Not only can children learn about the use of violence through their parents, but more important, in terms of developing children's skills to deal with conflict, the tendency for children to withdraw may preclude their ever viewing rational argument as an alternative way of ending disputes. When women and men possess good communication skills, unmet expectations can be clarified, behavior can change, and compromises can emerge. Children, by withdrawing, may fail to develop an understanding of the positive role of communication. Differences in childhood socialization of boys and girls, particularly in the areas of aggression and verbal skills, may tend to reinforce what children learn about the appropriateness of violence and communication in male and female sex roles. If mothers are tolerant (and the object, as well) of their sons' physical aggression, and if mothers are more likely to talk with their daughters, men and women may enter adulthood with different expectations about the use of physical force and different expectations concerning the importance of communication in conflict.

When women decide to move beyond the confines of the immediate family to seek help and support, there are a variety of potential listeners for their complaints. Not all of these prove equally helpful or supportive to women. Nearly all the women had talked to someone about their husbands' violence, and 81% of the respondents indicated that they had contacted friends. Relatives and lawyers were the next most frequently contacted (59% each). Of the contacts made, those that women indicated to be supportive and those that were not helpful revealed the strengths and shortcomings of traditional community groups that are now charged with handling domestic violence. Table 1 shows the number of women contacting each group, the percentage of these contacts which were rated as "helpful" or "supportive," and the percentage of women who contacted a source and had a negative experience with that source group.

TABLE 1.   GROUPS OR AGENTS WOMEN CONTACTED REGARDING THEIR PARTNERS' VIOLENCE

GROUP/AGENT	NUMBER OF WOMEN CONTACTING GROUP	NUMBER OF WOMEN WHO FOUND GROUP HELPFUL	NUMBER OF WOMEN WHO HAD NEGATIVE EXPERIENCE
		$N = 38$	
Friends	30	12	2
	(81%)	(40%)	(7%)
Relatives	22	9	8
	(59%)	(41%)	(36%)
Lawyers	22	4	7
	(59%)	(18%)	(32%)
Police	15	3	4
	(41%)	(20%)	(27%)
Marriage counselors	15	6	4
	(41%)	(40%)	(27%)
Women's group	12	8	1
	(32%)	(66%)	(8%)
Psychotherapist	11	7	1
	(30%)	(64%)	(9%)
Minister, priest	10	1	6
	(27%)	(10%)	(60%)

Factors Affecting Marital Violence and Help-Seeking

Previous studies have suggested that employment and financial problems are contributors to family violence. The expectations of men and women regarding employment, the role of husband as provider, the importance of achievement in occupations, and satisfaction with family income, may lead to the appearance or escalation of violence in the relationship and may have direct effects on wives and children. Our results point to the importance of economic factors as contributors to marital disputes.

Occupation and career success for men may be threatened during times of unemployment or when job opportunities do not match expectations for success and achievement. For most women, the most recent instance of violence occurred between 1970 and 1975, a period of rising unemployment and job insecurity. Marital violence was reported to increase during a period of unemployment in British history.

Men who were only employed part-time or were unemployed at the time of the most recent conflict were more violent toward their wives than men who were employed. Women whose husbands were unemployed experienced more varied types of violence than women whose husbands were employed, as can be seen in Table 2.

Husbands who experienced low job satisfaction were more likely to punch or kick their wives than husbands who were satisfied with their job. Seventy-three percent, or 16, of those women whose husbands were described as having low job satisfaction were punched or kicked, while only half of the women whose husbands were satisfied with their jobs were treated in this way.

While husbands' lack of job satisfaction may be frustrating to both men and women, for men, the lack of success in their careers may be compensated for by exercising control in their marriages. Rather than ignore their wives' failure to meet their expectations, husbands increase the cost to wives of violating their expectations by expanding their use of physical force as a means of punishment. In the present study, this is supported by the tendency of wives whose husbands experienced job dissatisfaction to more often mention that specific sex role violation led to the most recent incidence of violence in their marriage. (Table 3.)

The importance of job satisfaction is described by one respondent:

> He states that his job is frustrating and unsatisfactory. It is low paying and boring; few challenges. He never sought another job as he says, 'No one would hire me.'

Men who fail to find employment may attempt at home to prove their superiority over their wives. Of the 11 wives of unemployed men, 64% ($N = 7$) of the wives reported feeling "inadequate," "unworthy," or "unattractive," while only 36% ($N = 4$) of women whose husbands were employed reported such feelings.

The actual stress of diminished or inadequate financial resources may also contribute to conflict. Women who reported financial problems to be moderate or very severe were more often assaulted with weapons than those with limited or no financial worries. Understandably, these women reported anxiety more often than women experiencing less threatening forms of violence. Of the nine women who had been assaulted with a weapon, six reported severe financial problems. Stereotypes often link family violence with social class or ethnic background; in truth, these stereotyped groups are more likely to experience financial stress. Even though class and ethnicity

TABLE 2. RELATIONSHIP BETWEEN HUSBAND'S EMPLOYMENT AND LEVEL OF VIOLENCE EXPERIENCED BY WIFE.
$N = 38$

	HUSBAND EMPLOYED FULL-TIME	HUSBAND NOT EMPLOYED FULL-TIME
High violence	10 (37%)	8 (73%)
Low violence	17 (63%)	3 (27%)

Gamma = 0.63, which indicates a moderately strong association between the level of violence and a husband's employment. "High violence" women were those who experienced more different types of violence (e.g., greater than the average number of different forms of violence).

were not controlled for in the current study, our largely middle class respondents demonstrated the important role financial strain can play in relation to marital violence.

Mothers who reported severe financial problems were also more likely to report that their husbands were violent toward their children. Of the 14 women who reported severe financial problems, 9 reported that husbands had acted violently toward the children. Violence aimed at the wife was likely to cause a reaction among children who had observed the violence, but children who were not affected were more likely to have fathers with good job satisfaction than children who were affected. Of the 7 women whose children

TABLE 3. HUSBAND'S JOB SATISFACTION AND CONFLICT OVER SEX ROLE EXPECTATIONS.
$N = 36$

MOST RECENT EPISODE	HUSBANDS NOT SATISFIED WITH JOB	HUSBANDS SATISFIED WITH JOB
Sex role behavior expectations violation	12 (71%)	5 (53%)
Other causes (emotional confusion, frustrations outside marriage, drinking)	10 (29%)	9 (47%)

Gamma = 0.37, which indicates a moderate association between a husband's job satisfaction and the cause of the most recent violent episode.

were not affected, 4 had husbands who were satisfied with their job, while two-thirds, or 14, of the wives whose children were affected by marital violence had husbands who experienced low job satisfaction.

Three-fourths of the women indicated that they and their partners had no religious affiliation at the time of their most recent conflict. In comparisons of those with religious orientation and those without an orientation, few associations appeared. Two-thirds of the small sub-group of women with a religious orientation said that their husbands' violence affected their self-confidence or self-esteem, while only 22% of the non-religious group reported these feelings. Religious groups frequently stress traditional sex role behaviors which emphasize women's responsibility in marriage and the home. Women who have broken ties with religion appear less likely to continue accepting traditional roles and less likely to agree that stepping beyond the boundaries of traditional roles is blameworthy. In contrast, religious orientation of women's husbands was not related to women's feelings of self-esteem. It appears that women with a religious orientation have internalized traditional sex roles, while husbands' religious orientation made no difference in whether women felt guilty or not. The importance of religion as a social institution has been questioned in recent years, yet numerous studies have demonstrated the relation between belief in traditional sex roles and strength of religion. One study concludes that many feminist beliefs are more likely to be held by college students who do not identify with a particular religious tradition.[8] Belief in traditional sex roles that are embedded in religious traditions may affect not only women, but may also interfere with ministers' ability to help abused women. A change in adherence to older sex role prescriptions among ministers could help to relieve women from feelings of guilt and self-doubt.

Among the women in this study, nearly all had talked to someone about their husbands' violence. It is important to understand what prompts women to go beyond the confines of their families in order to find help. Some problems may increase the likelihood that women will seek help. Increasing severity of physical violence, severe economic problems, and the extension of violence to children may lead women to seek help.

Patterns of help-seeking show that specific problems do lead women to seek help from specific agents or groups. Those who contacted the police, ministers, and women's groups were experiencing more severe physical abuse. If violence in the family extends to children, women are more motivated to contact helping agencies. Women who contacted helping agents or groups other than lawyers and marriage counselors were more likely to report that violence in the family was affecting their children. Economic pressures also characterized those who sought help from specific agencies or groups.

Job satisfaction also affected the pattern of help-seeking among women. Those whose husbands were employed but reported poor job satisfaction were more likely to contact ministers, police, lawyers, and women's groups. Women who were married to men in high status, professional or managerial occupations were four times more likely to have contacted therapists than women whose partners were employed in low status, low paying occupations. Women whose partners contributed least to the family income were less likely to be able to afford the services of a therapist. As women tended to seek help in understanding and solving their problems, all sources were not equally available. Women's help-seeking was affected by their resources within the family and risks to their status in the community and their marriage.

The impressions formed by community agencies or other resources of abused women may differ, since women may choose contacts on the basis of the specific nature and severity of the problem confronting them and on the basis of their own resources. An understanding of the range of problems faced by abused women could help agencies to quickly identify the resources needed by women who seek help.

Many women who chose to contact someone outside the family reported having unpleasant or negative experiences. Women who contacted ministers, relatives, lawyers, police, and marriage counselors reported the greatest proportion of negative experiences. Several examples illustrate the inadequacy of these groups and the implicit value orientations of those now in helping roles.

One woman reported that her minister had supported her husband "since he is supposed to be head of the household under normal circumstances." Another woman reported that her minister had suggested she remain married at any expense and that she should adjust to her husband's inadequacies. Only one woman reported that her minister understood the seriousness of her problem. Her minister said, "Get away from this man before he kills you!"

Several women described the reactions of their relatives as supportive, but a high proportion who contacted relatives failed to receive either understanding or support, instead finding that their relatives suggested that they "patch things up" or assumed that the woman "must be crazy" or needed a lesson in how to perform the "ideal wife role." The reports of these women suggest that parents of abused wives too often have little understanding and resources to offer their abused daughters.

Women also reported that contacts with lawyers were painful. "He first told me that if there was another woman I should overlook it. He seemed to think I was making too much of nothing." Other women did acknowledge that their lawyers had provided them with some knowledge of their legal rights, had relieved them of anxiety, and had served as successful buffers between them and their husbands.

Women also reported negative experiences with police and marriage counselors. Among the comments made about police were: "They brought him home fighting drunk and refused to arrest him since he was from a prominent family in the community," or "They refused to help or take any action." One woman who visited a marriage counselor found that her husband received more support. Another woman was encouraged to stay with her husband, despite the risk of bodily harm, and two women mentioned that the counselor seemed uninterested in their problems.

Women were least likely to report having unpleasant experiences with women's groups or friends. Although supportive, often these groups did not possess the specific resources that women sought. As one respondent described her contact with friends: "They were understanding, emotionally supportive, and helped me get out of thinking that I was alone in my experience, but they really couldn't help with what I needed most—protection, a good lawyer, and a chance to make it on my own."

Resources for helping battered wives are limited, and often those agencies which should be helping women, do not. The Women's Movement may, in the short run, help to raise women's consciousness of the problem, provide women with emotional support, and help them to more clearly identify aspects of their own problems.

But if women are to receive the help they need, those who are now paid to provide help, such as police, lawyers, ministers, and counselors, will have to assess the way they currently play their roles, and increase the resources available to abused women. As a start, the implicit value orientations of men in these roles should be examined. Perhaps men in these roles hold much the same expectations for their wives as the husbands of women who have reported here. As one respondent suggests, an increased understanding might lead men to voluntarily give up the use of physical force.

> I resent the fact that he has the power to use physical violence and does resort to it occasionally. I have a feeling that if violence were not a possibility he would have to fight with more fairness—using his wits and perseverence. When violence develops, all fair fighting is over—there is no more communication. He has the power to call a halt to fighting that I don't have. He also has the power to stop some action of mine that displeases him. I have no such power. If I had such power I'm not sure whether or not I would use it. Knowing the results it has on its victims, such as rage and resentment, I would like to believe I wouldn't resort to physical violence even if I could.

One respondent reflected on current limitations and offered a preventive measure. She suggested that couples agree not to use physical force against each other as part of the marriage vows, or at least sign an agreement before they are married banning physical force as a method of ending disputes.

Summary

The reports from battered women presented here show how social stress, limitations in resources, and sex roles affect women, their children, their marriages, and subsequent help-seeking behavior. Greater understanding of the causes of violence and the input of marital violence on women, their marriages, and their children may be useful in bringing about change. Specifically, an awareness and understanding of the problem of wife abusc may help to relieve women of feelings of guilt and low self-esteem, as well as help them to identify specific targets for change and new goals which will expand opportunities for their growth in adulthood. Research on the psychosocial aspects of wife abuse can be helpful, especially when combined with a careful examination of legislatures, courts, police, and other segments of society and communities that have helped to keep women trapped in their marriages. Partly as a result of the Women's Movement, today many parents feel that their sons and daughters should have equal opportunities. Greater knowledge of the causes of marital violence may relieve women in distress, help to give women new opportunities, and insure that the success and achievements of young women do not abruptly come to a halt after marriage.

REFERENCES

1. Allen, Craig M., and Straus, Murray A., "Resources, Power, and Husband-Wife Violence." Paper read at the 1975 annual meeting of the National Council on Family Relations.
2. Gelles, Richard J., *The Violent Home: A Study of Physical Aggression Between Husbands and Wives*. Beverly Hills, California: Sage Publications, 1974.
3. Gelles, Richard J., "Violence and Pregnancy: A Note on the Extent of the Problem and Needed Services," *The Family Coordinator* **24:** 81–86 (January 1975).
4. Gelles, Richard J., "Abused Wives: Why Do They Stay?" Revised version of a paper presented at the meetings of the Eastern Sociological Society, Boston, Massachusetts, March 1976.
5. Gelles, Richard J., and Straus, Murray A., "Toward an Integrated Theory of Family Violence." Paper presented at the 1974 conference of the National Council on Family Relations.
6. O'Brien, John E., "Violence in Divorce Prone Families," *Journal of Marriage and the Family* **33:** 692–698 (November 1971).
7. Owens, David J., and Straus, Murray A., "The Social Structure of Violence in Childhood and Approval of Violence as an Adult," *Aggressive Behavior* **1:** 193–211 (1975).
8. Schmid, Margaret, "Feminist Attitudes: Dimensions and Distributions by Gender, Religion, and Class," doctoral dissertation, Northwestern University, 1974.
9. Snell, John E., Rosenwald, Richard J., and Robey, Ames, "The Wifebeater's Wife—A Study of Family Interaction," *Archives of General Psychiatry II:* 107–113 (August 1964).
10. Steinmetz, Suzanne K., and Straus, Murray A. (eds.), *Violence in the Family*. New York: Dodd, Mead and Co., 1974.
11. Straus, Murray A., "Some Social Antecedents of Physical Punishment: A Linkage Theory Interpretation," *Journal of Marriage and the Family* **33:** 658–663 (November 1971).
12. Straus, Murray A., "A General Systems Approach to a Theory of Violence Between Family Members," *Social Science Information* **12:** 105–125 (June 1973).
13. Straus, Murray A., "Leveling, Civility, and Violence in the Family." *Journal*

of Marriage and the Family **36**: 13–29 (February 1974), plus addendum in August 1974.

14. Straus, Murray A., "Cultural and Social Organizational Influence on Violence Between Family Members," in *Configurations: Biological and Cultural Factors in Sexuality and Family Life*, Raymond Price and Dorothy Barrier (eds.). New York: D. C. Heath, 1974.
15. Straus, Murray A., "Societal Morphogenesis and Intrafamily Violence in Cross-Cultural Perspective." Paper presented at the Conference on "Issues in Cross-Cultural Research," New York Academy of Sciences, October 1975.
16. Straus, Murray A., "Sexual Inequality, Cultural Norms, and Wifebeating." Paper presented at the International Institute on Victimology, Bellagio, Italy, July 1975.
17. Straus, Murray A., Gelles, Richard J., and Steinmetz, Suzanne K., "Violence in the Family: An Assessment of Knowledge and Research Needs." Paper read at the annual meeting of the American Association for the Advancement of Science, Boston, February 1976.

4 Neurological Factors

Tell me then I pray (since every action of man must be tutored by some virtue or other) what appearance can it be for a man to beat a woman. It is not wisdom because that depends on a staid carriage. It is not justice because that requires a serious deliberation. Temperance because that wants unsettled passion. And if none of these then no virtue at all: for all other virtues are comprised under them, as some lesser dignity under a more ample style.

HEALE, WILLIAM, 1609

THE NEUROLOGY OF EXPLOSIVE RAGE: THE DYSCONTROL SYNDROME*†

Frank A. Elliott, M.D., F.R.C.P. Pennsylvania Hospital

Explosive rage triggered by seemingly minimal provocation and accompanied by physical or verbal aggression occurs in two groups of conditions: functional psychoses and personality disorders on the one hand, and neurological and metabolic diseases on the other. The term 'dyscontrol syndrome' is sometimes used for symptoms arising from poor impulse control, whether the cause is organic or functional. It is an important cause of wife and child battery, senseless assaults, motiveless homicides, self-injury, dangerously aggressive driving, domestic infelicity, divorce, and (in children) educational and social difficulties. Even if the violence is only verbal, it can destroy domestic relationships and wreck careers. All these disasters, including homicide, are represented in the cases of organic dyscontrol listed in this report.

Prevalence

The prevalence of explosive rage, whether psychogenic or organic in origin, is much underestimated. In the first place, it is often regarded as a quirk of personality rather than a matter for medical concern, especially in strata of society in which violence is so common that it excites little comment. Secondly, few patients are willing to admit to an uncontrollable temper, whether from a sense of shame, fear of commitment, or fear of legal sanctions, and the family often helps in the cover-up. Consequently the true state of affairs does not emerge unless the physician asks the right questions: 'Do you have difficulty in controlling your temper? Have you been charged with traffic violations or dangerous driving? Are you especially sensitive to alcohol? It is also necessary to inquire, but at a later interview, about the more delicate question of inability to control sexual impulses, which is present in a few cases.

A third cause of under-reporting is that, despite the extensive

---

*Reprinted from *The Practitioner*, July 1976, **217.**
†The following article is included in this anthology because physical disorders of the brain are sometimes responsible for wife battery, though, as yet, there is no data on what proportion of wifebatterers are so affected.

MARIA ROY

literature on violent behavior, little of this information has found its way into medical teaching; we are not taught what to look for, and therefore fail to realize the significance of what we see. More-over, as several authors have pointed out, we tend to shun violent patients because they can be troublesome. Symptomatic of this atti-tude is the frequent use of euphemisms in the literature. Patients are described as 'irritable' or 'hyperresponsive', or 'explosive personalities'.

The Anatomy of Explosive Rage

Experimental and clinical evidence links explosive rage to disor-ders involving the phylogenetically ancient limbic system, which includes the amygdala and hippocampus of the temporal lobe, the hypothalamus, the fornix, the cingulate gyri and cingulate bundle, the septum pellucidum, and the septal area (see illustration). The

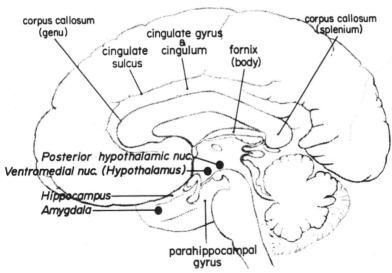

Diagrammatic view of some limbic structures.

first hint of this relationship was given by Boerhaave[5] who noted that in rabies, which involves the brain-stem and hippocampus, the patient may gnash his teeth and snarl like a dog, and in 1892 Gowers[12] spoke of them as 'exhausted by attacks of fury'. In the same year Goltz[11] reported that in dogs the removal of a large portion of the forebrain gave rise to savage behaviour in response to minor provocation. Since then it has been shown that electrical stimulation of the amygdala can produce either rage or tameness, depending upon the precise placement of the electrodes, and that in man and animals explosive rage can be abolished by bilateral amygdalotomy. In the cat, damage to the ventro-medial nucleus of the hypothalamus produces—after a delay of many weeks—a permanently savage animal; paradoxically, electrical stimulation of the same nucleus can elicit aggressive behavior.[10] In man, tumors of the third ventricle and other midline structures can give rise to either rage or profound apathy,[8] and pathological aggression can be abolished by bilateral postero-medial hypothalamotomy. Tumors of the corpus callosum which spread to involve the overlying cingulate gyri usually cause apathy, but explosive rage can occur if the septal area is involved. Bilateral cingulotomy can control aggressive behavior. Repeated attacks of rage were the outstanding feature of a case of a cyst of the septum pellucidum described by Leslie.[18]

These few examples, drawn from an extensive literature, indicate that the limbic system contains within itself mechanisms for the production and control of angry aggression. This does not mean that the system is an autonomous 'centre' for aggressive behavior, or that all forms of aggressive behavior are due to disorders of the limbic system. In mature individuals anger is subject to a measure of cortical control and some patients who are given to explosive rage can learn to contain it. On the other hand, in man at any rate, cold, calculating, predatory aggression, carried out for profit, is properly viewed as originating in the neocortex.

Etiology

Explosive rage occurs in a minority of patients affected by any given disorder—for instance, it was present in only ten out of 2000 cases of head trauma in adults studied by Hooper and colleagues,[16] and in temporal-lobe epilepsy the incidence is in the region of 20%. Clearly, other factors play a role. Of these, sex is important—males are more often affected than females, at all ages. Aggressive behavior is linked to high androgen levels in the plasma and in most male animals castration (which lowers androgen levels) has a taming effect.

The family background is important. An uncontrollable temper sometimes runs in families, involving several generations. Daven-port[7] found that about half the progeny of such parents suffered from violent attacks of rage. All observers agree that some—but not all—of the children reared in an atmosphere of uncontrolled temper, parental dissension or separation, and emotional depriva-tion, become violent themselves, but it is not always easy to decide whether the effect is due to heredity, emotional trauma, bad exam-ple, or a mixture of all three.

Patients fall into two groups. In the first there is a history of tem-per tantrums in infancy and childhood which have persisted as more formidable explosions of rage in adolescence and adult life. In the second group, formerly normal individuals become subject to explosive rage as a sequel to a brain insult or metabolic disorder.[1]

In the first group, emotional dyscontrol dating from early life can often be traced to prenatal, natal, or postnatal events—including birth injury, foetal anoxia, and infantile convulsions. It is com-mon in epileptics and children with minimal brain dysfunction such as specific learning defects, constructional apraxia, difficulty in learning geographical relationships, poor attention span, incapacity for abstract thought, imperception, excessive synkinesis, clumsi-ness, mild choreiform movements, impairment of stereognosis and graphaesthesia, hyperkinesia, and visual field defects. It is a promi-nent feature of the hyperkinetic syndrome of children, some of whom have organic defects. It also occurs in more severely affected individuals with cerebral palsy, mental retardation, and arrested hydrocephalus.

In the second group explosive rage appears in a previously nor-mal subject after head trauma or other cerebral insults. The most dramatic example of this was provided by epidemic encephalitis lethargica in the second and third decades of this century. This dis-ease could change a normal, pleasant child into a cruel, aggressive psychopath given to temper tantrums, cheating, stealing, and other forms of juvenile depravity.

Kinnier Wilson[29] reported the case of a young woman who 'used suddenly to become conscious of a rising surge within her, a seemingly physical wave which flooded her brain and caused her to clench her fists, set her jaws, and glare in frenzy at her mother: 'Had my mother said anything then to cross me, I would have killed her'". These attacks were followed by remorse.

The same constellation of symptoms can occur following head injury, especially in children.[4] In some cases explosive rage is the only sequel, and it may occur for the first time many months after the injury. It can also occur following repeated minor head injuries, as in the punch-drunk syndrome. Clinical, surgical, and electroencephalographic evidence suggests that this delayed effect of closed-head injury is related to contusion of the temporal lobes, which is so often involved by contrecoup lesions. On the other hand, the extreme belligerence which often occurs as a temporary phenomenon as the patient emerges from coma probably has a different origin. In such cases the blood-brain barrier is breached and it is possible that catecholamines gain access to the limbic system and stimulate the alpha- and beta-receptors which are involved in rage.[10,23] I have have found that this type of belligerence can sometimes be controlled rather dramatically by large doses of an adrenergic blocking agent (propranolol, up to 80 mg four times daily). On the other hand, although propranolol has been found to prevent fighting behavior in rats (induced by foot shocks and by septal lesions), beta-receptor blockade was not involved in the effect.[2]

Temporal-lobe epilepsy (synonyms: psychomotor seizures, complex partial seizures) is the most common of the organic conditions associated with explosive rage. It is often due to sclerosis of the medial part of the temporal lobe, including the hippocampus (Ammon's Horn sclerosis), the result of an anoxic incident in early infancy. Less common lesions include infarcts, porencephaly, small vascular malformations, traumatic scars, indolent gliomatous tumors, and cortical dysplasia akin to tuberous sclerosis.[9] Angry, aggressive behavior is sometimes seen during post-ictal automatism, especially when attempts are made to restrain the patient. It can occur in the absence of the ictal symptoms characteristic of that particular patient and it is often difficult to know whether an attack is ictal or not. Denis Williams[27] identified 17 cases of ictal aggression in a hundred cases of temporal-lobe epilepsy and Bingley[3] found it in 27% of 90 cases. Others believe that ictal rage is rare, or deny its existence.[6] In one well-documented case, an attack of rage coincided with an epileptic discharge in the amygdala.[20] Even more persuasive is the fact that both seizures and attacks of rage are sometimes reduced or abolished by the use of hydantoinates or carbamazepine.

In a third group, attacks of explosive rage are inter-ictal. The patient is aware of a gradually mounting dysphoria before the explosion, there is no amnesia, and psychotropic drugs may be needed in addition to anti-seizure medication to prevent outbursts. In a fourth type of case, first described by Kaplan in 1899,[17] an attack of rage terminates in a convulsion.

> For example, a woman aged 33, who had occasional temporal-lobe seizures and frequent attacks of inter-ictal rage, was trying to get a tablet of aspirin out of a bottle when the cap stuck. Instantly she became insanely angry and screamed with rage. She recalls that she literally 'saw red.' She then lost consciousness and was found having a generalized convulsion. Since chromatopsia can occur as the aura of temporal-lobe seizures, it is probable that the attack of rage was part of the seizure.

Explosive rage has also been seen as a sequel to viral encephalitis, brain abscess, stroke, subarachnoid hemorrhage, pre-senile dementia, Huntington's chorea, normal pressure hydrochepalus, arrested internal hydrocephalus, and, rarely, in multiple sclerosis. It can follow cerebral anoxia in patients who survive cardiac arrest. It can be an early symptom of deeply situated tumors in or near the midline of the cerebral hemispheres—that is, tumors which are in a position to implicate the limbic system. It can also occur for the first time some months after surgery for removal of such tumors. In the present series this occurred in 3 cases: a parasaggital meningioma, a meningioma of the sphenoidal ridge, and a glioma of the temporal lobe. The delayed onset of symptoms in these cases is reminiscent of the delayed onset of belligerence in cats following the destruction of the ventro-medial nucleus of the hypothalamus. Possible reasons for this delay have been discussed by Glusman.[10]

Of the metabolic disorders that can cause explosive rage, hypoglycaemia is the most common, whether it be functional, iatrogenic, or due to endogenous hyperinsulinism. Wilder[26] has assembled a formidable bibliography on violent rage triggered by this condition, including a case of matricide triggered by hypoglycaemia in a man who had suffered brain damage at birth or in infancy.[14] Hypoglycaemia induced by intravenous tolbutamide can activate abnormalities in the electroencephalogram in some patients with temporal-lobe seizures.[13] The fact that rage is not induced by the hypoglycaemia which can occur during a five-hour glucose-tolerance test, even in people who have hypoglycaemic reactions outside the laboratory, emphasizes the role of the social setting. In the same way, patients liable to pathological alcoholic intoxication in social life do not develop symptoms from the same amount of alcohol when it is given to them in the laboratory.

Premenstrual tension is a common example of the effect of endocrine and metabolic factors on the rage threshold, a situation which is familiar to many families. Morton and his colleagues[22] found from a study of women prisoners that 62% of the crimes of violence were committed during the premenstrual week, and only 2% at the end of menstruation. The feelings of depression, irritability, futility and persecution are accompanied by a decrease in the plasma progesterone: estrogen ratio.

Symptoms and Signs

This report is based on a study of 54 cases, of whom 37 were men and 17 women; 51 were white and 3 were black. They came from all social classes. Ages ranged from 13 to 68, and 45 were below the age of 40. There were 15 cases of temporal-lobe epilepsy, 11 of head trauma, 12 with minimal brain damage dating from infancy, 2 each of viral encephalitis, multiple sclerosis, stroke, and cardiac arrest, 1 of suprapituitary tumor, 3 who developed rage attacks following the removal of a brain tumor, 1 each of Alzheimer's disease and arrested hydrocephalus, and 2 with unilateral temporal-lobe spikes, without seizures. In addition to the 15 cases of temporal-lobe epilepsy, an additional 11 cases gave a history of seizures: 3 after head injury, 3 with minimal brain damage, 2 with multiple sclerosis, 2 after viral encephalitis, and 1 after removal of a temporal-lobe glioma.

The features of the dyscontrol syndrome vary little from case to case.[20] In the 'organic' type there are frequent episodes of intense rage which are triggered by trivial irritations and are accompanied by verbal or physical violence. Speech is explosive and marked by unwonted obscenities and profanity. The attack is usually followed by remorse, but in some cases the patient—like the aggressive psychopath—is untroubled by his behaviour, or denies it. It must be emphasized that the background of these individuals is not one of chronic malevolence. On the contrary, most of them have a warm, pleasant personality, which may account for the extraordinary degree of forbearance extended to them by family and friends.

The violence itself has a primitive quality—biting, gouging, kicking, spitting, multiple stabbing and so on.

> One patient, who has occasional temporal-lobe seizures, completely demolished his victim's skull with a hammer, then stabbed her repeatedly, and finally tried to set fire to her body. A cultivated woman of 25 bit a policeman who had reprimanded her for a parking offense. A young man pushed his fist through the windscreen of his car, breaking bones in the process.

There is often a history of traffic accidents resulting from aggressive driving; the patient uses his car as a weapon. A smaller number of patients also exhibit poor impulse control in sexual matters, which may lead to sexual assaults. These are not necessarily carried out in anger; a literary example is Emile Zola's Jacque, a man with the symptoms of temporal-lobe epilepsy who could not always control an urge to kill women who attracted him. Pathological intoxication is common; a small amount of alcohol either triggers an attack of rage or produces drunkenness.

In the majority there are additional features of the underlying condition, whatever it may be. Neurological signs are usually 'soft' and subtle and will escape notice if neurological examination is cursory. In a few patients explosive rage appears to be the only sequel of a cerebral insult, and it is especially in these cases that the rage is apt to be regarded as psychogenic, because the attacks and the damage that results from them produce a train of emotional disturbances which can be mistaken for the cause, rather than the result, of the outbursts. Half of a large group of patients studied by Mark and Ervin[20] had made serious attempts at suicide. Moreover, some individuals who have had temporal-lobe seizures for many years come to display persistent or episodic schizophrenia-like symptoms.[24]

Special Investigations

Psychiatric examination and psychological testing designed to detect organic damage are desirable. Psychogenic and organic symptoms often coexist. Electroencephalography is obligatory. A single test, if normal, means little because the abnormalities appear intermittently;

repeated tests increase the percentage of positive results and the yield is further improved by the use of sleep records using nasopharyngeal electrodes. Chemical activation techniques are important. Even then the results may be negative, despite the presence of epileptic discharges as recorded by depth electrodes.

When electroencephalographic abnormalities are present in the organic type of dyscontrol, they usually take the form of focal temporal spikes (which may be unilateral or bilateral) or focal slowing. In cases without structural disease or epilepsy, bilateral temporofrontal theta-rhythm (4–7 Hz) predominates, especially in persons under the age of 40.[21,28] This is interpreted as the result of maturational lag, a 'constitutional' defect.

A five-hour glucose-tolerance test should be carried out if there is any reason to suspect hypoglycaemia. X-ray studies should include basal views of the skull because the middle fossa is sometimes reduced on one side if the temporal lobe on that side was injured early in life. Computerized axial tomography (the EMI scan) is proving useful in detecting unsuspected abnormalities.

Treatment

Psychiatric supervision, which is obligatory when the dyscontrol syndrome is a symptom of mental illness or personality disorder, has somewhat less to offer the organic cases but is often helpful in adjusting the attitudes of the patient and the family, and in uncovering hidden emotional conflict which is contributing to the dyscontrol.[19]

The frequency and severity of the attacks can usually be reduced by pharmacological agents. These should be given on a maintenance basis when the attacks of rage come on without warning, but can be taken intermittently during periods of mounting tension in patients who recognize that these precede an attack.

The hydantoinates and carbamazepine are effective in reducing both seizures and inter-ictal rage in epileptics, and also help to prevent attacks of rage in patients who do not have seizures but in whom there is electroencephalographic evidence of a seizure focus. Primidone is less desirable, not only because it sometimes produces an unacceptable degree of general sedation but also because it can have the paradoxical effect of increasing the number of emotional outbursts. The same thing applies to barbiturates. Surprisingly, methosuximide and ethosuximide have been found to be effective by some workers.

In non-epileptics, drugs which have been found to be effective are haloperidol, meprobamate, and the benzodiazepines (chlordiazepoxide hydrochloride, diazepam, oxazepam). Meprobamate is particularly effective in small doses (400 mg twice a day); in experimental animals it has a greater impact on the thalamus and limbic system than on the cortex. As mentioned before, propranolol has proved effective thus far, in both epileptics and non-epileptics, but the number of cases treated is too small to warrant a conclusion as to its value.

Amphetamines and methylphenidate are useful in some hyperkinetic children. The phenothiazines, so effective in the control of psychotic hostility, can aggravate the situation in epilepsy by lowering the seizure threshold, and they should not be used except in conjunction with antiseizure medication.

Both alcohol and barbiturates should be avoided; whether taken singly or jointly, they tend to increase aggression. Tinklenberg and Woodrow[25] reported that 'pharmacologically experienced' delinquents choose quinalbarbitone as the drug most likely to increase aggression. On the other hand, drug users agree that marihuana decreases aggression, and two of my patients who suffer from explosive rage volunteered that their attacks were more effectively aborted by smoking a single 'joint' than by any of the medications that had been prescribed for them. This merits further study.

Individuals vary widely in their sensitivity to pharmacological agents and it may take a little time to find the best drug or combination of drugs. This should be explained to the patient; otherwise, dissatisfied by the lack of immediate results, he may impulsively seek help elsewhere. Many of these people are hostile and skeptical, either because they do not see why they should consult a doctor at all or because they have previously sought help in vain. Some refuse to consult a psychiatrist. Many can be taught to recognize premonitory symptoms and to take evasive action by simply walking away from a provocative situation. Most patients are relieved to hear that their attacks of rage have an organic origin and can be treated by physical means.

Attempts to raise the threshold of aggression by reducing androgen levels have met with varying success. Methods range from the use of antiandrogenic drugs and estrogenic substances to male castration. If premenstrual tension is an aggravating factor, it is treated with progesterones. The addition of diuretics may make the patient feel more comfortable in a physical sense, but it does not appear to alter the irritability. The use of minor tranquillizing drugs such as meprobamate during the premenstrual week can be most helpful.

Hypoglycaemia is treated according to its causes. Morton and his colleagues[22] have reported that a glucose-tolerance test carried out during the premenstrual period resulted in a typical hypoglycaemic curve in many of the violent prisoners they studied and found that improvement in behavior and attitude followed the use of a high-protein diet coupled with ammonium chloride.

Psychosurgical treatment should be limited to severe cases which do not respond satisfactorily to conservative measures. The procedures include unilateral temporal lobectomy, bilateral anterior temporal lobotomy, unilateral or bilateral stereotaxic medial amygdalotomy, stereotaxic posteromedial hypothalamotomy, anterior and posterior cingulotomy, anterior thalamotomy, and orbito-frontal tractotomy. The long-term merits and demerits of these operations are still being weighed.[15]

REFERENCES

1. Bach-Y-Rita, G., Lion, J. R., Climent, C. E., and Ervin, F. R., *Amer. J. Psychiat.* **127:** 1473 (1971).
2. Bainbridge, J. G., and Greenwood, D. T., *Neuropharmacol.* **10:** 453 (1971).
3. Bingley, T., *Acta. Neurol. Scand.*, suppl. 120, **33:** 1 (1958).
4. Blau, A., *Arch. Neurol. Psychiat.* **35:** 723 (1936).
5. Boerhaave, H., "Aphorisms Concerning the Knowledge and Cure of Diseases." Translated by G. Delacoste, London (1715).
6. Daly, D. D., in *Advances in Neurology*, vol. 11, Chapter 4. Raven Press, New York (1975).
7. Davenport, C. B., *J. Nerve. Ment. Dis.* **42:** 593 (1915).
8. Elliott, F. A., in *Handbook of Neurology*, vol. 2, Chapter 24. North Holland Publishing Co., Amsterdam (1969).
9. Falconer, M. S., Serafetinides, E. A., and Corsellis, J. A. N., *Arch. Neurol.* **10:** 233 (1964).
10. Glusman, M., *Ass. Res. Nerv. Dis. Proc.* **52:** 53 (1974).
11. Goltz, F., *Pflügers Arch. Ges. Physiol.* **51:** 570 (1892).
12. Gowers, W. R., *Diseases of the Nervous System*, vol. 2, p. 928 (1892).
13. Green, J. B., *Neurology* **13:** 192 (1963).
14. Hill, D., and Sargant, W. A., *Lancet* i: 526 (1943).
15. Hitchcock, E., Laitinen, L., and Vaernet, R., *Psychosurgery*. Charles C Thomas, Springfield, Illinois (1972).
16. Hooper, R. S., McGregor, J. M., and Nathan, P. W., *J. Ment. Sci.* **91:** 458 (1945).
17. Kaplan, J., *Allg. Z. Psychiat.* **56:** 292 (1899).
18. Leslie, W., *Canad. Med. Ass. J.* **43:** 433 (1940).

19. Lion, J. R., *Evaluation and Management of the Violent Patient*, Charles C Thomas, Springfield, Illinois (1972).
20. Mark, V. H., and Ervin, F. R., *Violence and the Brain*, Harper & Row, New York (1970).
21. Monroe, R. R., *Episodic Behaviorial Disorders*, p. 176. Harvard University Press (1970).
22. Morton, J. H., Additon, H., Addison, R. G., Hunt, L., and Sullivan, C., *Amer. J. Obstet. Gynec.* **65:** 1182 (1953).
23. Reis, D. J., in *Neural Bases of Violence and Aggression*, edited by W. S. Fields and W. H. Sweet, Warren H. Green Inc., St. Louis, Missouri (1975).
24. Slater, E., Beard, A. W., and Glithero, E., *Int. J. Psychiat.* **1:** 4 (1965).
25. Tinklenberg, J. R., and Woodrow, K. W., *Ass. Res. Nerv. Dis. Proc.* **52:** 209 (1974).
26. Wilder, J. in *Handbook of Correctional Psychology*, edited by R. Lindner and R. Slieger, Philosophical Library, New York (1947).
27. Williams, D., *Brain.* **79:** 29 (1956).
28. ——, *Ibid.* **92:** 503 (1969).
29. Wilson, S. A. Kinnier, *Neurology* **1:** 662 (1940).
30. Zola, E. (1872). *La Bete Humaine* (*English translation, The Beast in Man*, Elek Books, London, 1969).

5 Psychiatric and Psychological Factors

Jealousy is a child conceived of self-unworthiness, and of another's worth, at whose birth fear made it an abortive in nature, and a monster in love. For the jealous man unworthily loving a worthily beloved object, stands in fear of communicating his good unto another more worthy. So that neither is his love perfect, because conjoined with love which fear poisons. But of both arises this mongrel kind of jealousy a loving fear or a fear of full love.

HEALE, WILLIAM, 1609

PSYCHOLOGICAL ASPECTS OF WIFEBATTERING

Natalie Shainess, M.D. Faculty, William Alanson White Institute of Psychiatry, Psychoanalysis, and Psychology
Lecturer in Psychiatry, Columbia University College of Physicians and Surgeons

It seems incongruous that while we have presumably become more enlightened and "free-er," wifebattering has not decreased in recent years, not only in this country, but throughout the world. At the same time little professional literature has been paid to this problem. However, at the annual May meetings in Toronto this year (1977), the American Psychiatric Association devoted a whole section to papers on the problem of wife assault.

The *Birmingham Post*, in 1975,* reported that 25,000 women in Britain are assaulted annually by their husbands, and that about 30 sanctuaries for women have been established. In addition, a bill was introduced in the House of Commons to give an assaulted woman temporary rights to exclusive possession of her home, through the courts. In this country, some shelters are being established, but they are few in number.

Historical Background

Before going into the factors which effect violence, it is helpful to remember that the male is the physically stronger sex, and while there are individual variations, the knowledge of his superior strength is something very much within masculine awareness. In Jungian terms, one would say it is part of his "archaic unconscious." Old cartoons of Neanderthal man carrying a club and pulling his woman along by the hair to their sexual rendezvous made a statement about this awareness—but the club was unnecessary, at least where the woman was concerned; his brute strength was sufficient for subduing her. In the dawn of history, and in a primitive sense, one could say that all males regarded females as need-servers; this too may play a part in the male discontent that results in battering.

Legal codes have also played a part in making a woman a man's chattel, to do with as he wished; from the Napoleonic codes (see Davidson in Chapter 1 of this book), where women could not inherit, vote, sue their husbands, or sign contracts alone, to English law, which, for the most part, supports the husband, to laws in this country,

---

*"Aid for Battered Wives," *Birmingham Post* (July 12, 1975).

where, as attorney Marguerite Rawalt pointed out, in the nineteenth century, a woman could be committed to a mental hospital solely upon her husband's petition. Rawalt has called women "constitutional outcasts," saying that even today, "the hidden truth about the U.S. Constitution is that it applies to men only."[1] The point of this is that in the face of women being treated legally as a class apart, the effect of such legal codes upon the treatment of women is far-reaching, permeating concepts of gender-identity, social and work roles, and views of healthy and neurotic character. It also subtly dictates who can get away with what; in short, in a sense, it encourages men to take advantage of women, by physical force or in other ways.

In England, a country we have long been accustomed to viewing as democratic, it comes as a surprise that women are no better—and possibly worse—off. I spent some time in Stratford-upon-Avon, doing research for a paper on Shakespearean women. Women were chattels in Shakespeare's time. In "The Taming of the Shrew," Petrucchio, who weds Katherina for her money, "magnanimously" overlooking her bad temper, makes it clear that he can do anything he wants to her: "I will be master of what is mine own. She is my goods, my chattels; she is my house [this has sexual implications], my household stuff, my field, my barn, my horse, my ox, my ass, my anything.

In reviewing literary criticism of 'The Shrew' I came across a very interesting report by Winter in 1892. Shakespeare's Shrew, Winter noted, calls attention to the fact that long ago it was a settled principle of common law in England that a man may beat his wife, provided that the stick was not thicker than his thumb. The ducking stool could be repeatedly soused in a pond or river to punish a scolding woman as late as 1809. John Taylor, one of the so-called water poets, counted 60 whipping-posts within one mile of London, prior to 1630, and it was not until 1791 that the whipping of female vagrants was forbidden by statute. The brank—a particularly cruel gag—was in common use to punish 'a certain sort of woman.' This affords an instructive view of British law towards women. Winter stated: "It is not that the gentlemen of England are tyrannical and cruel in their treatment of women; but the predominance of John Bull in any question between him and Mrs. Bull is a cardinal doctrine of British law."*

This acceptance of brutality to women and wives is a cultural phenomenon which promotes the position of women as underdogs,

---

*Winter, W., *Old Shrines and Ivy*. Boston: Macmillan Co., 1892.

and gives a feeling of self-righteousness to the indulgence of male whim or temper.

Cultural Trends

In addition to the background material presented, which includes elements in culture which tolerate or promote assault upon women, there are specific changes in society today which account for the rise in wifebattering. In contrast to the late Victorian, patriarchal and *repressive* society of Freud's time, there have been enormous changes in the last 15 years, including the "sexual revolution," which warrant our society to be called the "*expressive* society." The changes have been world-wide, because the mass media are instruments disseminating information on a world-wide scale. Business and advertising play a large part in shaping attitudes and beliefs. As a result, there has been a general lowering of social goals, much greater impulsiveness, and an "accept yourself as you are" philosophy; all of which tend to do away with striving, not only for personal improvement (other than that directed to appearance), but to interfere with the wish to be, or appear to be, a better or more worthy person. Thus, the wifebatterer feels less concerned about giving in to rage or impulse, and anticipates less condemnation from society. Billions of words have been spent in debate concerning whether punishment is a deterrent from crime, especially in relation to capital punishment. I have no doubt that anticipation of punishment is a deterrent to some extent; but even more to the point, the law is a forthright indication of society's goals and beliefs.

Another important factor is the loss of serious interest in parenthood. This is not to say that very involved parents have not reared young who have become disturbed and at times dangerous people, but tendencies today are such that children are often reared with considerable neglect, lack of love, and treatment which interferes with socialization—all furthering more negative personality traits and impulsivity.

Personality Problems of the Wifebatterer

In general, people tend to take out their frustrations on those to whom they are closest, the people they see every day. When, in addition, the tie is a relatively indissoluble one, such as marriage, and there are added related problems, such as difficulties with children, wife-assault becomes more understandable (but not acceptable!). It cannot be stressed enough that the degree to which there was chaos in the man's early life, and lack of exposure to any collaborative living between parents, is a major element in promoting the tendency to assault. I believe that many of the background factors pertaining to the rapist apply here. Freud, in his paper, "A Child is being Beaten,"[2] noted that feelings of pleasure were connected with this beating fantasy (and memory), and that violent feelings became fused with erotic ones. Sometimes this is enacted through assault in which "making up" with the wife sexually is the second and hidden component of the assault. But it is essentially the experience of corporal punishment and the development of an identification with the aggressor, which is an important causative element in the tendency to assault in later years.

The so-called "passive-aggressive" male has a personality in which the tendency to feel helpless and vulnerable is basic. But as these self-concepts grow and are elicited in interactions with the mate, they may trigger feelings of anger and rage which result in irrational aggressive actions, of which assault may be a part. The "obsessive-compulsive" man is not likely to assault when his defenses are working well. But with added threat, which taxes him to the limit, the result may be an explosion, or, as some have described it, an *im*plosion, which also has outer-directed effects, and may result in attack upon the mate. Or, the man living with congealed rage—usually paranoid—is particularly likely to assault his wife or any person close to him.

The sadistic man may use assault as one element in an ongoing attack on the person with whom he lives in greatest intimacy (or perhaps "proximity" is a better term, because the sadist is close to no one). Here, his assaults may be physical, but they are calculated, and only a part of what is the central core of his relationship: the ongoing destruction of another person. Such assaults are not "heated," but involve the administration of punishment in cold, icy calm (on the surface, at least). Fromm has described in detail the personality involved in "malignant aggression."[3]

The use of brute force is always an indication of resources taxed to their limit, of process impoverishment, whether we are considering an individual or a nation. It also indicates insistence on having the other defer, and of refusal to compromise; it is insistence on power as a means of resolving differences. As already indicated, infantility and the inability to tolerate frustration, resulting in low impulse

What Can Be Done About the Problem Generally?

As far as the existing problem is concerned, women need to learn that there is no cause for shame, and that if they are assaulted, they must take action—*court action*. As with rape and many other violent situations, women tend to blame themselves, and take on a burden of guilt which is inappropriate. They must realize that to be victimized is *not* to be guilty. Here women's consciousness-raising groups can be helpful, as may be efforts made through the media and public protest. Women must have adequate protection in the courts; but before this, they must have a place of refuge which also accommodates their children, so that they are not exposed to further danger after an assault has taken place. The establishment of AWAIC (Abused Women's Aid in Crisis) in New York City by Maria Roy, where women can call in and receive guidance, is an important first step.

From a psychological point of view, such women need supportive counseling, and if they are capable of benefitting from it, psychoanalytically oriented psychotherapy, to help them build their self-esteem and develop their resources. Battered wives must be helped with starting independent lives and developing their abilities to make life reasonably satisfactory for themselves, should they not remarry.

Ultimately, preventive education can be the most important means of eliminating the problem of wifebattering. In a society that has learned to solve its problems, without resorting to force, wifebattering is not likely to be a problem.

REFERENCES

1. Rawalt, Marguerite, "Women are Constitutional Outcasts," *The Woman Physician* **26** (12) (December 1971).
2. Freud, Sigmund, "A Child is Being Beaten" (1919), *Collected Papers* **II**. New York: Basic Books, 1959.
3. Fromm, Erich, *The Anatomy of Human Destructiveness*. New York: Holt, Rinehart and Winston, 1973.

MEN WHO ASSAULT THEIR WIVES*

M. Faulk, M.R.C., Psychiatrist, Consultant Forensic Psychiatrist, Hampshire Area Health Authority, Southampton and South West Hampshire Health District, England

While there is now a substantial amount of literature on the nature of the battered baby phenomenon and the psychiatric disturbances

---

*Reproduced from *Medicine, Science and the Law* (1974), 14, 180–183, by permission of the British Academy of Forensic Sciences.

in the parents involved, there is virtually no literature on the psychiatric disturbance of men who assault their wives. The following paper is an account of a group of men seen during the period of remand in custody awaiting trial on charges of seriously assaulting their wives.

Method

Twenty-three men remanded in custody for charges of seriously assaulting their wives or cohabitees were interviewed. Information available in the prison records and depositions was incorporated where available. A questionnaire on each subject was then completed by the interviewer. An attempt was made to collect all the cases of this type on remand in that prison at the time. Chance factors would have played a part and this survey could not be regarded as complete. However, it illustrates the types of cases and problems which may be seen.

Results

The ages of the men varied from 20 to 70. The average age was 39 years. Seventeen of the men were married to the victim and eight were cohabiting. The charges are shown in Table 1. In nearly all cases the charges were of the most serious nature. The results of the trials were that only one was found not guilty, a number were found guilty of lesser charges (e.g., manslaughter), and none was found guilty of murder. The eight cases charged with murder were all reduced to manslaughter, six of which were due to diminished responsibility.

At the time of the offense, 16 were found to have psychiatric disorder as shown in Table 2. When compared with the age of the subjects, it was found that 7 of the 8 over 40 years of age had serious psychiatric illness. Four had depression which was diagnosed by a marked lowering of mood, loss of hope, and suicidal feelings. One had dementia as shown by a deterioration in intellectual activity. Three suffered from delusional jealousy, one associated with depression and the other with a paranoid personality. Of the 15 below 40 years of age, 7 had a psychiatric disturbance. Of these two had a marked disturbance of personality, two had a severe anxiety state, and one a post head injury syndrome. Only two had the more severe forms of mental illness, i.e., one was depressed, and the other suffered from a paranoid illness.

TABLE 1. NATURE OF CHARGES IN ASSAULTS ON WIVES

NATURE OF CHARGE	NUMBER OF CASES
Murder	8
Attempted murder	9
Grievous bodily harm	3
Actual bodily harm	2
Malicious wounding	1
Total	23

An attempt was made to understand the dynamic relationship of the offender to the victim. Five types of relationship could be categorized:

1. Dependent passive husband: in this type of relationship the husband characteristically gave a good deal of concern and time to trying to please and pacify his wife, who often tended to be querulous and demanding. The offense was an explosion which occurred after a period of trying behavior by the victim. There was often a precipitating act by the victim.

2. Dependent and suspicious: in this type the husband had a long history of being unduly suspicious of his wife's fidelity. The husbands were controlling and jealous but they would not leave their wives despite their suspicions, i.e., they had a great need to stay. This built up an intolerable tension which led to a violent outburst, often preceded by increasing violence.

3. Violent and bullying: these men attempted to solve their problems or gain their end in many aspects of their lives by violence

TABLE 2. PSYCHIATRIC STATE AT TIME OF OFFENSE

NATURE OF STATE	NUMBER OF CASES
Depression	5
Dementia	1
Delusional jealousy	3
Post head injury syndrome	1
Anxiety state	2
Personality disorder	2
No psychiatric abnormality	9
Total	23

TABLE 3. DYNAMIC RELATIONSHIP WITH VICTIM

RELATIONSHIP	NUMBER OF CASES
Dependent and passive	9
Dependent and suspicious	4
Violent and bullying	1
Dominating	5
Stable and affectionate	4
Total	23

and intimidation. Sometimes this behaviour was intimately associated with alcohol abuse. The offence was often just the last violent incident in a long chain of violent incidents many of which might be quite minor.

4. Dominating husband: these husbands had a great need to assert themselves and would brook no insubordination from their wives. They were often quite successful in other aspects of their lives. Their offence might be precipitated by some trivial affair which they interpreted as a threat to their position of power.

5. Stable and affectionate group: this included couples who appeared to have enjoyed a long-standing, stable relationship. The violence occurred at a time of mental disturbance, characteristically during a depressive episode.

Representatives of all these groups were found (Table 3). Interestingly, the commonest type was the dependent and passive (nine cases).

TABLE 4. PREVIOUS OFFENSE

TYPE OF OFFENSE	NUMBER OF CASES
Property	5
Violent	3
Drugs	2
Alcohol	1
No previous offences	13
Total	24

TABLE 5. NUMBER OF PREVIOUS OFFENSES

NUMBER OF PREVIOUS OFFENSES	NUMBER OF CASES
1	4
2	1
3	3
4	1
5+	1
None	13
Total	23

Preceding Offense. Fifty percent of the group had no previous offenses (Table 4). When divided by the age of 40 years, the younger group had relatively more offenses, i.e., 66% of the younger group had offended and almost 25% had an offence of violence. In the older age group, 25% had offended and only one for violence. This finding is in keeping with the idea that the older age group were more mentally ill and more likely to have a history of a stable partnership. The number of previous offenses is shown in Table 5. Only six men had more than one offense.

Previous Threats. From a prophylactic point of view, it is interesting to note that overall almost 75% had behavior which warned of the final explosion (Table 6). The "warnings" took the form of threats or assaults. A warning occurred most commonly in those with personality disorders in which it seemed that the violence was often a means of manipulating or intimidating the victim and in those with delusional jealousy. Attacks without warning occurred most frequently in those with mental illness or in those cases in which "the worm turned." The warning was brought to the attention on

TABLE 6. PREVIOUS "WARNINGS"

NATURE OF WARNING	NUMBER OF CASES
Threat	11
Beating	13
Wounding	1
No previous warning	7

TABLE 7. AGENCY AWARE OF WARNINGS

AGENCY	NUMBER OF CASES
Victim only	7
Police	8
Doctor	1
No warning	7
Total	23

the police in eight cases, to a doctor in one case, and in seven cases only the victim was aware of the preceding violence (Table 7).

Outcome of Trial. A variety of sentences were passed which reflected in part the mental state of the offender and in part the degree to which the court was sympathetic to the tragic situation (Table 8). It reflects the mentally disturbed nature of the population that six were placed in a mental hospital under s. 60 of the Mental Health Act 1959 with restrictions under s. 65. Five were placed on probation including two who had been charged with murder. The impression was that the men who had a previously good personality and were under stress at the time of the offence were the ones with which the court might sympathize and whom the court sought to sentence lightly. One of the accused died before trial and one was found not guilty.

TABLE 8. OUTCOME OF TRIAL

SENTENCE	NUMBER OF CASES
Probation order	5
Suspended sentence	1
Up to 1 year	2
2–5 years	6
6–10 years	1
S. 60/65	6
Not guilty	1
Died before sentence	1
Total	23

Discussion

There is a dearth of reports on this particular type of violence, although reports of specific syndromes, e.g., delusional jealousy may be found. In this series, delusional jealousy occurred in three men and resulted in hospital orders being made. There is a real difference between the men in this series and those described in association with battered babies. Scott[1] found three groups of battering fathers: an immature, an aggressive, and a heterogeneous group. Although very immature and aggressive personalities were recognized in this series, they formed a minority of the cases and many more were apparently stable people responding to prolonged strain, or psychotic people responding to the effects of severe mental illness. Similarly, there was a lower incidence of previous offenses in the wifebattering group than in the babybattering group. It may be a combination of these reasons which leads the court to a sympathetic approach to these offenders, seeing the situation frequently as a particularly tragic one.

The treatment requirements of the group must be sufficiently wide to encompass the severe psychotic and the psychopathic. The group of men who seemed essentially normal in other aspects, tended to receive noncustodial sentences which seemed appropriate to their dangerousness. Hospital orders were much more common in the battered wife group than in the battered baby group (6:0). Only one of the custodial sentences was longer than five years though the hospital orders were accompanied by restriction orders unlimited in time in six cases.

Of particular interest is the opportunity for prophylactic intervention. It has already been noted that there were premonitory signs of violence in almost 70% of cases and in this respect there is a similarity to the battered baby situation. The police were the agency most often contacted after an episode of violence and doctors were rarely involved. It is difficult to assess the significance of the fact that seven wives had had a "warning" but had not acted on this. It may be that they were frightened of the consequences of reporting their fears, either for themselves or for their husbands. It may be, on the other hand, that the initial assaults are so common in some sectors that their prophylactic significance is missed.

Clearly, further investigation is required to discover what proportion of domestic assaults reported to the police end in serious violence. It would further seem worthwhile developing a crisis intervention service, backed by inpatient facilities, to attempt to reduce this sort of violence. It may well be that publication of the problems and cooperation with bodies such as the Samaritans and the police could make an impact as it may have done for suicide.

REFERENCE

1. Scott, P. D., *Medicine Sci. Law* **13**: 197 (1973).

CLINICAL ASPECTS OF WIFEBATTERING

John R. Lion, M.D., Associate Professor; Director, Clinical Research Program for Violent Behavior, Institute of Psychiatry and Human Behavior, University of Maryland School of Medicine

Wifebattering is a relatively new term in the lay press; it is actually a behavioral event more than a medical entity and its heritage springs from the widely publicized topic of child abuse.[1] It is interesting to review the history of child abuse, since the latter has direct relevance to the conceptualization of wifebattering. Child abuse existed long before it became a formal term through legislation; it required the diligent efforts of protectors of children's rights to bring the phenomenon to public awareness. Prior to that, a good deal of denial, coupled with the perception that what happened to children was the individual family's business and no one else's, made child abuse remain an untouchable subject. The revelation that child abuse frequently occurred led to much anxiety and revulsion on the part of the public; the impetus for child abuse legislation was social, catalyzed and shaped by medical forces often called upon to intervene. However, only when legal liability of physicians who saw child abuse and did not report it became part of reporting laws, was child abuse considered as a communicable disease. The concept of child abuse then became accepted by the medical profession as well as the social and legal professions. Wifebattering is not formally recognized by any profession as yet.

Child abuse legislation generally focused on protection for the child and treatment for the adult since it was assumed that children were innocent parties to abuse and played little or no role in provocation. The burden of guilt is thrust upon the parents, who are held legally responsible for the act.

Despite the forensic structure surrounding the child abuse concept, it is, strictly speaking, still a quasi-legal and quasi-medical phenomenon, lying in that borderland between true medical illness and social deviance. Forensic psychiatrists are accustomed to this dilemma; they often try to straddle the chasm between criminal responsibility and irresponsibility. In child abuse, clinicians are often faced with the same psychological dilemma. They must decide whether a phenomenon is reportable or is instead the private business of the parties concerned. This is particularly the case when the battering is minimal, questionable, or the parents appear otherwise responsible. In short, subjectivity enters into the picture.

These brief comments serve as an introduction for wifebattering. In wifebattering, the victim plays a crucial role. Indeed, the entire social movement leading to the recognition of wifebattering has to do with the fact that the victims have remained in battering situations for so long. This observation is frequently made by social workers and physicians alike. They ask the victim, "Why have you let this occur so long?" The answer to the question has to do with complex, interlocking, hostile dependencies between two adult partners. This makes wifebattering different from child abuse. In child abuse, a pathological relationship exists between a strong adult and a psychologically and physically weaker child. Helplessness is often a key dynamic theme in child abuse. It can play an important role in determining why a mother or father mercilessly beats a child who is screaming and crying. This behavior may betray the fact that she/he cannot tolerate helplessness because it reminds her/him of her/his own fragility. These types of dynamics do not usually operate in the case of wifebattering. In the latter, dynamics lie in another direction. A wife, in many instances, tolerates an abusive husband because she has seen her own father abuse her own mother, the other children, and herself. She may see this violent behavior as a norm. Provocation may be superimposed upon this, and impaired social awareness may perpetuate it. But the husband's dynamics are equally relevant. Those may relate to his need for superiority, which shields massive insecurity. All these dynamics are given as examples; the crucial point is that there are *two* sets of dynamics to consider in the diagnostic process. In both cases, however, the victim may evoke violence in a vulnerable person.

Obviously, wifebattering may reflect abuse because the wife may play no provocative role, but may instead be a captive of her husband. I compare this to slaves who were once victims of their masters. In this sense, wifebattering is a social issue drawing attention to the plight of certain women in bad marriages. Raising the wife abuse issue may result from consciousness raising begun by the Women's Liberation Movement (as cited by Dr. Shainess in the preceding article). Many women have attempted to gain dignity and self-esteem for themselves and other women within the last decade. In an adult marriage, one should focus on abuses inflicted *by* female spouses, as well as *on* them. (Refer to Steinmetz, S., in Chapter 3 of this book, for a comparison of violence on the part of both spouses.) On examination, we find that husbandbattering occurs, too, though it is not often physical; more likely, it is emotional battering. One has only to study marriages in a clinical way to determine that some wives may hold great power over their husbands and manipulate them, exploit them, withhold sexual contact for long periods of time, and behave so as to keep husbands dependent upon them. Wives are usually physically weaker, and battering in its truest sense takes different forms among men and women; thus, men can batter wives both physically and emotionally, and women can batter men emotionally. The pathological relationships between paranoid women and dependent men have, in fact, been described in literature.[2] Seeing how some wives treat husbands gives clues to the subtleties and complexities of this kind of relationship. Unfortunately, one cannot easily observe the physical battering that goes on within the household, which occurs behind closed doors, usually in the evening, and often with the involvement of alcohol.

Wifebattering should not come as a surprise to anyone since it involves violence between people who are intimate with one another. Most crimes of violence occur between people who know each other. In most healthy marriages, a certain amount of mutual emotional battering goes on, and disagreements are resolved in healthy and respectful ways. In pathological relationships, the intensity of bonds between the combatants shifts the wounding into the physical realm because so much is at stake.

Duration of time appears to play some role in the delineation of wifebattering. Unlike child abuse, where one fracture confirms the diagnosis, one black eye sustained by a wife does not usually legally constitute wifebattering. One must again recall that wifebattering is still not, though perhaps should be, a diagnosis which must be reportable. (Refer to Kutun, B., Chapter 7 in this book, for legislative suggestions.) The burden of proof to report this event is, at present, left entirely to the wife. Therefore, the clinician is dependent upon history to assess when a wife should be labeled as "battered." Until such time, it is difficult to treat her. Happily, the large publicity given wifebattering will undoubtedly bring forth women who have been battered but frightened to report such battering. It will also bring forth women who are ambivalent about any kind of change. Reducing the battering relates to raising self-esteem to the point where women will do something to stop the husbands who batter them. One does not raise self-esteem in one session, and this is a process which may require months, or even years, of therapy. To this extent, identification of wifebattering does a service for those women who are at the brink of leaving but need the impetus afforded them by this social movement. But bringing wifebattering into the public eye does a disservice, and could be dangerous, to those women who feel that a tremendous promise for a quick change in life styles has been given them. In reality, it is not simple or safe for a woman to leave her husband, take her children, get legal aid and psychological counseling, initiate court proceedings against her husband, find a new place to live, acquire financial assistance, and relocate her children in a new school. Furthermore, such a woman may need police aid against retaliatory threats made by her husband. The wife may have to struggle to convince police authorities, who are often reluctant and passive-aggressive with their help, that she is truly in danger.

As mentioned above, the phenomenology of wifebattering involves the victim playing a major role. Recognition of this is mandatory, and should not be construed as pejorative.[3] The fact remains that wifebattering, as an event of violence between two adults, resembles any other kind of assault where it is recognized by law that provocation by the victim mitigates the legal charge. Thus, if it can be shown in the case of murder that a victim played a provocative role, the charge can be reduced from murder to manslaughter. This is an extreme example, but should be kept in mind when looking at cases of wifebattering. There is more to wifebeating that a husband who harms his wife and a wife who will not speak up against the hurt. The issues involve the ambivalences and pathologies of both partners. These complexities are illustrated by the following example.

Example 1

A 34-year-old, twice married mother of five came into the psychiatric emergency clinic with the chief complaint of being battered by her 53-year-old husband. The history revealed the husband to be a chronic alcoholic, legally blind, with previous psychiatric hospitalizations for drinking. The woman's first marriage terminated after a five-year-period because of infidelity on the part of the husband. The second and current marriage of eight years' duration had been characterized by intermittent violence. During that time, the woman had become quite close with her father-in-law and mother-in-law, who supported her extensively and always sided with her when her husband mistreated her. The woman stated that her relationship with the husband's mother had been like that of a "daughter" and that she valued the relationship a good deal. Regarding the question as to why she remained in an abusive and assaultive marital situation for an eight year period, the patient stated "I still love my husband but my love has begun to turn to hate."

Despite this long period of ongoing assaultive behavior, the precipitant for her finally seeking psychiatric evaluation remained unclear. There appeared to be no clear psychodynamic explanation, but instead a simple one; the husband was becoming more injurious and had threatened to kill the wife, hitting her on the head with a broom, and physically assaulting her in other ways.

The woman described her husband as a very possessive and suspicious man who constantly accused her of infidelity. In addition to drinking, he also smoked marijuana frequently. The husband was contacted. He became angry on the telephone and claimed that his wife had "all the problems." He eventually agreed to come for psychiatric counseling, at which time he was intoxicated, paranoid, argumentative, and denied serious aggressive behavior. The wife showed ambivalence towards the husband; she displayed some warmth and affection combined with anxiety over the assaults and alleged homicidal threats.

Marital counseling seemed impossible. The woman was accordingly placed in a group psychotherapy situation in order to come to grips with her own ambivalent feelings about her husband. She attended group therapy sessions regularly for several months. Eventually she appeared to gain some self-esteem and came to the resolution that she might be better off without her husband, despite the fact that separation from him would involve potential harassment and even possible danger. However, before this could be accomplished, the husband himself moved out of the house, stating that "there's nothing wrong with me and if she wants to be alone, that's OK with me."

This case illustrates a number of important aspects already alluded to in the above discussion. First, the woman was obviously ambivalent about her husband. She enjoyed the company of his family to the extent that this diluted the negative effects of the husband's abusive behavior. One might wonder about her tolerance for abuse in the second marriage and her tolerance for infidelity in the first marriage.

Such tolerances are not uncommon in marital situations. In severe cases, wives who experienced parental alcoholism and violence expect and evoke such behavior from their own husbands. Intimacy, gentleness, and compassion mystify and frighten such women. In a psychotherapeutic situation, the above woman was able to see that her own dignity had some merit. This crucial step enabled her to work towards asserting her dignity, gaining independence, and deciding to leave her husband. Interestingly, the husband must have sensed this new resolve. He made the first move to separate in a manner typical of an assertively paranoid person.

The outcome of this case is still uncertain. This case involved a husband who was quite sick and a wife who allowed the sickness to persist. Many of us would tolerate a situation "for better or for worse," to a limited degree, and then take some kind of drastic steps to correct it. There are some individuals who remain within a pathogenic situation for years, seeking some kind of comfort from those around them.

This is an important point. Pain, discomfort, and suffering may form the bases for some people's life styles. Without such misery and discomfort, individuals are faced with the more pressing obligation to make their own decisions. Being the underdog and having one's life decisions made by someone else are, in an unhealthy way, psychologically comforting. This is true both for men and women and should be considered in the phenomenon of wifebattering.

In this day and age, when people live together and are not married, one also sees evidence of "matebattering." This has the same psychodynamics and illustrates the same principles of management.

Example 2

A 26-year-old divorced female technician formed a relationship with a man whom she knew had a previous history of assault. She had made contact with the man when he made a random obscene phone call to her one night. She got involved in a discussion with him and agreed to meet him. The man became increasingly demanding of the woman's affections and belligerent when she withdrew. After mild assaults (slapping), the man threatened to harm the woman and expressed a veiled threat to kill her. The woman responded to this threat by going to the police station. She told policemen on duty that she had been threatened, but she was not taken seriously by the officer in charge. The man's threats continued, and the woman eventually related her problem to her physician. He advised her that since her life was in danger, she should retain a lawyer. With his help, he said, she should again go to the police officers in her neighborhood. The woman became quite frightened by these suggestions fearing retaliatory violence as a result of these assertive steps. Also during this crisis period, she received a phone call from the man, and responded by telling him that she would like to help him but couldn't and that he needed professional help; this statement betrayed the obvious ambivalence. It was pointed out to her that limit-setting and controls were important. This situation could have escalated to dangerous levels if such limits were not set. The woman eventually did retain counsel, who advised her of her rights, and she sought out the magistrate of the local court with a formal complaint. A summons was issued to which he responded immediately with a counterthreat via telephone, witnessed by the woman and a friend. A second summons was issued. The man was eventually brought to court. There, the judge ordered the man to leave the woman alone or face certain incarceration. Save for one phone call, no further word was heard from the man.

This case illustrates the complexity of getting a "battered wife," who, in this instance, was a companion, to seek aid. Police do not sympathize with those who seek aid during domestic quarrels. They often act as though the wife or mate has deliberately brought such harm on herself. Retaining a lawyer lent credence to the woman's complaint. The support of a physician diminished retaliatory fantasies so prevalent in the management of wifebattering. Perpetuation of a violent situation through ambivalence is also illustrated by this example.

Unfortunately, this case did not resolve the psychodynamic question of why the woman chose this mate to begin with. Her previous marriage had some elements similar to this relationship. Tragically, some battered wives repeat early mistakes in their subsequent marriages if they fail to learn the origins of their poor choices and their unconscious needs. Furthermore, choosing a mate who is gentle both physically and emotionally may be difficult. The sudden change from an alcoholic, abusive mate to a compassionate, kind one, requires supportive help. Some women fear kind husbands and good men, lest such individuals go away or otherwise hurt them. It is easier to choose someone who is already mean because there is less to lose. This curious equation operates all too often when self esteem is at its lowest.

This second case illustrates an interesting aspect of the battered woman, a tendency for the person to "feel sorry" for her husband, particularly if he is an alcoholic. I have seen this in the case of *"explo-*

sive personalities." (Refer to Elliott, Frank A., in Chapter 4 of this book.) Such men, with epileptoid-like disturbances, fly into rages perceived by the mate or spouse as manifestations of a disease process, a "Dr. Jekyll/Mr. Hyde" transformation. Thus, the batterer is not really himself and can be excused.

The male who exhibits explosive rage outbursts may have treatable psychopathology and should be evaluated by a psychiatrist. The diagnostic process for this is reviewed elsewhere.[4] This discussion relates to the battered wife because it is necessary to recognize that despite existing illness, abuse is nonetheless occurring. Danger and risk exist in the face of alcoholism; sometimes the "feeling sorry" aspect of the wife's behavior should be seen as a defense to protect her from her own anger and assertiveness.

Example 3

A 30-year-old government worker and his wife were seen for psychiatric evaluation because of extreme temper outbursts accompanied by physical abuse by the husband. The husband was a pleasant and obsessional individual, very guarded in his emotions and having little insight. He was a highly skilled intellectual who tended to handle stress in an all-or-none fashion. He exploded when his wife made demands upon him. For example, if she asked him to take out the trash while he was watching the ball game, he would explode with fury and strike her.

The husband was seen in therapy for more than six months. In treatment, he expressed feelings about his reactions to an overbearing possessive mother and rather harsh father from whom he, an only child, had obtained early independence. The psychotherapy also revealed that the wife had many of the same neurotic traits as the husband's parents. She was strongly domineering and yet had considerable dependence on her parents. She called them several times a day for advice and counsel. Small imperfections in the house, furniture, appliances, or the making of meals would cause the wife to become very self-doubting. She would pass the criticism on to the husband, who would explode. The wife often became overprotective with her husband when it rained or snowed or when he smoked cigars. The husband, an obsessive, intensely disliked weakness and resented these intrusions.

Both parties were seen together. The wife had numerous criticisms of her husband and could not mention any of his positive attributes at all. Finally, she acknowledged that "I'm glad that I found him." She stated that he was too close to his parents and this bothered her. Her own awareness regarding her parental dependency was lacking. It was quite evident from observation of the complicated interaction between the two parties that the wife lacked a good deal of insight into her own neurotic traits and bubbling angers.

This account illustrates a complex situation between two people without backgrounds of violence or deprivation. The dynamics of this case ultimately could be interpreted in the following way. The husband would explode and hit the wife, which in turn caused the wife to seek support and comfort from her parents. They soothed her and gave her the confidence she lacked. The child-like reinforcement the wife received led her to march back into the marriage and unwittingly trigger another incident. Prior to therapy, the husband accepted each new challenge and responded predictably. He behaved as the bad little boy he had been as a child with his own parents, while the wife behaved as a mistreated little girl who could run crying to her parents. Both parties, then, were essentially living as children within the marital situation. Intensive psychotherapy was required to break this vicious circle. Specifically, the husband was counseled as to how to handle his wife's complaints in non-violent ways and the wife was told alternate ways of seeking grievance and redress by talking both with the husband and psychotherapist about her complaints, rather than going to her parents. These efforts required time and patience, but were beneficial to the marriage.

Interlocking dependencies form the basis for interlocking hatreds and animosities. The ambivalences—the love and hate—created in such situations often go unnoticed. Whenever there are abuse and hate, there is love at some level, though it may be difficult to find. Each case of wifebattering, matebattering, or husbandbattering, requires that the clinician see each party individually, then together, to see the quality of the interaction. This is not a simple matter; often, several interviews are required before a therapist learns what makes each person function adequately and what the underlying dynamics are.

These examples illustrate the complexity of wifebattering. When one examines murderers or rapists, one must understand each case separately. Wifebattering, though becoming a social movement, involves individual study of clinical cases. There is an added complexity of countertransference. Women have traditionally been viewed as objects, possessions of men. When women who have been abused go to male physicians for help, there is a danger that the clinician may side with the man and see the woman as provocative. The doctor must guard against such a simplistic diagnosis. He must also not automatically see the woman as the underdog. The physician must be open and objective in assessing a wifebattering situation.

The treatment of wifebattering involves treatment of both parties to the extent that this is possible. (Refer to Straus, M., in Chapter 7 of this book.) When treatment of both husband and wife is not possible, the aim of treatment is to take the battered person and place her or him in a situation where consciousness can be raised. Then an intelligent choice can be made about whether or not to remain in the situation. In addition, clear legal guidance and firm support with regard to the authorities are necessary accompaniments to vigorous psychotherapy. The ultimate aim of any therapeutic process to alleviate battering is to raise self-esteem. For where there is poor self-esteem, there is a tendency to stay in a bad situation, or to seek one. Beyond this global therapeutic end point, wifebattering or mate-battering involves getting both parties to verbalize emotions rather than act them out. Alternatives to swearing, screaming insults, and hitting need to be learned. *One of the things I do with patients prone to temper outbursts and paroxysmal rage attacks is to teach them to recognize their own inner affective states of anger.* Then, they can inform a potential victim when something occurs which makes them angry. It may seem mundane, but it is of crucial therapeutic importance for a husband to tell his wife, "That makes me angry," rather than slap her. This conversion from physical action to verbal confrontation is a profound one.[5] Medications for patients who are prone to rage attacks can be useful, and this matter has been reviewed.[6] Medications may be particularly useful in tense situations where both parties can recognize that the propensity for anger exists. Such conditions of stress occur when a child is sick, when there are economic crises, when a spouse is laid-off from work, and the like. Again, the aim of treatment is to teach partners in a marriage to recognize when stressful points occur and to work them through together.

For the battered wife, some aspect of treatment must focus on her background and any existing heritage of violence which forms the basis for violence in the current marriage. The same kind of background evaluation is necessary for the husband who may need to prove his masculinity and superiority by aggressive and physically abusive means. With this treatment process comes an ability to express compassion and gentleness. This is the most difficult thing to work out. Those that value "might and right" have a poor ability to hold the hand of someone who is sick and weak. Thus, the participants of a pathologic and violent marriage must come to grips with their inner needs for warmth and tenderness and be able to express them.

Videotaping and videotape confrontation are extremely useful in situations where insight of partners is lacking. When a man can see how angry he gets, a great deal can be accomplished. Role playing may be another useful tool for teaching patients to anticipate the consequences of daily family stresses or particular family conflicts.

REFERENCES

1. Helfer, R. E. and Kempe, C. H., *The Battered Child.* Chicago: University of Chicago Press, 1968.
2. Dupont, R. L., and Grunebaum, H., "Willing Victims: the Husbands of Paranoid Women," *Amer. J. Psychiat.* 125: 152–159 (1968).
3. Symonds, M., "The Accidental Victim of Violent Crme," in *Violence and Victims*, S. A. Pasternack (ed.). New York: Spectrum Publications, 1975.
4. Lion, J. R., *Evaluation and Management of the Violent Patient.* Springfield, Ill.: Charles C Thomas, 1972.
5. Lion, J. R., "The Role of Depression in the Treatment of Aggressive Personality Disorder," *Amer. J. Psychiat.* 129: 347–349 (1972).
6. Lion, J. R., "Conceptual Issues in the Use of Drugs for the Treatment of Aggression in Man," *JNMD* 160: 76–82 (1975).

Acknowledgment: I thank Jill A. Lion for editorial assistance.

6 The Law and Law Enforcement

. . . . I have found a certain kind of strictness and obdurity against no condition more than against the estate of wives. For instance, it (the law) decrees, a wife shall lose her dowry for giving a lascivious kiss. That a wife is legally bound to follow her husband wandering at his pleasure from city to city. Be it from one land into another region. Be it from her own country into banishment itself. Especially if it be in pilgrimage into the Holy Land. That the wife is only dignified by the husband, and not in any ways the husband graced by the wife. That the husband's suspicion of his wife's lightness may be the wife's expulsion from her husband's company. Lastly, if a wife play the adulteress (a fault indeed deserving no excuse), her husband may then produce her into public judgement, deprive her of her promised dowry, and expose her to perpetual divorcement. But if the husband commit the like offense, though it were as open as the sun, and as odious as hate itself, yet the wife may not in public as much as open her mouth against it. Infinite such other. Hard impositions in my weak sense for so weak a sex . . . For in the whole body of either law, Canon or Civil, I have not yet found (neither as I think has any man else) set down in these or equivalent terms, or otherwise passed by any positive sentence or verdict <u>That it is lawful for a husband to beat his wife.</u>

HEALE, WILLIAM, 1609

SOME THOUGHTS REGARDING THE CRIMINAL JUSTICE SYSTEM AND WIFEBEATING
Maria Roy

Underlying the criminal justice system is the covert toleration of wifebeating, as indicated in the policy and personal attitudes of the police, prosecutors, and judges; and through the inefficient procedures which render even the existing legal remedies inadequate. The family, for all practical purposes, is immune to the benefit of intervention from the law. Because the family is still looked upon as an entity that is beyond reproach, and that must continue as an entity in spite of the presence of violent conflict; because women are still thought of as the property of men (as evidenced by statutes declaring the husband as head of the household); and because of the sexist organization of society, wherein the male dominated criminal justice system insures very little legal remedy for women who seek it, very serious attempts must be made to eradicate the all pervasive tolerance of wifebeating in the statutory and common law.

Police policy of arrest avoidance; the incredibly lengthy response time to calls for help, the "take a walk around the block" recommendations of police, prosecuting attorneys, and judges; and the policy of "cool off" the husband and "turn off" the wife all contribute to the perpetuation of violence behind closed doors within the sanctity of the family.

In addition, the denial of compensation, even when injury results in permanent disability, when inflicted by the *husband*, further testifies to the sex discrimination inherent in the legal system.

Since the judicial system is intent upon "preserving the family"— even when the family does not function as a healthy, loving unit; and since the judicial system does not attempt to determine which cases among those brought up demonstrate a high potential for violent crime; and finally, since the judicial system fails to differentiate between those women who are serious about pursuing legal remedy from those who are not; then efforts should be made to re-focus the criminal justice system on the nature of violence within the home. It must be identified and recognized as *criminal*, not viewed euphemistically as a "domestic disturbance," and thereby beyond the jurisdiction of the law enforcer. When assaults in the home are *not* considered as crimes, they are most often not likely to be prosecuted; women are dissuaded from lodging a complaint and following through, thus perpetuating the treadmill of violence.

When law enforcement agencies and the courts impose their prejudices on the cases brought before them, they, through "sins of omission," condone the husband's violence and give him a license to continue his violent actions. What results is a continuation of violence in the home, perhaps leading to homicide, suicide, and infanticide.

Uniform Crime Reports (1974) indicated that one-fourth of all murders in the nation are from some type of family dispute; and *over* half of these domestic assaults were spouse killing spouse. Aggravated assaults between husbands and wives account for nearly 12% of all reported assaults in the U.S. Some say violence occurs in 50–60% of all marriages.

In short, the family becomes an armed camp: the nuclear family evolving into a nuclear holocaust.

Women without legal recourse and lacking the benefits of the extended family have little alternatives. They are forced to remain on the battlefields, "protecting" themselves and their children without the proper means to do so.

The men who engage in gratuitous violence are encouraged; the women are discouraged and defeated; the children are scarred for life. These children inherit a legacy of violence, a gift of tyranny which they in turn will pass on to their children.

One generation of violence begetting another—and so on.

LEGAL SOLUTIONS: EQUAL PROTECTION UNDER THE LAW

Emily Jane Goodman, New York attorney and co-author of
Women, Money and Power

There is a sex crime committed more often than rape. Though not necessarily sexual, in the sense of forced intercourse or other non-consensual genital contact, there is a crime which, by definition, is perpetrated by one sex upon the other. This sex crime need not take place in the bedroom, on streets, rooftops, or auto seats. But it is taking place all over America—without regard to income, race, or ethnic background. The crime is one in which the victim is constantly exposed to the perpetrator, often dependent, and in fact, under contract to him.

Wife abuse.

The questions of how hard and how often a woman is assaulted by her husband are, for the most part, irrelevant. It has been said that there is no such thing as a wife who has been beaten *once*. The issue to be dealt with is the victim's options when she is attacked at all.

There cannot be any doubt about the widespread nature of the problem, despite the absence of statistical data. We know that abused wives are ever more reluctant to report, or even admit, their victimized status than are women who have been raped. There is even greater guilt experienced, there is surely dependency, and even a belief that "it's all part of marriage."

The woman who has been beaten and battered often goes to great lengths to deny to herself and to others that the man she is "supposed to love" sees her as a punching bag. The woman who reports her injuries as resulting from falls, muggings, and accidents such as walking into doors is often too ashamed and frightened to say, "My husband did it."

There are no limitations in terms of age, race, class, or nationality. The variable here is gender. Among the men who beat their wives are doctors, lawyers, bankers, and businessmen; and the husband-assailant is not necessarily a drinker acting under the influence of alcohol.

The abused wife, whose bruises may or may not show, has—as she sees it, and in some ways, in fact—very limited options.

For the wife who has been physically abused, shame, guilt, economic and emotional dependency, and the belief that it's all part of the marriage are only some of the problems. In addition, she is without adequate legal remedies.

"Laws," wrote John Stuart Mill, "convert what was a mere physical fact (masculine strength) into a legal right . . . In no other case (except that of a child) is the person who has been proved judicially to have suffered an injury replaced under the physical power of the culprit who inflicted it."

At day-long hearings on battered wives, a New York City councilman asked, "Do we break up a marriage merely because a man beats his wife?" Repeatedly, the same elected official asked, "Doesn't our public policy reflect the sanctity of the marriage?"

The theory, and the problem, is that the laws and courts are supposedly acting in the interests of the family unit, though at the expense of married women. The attitude of the legislature, police, and judges is that they are dealing not with a public crime, but with signs of a "troubled marriage."

The laws reflect the dehumanizing private-property aspects of marriage and family. Special treatment for violence toward spouses reflects our social order and acceptance of male prerogatives. But, just as sex is a suspect classification for determining abilities, talents, intelligence, potential, jobs and, legal rights, marital status is a suspect classification for "law enforcement."

In a clear example of how women are thought to be at fault in causing their own abuse or in misusing "The System," the chief judge of the State of New York has written:

> . . . many family confrontations, although, technically taking the character of a criminal offense, are lacking in the elements, public or private, that justify the use of criminal procedures and sanctions.
>
> . . . criminal charges brought by wives fell into three discernible patterns:
>
> 1. Wives who lodge complaints to compel their husbands to leave home and to obtain protection, support, and custody of the children;
>
> 2. Wives, normally married less than five years, who treat the assault of disorderly conduct as a sign of troubled marriage and who use the courts to seek resolution of the difficulty and effect conciliation;
>
> 3. Wives, usually married more than five years, and willing to settle for less than an ideal marriage, who seek to use the proceeding only to get their husbands to stop beating them or to stop drinking heavily.

The wife, then, is left without legal remedies at every step of the way. Although almost half of the calls to the police are for assistance in marital disputes, the police—virtually all male—do everything possible to dissuade the wife from pressing charges. Their arguments cover a wide range: "Who will support you if he's locked up?" "He could lose his job." "You'll have to spend days in court." "Why don't you kiss and make up?" "Why'd you make him slug you?" "If you make trouble, think of what he'll do to you the next time."

If the wife signs a complaint, her husband, if arrested (unlikely), would probably be released and given a future Criminal Court date. In the intervening time, much can happen to mollify the assaulted woman, but if the couple ever gets to Criminal Court, the case, unless dismissed, will (in New York, for example) be referred to the Family Court, because the defense counsel, the district attorney, and the judge are likely to agree that "this is just a family matter."

A powerful prosecutor is quoted as saying:

> There is no way in hell we can try 6,000 cases a year with our staff, so which
> ones should we try? Take a felonious assault case involving a domestic quarrel.
> Does this deserve to be tried by a 12-man jury? No. We are much better off if they
> kiss and make up rather than if we put them in jail.

In New York, until just recently, the Family Court had "exclusive original jurisdiction" over husbandly assaults; only a Family Court judge had the discretion to make an exception and have a case handled by Criminal Court. The District Attorney's office often took the position that wife abuse is not a sex crime and does not concern the prosecution. On July 20, 1977, Governor Hugh Carey of New York signed into law a bill that would give *women* the option to bring criminal charges against husbands who beat them. This new law, which takes effect September 1, 1977, gives the wife a choice between Family Court or Criminal Court. The purpose of the Criminal Court proceeding will be to punish the offender, while the interest of the Family Court proceeding will be to keep the family together.

Though assaults by a spouse and other specified offenses were not viewed as "crimes," the assailant enjoyed the best protection provided by criminal law, such as the right to counsel (court-appointed, if necessary). Because of the civil nature of the Family Court, the "respondent" does not face the penalties available if he assaults a stranger, rather than his wife.

A woman passenger in an auto accident may sue the driver for damages, whether they are married or legal strangers. But if she's punched in the nose, her legal options depend on her marital status. A wife hit by her husband traditionally loses access to courts and laws available to others. Hopefully, the new option available to her in New York State will change her status.

The wife, who is unable to obtain free legal services, will be discouraged by the prospects of representing herself or having to retain—and pay—a private attorney. The courts will be alien and unfamiliar to her. She may be surprised by the sexist attitudes of both male and female judges.

Whether the matter arrives in Family Court through the so-called criminal process, or by the wife seeking an "order of protection," the judge may issue such an order, which theoretically requires the husband to stay away from his wife or simply to abstain from the offensive conduct; set bail; require conciliation proceedings; place the husband on probation; suspend judgment; dismiss the petition; or, in circumstances apparently bordering on attempted murder, send the case to Criminal Court.

If not for the fact that wife abuse is all but condoned by our laws, it would not have been startling when, in October of 1976, a Brooklyn Family Court judge ordered a husband charged with assaulting his wife to be tried as an accused criminal rather than as a party to a troubled marriage. However, it is not at all clear that this would have been done if a weapon had not been used.

In any event, during all of the proceedings, delays, and adjournments, the wife's evidence—her bruises and other injuries—may be fading (physically and psychologically). She may still be living under the same roof as the assailant; a highly unlikely situation involving the parties to a non-marital assault. If she has a Family Court "order of protection," the husband may keep away; this, in turn, can cause the wife and children renewed emotional and economic problems.

Moreover, the Family Court cannot remand the husband to jail for the "original misbehavior," but only for willful violation of its own order. According to the Department of Corrections, on a recent, typical day, there were—in the entire City of New York—only seven men in custody as a result of any Family Court order.

There is no valid, rational reason that wives should in most states be denied equal protection under the law. And yet they are—clearly in violation of the Constitution. There is no reasonable distinction between "public and private violence," as it has been put.

It is possible that our lawmakers, who are predominantly male, prefer to preserve the status quo, not only for sexist reasons, but also for other political and economic considerations. Psychologists, the police, even the couples involved, recognize a connection between violence in the home and outside frustrations, particularly financial ones.

Although the problem crosses class lines, for many men, assault is the only opportunity to reverse their own life pattern, and to be among the oppressors rather than the oppressed. If men could not beat wives, the handy victims, there might be revolution in the work places.

Yet even if legislatures acted to change laws, the unsatisfactory result here, as in penal areas, would probably be just more incarceration without ever dealing with the underlying cause: sexism.

Legal reforms for the interim period during which wives are still intimidated and dependent on husbands are difficult to arrive at. However, this is an area in which the void might be filled with experiments in lay tribunals operating on principles of community control and peer-group justice.

But since the laws pertaining to wife abuse, and domestic relations in general, are governed by our society's indulgence in "male supremacy," statutory modifications are unlikely to solve the problem. Only radical social and legal changes in prevailing attitudes toward women, the family, and marriage can make any significant difference.

INTERNATIONAL ASSOCIATION OF CHIEFS OF POLICE TRAINING KEY*

Violence within families is a complex and perplexing social problem about which there currently exists no definite knowledge. Researchers have related family conflict to many factors including societal violence, personality, economic condition, occupational role, and personal history, but there seems to be no specific set of conditions that are peculiarly linked to familial violence. Family violence occurs at all levels of society, within the homes of educated and the illiterate as well as the wealthy and deprived.

Although there now may be no answers to the many questions that surround family violence, there is no doubt about police involvement in such emergencies. Every police officer knows that a large part of his job is to intervene in family disputes, and every officer is aware of the danger he faces when entering a violent home. Previous Training Keys[1] have discussed the police role in cases of child abuse and family disturbances where the potential for violence is clearly evident. This Key focuses on a third form of family violence—wifebeating.

Wifebeating is probably as old as the institution of marriage and historically has been accepted to varying degrees in most cultures. Until relatively recently, physical abuse of a wife was tolerated or at least ignored in this country. As women gradually become more independent of their husbands, they began to institute civil damages suits against their husbands for personal injuries.[2]

Many states have passed what are commonly referred to as the "Married Women's Acts." These acts give married women the right to

---

*Training Key #245.
[1]See Training Keys #207, "Child Abuse," and #209, "Crisis Intervention."
[2]*Johnson v. Johnson*, 201 Ala. 41, 77 So. 335 (1917); Brown v. Gosser, 262 S. W. 2d 480 (Ky. Ct. App. 1953).

own property, to sue and be sued, and generally to be regarded as persons separate from their husbands. Under these laws, wives remain in a legal sense, independent of their husbands and can bring criminal charges against their spouses. Even in the states that have adopted specific statutes that apply to wife beating, however, such incidents are still considered by large portions of every segment of society as being extralegal "family matters" in which the law should not interfere. The fact that many persons condone a degree of spouse assault is evident from a National Commission on the Causes and Prevention of Violence survey which found that 25% of the men and 16% of the women surveyed approved of slapping a spouse under certain circumstances.

Although there are incidents of husbands being beaten by their wives, physical violence that the police typically encounter is directed by husbands toward their wives. The incidence of wifebeating cannot be determined with any precision because assault, battery, or similar terms are used to officially report and categorize such incidents in police files, emergency room records, and court dockets. Wifebeating *per se* is not recognized as a specific crime. To determine a valid approximation of the incidence of wife assault would therefore require a case by case study of every assault. Even if all reported wife assaults were known, the total number would be an unreliable figure since it is recognized that wifebeating is largely an underreported crime.

The Partners

Wifebeating is a multi-dimensional problem. Psychologists and sociologists believe that the root causes of wifebeating lie deep within the personalities of those involved and within the society at large. The economic dependence of most wives, the cultural sexism that pervades institutions, and the psychological make-up and personal histories of the victims and assailants seem to play a major part in stimulating most assaults and in keeping the abused wife trapped in a violent relationship.

The specific factors that produce an abusive relationship within a home vary in each instance; however, social research and police experience indicate that there are certain general characteristics prevalent among reported cases of wife abuse. It cannot be known whether these characteristics are typical of marital assault in the thousands of cases that go unreported. It should be stressed that the following factors do not describe a typical victim or assailant; they represent commonly encountered facts in wife-abuse cases.

Victim. Most people cannot understand why some women tolerate marriages of violence, particularly those chronic cases in which accepting abuse has become a routine in the victim's life. Nonetheless, many abused wives are reluctant to report incidents, electing to endure an unbearable situation rather than to seek assistance.

Economic dependence is perhaps the single most common reason why many abused wives choose to stay within a violent marriage. Quite often it is the husband who directs the finances of a household. This is especially true of violent homes where the husband tries to maintain the wife's dependency through economic control. In destitute homes, the abused wife's economic dependency on her spouse may be complete because of a general lack of funds to meet basic needs.

Abused wives of affluent husbands may not suffer the same total dependency or deprivation, but seldom do they have their own checking accounts or other cash sources. Such wives, who may have avenues of escape from a violent marriage, often choose to remain with their assaultive husbands to maintain their high standard of living. This is particularly true where children are involved. Although the wife may be personally willing to face economic hardship, she may not be willing to allow her children to suffer in the same way.

Most abused wives do not possess marketable skills that could be used to establish financial independency. But even those wives who are principal providers or who earn supplemental incomes can also be financially trapped within a violent marriage when their husbands control the family's finances.

A history of violence in the family seems to be another factor that is part of the battered wife phenomenon. Many abused wives are from homes where their mothers were battered. Thus they may be more inclined to accept abuse as a "normal" part of marriage than others who do not grow up in the same atmosphere of wife abuse. Such abused wives may rationalize that being beaten is part of a wife's role. In these cases, realization that a marriage should not be violent often comes after the wife has suffered for many years.

Low self-esteem appears to be another common denominator among battered wives and clearly is related to the other factors just mentioned. Economic dependency decreases the self-esteem of all adults and the battered wife proves to be no exception. A childhood history of experiencing parental abuse can lead to the expectation and acceptance of rigid male domination.

What contributes most significantly to the lack of self-esteem among battered wives is, however, the physical abuse itself. The humiliation and shame of being assaulted time and again by someone who is intimate must create grave doubts about one's worth. The self-image of the abused wife may drop to the point where she believes she is responsible for and deserving of abuse.

Fear is the constant companion of the battered wife. The abused wife is often immobilized emotionally and mentally by the knowledge that she may be assaulted at any time. Contrary to the popular image of the enraged, drunken husband returning home on a Saturday night to beat his spouse, wife assault occurs with no predictability and any event may trigger abuse.

Fear of husband reprisal stops many battered wives from reporting assaults to the police or contacting social service agencies or professional personnel. Frequently, fear also prevents abused wives from discussing the matter with friends or family.

Social isolation is characteristic of the abused wife for she is typically trapped both emotionally and physically. She may not have the minimum funds needed to socialize and develop friendships, and, more importantly, she may not have the desire to do so. Abused wives frequently are withdrawn and avoid contact with neighbors, friends, and relatives because of the nature of their problem and their reticence to discuss it. The abused wife knows that friendship means communication. She also knows that a black eye or an unusual bruise can be explained away as an accident only once.

Not all abused wives are completely without fault in provoking and maintaining violent relationships with their spouses. There is indication that victims of chronic wife abuse have a greater tolerance for violence and are more violent themselves than women who never experienced marital assault. Whether the attitudes of some victims toward violence is a result of their marriage or whether they are belligerent for other reasons has not been determined.

Assailant. Determining what causes men to assault their wives can only be speculated upon since there is even less information about assaultive husbands than about their spouses. Of significance is an apparent pattern of similarities between the victim and the assailant.

Frequently, their personalities are complementary, and there is some evidence of general violence by both spouses. That divorced victims of abuse often remarry assaultive partners indicates the importance of personality factors in understanding family violence.

The assaultive husband, like the battered wife, is likely to have grown up in a violent home. The wife batterer may have been a battered child and has a higher tolerance for violence which follows him through life. The assaultive husband often believes he has the right to beat his wife. Many wife batterers have police records, and a substantial number have been arrested for violent offenses other than wife assault.

While the battered wife is typically passive, the assaultive husband often is overly concerned with living up to the role of the dominating male—at least in his home. Frequently, this compulsion to exercise stereo-typical masculine traits, such as physical aggressiveness, is related to the husband's failure outside of the marriage. Many battering husbands are unsuccessful financially, occupationally, and socially. Like their wives, they also suffer from low self-esteem. Their frustration and anger is sometimes directed violently toward the wife.

The overconsumption of alcohol and the use of drugs by the assailants are recurring factors in wifebeating cases. However, alcohol and drugs are closely linked to most crimes of violence, and the fact that they are sometimes used by assaultive husbands immediately prior to or during an attack reveals little about the true causes of wifebeating.

The Children

The children of a violent household are often more seriously affected than their parents. Children who are forced to witness violence between their parents may suffer emotional trauma and develop attitudes that persist throughout their lives. As was indicated previously, exposure to family violence as a child increases the likelihood that the person will act violently as an adult.

Children may be victims of physical as well as psychological abuse. The battered wife may strike out at the children, using them for scapegoats, or the assaultive husband may beat his children as well as his wife. The consequences of abusive treatment go deeper than the physical injury and can seriously impair the child's proper development.

For these reasons, the police officer should not overlook the well-being of children caught in a violent home. In considering the child as a possible victim of abuse, the officer should evaluate the physical well-being of the child, his environment, and the parents' attitude toward him. When necessary, officers should act to separate the children from the abusive parent and proceed with criminal charges. In all cases, the ramifications of children witnessing violence should be explained to the parents.

Children may sometimes be considered as witnesses to an assault. To be competent as a witness, the child must be able to accurately relate the event and distinguish between fantasy and reality. With older children of average ability this is not a serious problem; however, retarded or younger children present additional concerns.

The Police Role

A critical difference exists between the police response to family disturbances where no physical violence has occurred and a wifebeating. Although the application of crisis intervention skills are required in both cases, the primary purpose of mediation to help resolve family problems is to prevent violence and therefore make arrest unnecessary. Where an attack has already taken place, however, the police officer must be prepared to conduct an assault investigation while recognizing the special sociological and psychological factors that surround wife abuse incidents. "Family disturbances" and "wife beatings" should not be viewed synonymously; nor should wife abuse be considered a victimless crime or solely a manifestation of a poor marriage. A wifebeating is foremost an assault—a crime that must be investigated.

Past experience shows, however, that many victims of marital assault do not cooperate with the police. Many victims will not sign a complaint or, if they do, will later refuse to testify against their spouse.

Some of the reasons why battered wives do not seek assistance or refuse to cooperate fully with the police have already been mentioned. Certainly the economic circumstances of a family represent the most influential of these factors. A battered wife who cannot survive without her husband is under tremendous pressure to "overlook" his violence, especially if there are dependent children. On a more personal level, the battered wife may to some degree love her husband despite his behavior. It is understandably difficult to have arrested someone with whom you have been intimate or have feelings for.

Frustrated by the pattern of victim uncooperativeness, some police officers have developed an indifferent attitude toward arresting assaultive husbands. Battered wives in turn point to this attitude as one reason why they fail to proceed legally against their spouses. The two conflicting views produce a "chicken-versus-the-egg" controversy that is useless to pursue. A more constructive view is to find an approach that will accomplish the police mission in such cases and provide the victim with the best possible service.

An assault cannot be ignored by the police regardless of the victim's attitude or motive for not cooperating. Each wifebeating incident must be investigated, and the officer's decision to make an arrest or a referral to an appropriate social service agency should be based on the nature of the assault. Specific laws that are applicable to wife abuse differ among states, but the offenses are generally categorized in the assault and battery statutes. The following offenses vary in degree according to their seriousness: simple assault and battery, aggravated assault, assault with intent to maim or disfigure, and assault with intent to murder.

In cases where the wife refuses to cooperate with the officer, it is exceedingly difficult to proceed. Felony cases, however, can be pursued if there exists strong circumstantial and physical evidence. In a few cases there may be an independent eyewitness to the assault. Based upon the available evidence, the officer may be able to make a probable cause arrest in a felony case regardless of the lack of the wife's cooperation.

A policy of arrest, when the elements of the offense are present, promotes the well-being of the victim. Many battered wives who tolerate the situation undoubtedly do so because they feel they are alone in coping with the problem. The officer who starts legal action may give the wife the courage she needs to realistically face and correct her situation.

From the viewpoints of the prosecutor, courts and social service agencies, the positive steps by the police to make every contact with a battered wife a matter of official record may not be very well received. Regardless, the individual officer should not take it upon himself to dismiss wifebeating incidents, even when such enforcement may seem utterly futile. When no better way of handling family assault incidents is available, the police must follow the law and document the problem. Also these case reports help to build a record of the husband's actions and intent, which may be useful for future prosecution.

To minimize pressure on the prosecutor, courts, and social service agencies will only delay the time when adequate remedies and programs are provided. Ignoring the problem is an improper action of the police. Even if each family processed through the legal and social service systems receives no help from them, initiating the process remains the proper action for the police until a better system exists.

Discussion Guide

1. Battered wives often take property with them when leaving their spouses. Discuss the larceny laws as they apply to husband and wife.

> . . . Courts now generally hold that a husband can be charged with larceny, or embezzlement of his wife's separate property—*People v. Morton*, 308 N. Y. 96, 123 N.E. 2d 790 (1954); *Whitson v. State*, 181 P.2d 822 (Ariz. Sup. Ct. 1947).
> . . . Similarly, a wife can be convicted of misappropriating her husband's property—*State v. Koontz*, 124 Kan. 216, 247 P. 949 (1972); *People v. Graff*, 39 Cal. App. Dec. 487, 211 P. 829 (1922).
> . . . Some courts have suggested that it would not be larceny if money were taken to obtain food, shelter or other necessities—*State v. Herndon*, 158 Fla. 115, 27 So. 2d 833 (1946).
> . . . In a few states, it is still impossible for one spouse to be guilty of stealing from the other.
> . . . What is the law in your jurisdiction?

2. Requests for police intervention in family problems are not limited to incidents of assault or larceny. Another common situation is where one of the spouses desires to have the other removed from the premises. So far as the parties' rights to the same property are concerned, trespass action against a spouse is possible if:

> . . . The property belongs solely to the other spouse.
> . . . A spouse has been deprived of property because she has been forced to live apart from her husband due to his unlawful acts.
> . . . What is your jurisdiction's procedures in common law situations?

3. When police officers enter a home in a family disturbance inci-

dent, they may observe evidence of another crime. Discuss the doctrine of plain view.

> . . . Anything seen in plain view during the normal course of an authorized entry
> or search can be seized and used in evidence so long as there is probable cause
> to believe that a crime has been committed.
> . . . If a person only permits entry but refuses his consent to search, incriminat-
> ing items observed in plain view may suffice to establish an officer's probable
> cause to make an arrest or to return with a search warrant.
> . . . Things seen in plain view are not the product of a "search."

Questions

The following questions are based on material in this Training
Key. Select the best answers.

1. Studies of wifebeating show that family violence occurs in:
   (a) homes of well-educated persons
   (b) economically deprived areas
   (c) all levels of society.
   (d) among mentally retarded persons.

2. Wifebeating is generally considered an underreported crime.
Which of the following answers best explains why some abused
wives are reluctant to seek assistance?
   (a) Women by nature are masochistic and thus expect and en-
       joy physical abuse.
   (b) Economic and psychological dependencies make some
       women endure abusive treatment rather than seek aid.
   (c) Available legal remedies do not provide a means by which
       victims can escape the situation.
   (d) Wife abuse is a victimless crime, solely a manifestation of a
       poor marriage which should not be reported.

3. The proper police role in a wifebeating case is to:
   (a) Investigate the cases in which the wife will initiate prosecution.
   (b) Answer calls only if a third party is the complainant.
   (c) Make a referral to the proper social agency and avoid an
       arrest in these family cases.
   (d) Investigate the case, regardless of the victim's attitude, and
       dispose of the case by making an arrest or referral based
       upon the investigation.

Answers

1. (c) Wifebeating, like other forms of family violence, occurs at all levels of society, among economically deprived families as well as in affluent homes.
2. (b) Wifebeating is a multi-dimensional problem involving economic and psychological factors.
3. (d) An assault cannot be ignored by the police. Each wifebeating incident must be investigated and appropriate action taken.

INTERNATIONAL ASSOCIATION OF CHIEFS OF POLICE TRAINING KEY*

Intervening in wife assault cases is a formidable task. The police officer is exposed to the threat of personal injury every time he responds to a family disturbance call. He witnesses and becomes a part of personal tragedy that frequently involves not only a husband and wife but also their children.

Initial Response

Although assaults on wives occur as a result of a variety of circumstances, there are a few characteristics that point out the seriousness of wifebeating and should influence the police response. A prevalent factor that surrounds wifebeating is alcoholic intoxication. In a majority of cases, the abusive husband is drunk when he assaults his wife. This is not surprising since overconsumption of alcohol and violent crimes of all kinds are closely linked. What it means to the officer is that the victim is in real danger and the suspect typically is not in a condition to accept a reasonable resolution of the situation. The intoxicated man who has already acted violently is a threat not to be underestimated. This applies especially to the victim as well as the police officer. Supporting this view is the fact that homicides occur in a significant number of homes where wifebeating is chronic. The husband may increase his violence to the point of murder, or the wife's felt need to protect herself may lead to homicide.

In 1975, murder within the family made up approximately one-

---

aining Key #246.

fourth of all murder offenses and over one-half of these family kill-
ings involved spouse killing spouse. The wife was the victim in 52
percent of these murder incidents and the husband was the victim
in the remaining 48 percent. Police officers must be aware of the
danger involved in disturbance calls. Since 1966, 157 officers have
lost their lives responding to disturbance calls.[1]

Receiving the Complaint. The dispatcher can contribute significantly to the safety of the victim and police officers. He has an opportunity to obtain from the caller valuable information concerning the nature of the assault and the emotional state of the
parties involved. Failure to obtain such information makes the
responding officers' task more difficult and more dangerous.

In a wifebeating case, the dispatcher should try to keep the calling
party on the phone and instruct the person to keep the telephone
line open even after the officers arrive. By keeping the telephone line
open, the dispatcher can monitor the assault and provide additional
information to the responding officers as the situation changes.
Once the officers are inside the residence, the dispatcher can continue to monitor the activities and maintain communication with
the responding officers.

In questioning the caller, the dispatcher should attempt to determine the extent of the injuries and what type of medical assistance
is needed. The dispatcher should ask whether or not any of the
parties are armed, and if so, with what kind of weapon, where the
parties are located, and what they are doing. In agencies that maintain a cross reference file of incidents by names and addresses, the
dispatcher should check it to determine previously reported incidents involving the same parties and the probable danger involved.

By listening to the background noises, as well as the complainant's
description, the dispatcher can make further determinations about
the extent of the danger. Threats, screams, breaking glass and furniture or shots indicate the seriousness of the incident. In some
cases, the dispatcher may urge the wife to leave the residence and
meet the responding officers outside.

Arriving at the Scene. Officers should approach the residence
from a direction which offers the greatest protection from an attack. When a house is the incident location, the officers should stay

---

[1]*Crime In the United States—1975*, *The Uniform Crime Reports* (Federal Bureau
of Investigation; Washington, D.C.) pp. 18, 19, 22.

close to the residence and pass beneath windows. Since the officers will not know exactly what is taking place inside, whether the incident scene is a house or an apartment, they should stop and listen to determine if the disturbance is in progress and to pinpoint the location of the parties involved. Persons encountered in the hallways of an apartment building should be briefly questioned about the incident and the parties involved.

The officers should also try to view the inside of the residence before announcing their presence. Such observations of officers, when made without unusual action such as standing on top of boxes to peer through a window, fall under the plain view doctrine and can be used to establish probable cause that a crime has been committed.

When the officers reach the door, one officer should position himself near a window where he can observe the persons who answer the door. The officer at the door should stand to the side to avoid gun fire or other attack. He should be prepared for any circumstance when the door is opened since he is often met with hostility or violence.

Gaining Entry. When conditions permit, the officers should introduce themselves, give an explanation of the police presence, and request that they be invited into the home. If entry is refused, the officers should calmly explain that they understand the citizen's feelings, but that they must make sure there is no serious trouble inside.

The emergency nature of the complaint and the refusal of the citizen to allow the officers into the home may require them to make a forced entry. Whenever practicable, a warrant should be obtained before entry is made. However when it can be reasonably believed that the reported victim is in danger, the process of obtaining a warrant may prove to be too time-consuming, and the officers may lawfully force an entry into the home. Among the circumstances that can provide the officers with the necessary probable cause to force an entry includes cries for help, weapons displayed, obvious signs that a struggle occurred and an eyewitness account that a felony occurred and the victim is still in the home.

Establishing Control. Nothing positive, not even rendering first aid, can be achieved until the police officers have the emergency situation under control. The officers should immediately locate all parties, determine whether they are armed, and determine the extent of their injuries. The parties should be separated so that they are out of normal hearing range of each other but within continuous viewing range of the officers. The kitchen area should be avoided because of the many potential weapons located there. Children or others not directly involved should be separated from the parties and kept out of hearing range so that their witness status will not be compromised.

In these incidents, the parties frequently make spontaneous statements to convince the officers that they are blameless and the other person is at fault. The officers should not discourage such statements; in fact communication of this sort can serve to distract the parties while being separated. It is appropriate for the officers to encourage initial comments by simply asking "What happened?" Any incriminating answers would be considered as volunteered or "Res Gestae" statements. Volunteered statements are those made without police questioning, therefore, when a person becomes the target of direct questioning or when he begins to incriminate himself beyond a spontaneous statement, he should be stopped and advised of his rights.

Protecting the Victim. Police officers need to protect the victim from further battery and administer first aid where required. Use of physical force to protect the victim is not typically required since the assault will usually have stopped by the time the officers intervene; however, the police officers must always be prepared to counter violent resistance. The officers should determine the extent of injuries suffered by the victim and obtain the necessary medical aid.

Battered wives frequently sustain internal injuries to the stomach, breast area, portions of the head covered by hair, and the back. Pregnant women are often hit or kicked in the stomach. The absence of external injury, therefore, does not mean that the victim has not been assaulted. Officers should always ask the victim if she has sustained injuries that do not show.

In some incidents where the wife is obviously hurt, she may refuse medical attention. The officer should tactfully determine whether she is rational, the injury is obvious, or the victim is unable to care for herself. It is the police officer's responsibility to obtain the proper medical attention for her, even if she protests receiving it.

Proper investigation of a marital assault requires that the officer establish that a crime was committed and that the elements of an offense are present. The circumstances of each case affect the officer's determination of the type of offense, if any, that has been committed. Each assault category has specific elements that must be present to constitute a crime. For example, to charge a person with assault and battery with intent to kill, the officer must determine that the means or force used was capable of causing death.

Interviewing the Victim. Throughout his contact with the victim, the officer should display concern for her physical and psychological well-being. The victim should be permitted to wash or care for other needs before being interviewed.

The victim should be given an opportunity initially to relieve her emotional tension. The officer should be aware that during this "ventilation" period, the trauma of the assault and stress she has suffered may distort her self-image. She may talk and act as if she were helpless. If this occurs, the officer should offer the victim encouragement and assure her that she is now safe.

After the ventilation period, the victim should be allowed to describe the incident without interruption. The officer's actions here can either discourage the victim or build her confidence in his sincerity to help her. The officer should be attentive and utilize the types of positive verbal and non-verbal communication techniques that encourage the victim to give him the information he needs.

Critical to the success of an interview is the manner in which the officer shows interest in the victim's account and predicament. This requires effective listening, and effective demands concentration, an understanding of what is being said, and an awareness of the importance of non-verbal communication.

Eye contact is an important non-verbal communicator. To maintain good eye contact, the officer should look at the victim in a spontaneous manner. Natural glances that express the officer's concern and interest will reassure the victim. Head and facial movements are also important non-verbal communicators. A slight nod demonstrates interest and encourages the speaker to continue the conversation.

Verbal responses of the officer also greatly influence the interview's success. The officer should use neutral words and phrases to encourage further statements. Phrases such as "yes," "oh," "I see," and "please continue" will encourage communication yet will not interrupt the person's thought. When the victim needs to be prompted to continue the statement, the officer should repeat the victim's last phrase in a questioning tone.

The physical violence and emotional stress suffered by victims of marital violence are manifested in various verbal styles and emotional states. The physically abused wife's verbal pattern can range from quiet to talkative. Some wives find it difficult to discuss the incident and may omit embarrassing details. Others are relieved to have the opportunity to discuss the incident. It is not uncommon for a victim to "substitute" her true feelings with laughs or smiles or, at the other extreme, with highly controlled behavior which hides her stress. Some victims will graphically express their reactions through verbal and physical behavior, displaying fear, rage, and anxiety.

When the victim has completed her account of the incident, the officer should ask about details of points he needs clarified and then summarize her communication. Summation gives the victim a chance to point out statements that she feels were misunderstood and may help her to better understand her situation.

Interviewing Witnesses. Witnesses to the assault—typically children, other family members, or neighbors—should be interviewed as soon as possible. The statements of witnesses who are related to or are friends of the victim or assailant must be carefully evaluated for bias. Such witnesses may well be under significant emotional stress that influences the accuracy or truthfulness of their accounts.

It may be necessary to conduct a neighborhood canvass to locate witnesses. During this canvass, officers should not overlook the possibility of witnesses providing information about prior assaults that can establish a pattern of chronic abuse.

The officer should remember that a witness's knowledge of an offense must be based on one of his physical senses. In wife beating cases, the senses of sight and hearing would be most applicable. At times some individuals have a tendency to tell what they believe occurred, not what they observed or heard; therefore, the officer should verify whether a witness could physically experience what he claims.

Interviewing the Assailant. The interview of persons at the scene, which may include the assailant, consists of the general on-the-scene questioning as a fact-finding process and the interrogation of the assailant as a criminal suspect.

Most states have held that general "on-the-scene" questioning is not interrogation within the meaning of the Supreme Court decision in the Miranda and Escobedo cases. Since the officers need to determine if the incident is accidental, a matter of self-defense, or criminally committed, general questioning of all persons, including the husband, at the scene is part of the fact-finding process. However, if the purpose of the officer's questioning is to elicit incriminating information, it is assumed the questions constitute "interrogation." Officers will find themselves in the area known as "threshold confessions" in many family-related offenses. Such confessions are made at the beginning of the police involvement and are usually in response to an innocuous inquiry, such as "What's wrong here?"

When the interview has progressed to the point that the husband is a criminal suspect, and he will be interrogated for incriminating statements, then he must be advised of his Constitutional rights. Before interrogating the suspect, the officer must review all available information.

The officer must be alert to both what the suspect says and what he avoids relating. During the interview a sudden silence, shifting of conversation, or a sudden outburst of indignation or anger on the part of the suspect will indicate that the officer is discussing a sensitive area that should be explored. At such an opportunity, the officer could remain silent and use the long-pause technique to make the suspect feel obligated to continue the statement. If this fails, the officer should review the sequence of the discussion to the point where it became uncomfortable for the suspect.

Gathering Evidence. Physical evidence typically takes three forms in cases of wife assault: the injuries of the victims; evidentiary articles, such as a blood-stained blouse or weapon, that substantiate the attack; and the crime scene itself. The victim's account of the injuries sustained can be corroborated by a doctor. Information about the injuries should be obtained from him, including descriptions of the location, shape, size, and direction of all cuts and bruises. Whenever feasible, photographs of the injuries should be made. The officer should remember that any part of the female body that is normally covered cannot be photographed without the victim's written consent. Photographs should be taken under the direct supervision of the examining physician, whose testimony the photographs are intended to illustrate. Besides photographing external injuries, the officer should either photograph the crime scene to show that a struggle occurred or make a written description of it. All articles of evidence should be collected as in other investigations.

The Arrest. The decision to arrest depends on whether the specific elements of an offense are present. The officer is typically concerned about "false" arrest. However, charges of neglect of duty can result if the officer fails to make a necessary arrest.[2]

It is recognized that without victim cooperation wifebeating cases are difficult to investigate. However, if strong circumstantial and physical evidence exists in felony cases, the officer can conduct an investigation under his own authority and can make an arrest without the wife's cooperation when probable cause exists.

In misdemeanor cases that do not occur in the officer's presence, the victim will have to secure the arrest warrant. In this situation, the police investigation can serve to validate or disprove the complaint.

As with all arrests, the officer should try to avoid the use of physical force. The arrested person should be given the opportunity to accompany the officers peacefully. Any action which may provoke a violent response from either spouse should be avoided.

Exploring Alternatives

For a variety of reasons, many battered wives will not proceed criminally against their husbands. The officer's only positive course of action in these cases is to explain to the victim the types of noncriminal assistance that is available locally. The primary concern of the officer in suggesting alternatives is the future safety of the victim.

Social Service Agencies. Although only a few communities have agencies that deal specifically with battered wives, most social

---

[2]*State v. Lombardi*, 8 Wis. 2d 421, 99N.W. 2d 829 (1960). In this case, a sheriff was found guilty of willful neglect of duty when he did not pursue an investigation, at the request of the victim, against the victim's father.

service agencies offer a wide variety of services that may be useful to the victim. Unfortunately, these services are fragmented, and often it is difficult to sort out what help is actually available. In addition, there is the ever-present problem of the agencies being open only from 9 to 5 during weekdays.

To make a proper referral, the police officer must be provided with the information that both he and the victim need to identify the assistance available. Crucial information needed by the police officer to provide to physically abused wives includes how to obtain financial aid, legal assistance, and counseling.

Civil Action. Rather than pursue a criminal charge, the victim may choose a divorce or legal separation. The wife should obtain the assistance of a private attorney or Legal Aid Agency when initiating a separation. At the same time she may also wish to secure a peace bond or restraining order—court orders directing the assailant not to interfere with the wife.

Another alternative for the battered wife is to seek a mental illness commitment of her husband when he is mentally ill and dangerous to himself or others. If this course is followed, the wife will need to enlist the services of mental health agencies. A psychiatric assessment and court action are needed to determine whether the abusive husband is mentally incompetent and should be institutionalized.

Emergency Housing. Women's task forces across the country are presently establishing refuges for battered wives. The goal of these shelters is to provide 24 hour housing to battered wives. In addition, many of these shelters have developed general education efforts to inform the public about the problem and to make women aware of the shelter. Some shelters provide a telephone hotline, counseling, and legal services.

As of now, few such shelters are in operation; however, emergency housing facilties may be available locally through the YWCA, Churches, Salvation Army, Department of Social Services, or Community Mental Health Agency. It is necessary for the police, social service agencies, or women's groups to survey each community to determine what facilities are available and what are needed. Survey results should be passed onto all officers so that they are aware of the services available.

Separation. Where an arrest cannot be made and the victim wants to leave the premises, the police officers should remain to ensure her safety. Most abusive husbands are extremely possessive and may try to prevent their wives and children from leaving. The potential for violence in these situations is real. Officers should try to explain to the husband that a temporary separation is in the best interests of the family. Officers should also be prepared to meet any violent resistance.

Officers should not assist the wife in packing or removing articles from the home. Officers should advise the wife that she can remove property which she alone owns and common property that the husband agrees to release. Officers should advise the wife not to take property owned solely by the husband. The officers may wish to remind the wife of items, such as birth certificates, insurance policies, and identification cards, that she may overlook when leaving under emergency conditions.

The procedures followed when the husband leaves the home are essentially the same as when the wife departs. Officers should ensure that the husband takes with him all property that he will need for a reasonable length of time so that he cannot return under the pretext of having "forgotten" articles such as a razorblade.

Explaining Responsibility

Many victims of marital assault choose to stay with their husbands. Their reasons for doing so may be sound or frivolous. Regardless of the case, it is not the job of the officer to judge the victim; it is his duty, however, to explain that at a given point his responsibility stops and hers begins.

When a victim continually refuses to take legal action against her spouse and displays an indifference toward seeking other remedial alternatives, the police officer should explain that he cannot be her personal bodyguard. The officer should assure the victim that his assistance during emergencies will always be forthcoming. However, the victim must be made to understand that, by refusing to pursue a solution to the problem, the beatings may continue to occur and may become more severe. The victim must be made to realize that ultimately she is responsible for seeking her own safety.

Questions

The following questions are based on material in this Training Key. Select the best answers:

1. The decision to make a warrantless forced entry into a home during a family disturbance should be based primarily on the officer's evaluation of
   (a) Whether the stringent requirements of a warrant can be met.
   (b) Whether the entry to the house is refused by both spouses.
   (c) Whether the reported victim may still be in danger.
   (d) Whether local judicial officers are lenient in issuing warrants.

2. Which one of the following is *not* a consideration when investigating a wifebeating?
   (a) A medical statement from the attending physician is needed to prove that a battery occurred.
   (b) The suspect needs to be advised of his Constitutional rights prior to an interrogation.
   (c) Physical evidence may include photographs of the wife's injuries.
   (d) The trauma of the assault and stress may destort the wife's self-image, and she may talk and act as if she were helpless.

3. For a variety of reasons, many battered wives will not proceed criminally against their husbands. In these situations, what is the primary concern of the officer?
   (a) Suggestive alternatives for her future safety.
   (b) Making sure that she is aware that she is refusing legal assistance.
   (c) Recommending civil actions, such as a divorce or separation.
   (d) Assisting the wife in packing her belongings and leaving the residence.

Answers

1. (c) In family disturbances the emergency nature of police intervention is to prevent injury.

2. (a) Although a medical statement is corroborating evidence, it is not necessary to prove a battery offense.

3. (a) The officer's only positive course of action is to make suggestions that will offer the greatest protection in the future.

DOMESTIC ASSAULT: THE POLICE RESPONSE
Darrel W. Stephens, Assistant Chief of Police, Lawrence, Kansas; formerly with Kansas City, Missouri Police Department, serving as the Commander of the department's Operations Resource Unit.

One of the most frequently called-upon services the police provide is intervention in interpersonal conflict situation. Intervention in disputes between husband and wife are by far the most common of these interventions and one of the most dangerous for both the participants and the police. The F.B.I. Uniform Crime Report indicates that 27.5% of the police officers assaulted in the United States were assaulted while responding to complaints of disturbances.[1] Research by the Kansas City, Missouri Police Department has found that 33.6% of the homicides and 31.6% of the aggravated assaults in Kansas City occur in domestic disturbance situations.[2] Although these statistics suggest a serious problem, the police have not traditionally dealt with it as such.

Given the nature of domestic assault, it is not surprising that many police officers believe that these matters ought to be handled by social workers. The police argue that they do not have the time to deal with family disputes when they should be addressing the more serious crime problems. This feeling seems to be supported by the American public, as evidenced by a statement of the Mayor of Cincinnati, Bobbie Sterene, at the 1976 National Conference on Women and Crime:

> According to a Harris poll, 20% of all Americans approve of hitting a spouse on appropriate occasions, but among the college educated, this percentage rises to 25%. In my innocence, I always thought that even the perpetrators of the crime really didn't think that it was good social practice. Harris is quoted as saying physical violence is equally common among all income groups and education levels. If anything, the middle class is more prone toward physical assault than the poor. Another startling statistic is that women really are twice as safe on the street as they are in their homes.[3]

If 20% of the American public believes that it is acceptable to strike one's spouse, one would expect that the police would not take the problem too seriously. Nevertheless, some police departments have made attempts to deal with the problem. This paper will discuss the traditional police response to domestic assault; recent attempts of the police to improve the manner in which they respond to the problem; research by the Kansas City Police Department; and the views of the author on the deficiencies of the system and how improvements might be made.

The Traditional Response

The police generally become aware of a domestic dispute when one of the participants or a neighbor calls the police. In almost all cities, two officers are dispatched on the call for service. On arrival, the officers usually separate the parties involved, apply first aid if required, and attempt to determine what has happened. The police officer has traditionally had two alternatives available to resolve the problem. The first is the informal alternative, in which the officers attempt to resolve the immediate situation using a variety of methods. The second is the formal alternative; the arrest of one or both of the parties in the dispute.

The informal methods used by police officers range from persuading one of the participants to leave to threats of arrest if the police have to return the same day. Officers have even used the alternative of "instant divorce" that one sees on television. Although this type of disposition is not the best in some cases, it is the most expedient for the police and is preferable, in many cases, to the formal alternative of arrest.

The police generally use the formal alternative when one of the parties involved in the dispute wishes to sign a formal complaint. It is also used when a serious assault has taken place. An arrest is generally not the most desirable resolution of the conflict. In most cities, the party arrested can obtain an immediate release by posting a small cash bond or simply signing a citation promising to appear in court on the charge. This quite often results in the individual returning to the scene of the conflict with a different reason for renewing the dispute.

The alternatives traditionally available to the police for addressing the domestic assault problem obviously fall short of the needs. Neither allow for dealing with the causes of the problem or provide any relief or assistance to the individuals involved. Therefore, the police find themselves returning to some households time after time to deal with a problem that they cannot begin to provide assistance in resolving with the alternatives available. It is not difficult for one to understand how a police officer might get frustrated with family disturbance calls, given the situation described above.

One needs, however, to carry the traditional response further to appreciate the futility of the formal alternative available to the police. Arrest requires that the parties appear before the court. (This is usually a municipal court.) An individual is generally charged with disturbing the peace or common assault.* The judge will hear the case and dispose of it, if the individual is found guilty, with one of the alternatives available by law.

Although the court usually has a wide range of alternatives available, one will quite often see this type of case adjudicated by the imposition of a fine or a peace bond. One may, on rare occasions, see a jail sentence imposed. The system has not, however, dealt with the problem even when an individual has had full exposure. One suspects that the criminal justice system does more to aggravate the problem than to assist in resolving it.

The traditional response to domestic assaults is clearly not adequate to deal with the problem. Nevertheless, the vast majority of police departments continue to respond in this manner. The need for the police to modify their response is obvious.

An Alternative Police Response

The police have had the responsibility for maintaining public order since the first municipal police force was formed in London in 1829. This order maintenance responsibility gradually evolved into the police responding to calls to quell domestic related disturbances. As is the case with many other types of service the police provide, it is not known exactly how or why the police began performing a service that many believe should be provided by a social service agency. One can, however, provide some logical reasons for responding to domestic disturbance calls for service. It has been pointed out that there is a high potential for an assault to be

---

*It is at this point that the complaining party quite frequently dismisses the complaint. Data are not readily available to indicate how many cases are dismissed. It is apparently a common occurrence because police officers in many cities cite this as another reason for not being too concerned with the problem.

committed and it is a police responsibility to make an arrest if one has occurred. If the assault has not occurred, the police may be able to prevent a crime. Moreover, the police are one of the few municipal services that make "house calls" and are available 24 hours a day. Regardless of the reasons why the police provide this service and the notion by many in the police profession that social service agencies should handle these situations, it seems quite clear that the police will continue to have this responsibility. In fact, some argue that the police are the most appropriate agency to handle these incidents because they have a system already established to provide immediate service on a 24 hour basis and these incidents often require the authority that police officers have. Furthermore, it is argued, the only thing the police lack is the training necessary to adequately handle these incidents. The first proponent of this argument was Dr. Morton Bard, professor in the Department of Psychology in the Graduate Center of the City University of New York and formerly a New York City police officer. His research on Family Crisis Intervention follows this article in this book.

In 1966, Dr. Bard presented the above argument to the New York City Police Department and the Office of Law Enforcement Assistance in Washington, D.C., along with the assertion that responding to family disturbances is one of the most frequent activities the police officer performs and one of the most dangerous.[4] Bard proposed a twofold experiment. First, the experiment would test the impacts of providing police officers with training on how to intervene in family disturbance situations. Second, he proposed establishing referral mechanisms for the police to send families to social service agencies to provide ongoing assistance in resolving family problems. Bard hypothesized that this program would reduce the number of injuries to officers while handling these calls; would reduce the number of call backs to the same family; and would reduce the number of homicides and assaults in the experimental precinct when compared to the control precinct. In order to carry out this experiment, Bard proposed the establishment of a Family Crisis Intervention Unit, composed of carefully selected officers who would receive the necessary training and would handle all of the family disturbance calls when they were available.[5] When the officers were not responding to these calls, they would be on routine patrol in the precinct. Bard's proposal was accepted and the experiment was conducted. Although the experiment produced no conclusive findings, it did suggest that selected police officers could improve the quality of this service and reduce the chances for personal injury.[6]

Dr. Bard followed this experiment with a similar experiment with the New York City Housing Authority Police. The significance of this experiment was that the officers were not specially selected for the training; the training was provided to a class of recruit officers. The findings were essentially the same as in the first experiment. From this beginning, the concept of training police in family crisis intervention techniques has spread to a number of police agencies. The concept has been operationalized by police departments in two different ways. The first is using specialists, such as Bard did in his first experiment. The second has been the use of generalists, whereby all officers receive crisis intervention training.

The generalist method has been encouraged by Dr. Jeffery Schwartz and Dr. Donald A. Leibman in California.[7] They have developed training programs to provide all officers with these skills. They have also developed a training program to train police officers as instructors for crisis intervention training. These programs have been used in a number of cities on the west coast. Moreover, Schwartz and Leibman argue that this type of training is useful to a police officer in almost all types of encounters with the public, because most of the interactions an officer has with a citizen are likely to be crisis situations for the citizen.[8] Bard has also advanced the notion that crisis intervention would be useful in dealing with rape investigations.[9]

Providing police officers with training in crisis intervention and developing programs utilizing referral agencies are obviously significant improvements over the traditional response. The training and programs not only provide improved service to the public; they make the police officer's job safer. Nevertheless, many police departments do not provide this type of training and continue to rely on the traditional methods of addressing the problem of domestic disturbances.

Domestic Violence Research

In 1972, several officers from the Kansas City Police Department challenged the age-old assumption that domestic homicides and assaults could not be prevented. The assumption is that since these events occur spontaneously in the privacy of the participants' homes, there is nothing the police can do. The officers believed, however, that if the police had contact with the victims or the perpetrators prior to the assault or homicide, there might be something that could be done to prevent them from occurring. This launched a research effort that was supported by the Police Foundation. The major findings of this initial research are as follows:

1. 33.6% of Kansas City's homicides and 31.6% of its aggravated assaults occur in domestic disturbance situations.
2. In 26.5% of the homicides and 37.02% of the aggravated assaults, one of the participants had been arrested for disturbance or assault in the preceding two years.
3. In the two years prior to the domestic assault or homicide, the police had been at the address of the incident for disturbance calls in 85.4% of the cases at least once, and in 53.9%, five or more times.
4. In the two years prior to the domestic assault or homicide, the police had been at the residences of the victims and suspects for disturbance calls at least once in 85% of the cases, and five or more times in 49.7%.
5. Discriminant analysis indicated that the presence of a gun, the prior disturbance history of the individual, and the use of alcohol were the strongest factors accounting for the variance between disturbances in which physical force and no physical force occurred.
6. Multivariate analysis of disturbance data identified patterns of situational interactions and the frequency with which physical force was employed in each.
7. In addressing disturbances, patrol officers normally seek temporary diffusion of the situation through two means. The first, informal disposition includes the separation or warning of the disputants and the possible reference of the parties to an attorney to resolve civil disagreements. The second disposition is arrest of one or both parties. Arrest usually occurs when certain single variables (i.e., the presence of a gun, the use of alcohol, or a dispute concerning a third party) are present.[10]

This research indicates that the police do have prior contact with the victims and the perpetrators of domestic homicides and assaults. It also suggests that the potential for the occurrence of these events might be predictable. The Kansas City Police Department is continuing their research with support from the National Institute of Mental Health in an attempt to develop and validate a prediction model.

The research of the Kansas City Police Department is significant in two respects. First, it confirms the seriousness of the wifebeating problem, in that one-third of the homicides in Kansas City stemmed from domestic problems. The domestic problem continued until one of the participants lost their life or was seriously injured. Secondly, the research magnifies the inadequacy of the Criminal Justice System's response to the problem. In over half the assaults and homicides, the police had been at the address of occurrence five or more times. The response of the system in these cases obviously fell short of the needs.

An Improved Response

Given the seriousness of the problem of domestic assault and the inadequacy of the police and Criminal Justice System's response, one obviously must ask if the response to the problem might be improved. The complexity of the problem is such that there are no easy answers. However, it is clear that improvements must come from several areas and these areas must be coordinated.

The most appropriate role for the police seems to be one of problem-identification. The police will continue to be the first to become aware of these situations. In order to adequately fulfill this role, police officers will have to receive the type of training pioneered by Dr. Morton Bard in 1966. Police departments that have not provided their officers with this type of training should be encouraged to do so by citizens in every community. The police will provide this training if the citizens' expectations are made clear. The police have responded in the past when communities have demanded a higher quality of service. The best examples of this occurred in the late Sixties and early Seventies in the human relations area and, more recently, in the treatment of rape victims. The proper training for the police is an important first step. If the police are to fulfill the role of problem identification, they must be able to recognize the symptoms of the situations that have a high potential for violence and be able to competently deal with the immediate situation without injury to themselves.

Given adequate training, the police must have formal alternatives other than arrest to deal with these situations. In Standard 3.3 of the American Bar Association's standards relating to *The Urban Police Function* it is suggested that the police be given authority to use methods other than arrest and prosecution to resolve conflict situations.[11] This authority would obviously have to be limited and would have to be supported with services outside the Criminal Justice System that have the capacity to deal with the problem.

There should be assistance available to the victims of domestic assault 24 hours a day. Most of these problems do not occur on Monday through Friday from nine to five and the victims cannot wait several weeks to make an appointment for assistance. Moreover, the assistance that is presently available with an appointment seems to be more concerned with reconciliation. Although there is nothing wrong with reconciliation, there are women who are faced with an intolerable situation and have no desire to reconcile the differences or have attempted it and failed. These women are essentially on their own at present and are often forced to continue to be victims of assault in their own homes because they have no other alternatives. There is obviously a need for shelters such as those established in England and in several areas of the United States. The shelters would provide the opportunity for a woman to start a new life free from beatings.

Volunteer groups should also be established to provide immediate assistance to the victim of domestic assault. These could be developed in the same way the rape counseling programs have been developed in cities across the nation. These programs have been successful in providing help to women in stressful situations, and it is likely that the same concept would be successful in assisting the victims of domestic assault.

Domestic assault has been neglected by the Criminal Justice System, as well as by society in general. This neglect stems, perhaps, from the attitude expressed in the Harris poll mentioned previously, whereby many people believe it is acceptable social practice to beat one's wife. These people clearly do not understand that this situation can, and often does, result in the death of one of the individuals involved.

Both the police and the public need to reassess this view toward the problem. The police should view their involvement in domestic disturbances as a crime prevention activity and accept the role of identifying the problem. The public needs to respond by encouraging and supporting adequate training for the police and adequate services outside of the criminal justice system for the victims of domestic assault. The problem will not receive the attention it deserves until both the police and the public recognize the need.

Without this joint effort, the outcome is quite clear, one of the individuals involved in the domestic dispute will become a statistic in the Uniform Crime Report:

> Criminal homicide is largely a societal problem which is beyond the control of police. The circumstances of murder serve to emphasize this point. In 1973, murder within the family made up approximately one-fourth of all murder offenses. Over one-half of these family killings involved spouse killing spouse.[12]

REFERENCES

1. Kelley, Clarence M., *Federal Bureau of Investigation, 1974, Uniform Crime Reports*. Washington: Government Printing Office, 1974, p. 243.
2. The Kansas City, Missouri Police Department, *Domestic Violence and The Police*. Unpublished report, 1973.
3. National League of Cities, U.S. Conference of Mayors, *Proceedings of the National Conference on Women and Crime*. Washington: NLCUSCM, 1976, p. 61.
4. Bard, Morton, *Training Police as Specialists in Family Crisis Intervention*. Washington: Government Printing Office, 1970, pp. 1–3.
5. *Ibid.*, pp. 4–7.
6. *Ibid.*, pp. 23–34.
7. Police Foundation, "Background Memorandum on Disputes or Disturbances Mimeographed material provided for conference on domestic violence sponsored by the Police Foundation in October 1973, p. 12.
8. Statement of Jeffery Schwartz, personal interview, November 1973.
9. Bard, Morton and Ellison, Katherine, "Crisis Intervention and Investigation of Forcible Rape," *Police Chief* **XLI**, *No.* 5: 68 (May 1974).
10. The Kansas City, Missouri Police Department, *Domestic Violence and The Police*. Unpublished report, 1973.
11. American Bar Association, *The Urban Police Function*, Approved Draft, 1973. Washington: American Bar Association, 1973, p. 7.
12. Kelley, Clarence M., *FBI*, 1973, p. 9.

FAMILY CRISIS INTERVENTION: FROM CONCEPT TO IMPLEMENTATION*†

Morton Bard, Professor of Psychology, The Graduate School and University Center of The City University of New York.

Foreword

One of the most hazardous assignments police officers face is dealing with family quarrels and disturbances. In 1972, 13% of all policemen killed in the line of duty died while responding to disturbance complaints. Twenty-seven percent of the assaults on police officers occurred in the same setting.

The risk is even greater for the participants in these quarrels. Of all murders reported in 1972, 24.3% occurred between family members, 7.1% during a "lover's quarrel," and 41.2% as the result of other arguments. The vast majority of all aggravated assaults involve relatives, neighbors or acquaintances.

Despite these dangers, techniques for dealing with such crises are rarely included in police recruit and inservice training programs. Research, however, indicates that police trained in crisis intervention are less likely to be injured or assaulted when handling fights and disturbances. Some researchers believe well-trained officers also serve to reduce homicide and assault rates.

The feasibility of training police as specialists in family crisis intervention was first tested by the Office of Law Enforcement Assistance in 1967. The National Institute has continued to support this work, expanding the training focus from a small group of selected volunteers to a broad range of officers and refining the experience of earlier projects.

The Institute believes that crisis intervention training can enhance police safety and make police service more responsive to community needs.

From a broader perspective, this sophisticated training technique changes the police function in concrete and positive ways. Success is measured in terms of police abilty to solve disputes rather than piling up felony arrests. As the police begin to view themselves as skilled conflict managers capable of defusing potentially explosive situations, beneficial effects are felt throughout the department.

Successful intervention in family disputes also can result in many economies, eliminating the time and expense involved in bringing a case to court.

This monograph explains the concept underlying the training and

*This project was supported by Grant No. NI-70-068, awarded by the National Institute of Law Enforcement and Criminal Justice, Law Enforcement Assistance Administration, U.S. Department of Justice under the Omnibus Crime Control and Safe Streets Act of 1968, as amended. Points of view or opinions stated in this document are those of the authors and do not necessarily represent the official position or policies of the U.S. Department of Justice.
†December 1973, U.S. Department of Justice, Law Enforcement Assistance Administration National Institute of Law Enforcement and Criminal Justice.

discusses some guidelines and problems in organizing such a program.

We hope it will be useful both as an introduction to crisis intervention techniques and as an aid to those agencies interested in adopting this training method.

> Gerald M. Caplan, Director, National Institute of Law
> Enforcement and Criminal Justice

Introduction

Police administrators today are constantly seeking to improve the quality and delivery of police services. However, because these services have become so diversified and complex, their improvement must involve certain new organizational strategies.

An important idea to consider in determining these organizational strategies is the concept of policing as a "person profession," that is, one which requires a facility in interpersonal relations. If one accepts this assumption, it follows that the training of police officers in the acquisition of interpersonal skills should occupy a high priority in the police system.

One area of police work that requires a skill in interpersonal relations is that of family crisis management. Although processing family disturbances constitutes an important aspect of police work, and although a significant proportion of injuries and fatalities suffered by police occurs in this area, police administrators have generally not addressed themselves to the realities of this problem.

Some years ago, however, a study indicated that the training of police officers in specific interpersonal skills could improve and facilitate the management of domestic disturbances.[1] Utilizing resources from both the behavioral and social sciences, this project in crisis intervention training demonstrated that there were more effective, safer, and more satisfying ways for police officers to handle family crises than the traditional means. What is more, there were some indications that skillful performance of family crisis intervention was viewed as a valuable service by the community. Given the frequency with which police departments are confronted by family disturbances, and given the limited competence of and unclear mandate for police officers in such situations, it was natural to find police administrators responding quickly to the implications of that initial study.

Unfortunately, however, enthusiastic implementation of family crisis programs often went forward with too little understanding of the underlying concept and with even less appreciation of the organizational pitfalls which can result from adopting these programs.

It is the intent of this monograph to help correct that situation by briefly explaining the concepts undergirding police family crisis intervention and by exploring some of the organizational implications inherent in a "go" decision by a police department. It is not expected that this discussion will be an exhaustive one; it is only intended to alert the interested police administrator to some of the important issues involved.

The Concept

The use of the term "family crisis" in our original demonstration study was intended to broaden the view of what was involved in the usual family fight. Typically, police officers have regarded the event as an alcohol-inspired "nothing" about which little could be done. The term crisis was intended to communicate a sense that a dispute is usually a tip-of-the-iceberg phenomenon, that is, a spontaneous and obvious expression of some deeper difficulty in the family. It was assumed that broadening an officer's perception of a family disturbance was a necessary first step to acquiring the skills for dealing more effectively with these events.

While the original study's results supported that assumption in most police departments the term "family crisis" merely became a new and perhaps more professional way of saying "family fight." A name change alone, therefore, is insufficient. The new name should reflect new knowledge and new understanding. If it does not, implementation of both training programs and organizational changes may be compromised.

In order to explain the importance of the term "family crisis intervention" as originally defined, two areas of human behavior which relate to this police function will be discussed. They are interpersonal conflict management and crisis intervention theory and practice.

Crisis Intervention. During the past three decades crisis intervention has occupied an increasingly important place in mental health applications. Lindemann,[11] an early contribution to crisis theory, posited that early skillful and authoritative intervention in critical personal events could forestall the possibly more serious, long-term consequence of such events. The logic of this formulation was subsequently supported by others[1,2,4,5,7] mostly in settings that lent themselves to his approach, that is, in hospitals and in clinics.

But intervention approaches based upon this theory posed an enormous challenge to mental health institutional practices. Long accustomed to operating by requiring people to "come in" for help, professionals were, and continue to be, hard put to develop methods of intervening at times of crisis when people are more susceptible to being influenced by others.[3] A variety of efforts have been made by institutions to achieve some outreach capability, including twenty-four hour walk-in clinics, telephone hot lines, mobile crisis units and local storefront clinics. These methods, intended to reduce the time interval between the crisis event and "laying on the hands," have brought to light some inherent flaws. For one thing, crisis services were usually secondary to the more central concerns of the mental health enterprise, namely diagnosis, treatment and training. Crisis intervention as a preventive strategy received little more than peripheral attention. (This phenomenon is no different essentially than the feat of preventive medicine in the priority system of the medical profession). Indeed, a crisis became virtually indistinguishable from an acute psychiatric emergency. And so, just as ideas tend to conform to institutional constraints and practices, crisis intervention became only a new term and was tantamount to putting old wine into new bottles.

Early efforts to deliver crisis services surfaced other difficulties as well. Often, the use of the service was determined by the prior knowledge or experience of the person in crisis, that is, by his recognition of need for the service or even by his knowledge of the service's existence. More important, perhaps, the methods employed rarely reached those who, by virtue of lack of education or impoverished circumstances, were unlikely to recognize their need and to reach out for help at the time of crisis. Further, since crisis services usually are a part of mental health facilities, they may not be positioned close enough to the site of a critical event to be of use to the victims. Finally, even when in crisis, many people are apprehensive about the implications of any psychiatric contact.

Those who have worked with the crisis concept have emphasized the importance of the *earliness* of the intervention in taking advantage of the openness of the person in crisis. However, the speed with which intervention can be accomplished is strongly influenced by how predictable the crisis was. As McGee[12] has suggested, crises fall on a continuum of predictability. There are those that can be seen coming, so to speak. They range from the normal developmental crisis to such events as a new job, a school examination or elective surgery. And then there are those crises precipitated by wholly unforeseen events such as natural disasters, serious accidents, or crimes. It would seem logical that crises that can be anticipated lend themselves to planning and that therefore earliness of intervention can be assured. But the unanticipated or sudden crisis event presents an extraordinary challenge. Since it cannot be predicted, how is it possible to plan for immediacy of intervention?

Leaving aside the answer to that question for the moment, let us consider the importance of authority. The perceived power of the care-giver has always been a secret weapon of the helping system. This phenomenon of power is even more important in the management of people in crisis—particularly those under the impact of a sudden, arbitrary and unanticipated crisis. The crisis has a chaotic effect; coping mechanisms are severely taxed and a sense of helplessness ensues. In a sense, the individual is, to a lesser or greater extent, so reduced in his ability to cope that his behavior may be regarded as regressed. Either actively or passively, he seeks help or direction. And, those in the environment who are perceived as powerful are apt to be seen as the source of order and stability in an otherwise suddenly chaotic world.

For the surgical patient undergoing the crisis of a sudden change in body form or function, only the surgeon is seen as having almost magical powers to order, to restore, to facilitate adaptation. What he says, what he does, how he says it and how he does it may be endowed with significance far beyond the real. Similarly, seeking the helpful power of authority is extremely important for a person in a crisis-induced emotional state.

Recognizing the significance of authority provides a context for answering the question about how it is possible to plan for prompt intervention in all crises. Clearly it is not possible to plan for the sudden, unpredictable and arbitrary stressful event. But it is possible to enlist the participation of an existing service delivery system whose domain is crisis, whose mode is immediacy and whose every essence is authority. These three attributes are all essential for effective crisis intervention. The irony is that they should be absolutely unique to an agency not usually identified as part of the helping system . . . the police.[10] Police officers usually are the first summoned when a sudden crisis occurs (appeal for help), they have a highly organized mobile response capability (immediacy), and they have the legal and symbolic power to "do something" (authority). The crises with which they commonly deal are natural disaster, crime and serious accident . . . events that can have shattering impact. These factors, when taken together, attest to the unique potentials of the police as a primary crisis intervention resource.

In effect then, the half-million police officers in this country constitute an untapped natural resource for the management of the unpredictable crisis event that so defies the mental health institutional capability. Indeed, it can be argued that this group is already delivering crisis services, however grudgingly and ineptly at the present time. This grossly inadequate service delivery is only the natural consequence of the dual role the police occupy in society. As the instruments of power, the police are encouraged to view themselves simplistically as "dirty workers" whose essential mission is to clean up or control the human flotsam and jetsam of society. At the same time, they have increasingly fallen heir to a vast array of helping functions, estimated to be between 80% and 90% of manhours.

The range of unpredictable crisis events that come within the purview of the police is almost infinite. Members of that service delivery system are positioned in time and place for an array of crisis intervention roles. The following typify the kinds of events that lend themselves to skillful crisis intervention as a preventive strategy by police officers:

1. *Crime victimization.* The victims of crimes, particularly those against the person, experience extraordinary stress reactions. A policeman trained in crisis intervention techniques can have the dual effect of helping the victim in stress while at the same time eliciting information necessary for the successful investigation of the crime.

2. *Natural disaster.* In this category are included such events as fire, flood, explosion, earthquake, tornado, etc. The suddenness and impact of the event leads to a "disaster syndrome." The dimen-

sions of this syndrome and specific techniques for combatting it are essential knowledge for the police who must restore order after such an event.

3. *Notification.* A frequent police activity with little recognition by laymen, this involves informing the family or next of kin of the death or injury of a family member. In this circumstance the police officer himself both causes the crisis and can act as an agent in its resolution.

4. *Accident.* Ranging from vehicular homicides to falling objects, these events differ somewhat from the "diaster syndrome" in that the chaos is personal and exists in an otherwise ordered and intact environment.

5. *Psychotic reactions.* These reactions have profound effects upon others, particularly family members.

6. *Suicides and attempted suicides.* As with psychotic reactions, these occurrences profoundly affect others. Skillful intervention by police may offer significant preventive opportunities.

Even a cursory examination of these crises communicates the unique potentials for crisis intervention in the police service delivery system. Further, it is suggested that the kind of immediacy in time and place that can be achieved by the police cannot be achieved by any other element in the helping system. In fact, given institutional constraints, the preventive mental health objectives of crisis intervention theory are unlikely to be realized by existing mental health operations. Ultimately it may be more rational, and indeed more economic to utilize the police system for the achievement of the objectives of crisis intervention. It really remains for the mental health professions to acknowledge that fact and to develop means by which the police may be used in an outreach capacity. It will require that mental health professionals conceive of new ways of "giving knowledge away" to those who are not trained in mental health theory but who are in a position to be more effective than theorists. If there is a commitment to prevention in mental health, then there must be a challenge to develop means for utilizing the immediacy and authority of the police system.

Interpersonal Conflict Management. The management of interpersonal conflict is probably the most time-consuming aspect of the police function. Cumming[8] monitored 82 consecutive hours of telephone calls to the Syracuse (N.Y.) Police Department and found that almost twenty percent of them were for disputes and fights in public and private places and among family members, neighbors, and total strangers. The police departments of Dallas (Texas), Kansas City (Mo.), New York (N.Y.), and Cambridge (Mass.) report similarly high percentage of time allocated to interpersonal conflict. Cumming concluded that although the "apprehension of law breakers may stand in the public mind as the crux of police work, most of a policeman's day is spent in more mundane matters such as . . . acting as an outside mediator in situations of conflict" (p. 170).

The word *mundane*, in this connection, has interesting implications. For one thing it is a reflection of the policeman's denigration of a dangerous and disagreeable function. For another, it reflects the television and detective-novel inspired public fantasy of what it is that occupies dramatic primacy in police work. However, the incredibly complex role of mediation is anything but mundane and the consequences of incompetent third party intervention are very serious; it can and often does contribute to violence rather than to pacification. A significant percentage of those police officers killed and injured in the line of duty were involved at the time in efforts to manage a human conflict. Both the dire effects on officers and the high homicide and assault rate among citizens may be traceable to the persistent neglect of the significance of the third party intervention role of the police.

The reluctance of both the public and the police to acknowledge the role of the police in conflict management is a costly misrepresentation of an important reality. More and more, the police, who are our most immediate representatives of a remote governmental authority, find it difficult to separate their duties in social regulation and public security from the day-to-day management of complex human problems. Conceptions of the police role which emphasize remoteness of authority by downgrading human services contribute to public disorder and insecurity, alienate the police from those they are charged with protecting, and, in a circular sense, negatively affect their crime control objectives. It can be reasoned that the goal of delivering human services can be regarded as an objective that, because of its profound effect upon public trust and cooperation, is equal with the objective of crime control.

The usual role of a policeman is one which leads naturally to his becoming involved as a third party in interpersonal conflicts. This function is one which can neither be readily delegated nor ignored. Both the urgency and destructive potential of interpersonal conflict requires the kind of timely and authoritatively lawful third party response capability that is absolutely unique to the police function.

Certainly it is no secret that when push comes to shove, the police enforce the political, economic and social views of the establishment. If the delivery of human services was acknowledged as being consistent with those views, policemen would be given the training and the encouragement necessary to deliver those services competently. Such training would serve not only to change potentially dangerous ways of reacting to a conflict, but also would result in a more satisfying job performance. Indeed, a recent study demonstrated that the performance of policemen trained in conflict management improved significantly as measured by traditional police criteria.[14]

Furthermore, a general sense of security in a community is not only the product of a lower crime rate. There is mounting evidence that citizens feel secure when they are convinced that government is responsive to their needs. The policeman is both the most visible and the most immediately available extension of governmental authority. As a crucial service which communicates responsiveness, conflict management goes far toward generating a sense of security.

Many of these observations result from a number of years spent directing action research programs that have sought, among other things, to test the feasibility of training police for third party interpersonal conflict.[3,5] During the course of these studies in New York City, it was possible to collect data on more than 1,500 cases of police management of conflicts among people. However, it should be noted that because of the nature of the original study involving family conflicts and the nature of the subsequent study's setting, (low income housing projects) most of the data relate to family disputes. Nevertheless it may be useful to touch briefly upon some of the findings.

Since training was a critical variable in these studies, a number of methods were used to assess training effects. Most striking was the finding that policemen, even when randomly selected, can learn and practice relevant interpersonal skills to affect their performance as conflict managers. What is more, the evaluation suggested that the changes in police behavior which are necessary for effective third party performance do not require a corresponding change in the attitudes and beliefs of the policeman. That is, despite changes in behavior our measures suggested that the changes occurred while attitudes remained constant.

It was our impression that the behavioral changes observed were related to the nature of the training. We call the training methods which we used "affective" and "experiential" methods. The methodology of such training differs considerably from the more traditional methods of the military-vocational training and from the academic model as well. In the military-vocational, instruction is along "how-to" lines and encourages the application of formulae to ensure job performance. In the academic, learning is highly abstract, verbal and passive; it rarely requires translation of knowledge into operational application. While the military-vocational admirably serves the purposes of mass troop movement or of assembly-line production, and while the academic model is ideally suited to contemplative and precise scholarship, neither can possibly serve the needs of a policeman who must make very rapid decisions in highly variable situations involving complex human interactions.

What then, given these needs, did our "affective" and "experiential" training program consist of? Most of the course content focused upon behavior within an actual social situation. The methods employed ranged from specifically prepared police social science information (communicated in a context which encouraged discussion) to real life simulations and video-taped role plays. A short period of intensive classroom training was followed by a period of field training over time. And the major thrust of the training was to encourage the kind of self-criticism which permits the practitioner to learn from his mistakes. Regularly scheduled case conferences were used which permitted the officers to continue the process of learning as they practiced in the field.

Perhaps it would be useful to take a closer look at the kinds of changes experiential training methods brought about in the officers in our studies. The following were among the training effects noted: 1) the officers were better able to regard both parties in conflict as contributing to the situation rather than to see the dispute as the responsibilty of one "crazy person"; 2) the officers were able to maintain objectivity in the way they behaved as well as in the way they perceived the conflict; 3) the response toward the police of those in conflict was positive; 4) there was little evidence of the need to employ force; 5) there was absence of injuries to officers; 6) the officers more frequently employed techniques other than arrest and/or court referral.

In one of our studies we attempted to determine whether conflict management training produced any measurable effects on the residents of a community.[5] An independently conducted community attitude survey revealed that the residents of the housing projects in which officers had been trained in interpersonal conflict management evidenced a greater sense of security after one year than residents in two control projects. It should be emphasized that the sense of security did not appear related to reported crime. It was our impression that the improved quality of police services (i.e., more sensitive interpersonal behavior by the police) communicated to the residents a greater sense of responsiveness by the authorities upon whom they were dependent for their security and welfare.

Our studies to date have confirmed the President's Commission[6] finding that in most disputes' "often the parties really want (the officers) only to 'do something' that will settle things" rather than make an arrest (p. 291). It appears to us that people in conflict want an objective, skillful and benign authority who can successfully negotiate, mediate or arbitrate a constructive outcome. The passions of the moment require a "here and now" legally sanctioned intervention which no other agency of the helping system is capable of delivering. Indeed, it can be shown that the police are even summoned to offices of psychiatrists, to social and welfare agencies and to hospital clinics for the purpose of managing disputes in those settings.

Also, our experiences to date have convinced us that we have only just skimmed the surface phenomena in third party intervention. We are aware that much of a policeman's behavior results from a mix of understanding, insight, knowledge and intuition. But exactly what is the full range of approaches used by officers in dealing with disputes? In order to learn the answer to that question and others, we must build bridges between the practitioner in the field and the researcher in the laboratory. A recently designed approach which we plan to put into effect soon is an elaboration of a strategy suggested by R. E. Walton.[13] The model proposed an active and intimate collaboration between police practitioners in the field and university based social scientists. The suggested collaboration would result in an instrument for knowledge-building for the police system and for social science as well.* The opportunities for studying aspects of human aggression in an actual social situation are limitless.

Finally, society's capacity for coping with the kind of violence that originates in interpersonal conflict can be enhanced by the use of a previously unacknowledged human resource. In a departure from the traditional view of their function, it is suggested that the police have a unique potential for delivering a service which can alleviate or prevent violence. Indeed, it is suggested that given their symbolic and lawfully authoritative role, the police, if provided with skill, competence and institutional support, can better serve the need for third party intervention in human conflict ("here and now") than any other agency of the helping system. Important functions related to training, to research, and to knowledge-building have been defined for social science in the achievement of these kinds of service roles by the police.

For society to encourage excellence of police performance in conflict management is one way of removing the stigma which we place on conflict in human relatoins. As Deutsch[9] recently said, ". . . the issue is *not* how to eliminate or prevent conflict but rather how to make it productive or at least, how to prevent it from being destructive." In providing a clear sanction for the police to deliver this much needed third party intervention service, we are acknowledging that conflict is not only a realistic and inevitable part of relationships among people, but can also present us with inherently constructive opportunities. In addition, by legitimating a human need whose traditional closet status has been so costly in terms of human life and social disorder, we are expressing our concern for and respect of the individuals in need.

Organizational and Operational Considerations

Ambivalence and Ambiguity. An organization can undertake changes in its operations for any number of reasons. Often the implicit and explicit reasons underlying the effort to change are closely

---

*Editor's Footnote: For a recent report on the collaboration of police officers and social scientists see: Bard, Morton and Zacker, Joseph, *The Police and Interpersonal Conflict: Third Party Intervention Approaches.* The Police Foundation, 1976.

related to the success or failure of the operation. Indeed, perhaps even more than the "nuts and bolts" of implementation, it is the underlying commitment that determines the outcome of organizational change. It is useless if not self-defeating, to pretend that ambivalence is not a factor inherent in change efforts. But failure to recognize and confront this ambivalence results in policies that are ultimately destructive to the success of an effort to change. It may be useful, therefore, to identify some of the sources of policy-making ambivalence that have subtle and corrosive effects upon the implementation of the family crisis concept by police organizations.

The social work myth. Even the most well-intentioned and best informed police executive may have difficulty in including helping services as an important function for a policeman. There somehow remains a residue of conviction that helping people is essentially a social work function that is discrete from the "real" work of the police. This attitude, while historically understandable, is associated with the belief that any helping function requiring the use of interpersonal skills diminishes the masculine authority image of the police. If this feeling of ambivalence exists in a police executive, it can wreak havoc with policy decisions and with administrative arrangements. It can result in him giving double messages and otherwise conveying his uncertainty to his subordinates, which can effectively subvert the most efficiently designed plan.

Before instituting a family crisis component, the police executive would be well-advised to expect this subtle form of unintentional subversion on the part of other policemen and deal with it openly. There is sufficient evidence by now that family crisis intervention *is* police work and not social work. Police have been doing the job grudgingly (and in most cases ineptly) to their own disadvantage, as police homicides and assaults will attest. Acknowledgement of the function does not make it social work; training for the function does not make it social work; and, organizational restructuring does not make it social work.

It must be understood that the family crisis approach to police training does not in any way alter the basic identity of the police. Instead, its major objective, as established by research, is for family crisis intervention to enable the policeman to do his job with greater effectiveness, with greater personal safety and with greater personal satisfaction. Unless that issue is clearly understood, successful implementation is endangered.

The community relations myth. In most cases the term community relations is a euphemism for public relations. Quite commonly, police officials regard a concept like family crisis primarily in terms of its value in changing the public's perceptions of the police in a positive direction. That is, it is seen as a concept which would appeal to the community in general and to "do-gooders-who-do-not-understand-real-police work anyway" in particular. If this motivation is the primary one for instituting a family crisis program, then the program can be expected to flounder. What is more, a program which is merely a short-term commitment to achieve a questionable public relations payoff contributes not only to cynicism within the police, but also to cynicism of the general public.

Community sophistication about public relations gimickry is now at a point where even subtle expressions of it are quickly detected. More than that, the ambivalent policy-maker whose primary concern is to sell the public fails to grasp a vital reality—to mount a program essentially to improve image is to condemn it to failure The image of any organization, and particularly that of a helping agency, is defined by the quality of functions performed; it is measured by the day-to-day activities of each of its practitioners. No amount of verbal game playing can convince a person that the actions he perceives are other than they appear. As with the "social work myth," any vestige of the "community-relations myth" as a source of ambivalent feelings about family crisis intervention, dooms it to failure.

The funding game. Society has recently begun to appreciate more fully the importance of law enforcement, and has become increasingly generous in supporting its efforts to upgrade itself. When increased public support first materialized, almost any reasonably designed "experiment" or "demonstration" program was looked upon favorably. Programs were usually undertaken on a trial basis using funds that were "added on" to existing budgets. This "soft-money" approach was particularly well-suited to organizational ambivalence in program policy-making. Often, without awareness, the decision to implement a new approach was taken without re-allocating any existing budget dollars, thus denying any commitment or permanence to a new program.

Given experience and research to date, the word "experiment" is no longer justified with respect to the significance of family crisis as a viable policing strategy. Organizational policy makers may still require add-on funds to launch such a program but any planning should acknowledge the need for reallocation of existing funds to ensure the long-term continuation of the change. Failure to do this is yet another expression of the subtle feelings of ambivalence which communicate themselves throughout the organization and are certain to be a factor leading to failure of the change.

Recommendations. The foregoing discussion was not intended to be comprehensive . . . only illustrative. It has only attempted to touch upon some of the subtle and hidden factors that may be at work when a decision is made to implement a new approach in a time-honored traditional system. Yet, unless these factors are understood, articulated and confronted, their influence in determining outcome is quite predictable. To undertake to implement family crisis as a police function requires, as a first step, recognition that ambivalence is a natural consequence of change in any organization. Inevitably, ambivalence leads to ambiguity which ultimately defeats the change effort.

The following recommendations may be helpful in countering the destructive potential of ambivalence:

1. The executive decision to "go" with family crisis, whether derived unilaterally by the Chief or by him in concert with his executive staff, must be reinforced by direct efforts to surface the sources of ambivalence. This means that a chief cannot just assign responsibility for this new program to a subordinate staff member and then treat the strategy as if it was the sole responsibility of that individual. Instead, we suggest that the Chief hold executive meetings with responsible staff on a regularly scheduled basis in order to tease out and confront those ambivalences that figure prominently in the organization. This paradoxically simple yet difficult exercise has a multiple payoff. It reinforces executive commitment and communicates readiness and willingness to confront any organizational ambivalence. Further it serves to reduce the isolation of responsible staff and reassures such staff that the commitment to this program is deep and not merely the product of executive whim.

2. Whatever the ultimate operational design might entail, it must have clearly defined incentives and rewards. Traditional rewards in police organizations are geared almost entirely to functions that constitute the smallest proportion of manhours. For example, promotion to detective (as a reward) may be based on a

particularly dramatic holdup arrest. This serves to reinforce the policeman's conviction that rewards are most likely to be related to crime-control functions. Means must be found to reward those myriad functions which require as high a degree of competence as do family crisis intervention techniques. One of the most telling statements of unequivocal commitment to an organizational change is through a reordering of reward priorities. Incentives and rewards can serve most effectively to reduce organizational ambivalence and its resultant ambiguity.

Models of Implementation. The execution of any idea requires a model which contains all the important elements of the concept and which can serve as the means for achieving the desired goal. Given the general structure of police organizations, three models will be discussed; the choice of a specific model, however, will depend upon the nature of each situation.

Generalist-Specialist Model. This was the model used in the original family crisis demonstration project. In essence, a selected group of general patrol officers processed all family disturbance calls in a specified area. These officers operated in uniform and on all tours of duty; when not engaged in the management of a family disturbance, they provided general patrol services in an assigned sector. This model has the following advantages:

1. Professional identity of the officer is preserved. In the eyes of his colleagues and of the public the officer charged with family crisis responsibilities is still a "real cop."

2. In a large organization, it appears to be an efficient way of delivering a needed service without sacrificing general uniformed patrol coverage.

3. It has implications for other generalist-specialist roles (e.g., youth, rescue, etc.) in which each officer has a specialized area of expertise. It avoids the need for each patrolman to be all things to all people.

4. It enhances the morale of patrolmen in that their area of special expertise is respected by both their colleagues and the public. Further, it defines a specific function for the exercise of professional discretion while maintaining general patrol capability.

5. It can take advantage of natural or latent talents of patrolmen.

Generalist Model. An alternate model, more suitable to small organizations is for all patrol personnel to be given training in family crisis theory and practice. This was the model employed in the housing study; as the research findings indicate, it can be useful as a strategy. The advantages of this model are:

1. It is suitable for small organizations that turn out too few men to have the luxury of a generalist-specialist on each tour.

2. It ensures involvement of all personnel in acquiring special knowledge.

3. While the quality of service delivered will show greater variance than it would with selected generalist-specialists, it will tend to maximize the impact on the department itself and on the public.

4. It minimizes the tendency to delegate all family intervention functions to a small unit; it reinforces family crisis as the ongoing responsibility of all patrol personnel.

Specialist Model. In contrast to the preceding models, we have not had any experience with the specialist model. However, our impressions gained in studying police operations and theory suggest that this may be the least desirable model. Indeed, assigning exclusive specialization for family intervention to selected officers who have no general patrol responsibilties appears to have few, if any, redeeming virtues. Therefore, the following disadvantages should be weighed before proceeding with this model:

1. This is the model through which organizational ambivalence is most likely to be expressed. The delivery of the service becomes the exclusive responsibility of the specialist and satisfies only the policy decision with no reference to the broader operating responsibilities of the organization.

2. It tends to create two classes of citizenship within the organization; those who do "real" police work and those who do social work. This encourages the public to think of the police as being either "bad guys" or as being "good guys"; that is, those who are aggressive enforcers and those who are benevolent authorities.

3. It is ultimately destructive to morale and hence destructive to the function of the specialist. The specialist feels alienated from his colleagues and confused in his identity as a policeman if his functions are restricted to a single dimension of service. Consider, for example, the derisive designation of "kiddie cop" for juvenile specialists in many departments.

Training. It must be clear by now that preparing policemen to deliver a highly complex human service requires unusual training for specific skills. Indeed, it requires a kind of training that is a synthesis of that which is traditional in police work and that which is found in fields which concentrate exclusively on human services. Once again, there are different training models that must be considered.

Intensive Training. In police organizations, the characteristic way of preparing personnel with specific skills is to run them through a brief and intensive training program. The methods of instruction are usually of a "how-to" nature, largely by lecture augmented by audio-visual aids. At the conclusion of the training experience, the patrolman returns to the field. There is usually little if any follow-up evaluation and even less likelihood of ongoing training in the field.

Field Training. Usually unsystematic, fragmented and methodologically questionable, field training can be found to range from the roll call exercise to informal "rap" sessions. It is this form of training that breeds the greatest cynicism since it comes across as "lip service" or "going-through-the-motions." This approach is most likely to communicate organizational ambivalence about the training itself, not to speak of the lack of commitment to the content of the training.

Combined Intensive and Field Training. This model, if properly conceived and employed, holds the greatest promise for human service functions. The brief and intensive training must be carefully designed to be consistent in content with the ultimate objectives of the program. But even more important, the intensive training should be regarded as *orientative* rather than conclusive. It should be the foundation upon which training in the field will build. Naturally, the methods employed in that training should also set the tone and prepare the officer for the kind of methods to be used in the field. It is unlikely, for example, that the exclusively lecture/audio-visual format will be feasible in the field.

At the conclusion of the brief intensive and orientative training, it is essential that there be follow-up in the field. It is here that the bulk of training occurs, in the human service professions . . . that is, in "learning-by-doing." In medicine the basic orientation afforded by the medical school is followed by years of continuous training in the clinic and hospital geared to practice. The methods used are essentially those of case study and self-critical analysis of practical applications of theory. If field training is possible in the kind of life and death emergency-oriented field that medicine represents, it is equally possible and necessary as an adjunct to the basic training of policemen.

A final word on training. Given the present transitional state of police training, and given its movement to a broader model than the traditional military-vocational one, few police organizations have the in-house capability to conceptualize or implement the kind of training that successful family crisis intervention entails. Hence, as much assistance as possible must be obtained from outside resources, that is, from the academic and professional communities. While it is true that most previous efforts at collaboration have been found wanting, it is also clear from recent developments that committed police leadership can inspire successful input from such outside resources.

Relationships With Other Agencies. A critical variable in making family crisis intervention a successful strategy is the establishment of working relationships between the police and other agencies of the helping system. However, given the fact that many of these agencies are already overburdened, it would be foolhardy to have unreasonable expectations of their ability to be of service. In order to ensure maximum participation though, agency representatives should be included as part of planning very early.

It should be noted that because a policeman is involved in a crisis when emotions are at their height, and is perceived as someone with authority, he may be in the best possible position to effect a constructive outcome. Because of this, a skilled policeman may be preferable to a community agency. But there will be cases which require services beyond the ability of the officer. In those instances, resources should be available and responsive. With proper training and judicious referring, these agencies can be effective backups. It is vital that the police executive ensure interagency liaison from the outset so that the necessary resources will be available.

Some final words are in order with respect to police family crisis intervention. This document has only touched upon some of the issues relevant to the implementation of such a program by police organizations. Acknowledgement of the highly complex functions performed by the police is inherent in the decision to develop such a program. It has been the position of this monograph that the questions of social regulation and public security are inseparable from the day-to-day management of complex human problems. The police are our most immediate representatives of a remote governmental authority. Conceptions of their role that reinforce remoteness contribute to public insecurity, alienate the police from those they are supposed to protect and, in a circular sense, negatively affect the objective of crime control. If citizens are to cooperate in the process of crime control they must trust the police. Such trust is engendered by the competent delivery of those human services that occupy so much of a policeman's time. It can be said, therefore, that the delivery of services like family crisis has parity with crime control as an objective of the police organizations.

REFERENCES

1. Bard, M. "Alternative to Traditional Law Enforcement," in Korten, E. F. et al. (ed.), *Psychology and The Problems of Society*. Washington, D.C., American Psychological Association, 1970.
2. Bard, M. "The Price of Survival for Cancer Victims," in Strauss, A. L. (ed.), *Where Medicine Fails*. Transaction Books: Aldine Publishing Co., 1970.
3. Bard. M., *Training Police as Specialists in Family Crisis Intervention*. Washington, D.C.: U.S. Government Printing Office, 1970.
4. Bard, M., "The Role of Law Enforcement in the Helping System," *Community Mental Health Journal* 7: 151 (1971).
5. Bard, M., Zacker, J., and Rutter, E., *Police Family Crisis Intervention and Conflict Management: An Action Research Analysis*. Final Report to National Institute of Law Enforcement and Criminal Justice, LEAA, U.S. Department of Justice, 1972.
6. Campbell, J. S., Sahid, J. R. and Stang, D. P., *Law and Order Reconsidered: Report of the National Commission on the Cause and Prevention of Violence*. New York: Bantam Books, 1970.
7. Caplan, G., *Principles of Preventive Psychiatry*. New York: Basic Books, 1964.
8. Cumming, E., *Systems of Social Regulation*. New York: Atherton Press, 1968.
9. Deutsch, M., "Toward an Understanding of Conflict," *International Journal of Group Tensions* 1: 42 (1971).
10. Janis, I., *Psychological Stress*. New York: John Wiley & Sons, 1958.
11. Lindemann, E., "Symtomatology and Management of Acute Grief," *American Journal of Psychiatry* 25: 213 (1944).
12. McGee, T. F., "Some Basic Considerations in Crisis Intervention," *Community Mental Healtn Journal* 4: 319 (1968).
13. Walton, R. E., *Interpersonal Peacemaking: Confrontations and Third Party Consultation*. Reading, Mass.: Addison-Wesley, 1969.
14. Zacker, J. and Bard, M., "Effects of Conflict Management Training of Police Performance," *Journal of Applied Psychology* 58: 202 (1973).

7 Future Trends and Prevention

And for the mitigation which is hereby some men interposed in a way of answer unto this objection (which is, that in the strictness of law, for a husband to beat his wife is lawful, but it is inconvenient in decency of manners) it is a plain and peevish contradiction and injuriously robs the law of the end of the law. For the end of the law is the happy government of a commonwealth which happiness is in nothing more eminently seen than in the decent conformity of manners and orderly behavior of all estates. And hence it is that the lawyer as a laborious traveller goes through all estates to bring all into decency. He orders the estates of monarchs and princes, of parents and children, of husbands and wives, of masters and servants. And in the whole body of a commonweal whatsoever is out of decent temper must by the law be ordered, as a sick part in a body natural by a physic cured. So that then an absolute indecorum in manners (as they confess the beating of a wife to be) is an absolute breach of the law.

HEALE, WILLIAM, 1609

A SOCIOLOGICAL PERSPECTIVE ON THE PREVENTION AND TREATMENT OF WIFEBEATING*

Murray A. Straus, Ph.D., University of New Hampshire

Our ideas about the causes of wifebeating influence the steps we take to prevent it. If wifebeaters are thought to be mentally ill, then psychotherapy is clearly needed; if husbands hit their wives because of the excessive strains a modern society puts on the nuclear family, then some reorganization of the family system and its relation to the society is needed; etc. Thus it is important to start by having a picture of what seem to be the fundamental causes. The first section of the article will do this at a general level by suggesting the extent to which wifebeating can be attributed to three factors: (1) the characteristics of individual husbands and wives, (2) the cultural norms and values concerning the family, and (3) the organizations of the family and society. Having laid out the general framework, the next six sections will describe specific causes and trace out the *preventative* steps which could be used to deal with each of these causal factors. Finally, the last two sections of the article are devoted to what, roughly speaking, can be called *treatment* steps; i.e., modes of dealing with existing cases of wifebeating (as contrasted with the preventative steps described up to that point).

The Causes of Wifebeating

This sketch of causal factor is likely to be controversial, and may even be denounced by some. The reason for the objections will not be that the sketch is largely speculative, but rather that it steps on the toes of the established disciplines of sociology, psychology, and psychiatry.

The first "toes" I will step on are those of psychology and psychiatry, and specifically, the view that men who beat their wives do so because they are "aggressive," "uncontrolled," or mentally ill. Some men who beat their wives are psychotic, or suffer from brain

*I am grateful to Maria Roy and to Professors Richard J. Gelles and Howard M. Shapiro, and Jean-Giles-Sims for comments and criticisms of the first draft; and to the National Institute of Mental Health for the financial support of the Family Violence Research Program at the University of New Hampshire through grants MH 13050 and MH 27557. A bibliography of books and articles growing out of this program is available on request.

damage which interferes with their being able to control aggression. But so are some men who drive trucks or teach sociology; my guess is that the proportion is no greater. In fact, to pick a figure out of the air (because there are no scientifically valid data on this), it is doubtful that more than 2 or 3% of all the wifebeating in the United States can be attributed to purely "intra-individual" characteristics such as those just described. Research on child abuse leads to the same general conclusion for that closely related phenomenon.[31]

The next "toe" is that of my own discipline: sociology. One of the most important contributions of sociology is to establish the extent to which a phenomenon such as wifebeating is caused by the very structure of society itself. There are two main aspects of social structure. The first aspect is the set of cultural rules and values which guide the behavior of members of a society. In the next section, I will summarize the evidence which shows that our society actually has rules and values which make the marriage license also a hitting license. But not everyone follows this particular set of rules and values. If they did, then every husband would hit his wife, rather than "only" about 60%.

There are many reasons why there is typically only a very rough correspondence between cultural prescriptions and what people actually do, one of which is that most cultures are full of contradictory and incompatible elements. Obviously, the expectation of marital love and tenderness co-exists with the "hitting-license" aspect of the way our culture defines marriage. So, for purposes of this chapter, I suggest that not more than 4 or 5% of wifebeatings can be attributed to purely cultural factors such as the implicit rule which gives spouses the right to hit each other.

The second major aspect of social structure is the way society is actually organized. Social organization and culture overlap, but are far from the same thing. For example, American culture does not value "red tape." But the complexity of a high technology society makes for more and more red tape, irrespective of whether we favor or oppose it. Similarly, there are many aspects of American social organization which probably influence wifebeating. An example is that we are a geographically mobile society. Couples tend to live separated from their relatives and from the intimate friends with whom they grew up. Thus, when the tension level between husband and wife is high, there are often no intimate friends or relatives who can either help to deal with the problem or intervene to prevent physical attack. The high unemployment rate of our society is another example. There is some evidence that wifebeating goes up with unemployment. To be unemployed in our society is terribly stressful, frustrating, and humiliating. But even so, not every unemployed man beats his wife. As in the case of intra-individual causes and cultural norms as cause, trying to pin the blame solely on the organization of society is not going to produce a high yield in our search for causal factors. For purposes for this discussion, I suggest that not more than 5 or 6% of wifebeatings can be laid at the feet of the organization of society *per se*.

Where does that leave us in the search for causes? The situation does not look very promising. Even if we take the high end of these estimates, it comes to 3% + 5% + 6%, or a total of only 14%, which means we have failed to explain 86% of the instances of wifebeating. But the situation is not nearly as unpromising as the 14% figure suggests. Explaining wifebeating by means of psychological, cultural, and social organizational factors *in isolation from each other* is like trying to watch TV with a pile of transistors, wires, and a tube stacked in front of you. It is only when they are combined, and in particular combinations, that a picture can be produced. Similarly, I suggest that the causal situation which accounts for most wifebeating is to be found in *combinations* of individual, cultural, and social organizational factors, rather than any one of these by itself. For example, some research[2,55] suggests that a particularly explosive combination is a man who takes seriously the role of husband as the head of the family, has been brought up to believe that women admire and prefer "tough" men, and whose wife has a better paying or more prestigious job. Such a combination of factors will create a situation which leads some men to use physical force to "show what's what around here."

Assuming that the hypothetical figures and the theoretical speculations just presented are correct, does this mean that psychological and sociological research on the causes of wifebeating should be abandoned? No—at least no more than it suggests that research on better transistors, wires, and TV tubes should be abandoned. Without those parts, there can be no working TV set, and without firm knowledge of the psychology and social structure of intra-family violence, it is unlikely that effective programs to reduce wifebeating can be designed.

This chapter must be viewed within the multidisciplinary framework just outlined. Specifically, although the purpose is to highlight the *social* causes of husband-wife violence, this does not deny the importance of other factors, particularly psychological factors. With this in mind, we can proceed with the examination of the ways in which wifebeating is produced by the very nature of our society and its family system, and at the same time attempt to formulate the specific policies which could be followed in order to reduce the level of husband-wife violence.

Cultural Norms Permitting Wifebeating

A fundamental aspect of American social structure which must be understood and confronted if there is any hope of dealing with marital violence is the existence of the cultural norm which, as previously noted, makes the marriage license also a hitting license. This is so much a taken for granted, unperceived, unverbalized norm, so contrary to the way most of us view marriage, that more space must be given to documenting it than will be possible for the social causes outlined in later sections. Even so, many readers will want to consult the more complete documentation in Gelles[31] and Straus[70,71,72] and Steinmetz and Straus.[68]

Once one is willing to entertain the hypothesis that there may indeed be cultural norms which legitimize physical violence between spouses, then evidence for the existence of this norm pop into view with startling frequency. The evidence can be found, for instance, in everyday expressions and jokes, such as the ditty:

A woman, a horse, and a hickory tree
The more you beat 'em the better they be

or the joke which has one woman asking another, "What makes you think he doesn't love you any more?" and the reply, "He hasn't bashed me in a couple of weeks." Many of the men and women interviewed by Gelles[31] expressed similar attitudes, as represented by such phrases as "I asked for it," "I deserved it," or "she needed to be brought to her senses."

But the marriage license as a "hitting license" is not just a matter of the folk culture; more important, it also remains embedded in the legal system, despite many legal reforms favoring women. In most jurisdiction, for example, a woman still cannot sue her husband for damages resulting from his assaults, because, in the words of a California Supreme Court judgment (*Self* v. *Self*, 1962), this "would destroy the peace and harmony of the home, and thus would be contrary to the policy of the law."! Of course, criminal actions can be brought against an assaulting husband, but here, too, there is an almost equally effective bar. This is inherent in the way the criminal justice system actually operates. Many policemen personally believe that husbands *do* have a legal right to hit their wives, provided it does not produce an injury requiring hospitalization—the so-called "stitch rule" found in some cities. If a wife wants to press charges, she is discouraged at every step in the judicial process, beginning with police officers (often the first on the scene) who will not make arrests, and going on to prosecuting attorneys who will not bring the case to court, and by judges who block convictions. (For that miniscule fraction of cases which do reach the court, see Reference 25.)*

Finally, there is evidence from surveys and experiments also pointing to the implicit license to hit conferred by marriage. Perhaps the most direct of this type of evidence is to be found in the survey conducted for the National Commission on the Causes and Prevention of Violence.[67] One of the questions asked of this nationally representative sample of adults was whether they agreed or disagreed with the statement that there are some circumstances in which it is permissible for a husband to hit his wife, and a parallel question about wives hitting husbands. About one out of four of those interviewed agreed with the proposition. Equally cogent are the results of an unpublished experiment by Churchill and Straus. This showed that when presented with identical descriptions of an assault by a man on a woman, those who were told that they were married recommended much less severe punishment.

There is a great deal of other evidence supporting the existence of the "marriage license as a hitting license" norm,[72] but I will have to assume that what was just presented at least makes the case plau-

---

*These comments should not be taken to be an argument for arresting, fining, and jailing assaulting husbands as *the* solution to the problem of wifebeating. Such actions, although necessary as an ultimate sanction, are more often self-defeating and ineffective—just as they are with most types of crime. Rather, the failure of the criminal justice system to act in the case of assaulting husbands (and wives) is stated as part of the evidence for the existence of an implicit cultural norm which makes the marriage license a hitting license.

sible. What, then, are the implications for prevention which follow from existence of this norm? There seem to be at least two parallel "policy implications."

1. Make the public aware of this largely unperceived norm.

There is a paradoxical quality to this policy implication, but its efficacy is based on the assumption that awareness can contribute to the demise of the hitting license norm because such a norm is so contrary to other norms and values about the family. If so, it will pave the way toward a second policy implication, focused more on individual husbands and wives, but especially the latter.

2. Redefine the marital relationship as one in which any use of physical force is as unacceptable as it is between those one works with, or with whom one goes bowling, or plays tennis.

For the individual wife, this means making clear to her husband that physical force simply will not be tolerated. In an unknown, but perhaps not insignificant, proportion of cases, this alone could serve to alter the situation, because the hitting license aspect of marriage is so much an unperceived, taken for granted norm, and is so contrary to other widely acknowledged and valued norms concerning marriage.

Despite the above, such attempts at redefining the marital relationship to render violence illegitimate are unlikely to be sufficient. In the first place, normative rules are only one of the structural determinants of behavior, and often a minor determinant. In the second place, such rules do not arise out of thin air. Rather, they reflect, and tend to be integrated with, a network of other cultural elements. Perhaps even more, they reflect the realities of daily living. Consequently, a truly fundamental approach to the problem of wifebeating must address these more fundamental causes. Each of these things is so closely interwoven with the others that it is almost as difficult to discuss them separately as it will be to change them. However, they can at least be grouped into somewhat meaningful patterns.

Wifebeating as a Reflection of Societal Violence

Governmental Violence. Even if one assumes that nation-states ultimately depend on at least the possibility of using physical force to uphold the law, this does not mean that the present level of physical force is either desirable or necessary.[35] The necessity for and efficacy of much governmental violence is highly questionable, as illustrated by the controversy over the efficacy of the death penalty, of police toughness (to say nothing of police brutality), and of the still widespread practice of physical punishment in the schools.[51,52] It is sobering to remember that at the very time this chapter was being written, the U.S. Supreme Court upheld both physical punishment and the death penalty. Finally, there is the fact that our government maintains a world-wide military establishment.

These examples of governmental violence provide powerful models for the behavior of individual citizens. They form an important part of an even more general normative system, which holds that violence can and should be used to attain socially desirable ends.[14,15] Of course, it is extremely difficult to prove that governmental violence provides a role model for individual violence, but an example of one type of evidence supporting this conclusion is found in the work of Huggins and Straus[41] and Archer.[3]

Huggins and Straus studied a sample of English language children's books covering the period 1850–1970. The original purpose was to see if the level of interpersonal violence depicted in these books showed an upward or downward trend over this 120 year period. The results showed no trend of this type. However, even though there were no "war stories" in the sample of books, during and immediately following each major war the frequency of interpersonal violence rose dramatically. Similarly, Archer and Gartner found a post-war increase in homicide rates for a large sample of nations. They concluded that the increase in murder rates was due to a carry-over of the wartime authorized or sanctioned killing. Thus:

3. Reduce to the maximum extent possible the use of physical force as an instrument of government.

Media Violence. Violence in the mass media both reflects the existing high level of aggression and violence in American society and helps perpetuate that pattern. The typical citizen watches "prime time" TV in which more than half of all characters are involved in some violence, including one out of ten in killing.[34] The amount of gratuitous violence in current motion pictures is also extremely high. The significance of these facts has been demonstrated by intensive research during the past ten years, including a number of excellent longitudinal and experimental studies. The studies have led almost all scientific reviewers of the accumulated evidence to conclude that violence in the media is part of a societal pattern which keeps America a high violence society.[74]

The message of the mass media is clearly that physical force can and should be used to secure socially desirable ends, not just in the "wild west" but in almost all aspects of contemporary life. Although it is rare for the media to depict husbands using physical force on wives, the more general message is easily transferred to the marital relationship. Thus, even though we know of no direct evidence that the implicit high value placed on both instrumental and expressive violence in the mass media is transferred to the marital relationship, this possibility seems so likely in view of the extensive evidence of the phenomenon psychologists call "transfer of training" that the following policy implication seems warranted:

4. Limit depiction of violence in the mass media to the maximum possible consistent with preserving freedom of expression and artistic integrity.

Essentially, policy implication *4* means that reduction in the extent to which TV and other fiction and non-fiction works "exploit" violence (i.e., makes extensive use of violence for the purpose of capturing as large an audience as possible).

Domestic Disarmament. It is by now commonly accepted that America is a violent society. But this acceptance does not automatically bring with it a realization that for the typical citizen, the problem is not violence in the streets, but violence in the home. For example, the largest single category of murderer-victim relationship is that of members of the same family. There are complex reasons why this is so,[73] some of which will become clear later in this article. However, for the moment, we will focus on the "gun-toting" aspect of American violence. One reason that domestic murders are so common is that more than half of all American households contain guns, most of which are "hand guns" rather than "sporting guns." Consequently:

5. Enact stringent gun control legislation, particularly directed at restricting hand guns, but also requiring that all guns be kept locked and unloaded.

Five has been aptly termed "domestic disarmament" by Amatai Etzioni. It can go a long way toward reducing the most extreme aspect of domestic violence: murder. Of course, domestic disarmament will not reduce violence *per se*, since one can still punch, kick, choke, or stab. But an attack with a gun is much more likely to be fatal than other modes of attack.

The Family as Training Ground for Violence

What has been said so far emphasizes the extent to which violence in the family reflects the level of violence in the society. But the other side of the coin is at least equally important; the level of violence in all aspects of the society, including the family itself, reflects what is learned and generalized from what goes on inside the family, starting at infancy.

Physical Punishment. The implicit models for behavior provided by actions of the government and depicted in mass media form two legs of the stool supporting American violence. The third leg is the family itself. In fact, the family may play the most crucial role. This is because the family is the setting in which most people first experience physical violence, and because of the emotional context accompanying this experience. Specifically, at least 90% of parents use physical punishment in early childhood. Moreover, for about half of all children, this continues through the end of high school—essentially until the child leaves home.[6,68,69]

When physical punishment is used, several things can be expected to occur. First, and most obviously, is learning to do or not to do whatever the punishment is intended to teach. Less obvious, but equally or more important, are two other lessons which are so deeply learned that they become an integral part of the personality and world view. The first of these unintended consequences is the association of love with violence. The child learns that those who love him or her the most are also those who hit and have the right to hit. The second unintended consequence is the lesson that when something is really important, it justifies the use of physical force. Finally, we suggest that these indirect lessons are not confined to providing a model for later treatment of one's own children. Rather, they become such a fundamental part of the individual's personality and world view that they are generalized to other social relationships, and especially to the relationship which is closest to that of parent and child: that of husband and wife. Therefore, it is suggested that early experiences with physical punishment lay the groundwork for the normative legitimacy of intrafamily violence previously noted, and provides a role model—indeed, a specific "script"[29,41]—for such actions. Gelles,[32] for example, found that one of the three main factors related to a wife tolerating abuse from her husband is the extent to which she was hit by her parents as a child (see also Lefkowitz et al.[47]). It should be almost self-evident, then, that an important policy implication of what has just been presented is:

6. Gradually eliminate physical punishment as a mode of child rearing.

I have used the term "gradually" in formulating this policy implication, even though my own values favor immediate cessation of physical punishment. Many practical difficulties stand in the way of an immediate cessation which, if disregarded, can have serious consequences. Specifically, we cannot expect to eliminate physical punishment until it is possible to provide parents with a proven alternative technology for controlling the behavior of children to protect them from danger and to teach the practical skills and ethical values for which society holds parents responsible. The fact that a few parents do manage to bring up children without the use of physical punishment is by no means the same as saying that most parents can do so. That remains to be proven before we risk undermining the vital task of socialization carried out by parents. Fortunately, such techniques are beginning to emerge (see policy implication 8).

Sibling Violence. Almost as universal as physical punishment is physical fighting between children in the family. Perhaps such fighting is inevitable in early childhood. But it is not inevitable that attacks by brothers and sisters on each other be regarded as much less reprehensible than attacks on or by unrelated children. This difference in the way identical acts of violence are evaluated and dealt with symbolizes and reinforces the legitimacy of violence between family members. As a result, such violence continues long after it has practically disappeared from the child's relations with their unrelated peers. For example, among the sample studied by Straus,[70,71] almost two-thirds had hit or been hit by a brother or sister during the year they were *seniors* in high school, compared to one-third of this sample who reported having hit or being hit by someone outside the family that year. Thus, right up through high school, many young people experience a second aspect of intra-family violence which implies that there is nothing terribly repre-hensive about the use of physical force between members of the same family. To the extent that this is correct, then:

7. Parents must take steps to reduce, and above all, not to ex-plicitly or implicitly define as permissible, acts of physical force be-tween their children.

As in the case of physical punishment, implementing policy im-plication 7 is not merely a matter of ceasing to do something. One of the things which the sociological perspective highlights is that any element of social structure is likely to be interwoven with other elements, and therefore cannot be dealt with in isolation. In this case, we must ask: "What is there about the situation of children in a family which gives rise to such a high level of violence?" and "How can children resolve their disagreements without physical fights?" Until children are equipped with the skills to do that, it is just as unrealistic for parents to implore "don't fight" as it is for family life educators to implore parents not to spank. Consequently:

8. Provide parents and children with techniques for coping with and resolving the inevitable conflicts of family life by means other than force and coercion.

There are many obstacles in the way of implementing policy implication 8, one of the most important of which will be dis-cussed in a later secton of this article: the failure to recognize the inevitability of intrafamily conflict, and hence to take steps for coping with conflict non-violently. But even if that were not a factor, what techniques are available? Although still a matter of research and controversy, the last few years have seen the development of methods which appear promising for resolving parent-child and sibling-sibling conflict.[12,13,18,56,61]

"Somato-Sensory" Deprivation. Harry Harlow once epitomized the results of his classic experiments with monkeys reared in iso-lation, by saying that monkeys deprived of warm social contact in infancy ". . . would rather fight than love." The same idea has surfaced in a number of different ways in the history of social science; for example, in the work on the authoritarian personality of Adorno et al.[1] Part of what Adorno's "F scale" measures is the propensity to use physicasl violence for socially desirable ends. People who get high "F scale" scores, for example, tend to favor the death penalty and to feel that sex criminals should both be imprisoned and ". . . publically whipped, or worse." Adorno et al. found that these same people also tended to have received relatively less love and affection from their parents than did those low on the "F scale."

Most recently, Prescott[62] has pointed to both neuro-physiological and cross-cultural evidence showing that the more a person is deprived of "somato-sensory gratification," such as intimate physical contact, love, and affection, the greater the level of aggression, including physical aggression. For example, a tabulation of data for 49 societies revealed that the societies which do not provide much physical affection to their children also tend to be those in which there is a high level of violence between adults. Since a loving and affectionate childhood tends to innoculate persons and societies against violence, it seems likely that this would be particularly true for violence in the family.

The policy implication which follows from this is not that parents should be warm and affectionate, because by now that has become part of the standard American child rearing ideology (as compared to the "school of hard knocks" and the "don't spoil the child" conceptions). Rather, the policy implication revolves around the fact that despite the warmth and affection ideology, millions of children are in fact deprived of just that.[1,37,48] Consequently:

9. Sponsor research to determine the social and psychological conditions which lead some parents to be cold and distant rather than warm and loving, and translate the results into programs to assist such parents.

The Inevitability of Conflict in Families

Conflict, in the sense of differences in objectives or "interests" between persons and between groups, is an inevitable part of all human association.[21,22,66] Some types of groups tend to be characterized by more conflict than others. Somewhat paradoxically, the more intimate the ties between members of a group, the higher the

average level of conflict.[21] Since the family is one of the most intimate types of groups, the level of conflict is particularly high within
the family.

A detailed analysis of the characteristics of the family which give
rise to its typically high level of conflict is given in Gelles and
Straus.[33] These include: (1) The large amount of time family members spend with each other—so called "time at risk"; (2) The wide
range of activities and interests which are included within the family, and hence the greater number of opportunities for conflict to
arise; (3) The fact that many of these activities overlap or compete
with each other; (4) The high level of emotional involvement in the
family. Since goals and activities which are central to the person are
involved, frustration of these activities hurts much more than does
frustration of activities in other spheres of life; (5) The presumed
right of family members to influence others in the family. If a friend
wears tennis shoes on a hike when you suggested hiking boots, it is
not nearly as likely to provoke an argument as if it were your husband, wife, or child; (6) The different outlook on life which comes
about because family members, at a minimum, represent the different outlooks characteristic of men and women (as compared to
same sex groups); (7) The fact that family roles are, to a large extent, assigned on the basis of age and sex, rather than chosen on
the basis of interest and/or competence; (8) The involuntary (for
children) or only semi-voluntary (for spouses) nature of membership in the family. Even if there were no legal barriers whatsoever, it would still be difficult to end a marriage. There are expectations held by oneself and others concerning the desirability of
stable marriages, the emotional trauma of leaving an established
relationship, fear of the unknown, financial difficulties, worries
about the children, etc. The problem with participation in a group
or activity which is not voluntary is that negative feelings and resentment are more common than in voluntary groups, if for no other
reason than the fact that voluntary groups (by definition) do not
contain people who don't like them; and (9) The privacy of the family plays an important part because it insulates the family from assistance by friends and relatives.

The nine characteristics of the family just listed are by no means
a complete account of the factors which produce conflict within the
family. However, they should be sufficient to indicate that the fam-

ily is typically the locus of a high level of conflict at the same time that it is also the locus of a high level of interpersonal support and love. The problem is that the nature of modern society does not provide adequate mechanisms for non-violent resolution of these conflicts. First, the privacy and the separation from close ties with neighbors and relatives characteristic of the modern family cuts it off from the assistance in resolving conflicts which such groups can provide. There is no one to turn to for help. Second, this same privacy and isolation from kin and neighbors also means there are few or no intimate and accepted outsiders who can serve as agents of social control to block the use of physical force. Consequently:

10. Reduce the impact of government programs and regulations which, directly or indirectly, encourage geographic mobility or reduce ties to the extended family.

This will be an even more difficult policy to implement than many of the others suggested in this chapter for a number of reasons. First, the art and science of "family impact analysis" is only now beginning to be explored.[53] Aside from a few obvious things (such as policies which give more encouragement to building new neighborhoods than to preserving the quality of existing neighborhoods), simply identifying the relevant programs and government regulations will be a slow and uncertain process. Second, those programs which are located will typically be found to be serving some important purpose. Consequently, it is not merely a matter of ending something, but more a matter of finding alternatives which do not encourage mobility and the reduction of extended family ties. Finally, the aid and support provided by an intimate community and kin are a mixed blessing. They can be stifling at the same time as they are helpful.

Returning to the high level of conflict within families, it has already been suggested that our unwillingness to recognize this fact is itself a source of violence. This is because as long as conflict within the family is viewed as atypical, wrong, or illegitimate, there will be reluctance to learn techniques for engaging in conflict nonviolently. Therefore:

11. Recognize the inevitability and legitimacy of conflict within family, rather than consider conflict an atypical deviation.

Once the inevitability and legitimacy of conflict within families is recognized, the way is open to learn efficient and constructive ways of resolving conflicts. Many of the methods cited in the references following Policy Implication 8, and those described in sections entitled: What Can a Battered Wife Do and What Can Others Do, are designed to do just that. One of the most important aspects of these methods is that they are intended for normal families. They make no assumptions about psychopathology. Instead, these methods assume that the family members need to learn more efficient methods of solving interpersonal problems and proceed to teach these methods by novel and non-moralistic behavioral methods. They focus on teaching people *how* to solve problems, not on *what* the solution to the problem is.

Sex Role, Sexism, and Wifebeating

Perhaps the most fundamental set of factors bringing about wifebeating are those connected with the sexist structure of the family and society. In fact, to a considerable extent, the cultural norms and values permitting and sometimes encouraging husband-to-wife violence reflect the hierarchical and male-dominant type of society which characterizes the Western world. The right to use force exists, as Goode[35] concludes, to provide the ultimate support for the existing power structure of the family, if those low in the hierarchy refuse to accept their place and roles. Nine of the specific ways in which the male-dominant structure of the society and of the family create and maintain a high level of marital violence are described in this section.

1. Defense of Male Authority. In the context of an individualistic, urban-industrial society, the presumption of superior authority for husbands is a potent force producing physical attacks on wives. This is because in such a society, male-superiority norms are not clearly understood and are in the process of transition, and because the presumption of male superiority must be validated by superiority in "resources," such as valued personal traits and material goods and services.[64]

If every man were, in fact, superior to his wife in such resources as intelligence, knowledge, occupational prestige and income, there would be a concordance between the ascribed authority and the individual achievements implicitly expected to accompany that authority in individual achievement-oriented societies. Clearly, that is often not the case, despite the fact that society gives men tremendous advantages in access to these traits and resources. Consequently, many men must fall back on the "ultimate resource" of physical force to maintain their superiority.[2,35,46,71]

Even if one were to argue that the physical and economic circumstances of past human history made male superiority necessary or reasonable, that is clearly no longer the case. Consequently, we need no longer be burdened with the violence necessary to maintain such a system, and it follows that:

12. Eliminate the husband as "head of the family" from its continuing presence in the law, in religion, in administrative procedure, and as a taken-for-granted aspect of family life.

Although progress is being made in respect to the achievement of husband-wife equality, the idea of the husband as head of the family remains firmly rooted in American culture (see the survey reported in *Parade;*[58] also Kolb and Straus[45]). In U.S. government statistics, the only way a women can be classified as the head of a household is if there is no husband physically present and there is no provision for listing joint head of household. It will only be through the continued active pursuit of the goals of the feminist movement that significant change is likely to occur. Moreover, the importance of the feminist movement goes well beyond husband-wife equality because it will be impossible to finally eliminate sexism in the family until it is also eliminated in the society at large.

Although the elimination of sexism in the family is a historical change of vast magnitude, there are aspects within the immediate control of individuals. For example, both for her own protection and as a contribution to the overall policy objective, no woman should enter marriage without it being firmly and *explicitly* understood that the husband is not the head of the family. Unless stated otherwise, the implicit marriage contract includes the "standard" clause about male leadership. Changing this contract after marriage is not only difficult, but gives rise to feelings of having been misled or cheated.

Although there may be objections to introducing these ideas in junior and senior high school classes dealing with the family (as indicated by recent congressional pressure on the National Science Foundation which resulted in terminating support for curriculum projects in Anthropology and Psychology), many local school districts will find such content appropriate. In addition, the feminist movement can continue to challenge the implicit support of male dominant family relations in magazines for young women such as *Seventeen*, *Bride*, and *Glamour*.

2. Economic Constraints and Discrimination. The sexist economic and occupational structure of society allows women few alternatives. The jobs open to them are lower in status. Despite antidiscrimination legislation, women continue to earn about 40% less than men in the same occupations. Without access to good jobs, women are dependent on their husbands. If there is a divorce, almost all husbands default on support payments after a short time, assuming they could afford them in the first place. Consequently many women continue to endure physical attacks from their husband because the alternative of divorce means living in poverty. Lack of economic alternatives to depending on the husband is one of the three main factors which Gelles[32] found associated with beaten wives remaining with their husbands. It follows that for women to be in a position in which they can refuse to tolerate physical coercion by their husbands, it is absolutely essential that there be occupational and economic equality. Consequently, one of the most fundamental policy implications is:

13. Eliminate the pervasive system of sex-typed occupations in which "women's occupations" tend to be poorly paid, and the equally pervasive difference between the pay of men and women in the same occupation.

3. Burdens of Child Care. The sexually based division of labor in society assigns child-rearing responsibility to the wife. This keeps the wife in the dependent, less powerful position as long as there are small children in the family. If the marriage ends, she has responsibility for rearing the children. But at the same time, society does not provide either economic provision for her doing so or child care centers which can take over part of the burden so that she can earn enough to support her children. The combination of occupational discrimination, lack of child care facilities, and inadequate child support from either the government or the father all coerce women into remaining married even though they are victims of violence.

The most fundamental policy implication of the above has to do with the sexual stereotyping of parental responsibilities. Under the present system, a husband does not need to fear that if he beats his wife and the wife leaves, *he* will be responsible for both the care of the child and the need to earn sufficient income. A husband can hit (and otherwise oppress) his wife with relative impunity from this possibility. He can be reasonably confident that if she does leave, he will not have the children unless he insists on it. Courts are reluctant to award children to fathers in any circumstances. It is no shame for a father to claim that the child will be best off with the mother, but for a mother to assert this is not only shameful, but in many cases will cause the child to be institutionalized or placed in a foster home. Therefore:

14. Reduce or eliminate the sex-typed pattern of family role responsibilities.

As in the case of sexual stereotyping in the paid labor force, interest and ability rather than sex needs to be the primary criteria for who does what. Moreover, this is a policy implication which, like that in respect to paid employment, is desirable irrespective of its effect on wifebeating. Just as many (but not all) women will find greater fulfillment through equal participation in the paid labor force; many (but again, not all) men will find greater fulfillment than they now experience in equal participation in the household labor force. That possibility is now denied to men because of the shame attached to household work and child care as major interests for men.

Policy implication *14* is a very long range type of social change, and we need not wait for that to come about. In the meantime, the entrapment of women in a violent marriage by expecting them to assume responsibility for the care of a child if the marriage breaks up can be addressed by other steps, and particularly:

15. Establish or subsidize a comprehensive and high quality system of day-care centers for pre-school children.

Again, this is a policy which is long overdue in its own right, and not just for its potential in preventing wifebeating. Such facilities are needed by millions of women who enjoy fully satisfactory marriages. (Refer to Varma, M., in this book.)

4. *Myth of the Single Parent Household.*   Another of the cultural norms which helps to maintain the subordination of women is the idea that children cannot be adequately brought up by one parent.

Thus, if a women is to have children, she must also have a man. To the limited extent that research evidence supports this view, it comes about because of the confounding of poverty and social ostracism with single parenthood.

It seems likely that if social pressure and constraints were removed, most women would want to live with a man and vice versa. Still, there is an important minority for whom this is not the case and who, in effect, live in a state of forced cohabitation "for the sake of the children." Thus, the fact that innumerable and (under present conditions) unnecessary social and economic constraints prevent the single parent family from being a viable social unit forces many women into accepting or continuing with a subordinate and violent relationship.

5. *Pre-eminence of Wife Role for Women.* Under the present system, being a wife and mother is the most important single role for a woman. Indeed, American cultural norms are such that one cannot be a "full woman" unless married. A man, on the other hand, has the option of investing much or little of himself in the husband-father role, depending on his interest, ability, and circumstances. In short, the stigma of being a divorced man is tiny compared to that of being a divorced woman—to which a special term with somewhat immoral overtones has in the past been attached: *divorcee*. this forced dependence on the wife role, as the basis for a respected position in society, makes it difficult for women to refuse to tolerate male violence by ending the marriage.

The policy implications of the single parent household myth and the dominance of the role of wife in establishing the human worth of women are difficult to put in specific steps, because they call for a broad re-orientation of the roles of men and women in our society. One cannot simply attempt to change these two aspects of the role of women, as important as that is. Change in these two roles, if it is going to occur, is only likely to happen as one part of the process of ending the subordinate and restricted status to which women are still relegated. These two aspects of sexually stereotyped roles are part of an overall configuration which, as will be noted below, tends to define women as children.

6. *Women as Children.* The conception of women as the property of men is no longer part of the legal system of industrial countries. However, elements of this outlook linger on in the folk culture. They also survive in certain aspects of the law, such as the statutes which declare the husband the head of the household and give him various rights over his wife; for example, the right to choose the place of abode, to which the wife must conform.* In addition, there is the related conception of women as "childlike." In combination, these aspects of the sexist organization of society give husbands a covert moral right to use physical force on their wives analogous to the overt legal right of parents to use physical force on their children.[31]

The implications, for wifebeating, of these three aspects of the sexist structure of the society and the family (plus others which cannot be included here for lack of space) suggest that the most fundamental policy implication of all is that:

16. Full sexual equality is essential for prevention of wifebeating.

At this point, it is necessary to make clear an important limitation to much of what has been said. Sexual equality, by itself, is almost certainly *not* going to end conflict and violence between husbands and wives. It will reduce or eliminate *certain types* of conflict, but at the same time, create new types of conflict. Issues which are *not* now the subject of disagreement in millions of families—such as who will work for wages and who will be in the household labor force, or more specific issues such as who will do the laundry—will no longer be determined by subscribing to the pattern of family roles which have been worked out over the centuries. Rather, they become open questions over which severe conflict can arise. It is by no means inconceivable that *neither* partner will want to be in the paid labor force, and that *neither* will want to do the laundry. Consequently, a reduction in the level of violence also depends on couples having the interpersonal and conflict-management skills necessary to cope with and realize the benefits of a less rigid type of family system. Millions of people lack these skills and almost all of us can improve them.

In addition, it will be shortsighted and dangerous to overlook the fact that freedom too has its costs. Freedom and flexibility in family patterns and sex roles remove some of the most important points of stability and security in life. These are costs that not everyone finds worth the benefits. Erich Fromm's classic book *Escape from Free-*

---

*It is pertinent that even in a state known for its social and familial experimentation, as recently as in 1971, the California State Bar Association voted *not* to repeal this legislation.

dom[28] was concerned with far more than issues of why fascism had such wide support. At the other end of the continuum, the opposition of millions of women to the Equal Rights Amendment and the feminist movement reflects the anxiety which many women feel over the possible loss of familiar and stable guides to life. Therefore:

17. As the society eliminates fixed sex roles, alternative sources of stability and security in self-definition will be needed.

Part of these needed social anchoring points will come from occupational identification which, in the past, was difficult or impossible for women. This difficulty was not only because so few women were in socially valued occupational roles, but also because for a *woman*, to be highly identified with an occupation raised doubts about her familial commitment, her love for her husband and children, and her femininity. But occupation as a source of identity and self-esteem has its limits. There are vast numbers of occupations unlikely to be valued as a means of establishing a personal identity—either by men or by women. Fortunately, there are other roles and identities which can give life the needed structure and social integration—particularly roles in relation to the community, special purpose groups, and the larger kin group. These will be discussed later. But before doing that, two final aspects of sex roles need to be considered.

7. Compulsive Masculinity. Talcott Parsons suggested that in modern industrial societies, the separation of the male occupational role from the family, and the predominance of the mother in child rearing, creates a fundamental difficulty for males in respect to achieving a masculine sexual identity:

> The boy has a tendency to form a direct feminine identification, since his mother is the model most readily available and significant to him. But he is not destined to become an adult woman. Moreover he soon discovers that in certain vital respects women are considered inferior to men, that it would hence be shameful for him to grow up to be like a woman. Hence when boys emerge into what Freudians call the "latency period," their behavior tends to be marked by a kind of *compulsive masculinity*. Aggression toward women who "after all are to blame," is an essential concomitant.[59]

Similarly, Parsons' analysis also suggests that the origins of *female* aggressiveness to be partly found in the particular structure of the family in industrial society, and postulates why much of this aggressiveness is focused against men—especially husbands—as the agents of women's repressed position in society.* The climate of mutual antagonism between the sexes, which is partly an outgrowth of the factors described by Parsons, provides a context which is not only conducive to attacks by husbands on wives but probably also underlies a number of other related phenomena, such as the growing evidence that in many instances, "rape is a power trip, not a passion trip."[10,16,17] Moreover, as in the typical homosexual rape in prisons,[23] the degradation and humiliation of the victim is often a major motivating force.

The female side of the pattern epitomized by the phrase "compulsive masculinity" can be called "compulsive femininity." Part of compulsive femininity is represented in the *Total Woman*,[54] but also, and probably far more typically, it is the internalization of the "women as children" social definition in the form of negative self-image.

8. Negative Self-Image.

Under the present social structure, women tend to develop negative self-images, especially in relation to the crucial trait of achievement.[39] As a consequence, they may also develop feelings of guilt and masochism, which encourage toleration of male aggression and violence, and in some extreme cases, to seek it. Full sexual equality would eliminate this as a sexually structured pattern of behavior, even though it may remain on an individual-to-individual basis.

Since compulsive masculinity and its associated violence, and compulsive femininity and its associated negative self-image, are patterns growing out of the experiences of men and women from early childhood on—and particularly the differences in the ways boys and girls are socialized for their respective sex roles—it follows that:

18. Parent-child interaction, parental expectations, and all other aspects of socialization should not be differentiated according to the sex of the child.

9. Male Orientation of the Criminal Justice System.

Not only is much male violence against wives attributable to the sexist organization of society, but the crowning blow is that the male-oriented or-

---

*See the discussion of the sex myth in Steinmetz and Straus[68] for other ways in which the pattern of male-female relationships built into the society helps to create antagonism between the sexes and hence the association between sexuality and violence.

ganization of the criminal justice system virtually guarantees that few women will be able to secure legal relief. There is often difficulty getting even basic physical protection, as is graphically shown in the following instance (*New York Times*, June 14, 1976):

> It was about 4 o'clock in the afternoon when a call came into the 103rd Precinct station house in Jamaica, Queens, from a woman who said her husband had beaten her, that her face was bleeding and bruised. She thought some of her ribs had been broken.
> "Can you help me?" she pleaded to the police officer who answered the phone. "My husband's gone now, but he said he would come back and kill me." She was also frightened, she said, that he would start beating the children when he returned.
> "It's not a Police Department thing," the officer told her. "It's really a family thing. You'll have to go to Family Court tomorrow. There's nothing that I can do."

But even if the woman were to go to Family Court, unless she has unusual understanding of and ability to manipulate the system, there will often be a three week delay before her request for a "peace bond" or an "order of protection" comes before the judge. Such orders are therefore of no greater help than the police officer in securing immediate protection from another assault. Even without these delays, many women cannot attend court because of the absence of child care arrangements during the long hours of waiting for a case to come up and the frequent repetition of these days when the case is rescheduled.

Among the many other impediments to securing legal protection against assault by a husband are (a) immunity from suit by ones spouse; (b) the requirement that, even though there is abundant physical evidence, the police officer must witness the attack before an arrest can be made; (c) the frequent failure of police to arrest even when they do witness an assault; (d) the "cooling out" by police, prosecuting attorneys, and judges, of wives who attempt to bring complaints; and (e) the refusal to make an award by public compensation review boards (even in cases of permanent disability) if the injury was inflicted by the husband.[72]

19. Eliminate from the criminal justice system the implicit toleration of wifebeating which comes about through statutory and common law; the attitudes of the police, prosecutors, and judges; and through cumbersome and ineffective procedures which make even the available legal remedies and protection ineffective.

Some movement in the direction of policy implication *19* is now taking place, but it is far from a general trend. Change in the legal system tends to take place where it is taken up as a priority activity by well-organized feminist groups, as in the "NOW Wife Assault Program" in Ann Arbor, Michigan,[27,63] or in the occasional enlightened police department which recognizes the need to reorient its mode of coping with "family disturbance" calls.[8]

Economic Frustration and Violence

American society, like most societies, is one in which, from early childhood on, people learn to respond to frustration and stress by aggression. This is not an inevitable biological fact, since there are a few societies in which people learn to, and typically do, respond to frustration in other ways. Nevertheless, that is how things are in this society—and also the way they are likely to remain in the foreseeable future. For this reason, and also because it is a desirable national objective in its own right, social policy should give high priority to enabling as many as possible to avoid situations of extreme frustration of important life goals. This is by no means the same as attempting to create a life without frustration. Such a life, even if it were possible, would be empty. It would probably also be a source of violence in itself (see the discussion of the "Clockwork Orange" theory of violence in Gelles and Straus[33]). However, a major blockage of a critical life goal is quite another thing.

There are many critical life goals which are (or perhaps should be) beyond the realm of social policy to facilitate. But a goal on which there is high consensus, as well as a high possibility of achieving change, is the provision of a meaningful occupational role and an adequate level of income for all families.

In industrial societies, the husband's position of leadership is based on the prestige and earning power of his occupation. Consequently, if the husband is unemployed or does not earn an amount consistent with other men in the family's network of associates, his leadership position is undermined. Data from a study by O'Brien[55] shows that when this happens, husbands tend to try to maintain their superior position through the use of physical force. Data from a study of the parents of university students shows that the percentage of husbands who struck their wives in the last year ranges from a low of 4 and 7%

for those whose wives are almost completely or completely satisfied with their family income, up to 16 and 18% for those whose wives are slightly satisfied or not at all satisfied. There is also some evidence that assaults on wives go up with unemployment.[58]

In discussing the roots of wifebeating in the sexist organization of the family, it was pointed out that if husbands no longer had the burden of being the "head of the family" and the main "breadwinner," they would not need to call on the ultimate resource of violence to maintain that position in situations where the wife is more competent, earns more, or has a more prestigious occupation. The same reasoning applies, and perhaps even more strongly, when the husband is unemployed. Clearly, the most fundamental change needed is male liberation from the bounds of traditional sex roles. But at the same time, we can also pursue a policy which, aside from its intrinsic worth, is also likely to reduce wifebeating. It is stark in its simplicity and powerful in its effect of human welfare:

20. Full employment for all men and women in the labor force at wage levels consistent with the standards of the society, and a guaranteed income for those unable to work.

Aside from its impact on wifebeating through avoiding one of the most severe frustrations a person can experience in an industrial society, and through bypassing issues of power within the family, full employment can also exert a powerful effect through its consequences for self-esteem. Kaplan[43] has shown that the lower an adolescent's self-esteem, the greater the likelihood of his being violent. Kaplan's data further suggests that this is because boys low in self-esteem seek to achieve recognition from others through violence. This, of course, is tied in with the tendency to equate masculinity with aggressiveness. Consequently, when there is lack of recognition through achievement in school, in sports, or in an occupation, males can and do tend to demonstrate their "manhood' through violence. Again, the more fundamental policy objective is to change the definition of masculinity. But as long as that definition continues to be a part of our culture, full employment can help avoid invoking this aspect of "manhood," by providing meaningful employment as a basis for self-esteem.

A more radical approach to this aspect of the relation between economic frustration and wifebeating focuses on what critics of American society see as the inhuman occupational and economic system itself. Such critics are not opposed to full employment. What they oppose is an economic and social system which hinges human worth on earnings and competative occupational achievement. As long as such a system prevails, the vast bulk of the population are denied the possibility of securing an adequate level of self-esteem because, by definition, only a minority can be at the top in occupational prestige and income. In addition, the striving to get to the top pushes more human values to subordinate positions. Ties of friendship, kin, and community, for example, are regularly sacrificed on the altar of moving to get a better job or to accept a promotion. Consequently:

21. Reduce the extent to which society evaluates people on the basis of their economic achievements and the occupational and economic competition which this entails.

Policy implication *21* does not signal the end to all competition. Competition can be pleasurable if one can choose the arena of competition and if there is a reasonable chance of winning. Rather, it suggests the need to end the forced and (for most of the population) no-win competition which now characterizes our occupational-economic system.

What Can a Battered Wife Do?

The emphasis in this article has been on prevention, rather than on what a specific woman can do when she has been beaten. Most of the preventative steps are relatively long-term and also beyond the resources of a single person. I have stressed these seemingly impractical things because of a belief that they *are* practical. In fact, preventative approaches which do not include the type of actions outlined here are not getting at the fundamental causes; they are a band-aid approach.

But a focus on changing the fundamental structural causes does not mean that we should ignore the desperate and immediate situation in which millions of women find themselves. Their need is urgent. Consequently, the two concluding sections will be devoted to steps which are applicable to specific individuals. Some of these steps parallel or compliment the preventative policies covered up to this point, except that they are things that an individual woman may have within her power to carry out. Others are steps which can be taken by communities and local groups. Although the steps that an individual wife needs to take are in this section, and the steps that groups and communities need to take are in the section which follows, this is merely for convenience in presenting things. In actuality, the two sets of steps are closely connected and one depends on the other. In fact, there are grounds for some misgivings over implications of the title of this section since in a large proportion of cases there does not seem to be anything a beaten wife can accomplish unaided.[4]

1. Get Help. The odds are strongly against any woman who tries to cope with wifebeating on her own. The husband holds most of the cards: the house for all practical purposes, is his; psychologically, he typically holds the upper hand because women are conditioned to regard the success of the marriage as their responsibility; morally, the status of women as semi-children implies the right of husbands to punish errant wives as that almost all women who have been hit by their husband ask the irrelevant question, "What did I do wrong?"

Since wifebeating is primarily a social problem, i.e., a socially patterned type of behavior, the best source of help is from persons or groups committed to change the sexist structure of the family and society. Therefore, a feminist group, even if it is not explicitly concerned with wifebeating, is likely to be immensely important in helping the beaten wife to regain the psychological and moral initiative necessary to change things. If one is lucky enough to live in a community with a "refuge," "shelter," or "safe house" for battered wives, that is obviously the place to go for information and psychological support, even if there is no immediate plan to use the physical facilities. "Hot lines" are being set up in a growing number of communities by women's groups, some of them specifically focused on wifebeating. In New York, Abused Women's Aid In Crisis (AWAIC, Inc.) operates such a service and serves as a national clearing house for information and referrals.[4]

There are also a number of other possible sources of assistance, such as a local branch of the Family Service Association of America; a private psychologist, psychiatrist, or social worker—provided they are trained in marriage counseling (as indicated, for example, by membership in the American Association of Marriage and Family

Counselors); or a minister, priest, or rabbi, or a church-affiliated social service organization. However, considerable caution is needed in respect to all of these traditional human service agencies because, besides being traditional sources of help, in the sense of being long established, they also tend to be traditional in the sense of an explicit or implicit commitment to a patriarchical family system.

Finally, in addition to such formal sources of help, it is important to get advice, assistance, and moral support from friends, neighbors, and relatives. Avoiding the involvement of such people is part of the husband's psychological advantage, because it insulates him from shame and from criticism of his behavior. Sooner or later they are going to find out in any case. In the meantime, the beaten wife has lost the psychological and moral support which they might provide, and also their assistance in the form of specific suggestions, help in settling disputes, and often, a place to go for physical safety. Even if the advice is worthless, and the moral support not forthcoming, just the act of getting the issue into the open can help to create the psychological readiness to take the initiative for whatever steps are necessary.

2. Cancel the Hitting License. A beaten wife cannot wait for the norms of the society to change so as to redefine marriage as not including the unstated right to hit. Nor can she do it herself unaided. Assistance in bringing about this redefinition is one of the most important reasons for involving others. Having brought the issue into the open, and hopefully, with their support, she can make clear that the use of physical force by a husband (or wife) is *never* justified, and will not be tolerated.

Part of this is the need to keep clear the difference between a conflict and how one settles conflicts, and between being wrong about something and how one changes the behavior of the person who does something wrong. Even if the classic complaints of being a "nagging wife" or a "lousy housekeeper" are correct in a particular case, that no more justifies a beating than being a "griper" or a "slacker" at work. In this connection, it is important to realize that friends, neighbors, relatives *and therapists* often start by trying to find out who or what is wrong. A beaten wife must reject that approach, even though these issues must ultimately be faced. Whatever else is wrong, all parties must acknowledge that hitting is wrong. So an essential first step is to make clear that irrespective of who is at fault, the use of violence is unacceptable.

3. Be Prepared to Leave. The redefinition called for above is unlikely to come about unless the wife also makes clear that she can and will leave if the new definition of marriage is violated. Leaving, rather than violence, must become the ultimate sanction for both parties to a marriage. But this should never be done as a bluff. One has to accept the fact that if it comes to that, it is better to live in poverty, or live with whatever other burdens the end of the marriage brings, than to be beaten. Consequently, an essential part of the process of ending wifebeating is to plan ahead for this eventuality. Without such plans (that is, without a specific place to go) the threat of leaving is basically a bluff and one which will be perceived by most husbands, and therefore ignored, with a consequent worsening of the situation.

4. Get a Job. Plans to leave, should the need arise, do not just involve a physical location. A critical element is some means of support. Public assistance is the right of a woman who has been driven from her home by her husband's violence and one must be prepared to use this method of support. But it is better to provide for one's self. In fact, getting a job, even if this is at the expense of other things which are highly valued, is probably as important a step as can be taken. It serves to further validate the threat to leave if violence occurs. It serves to bolster the resolve of the wife so that she is more likely to take other needed steps which could prevent having to actually leave. It avoids the choice between two undesirable states of dependency: the husband or the state.

But what about the wife who has no marketable skills, or has young children? This question points up precisely the reason why threats to leave are typically ineffective. If that is the case now, will it be any different after the next beating? Obviously not. So the issue must be faced immediately. It is better to start any needed job training at the very beginning, or to get started with what jobs there are at the very beginning, or to set up child care arrangements at the beginning. All will be more difficult later, and in the meantime, lack of a job undercuts other steps.

5. Don't Wait. It is important that the situation be faced immediately—at the very first slap. If the first slap or beating has occurred, don't wait until the next one, especially in the hope that there will not be a next time. There will be a next time. All the available evidence shows that the frequency of hitting and beating does not decrease with age. So the attacks are most likely to continue—or increase—unless steps are taken to alter the pattern. Recognizing this simple statistical fact is, by itself, an important part of the overall process of ending wifebeating, because so many women endure their situation in the false belief that their husbands will grow out of it.

6. Problem-Focused Assertiveness versus Catharsis. A dangerous aspect of one wing of the "encounter group" movement, which has its parallel among a number of marriage counselors and writers of marital advice books, is represented in Bach and Wyden's *The Intimate Enemy.*[5] Bach and Wyden urge their readers to drop "outmoded notions of etiquette" and ventilate their anger. During one group session, Bach urged the women participants: "Don't be afraid to be a real shrew, a real bitch! Get rid of your pent up hostilities! Tell them where you're really at! Let it be total, vicious, exaggerated, hyperbole!"[40]

Although Bach and Wyden's book has disclaimers to the contrary, the overall message of the book, as I read it, urges wives to do just what the quotation suggests. This advice is based on a "catharsis," or "ventilation" theory of aggression control. That theory starts with the assumption that all of us have built into our nature a greater or lesser tendency toward aggression which somehow must find expression. If we attempt to repress this deep, biologically-based motivation, it will only result in a more destructive explosion of the innate aggression drive at some later time.

Unfortunately for those who have acted on such advice, almost no empirical research with any pretense of scientific rigor supports the theory, and much of it shows the reverse: That opportunities to observe or to be aggressive tend to produce *greater* subsequent levels of aggression and violence.[11,38,68,70,71] In general, aggression against another (either verbally or physically) tends to (a) produce counter-aggression, (b) impedes getting to the real problem, and (c) if it does succeed in squelching the other person, reinforces the use of aggression as a mode of interaction.

There is, however, a kernel of truth underlying the "let it all hang out" and "ventilation" approaches to marriage. It hinges on the difference between assertion (standing up for one's interests) and aggression (acts carried out with the intention of hurting each other). Assertiveness is essential. But one can be assertive without being aggressive (although always with the risk of aggression being imputed). For example, the critical first steps of "Getting help," "Canceling the hitting license," and "Making clear that one is prepared to leave," are all highly assertive, but non-aggressive acts. Second, assertiveness is vital if there is to be any hope of correcting the problem over which the violence occurs. If it is conflict over the children, sex, money, or how the household is run, then these issues must be faced.

Procedures for rational conflict resolution of the type just outlined, often combined with systems for rewarding occurrences of desired behavior, are the focus of much of the recent "marriage encounter" movement[44,49] and of "behavioral" therapists such as Blechman, et al.,[12,13] Patterson,[60] and a number of others who are represented in the chapters of an important new book, *Treating Relationships*[57] (see also Jacobson and Martin[42]). One can say that a focus of these approaches to "treating relationships" is the improvement of interpersonal skills, including assertiveness, so that the legitimate interests of all parties can be optimized. This type of therapy may also have the advantage of being less threatening and more attractive to husbands. In accordance with prevailing masculine role models, men are more reluctant than women to have their childhood or present emotions and psychological status hashed over, as in the traditional "insight" therapy. They prefer to deal with actions and results more than history and personality, and these are precisely the focuses of the new marriage encounter, marriage enrichment, and marriage counseling approaches.

7. *Leave or Take Legal Action.* In an unknown, but certainly not small, number of instances, the type of steps just outlined will be ineffective. In that case, a woman probably has only three choices: leave, take legal action, or some combination of the two. All of these are extremely complex and uncertain. The seeming simplicity of leaving overlooks vast differences in how the act is defined and perceived. If it is an impulsive running out of the house to some highly tenuous alternative, husbands will realize that their position is not at all jeopardized. Then, with the typical return home, the beatings resume, though perhaps not immediately. Almost all of the 100 women studied by Gayford,[30] for example, had left at least once, many repeatedly. When a wife returns under such circumstances, it probably strengthens the husband's hand, because now he realizes more than ever that she truly has no long-term alternative.

Even a departure which is *intended* to be temporary must be defined in this way in advance, along with an indication that the wife's return will be *her* choice—her decision to give him another chance. Such a definition of the situation will only be believable if it is truly within the wife's power not to return, and the husband knows this. This is part of the reason for the emphasis a few paragraphs back on making specific plans to leave at the very beginning. Any putting off or any concealment of such plans is likely to so seriously undercut a wife's position that other things may be irrelevant.

As for legal steps, a number are available, but all are difficult and uncertain because the judicial system is focused on "preserving the family" rather than protecting wives from physical injury. In fact, in a number of crucial places, the law gives priority to the former.[72] Moreover, even when legal actions are initiated, so many are dropped by the complainant that this provides a ready excuse for the police, prosecuting attorneys, and judges to follow their "natural" inclinations of treating wifebeating as "domestic disturbances" (i.e., not really a crime) rather than assaults. This, in turn, sets up a vicious circle. Since the cases are defined as not really crimes, or as crimes not likely as to be successfully prosecuted, women are discouraged from filing charges and encounter foot-dragging when they attempt to pursue such charges. As a result, many who would bring charges if not dissuaded, or who would follow through if obstacles and foot-dragging did not occur, do not. Even attorneys, employed by beaten wives, tend to follow this pattern. Consequently, for legal steps, as for almost everything else, the assistance of a feminist group, and, if possible, a feminist-oriented lawyer (male or female) may be critical. Assuming that such assistance can be found (or for a woman with sufficient determination, without it) the main legal steps have been well summarized by Clasen:[20]

Criminal Charges. She may choose (in some states) to prosecute this assailant under the criminal laws of the state. Once a complaint has been filed, it is very important to follow through with all the court proceedings. There will usually be a court appearance to authorize a warrant for a criminal charge, arraignment in the District Court, a preliminary hearing, and the trial. In felony cases, there will also be an arraignment in Circuit Court and a trial.

Not following through on a court case is an invitation for further abuse. Following through the verdict establishes to the assailant and to the world that further violence will not be tolerated.

Civil Suit. She may choose a divorce or legal separation. The help of a private attorney or Legal Aid must be enlisted. When papers are filed for divorce, a restraining order can be included to order the assailant to "desist and refrain from beating, annoying, molesting, physically abusing, or otherwise interfering with the personal liberty of the other" during the divorce proceedings, usually 6–18 months. If the assailant disobeys this restraining order, the police can pick him up and put him in jail.

Civil Commitment. The possibility of a mental illness commitment may be pursued if the assailant is mentally ill and dangerous to himself or others. If this is the client's chosen route, she must familiarize herself with Community Mental Health Services and the Probate Court commitment procedures. NOW will assist in making contact with Community Mental Health to arrange for psychiatric assessment and help from Court Services.

A wife assault victim may use all the resources available to her. She may, in fact, do "all of the above" in an effort to end violence perpetrated against her, or she may decide on one or two of these.

What Can Others Do?

Just about every step suggested for women who have been beaten has a counterpart in steps which are needed by feminist groups, the legal profession, human service agencies, and individual practicioners, if real progress is to be made. To leave it to a lone woman to buck what amounts to the institutionalization of family violence by an entire society, is both cruel and unrealistic, despite occasional successes. Each of the groups just listed, plus every individual citizen, needs to push for the type of policies outlined earlier in this paper. But in this section, only those steps which are intended to assist specific wives, rather than the longer range changes needed for a truly preventative approach, are discussed.

1. Task Force on Wife Abuse. Generalities which are stated as the result of social science research have little meaning for the average citizen. They are not impressed by a rate of so and so per thousan the U.S. population. They *are* impressed when X or Y number of cases are uncovered in their own community. So a first job for such a task force is to start building public awareness and raising public consciousness through a local survey such as those recently done in Flint, Michigan[26] or Saint Paul, Minnesota.[75] These need not be elaborate, nor do they have to fit the criteria of scientific sampling. They simply need to demonstrate that there are lots of women being beaten, and possibly right next door.

A second job of such a task force is to use this information to mobilize existing human service agencies in so far as this is possible. It can provide a basis for establishing a policy that public assistance will be given to women who leave home because of violence, rather than forcing an individual woman to make the general case as well as herspecific case. It can encourage the police to explore in-service-training for more effective and realistic handling of wifebeating cases. It can sensitize social service agencies to the need for dealing with the problem. Finally, it can help muster the public support needed to set up new channels for dealing with wifebeating.

2. Hot Lines and Support Groups. The difficulty, and often the impossibility, of a woman coping with a violent husband without psychological and moral support has been stressed at so many places in this article that no further elaboration is necessary here. Information on the nearest hot line or support group can be obtained from AWAIC, Inc. or the National Organization of Women (NOW).

3. Safe Houses. If all women had the understanding of the general situation and of the steps outlined in the previous section, emergency shelters or safe houses might only rarely be needed. But the situation is just the reverse. Consequently, in my opinion, the most important single step which a community group can take is the establishment of such a house. This provides the only realistic way out for large numbers of women. Moreover, it can also serve an important educational and consciousness-raising function. The fact that there is a whole house full of women and children whose own homes are not safe to live in is dramatic. It can help pave the way for public support of other immediate steps, as well as the longer-range preventative steps. In this connection, even if it is decided to keep the address of the house confidential as a security measure, the activities of the house should be given maximum publicity. Every untoward event should be reported to the media, including the difficulties created by zoning rules and by antagonistic or foot-dragging public officials. In fact, one might almost wish for a certain amount of legal and bureaucratic troubles, or even a threatening husband, as occasions for statements before a city council and articles in the newspapers and on TV.

4. Legal Aid. The term legal aid usually means legal services for people who lack the money to employ a lawyer. That certainly applies to a large number of abused women. Ironically, legal aid is often denied such women because, in most areas, a woman is not eligible if *her husband* has a regular income, even though she has no way of getting a share of that income without legal aid. There is also a need to create a more sympathetic understanding and sufficient commitment to the issue by lawyers so that they will persist despite unsympathetic prosecuting attorneys, judges, and juries, and to a considerable extent, a legal system which is stacked against providing protection or relief for beaten wives. Despite these impediments, the legal system can be an effective tool. So there is a need for legal counseling, at least as a supplement to private lawyers and to the usual legal aid lawyer.

A momentous step toward providing women with legal protection against assault by their husbands began as this chapter was written. A group of twelve repeatedly beaten women in New York City initiated a class action to require that the police, court officers, and judges comply with the provisions of existing statutes which have so long been flouted (*New York Times*, December 8, 1976:2; December 12, 1976:73). The suit charges that the police not only refuse to arrest abusive husbands in most cases but also that they do not tell the wives that they are entitled to make citizen's arrest with the aid of the police. The police also decline, according to the suit, to give the women medical assistance and protection by removing abusive husbands from the home. State laws mandate all of these, the suit states.

Battered wives are frequently told incorrectly by Family Court personnel that they must take advantage of the court's family counseling services before seeking legal help, the suit charges. These services are under the direction of the probation service.

5. Public Assistance. Since a major reason why battered wives remain with their husbands is their financial dependence on them, the availability of public assistance as an alternative to being beaten must be established in the minds of both public assistance officials and the general public. Often, it seems as though a beaten wife is not eligible because eligibility depends on having already established a separate residence. But this is a matter of administrative procedure, not law. Homeless *male* vagrants are given food and shelter, and the same can be done for women who are homeless because of being driven out to protect their physical safety. Moreover, this assistance needs to be available immediately, rather than at the end of administrative and investigative procedures, which often take three to six months.

6. The Police and Wifebeating. The work of Morton Bard of the Graduate Center of the City University of New York with the New York City and other police departments has shown that it is possible to change the typical role of the police in wifebeating cases.[9] The typical role is to intervene to control the immediate physical conflict, to avoid arrest, and, perhaps unintentionally, to give implict legal approval to the wifebeater. The implicit approval occurs partly because many policemen think that a husband does have a right to hit his wife, provided the injury does not require hospitalization. This manifests itself in many subtle ways. Among the less subtle of these are focusing almost entirely on quelling the disturbance and almost never mentioning the fact that assault is a crime. It also manifests itself in the difference in what the police offer to do for the husband and for the wife. After the "disturbance" has been stopped, if the wife is concerned with her safety, they do not offer to help the husband leave. It is assumed to be *his* house. Consequently, even though it is the wife who has been attacked, they offer to help *her* pack and leave.* To top it off, there are instances in which wives who fled to a neighbor's house being refused police protection to reenter the house to obtain their belongings because the officer felt that he had no right to enter "his" house![5] They rarely attempt to mediate or help resolve the conflict or make referrals to human service agencies, and even more rarely offer to assist the wife in pressing charges. In fact, as previously noted, the police usually try to argue a wife out of pressing charges.

---

*Even in those jurisdictions which do not vest property in the name of the husband, and do not give husbands the legal right to determine the domicile of the family, the fact that the law does not protect a woman from the use of force by her husband (unless a weapon has been used or the wife needs hospitalization) effectively gives him these rights.

Bard's program (refer to his article in this book) focuses on training police officers to do more than just separate the couple. Officers are given an understanding of why conflict and violence in the family are so common, how to help a couple address the underlying problem, and also to make referrals to appropriate human service agencies. It is essentially a crisis-intervention training program. Experience with the program to date suggests that it has helped the families involved, since "in the 22 months of operation of the Family Unit . . . there has not been a homicide in any family previously known to the unit. While family homicides in the precinct increased overall, in each case there had been no prior police intervention."[7] Moreover, the 18-man Family Unit, although exposed far more to the dangers inherent in family disturbance calls, sustained only one minor injury.

7. Therapeutic Intervention. Just as wifebeating was ignored by academic researchers in psychology and sociology until quite recently, there has been a similar gap in clinical practice. Actually, it is worse than a gap, because under the influence of Freudian theory, psychiatrists, clinical psychologists, and social workers have tended to focus attention on such things as presumed aggressive "drives," acting-out of impulsive "needs," and female masochism. In short, to the minor extent that wifebeating has been dealt with clinically, it has been through attempting to diagnose and treat sick persons rather than sick *relationships*. As previously noted, recent developments have moved the field of mariage counseling to just such a focus on relationships. Nevertheless, as of this writing, little has been published on the specific marriage counseling methods to be used for husband-wife violence. But a start has been made. Several family service agency conferences were held in 1976 (for example, by the Family Service of Detroit and by the Jewish Family Service of New York) and there has been one paper which details specifics.[65]

Marriage counseling is undergoing a tremendous growth. It may be the fastest growing type of clinical service in this country. Considering the large population now served and the prospects for an even larger clientele in the immediate future—most of whom will have been involved in at least some violent incidents, the scope for a meaningful contribution to the elimination of wifebeating is evident. However, this potential contribution is not likely to take place unless therapists come to see wifebeating as primarily a problem of social relationships (especially power) rather than of mental illness. Marital therapy, to deal with wifebeating, must focus on treating the relationship. Of course, psychological problems, such as damage to a wife's self-esteem and sense of adequacy, do often accompany wifebeating, and the counselor can provide valuable assistance to these women.

The importance of therapy focused on reorganizing the pattern of husband-wife relationships is stressed because, as previously noted, marriage counseling still seems to be dominated by psychoanalytic and other "insight" type therapies focused on the presumed deep psychological problems of partners. At best, such treatments are likely to be ineffective. Usually, they divert attention from the here and now issues which must be resolved. At worst, traditional therapy tends to reinforce the society's penchant for blaming the victim— the wife—rather than the husband or the relationship. This is most apparent in the use of such concepts as "female masochism," and in a subtle and usually unintended (but nonetheless powerful) encouragement of women to follow traditional passive-accepting female roles.[19] Perhaps the direction in which therapy in wife abuse cases needs to go can be best illustrated by comparison with the treatment of the closely related (but far less common) problem of child abuse.

The still predominant method of treating child abuse consists of insight type psychotherapy, and if this fails or is not available, removing the child and punishing the parents by fine or jail. This approach is slowly being replaced by programs which, instead of trying to reorganize the personality of the abusing father or mother, teach parents how to "parent" and thus to avoid the kind of situation which leads to child abuse. The same shift in emphasis is called for in relation to wife abuse, and the larger pattern of less extreme husband-wife and wife-husband violence of which wifebeating is the most dramatic manifestation. That is, the treatment steps must continue to include the wife removing herself, as well as prison for intransigent assaultive husbands—just as these remain the ultimate mode of coping with the child abusing parent. But the more fundamental solution lies in changing the five aspects of the social structure discussed in this article and, for the therapist, in assisting husbands and wives to acquire the interpersonal skills which will enable them to negotiate the inevitable differences and frictions which arise in marriage, and hence to avoid the escalating sequence of events which lead to physical violence.

Summary and Conclusions

Physical violence between husband and wife is common but not an inevitable part of human nature. Only in rare instances is it an outgrowth of pathological male aggressiveness, or of female masochism. Rather, the typical pattern of husband-wife violence, and its extreme in the form of wifebeating, is largely a reflection of the nature of the society and its family system and of the sex roles and sex-typed personality traits characteristic of that system. More specifically, the focus of this chapter has been on the taken-for-granted (and therefore unperceived) cultural norms, which give family members the right to hit each other; the carry-over into the family of the high level of violence in other spheres of life; the part played by the family in training its members for participation in a violent society and a violent family system; the sexist organization of the society and the family which necessitates violence to keep women in their place, and which; denies women the resources necessary to effectively escape from violence on the part of their husbands. Each of these aspects of the social structure was described for purposes of deducing the social policies which, if adopted, would tend to reduce the level of wifebeating. In all, 20 different policy implications were deduced. These are summarized in Table 1.

TABLE 1. SUMMARY OF POLICY IMPLICATIONS FOR PREVENTION DERIVED FROM ANALYSIS OF SIX SOCIAL STRUCTURAL CAUSAL FACTORS.

Factor I. Cultural Norms Permit and Legalize Wifebeating
  1. Make the public aware of this largely unperceived norm.
  2. Redefine the marital relationship as one in which *any* use of physical force is as unacceptable as it is between those one works with, or with whom one goes bowling, or plays tennis.

Factor II. Wifebeating Reflects Social Violence
  3. Reduce to the maximum extent possible the use of physical force as an instrument of government.
  4. Limit depiction of violence in the mass media to the maximum possible consistent with preserving freedom of expression and artistic integrity.
  5. Enact stringent gun control legislation, particularly directed at restricting hand guns, but also requiring that all guns be kept locked and unloaded.

Factor III. The Family is the Primary Setting in Which Violence is Learned
  6. Gradually eliminate physical punishment as a mode of child rearing.
  7. Encourage parents to take steps to reduce, and above all, not to explicitly or implicitly define as permissible, acts of physical force between their children.

Table 1. (*Continued*).

8. Parents and children need to learn techniques for coping with and resolving the inevitable conflicts of family life by means other than force and coercion.
9. Sponsor research to determine the social and psychological conditions which lead some parents to be cold and distant rather than warm and loving, and translate results into programs to assist such parents.

Factor IV. The Inevitability of Conflict in the Family
10. Reduce the impact of government programs and regulations which, directly or indirectly, encourage geographic mobility or reduce ties to the extended family.
11. Recognize the inevitability and legitimacy of conflict within the family, rather than consider conflict an atypical deviation.

Factor V. Sexually Stereotyped Roles and Sexism in the Family and the Society
12. Eliminate the husband as "head of the family" from its continuing presence in the law, in religion, in administrative procedure, and as a taken-for-granted aspect of family life.
13. Eliminate the pervasive system of sex-typed occupations in which "women's occupations" tend to be poorly paid, and the equally pervasive difference between the pay of men and women in the same occupation.
14. Reduce or eliminate the sex-typed pattern of family role responsibilities.
15. Establish or subsidize a comprehensive and high quality system of day-care centers for pre-school children.
16. Full sexual equality is essential for prevention of wifebeating.
17. As the society eliminates fixed sex-roles, alternative sources of stability and security in self-definition will be needed.
18. Parent-child interaction, parental expectation, and all other aspects of socialization should not be differentiated according to the sex of the child.
19. Eliminate from the criminal justice system the implicit toleration of wifebeating which comes about through statutory and common law; the attitudes of the police, prosecutors, and judges; and through cumbersome and ineffective procedures which make even the available legal remedies and protection ineffective.

Factor VI. Frustrations Built into the Economic System
20. Full employment for all men and women in the labor force at wage levels consistent with the standards of the society, and a guaranteed income for those unable to work.
21. Reduce the extent to which society evaluates people on the basis of their economic achievements and the occupational and economic conceptions which this entails.

Although the primary focus of the chapter was on policies which will *prevent* wifebeating, the desperate immediate situation of millions of wives must also be addressed. Consequently, that last third of the article was devoted to steps which can be taken by individual wives who are married to assaultive husbands, and to steps which can be taken by feminist and community groups, and by the police and human service agencies, to cope with the immediate problem. These are summarized in Table 2. The prevention steps in Table 1, together with the treatment steps in Table 2, form the basis on which we can

TABLE 2.   SUMMARY OF ACTIONS WHICH CAN BE TAKEN TO DEAL WITH SPECIFIC CASES OF WIFEBEATING.

I. What a Battered Wife Can Do

1. Get help
2. Cancel the hitting license
3. Be prepared to leave
4. Get a job
5. Don't wait
6. Problem-focused assertiveness
7. Leave or take legal action

II. What Other Persons and Groups Can Do

1. Task force on wife abuse
2. Hot lines and support groups
3. Safe houses
4. Legal aid
5. Public assistance
6. The police and wifebeating
7. Therapeutic intervention

hope for the eventual elimination of the socially patterned aspects of intrafamily violence which is known as wifebeating.

Changing a phenomenon as deeply embedded in the social system as wifebeating is a vast undertaking. So many things are needed that one almost does not know where to start. In fact, a realistic approach recognizes that there is no one place to start. Rather, a broad public awareness and commitment to change is necessary so that individuals and groups in all spheres of life can attend to changes in each of these spheres. For example, change in the legal and law enforcement systems will not by themselves end wifebeating. But the police, lawyers, judges, and legislators can act to remove some of the many barriers which now prevent women from receiving legal protection from beatings. Thus, in most states, unless the assailant uses a weapon, the police cannot make an arrest, even if the wife is obviously injured and the husband makes no attempt to deny her charges. (She can, however, make a "citizen's arrest" and insist that the police help her—provided she has sufficient presence of mind, self confidence, and determination, and some place to hide when the husband is released from jail an hour or two later!) The law concerning the evidence needed to make an arrest for wifebeating can be changed, just as laws regarding the evidence needed for a rape conviction have recently changed. Similarly, the fact that putting a husband in jail deprives the wife of her means of support is often pointed out to women, and is one reason so few severely beaten wives press charges. But this need not be the case in those states where a prisoner can be released for employment during working hours, and in other states such laws could be enacted—if society is truly determined to end wifebeating.

REFERENCES

1. Adorno, T. W., Frenkel-Brunswik, E., Levinson, D. J., and Sanford, N., *The Authoritarian Personality*. New York: Harper & Row, 1950.
2. Allen, Craig M. and Straus, Murray A., "Resources, Power, and Husband-Wife Violence." Paper presented at the National Council on Family Relations 1975 Annual Meeting.
3. Archer, Dane, "Violent Acts and Violent Times: A Comparative Approach to Postwar Homicide Rates," *American Sociological Review* (1976).
4. AWAIC, Inc., *Information Packet*. New York: Abused Womens Aid In Crisis, 1976.
5. Bach, George R. and Wyden, Peter, *The Intimate Enemy*. New York: Morrow, 1968.
6. Bachman, Jerald G., *Youth in Transition*. Ann Arbor, Mich.: Institute for Social Research, University of Michigan, 1967.
7. Bard, Morton, "The Study and Modification of Intra-Familial Violence," pp. 154–164 in Jerome L. Singer (ed.), *The Control of Aggression and Violence*. New York: Academic Press, 1971. Reprinted in Steinmetz and Straus, 1974.[68]
8. Bard, Morton et al., *The Function of the Police in Crisis Intervention and Conflict Management: A Training Guide*. Washington, D.C.: U.S. Department of Justice, 1975.
9. Bard, Morton and Zacker, Joseph, "How Police Handle Explosive Squabbles: New Techniques Let Police Settle Arguments Without Force," *Psychology Today* 10: 71–74 + 113 (November 1976).
10. Bart, Pauline B., "Rape Doesn't End With a Kiss," *Viva:* 39–42 and 100–102 (June 1975).
11. Berkowitz, Leonard, "The Case for Bottling Up Rage," *Psychology Today* 7: 24–31 (July 1973).
12. Blechman, Elaine A., Olson, David H. L., and Hellman, I. D., "Stimulus Control Over Family Problem-Solving Behavior," *Behavior Therapy* (1976).
13. Blechman, Elaine A., Olson, David H. L., Schornagel, C. Y., Halsdord, M. J., and Turner, A. J., "The Family Contract Game: Technique and Case Study," *Journal of Consulting and Clinical Psychology* 44: 449–455 (1976).
14. Blumenthal, Monica, Kahn, Robert L., Andrews, Frank M., and Head, Kendra B., *Justifying Violence: The Attitudes of American Men*. Ann Arbor, Mich.: Institute for Social Research, 1972.
15. Blumenthal, Monica D., Chadiha, Letha B., Cole, Gerald A., and Jayaratine, Toby Epstein, *More About Justifying Violence: Methodological Studies of*

Attitudes and Behavior. Ann Arbor, Mich.: Institute for Social Research, The University of Michigan, 1975.

16. Brownmiller, Susan, *Against Our Will.* New York: Simon and Schuster, 1975.
17. Burgess, Ann W. and Holmstrom, Lynda Lytle, *Rape: Victims of Crisis.* Bowie, Md.: Robert J. Brady, 1974.
18. Caldwell Brown, Catherine, "It Changed My Life: A Consumer's Guide to the Four Major Parent-Training Programs," *Psychology Today* **10**: 47–57 + 108 (November 1976).
19. Chesler, Phyllis, *Women and Madness,* First Edition. Garden City, N.Y.: Doubleday, 1972.
20. Clasen, Carole, "Halt Assault NOW: A Guide for Assaulted Women." Ann Arbor, Mich.: Ann Arbor'Wastenaw County National Organization for Women (NOW), 1976.
21. Coser, Lewis A., *The Functions of Social Conflict.* New York: The Free Press, 1956.
22. Dahrendorf, Ralf, *Class and Class Conflict in Industrial Society.* London: Routledge & Kegan Paul, 1959.
23. Davis, Alan J., "Sexual Assaults in the Philadelphia Prison System," in John H. Gagnon and William Simon (eds.), *The Sexual Scene.* Chicago: Aldine, 1970.
24. Etzioni, Amitai, "Violence," chapter 14 in Robert K. Merton and Robert A Nisbet (eds.), *Contemporary Social Problems,* Third Edition. New York: Harcourt Brace Jovanovich, 1971.
25. Field, Martha H. and Field, Henry F., "Marital Violence and the Criminal Process: Neither Justice Nor Peace," *Social Science Review* **47** (2): 221–240 (1973).
26. Flynn, John, *Spouse Assault: Its Dimensions and Characteristics in Kalamazoo County, Mich.* Kalamazoo, Mich.: Field Studies in Research and Practice, Western Michigan University, 1975.
27. Fojtik, Kathleen M., "Wife Beating: How to Develop a Wife Assault Task Force and Project." Ann Arbor, Mich.: Ann Arbor-Washtenaw County NOW Wife Assault Task Force, 1976.
28. Fromm, Erich, *Escape from Freedom.* New York: Holt, Rinehart and Winston, 1941.
29. Gagnon, John and Simon, William, *Sexual Conduct: The Social Sources of Human Sexuality.* Chicago: Aldine, 1973.
30. Gayford, J. J., "Wife Battering: A Preliminary Survey of 100 Cases," *British Medical Journal* (January 25, 1975).
31. Gelles, Richard J., *The Violent Home: A Study of Physical Aggression Between Husbands and Wives.* Beverly Hills, California: Sage Publications, 1974.
32. Gelles, Richard J., "Abused Wives: Why Do They Stay." *Journal of Marriage and the Family* **38**: 659–668 (November 1976).
33. Gelles, Richard J., and Straus, Murray A., "Determinants of Violence in the Family: Toward a Theoretical Integration." Chapter to appear in Wesley R. Burr, Reuben Hill, F. Ivan Nye, and Ira L. Reiss (eds.), *Contemporary Theories About the Family.* New York: The Free Press, 1977.
34. Gerbner, George and Gross, Larry, "The Scary World of TV's Heavy Viewer," *Psychology Today* **9**: 41–49 + 89 (April 1976).

35. Goode, William J., "Force and Violence in the Family," *Journal of Marriage and the Family* **33:** 624–636 (November 1971). Reprinted in Steinmetz and Straus, 1974.
36. Gordon, T., *A New Model for Humanizing Families and Schools.* Pasadena, Calif.: Effectiveness Training Associates, 1971.
37. Henry, Jules, *Culture Against Man.* New York: Random House, 1963.
38. Hokanson, J. E., "Psychophysiological Evaluation of the Catharsis Hypothesis," in E. I. Megargee and J. E. Hokanson (eds.), *The Dynamics of Aggression.* New York: Harper & Row, 1970.
39. Horner, Matina S., "Toward an Understanding of Achievement-Related Conflicts in Women," *Journal of Social Issues* **28:** 157–175 (1972).
40. Howard, Jane, *Please Touch: A Guided Tour of the Human Potential Movement.* New York: Dell Publishing, 1970.
41. Huggins, Martha D. and Straus, Murray A., "Violence and the Social Structure as Reflected in Children's Books from 1850 to 1970." Paper read at the 1975 Annual Meeting of the Eastern Sociological Society.
42. Jacobson, Neil S. and Martin, Barclay, "Behavioral Marriage Therapy: Current Status," *Psychological Buletin* **83:** 540–556 (July 1976).
43. Kaplan, Howard B., *Self Attitudes and Deviant Behavior.* Pacific Palisades, Calif.: Goodyear, 1975.
44. Koch, Joanne and Koch, Lew, "The Urgent Drive to Make Good Marriages Better," *Psychology Today* **10:** 33–35 (September 1976).
45. Kolb, Trudy M., and Straus, Murray A., "Marital Power and Marital Happiness in Relation to Problem Solving Ability," *Journal of Marriage and the Family* **36:** 756–766 (November 1974).
46. LaRossa, Ralph, *Marriage Close Up: A Study of Couples Expecting Their First Child*, unpublished doctoral dissertation. University of New Hampshire, 1975.
47. Lefkowitz, Monroe M., Walder, Leopold O., Housemann, Rowell, and Eron, Leonard D., "Parental Punishment: A Longitudinal Analysis of Effects." Paper read at the International Society for Research on Aggression conference, Paris, 1976.
48. Lewis, Robert A., "Socilization into National Violence: Familial Correlates of Hawkish Attitudes Toward War," *Journal of Marriage and the Family* **33:** 699–708 (November 1971). Reprinted in Steinmetz and Straus (eds.), *Violence in the Family*, 1974.
49. Mace, David and Mace, Vera, *We Can Have Better Marriages—If We Really Want Them.* Nashville, Tenn.: Abingdon Press, 1974.
50. Martin, Del, *Battered Wives of America.* San Francisco: Glide, 1976.
51. Maurer, Adah, "Corporal Punishment," *American Psychologist* **29:** 614–626 (August 1974).
52. Mercurio, Joe, *Caning: Educational Rite and Tradition.* Syracuse: Syracuse University Press, 1972.
53. Minnesota Family Study Center, *A Program For Training Family Impact Analysis.* Minneapolis: University of Minnesota (mimeographed), 1976.
54. Morgan, Marabell, *The Total Woman.* Old Tappan, N.J.: Fleming H. Revell, 1973.
55. O'Brien, John E., "Violence in Divorce Prone Families," *Journal of Marriage*

and the Family **33**: 692–698 (November 1971). Reprinted in Steinmetz and Straus, 1974.

56. O'Dell, Stan, "Training Parents in Behavior Modification: A Review," *Psychological Bulletin* **81**: 418–433 (July 1974).

57. Olson, David H. L. (ed.), *Treating Relationships*. Lake Mills, Iowa: Graphic, 1976.

58. Parade Magazine, "A Special Rope Poll of Women's Rights," *Boston Sunday Globe:* **4** (September 26, 1971).

59. Parsons, Talcott, "Certain Primary Sources and Patterns of Aggression in the Social Structure of the Western World," 1947, pp. 298–322, *Essays in Sociological Theory, Revised Edition*. New York: The Free Press, 1966.

60. Patterson, Gerald R., *Families: Applications of Social Learning to Family Life*. Revised Edition. Eugene, Oregon: Castalia, 1975.

61. Patterson, Gerald R., Reid, J. B., Jones, R. R., and Conger, R. E., *A Social Learning Approach to Family Intervention*. **I:** *Families with Aggressive Children*. Eugene, Oregon: Castalia, 1975.

62. Prescott, James W., "Body Pleasure and the Origins of Violence," *The Futurist:* 64–74 (April 1975).

63. Resnik, Mindy, *Wife Beating: Counselor Training Manual #1*. Ann Arbor: AA NOW/Wife Assault, 1976.

64. Rodman, Hyman, "Marital Power and the Theory of Resources in Cultural Context," *Journal of Comparative Family Studies* **3**: 50–70 (Spring 1972).

65. Saunders, Daniel G., "Marital Violence: Dimensions of the Problem and Modes of Intervention," *Journal of Marriage and Family Counseling* (1976).

66. Simmel, Georg, *Conflict and the Web of Group Affiliations*. Glencoe, Ill.: The Free Press, (1908) 1955.

67. Stark, Rodney and McEvoy, James III, "Middle Class Violence," *Psychology Today* **4**: 52–65 (November 1970).

68. Steinmetz, Suzanne K. and Straus, Murray A. (eds.), *Violence in the Family*. New York: Harper & Row (originally published by Dodd, Mead & Co.), 1974.

69. Straus, Murray A., "Some Social Antecedents of Physical Punishment: A Linkage Theory Interpretation," *Journal of Marriage and the Family* **33**: 658–663 (November 1971). Reprinted in Steinmetz and Straus, 1974.

70. Straus, Murray A., "Leveling, Civility, and Violence in the Family," *Journal of Marriage and the Family* **36**: 13–29 (February 1974) + Addendum: 441–445 (August 1974).

71. Straus, Murray, "Cultural and Social Organizational Influence on Violence Between Family Members," in Raymond Prince and Dorothy Barrier (eds.), *Configurations: Biological and Cultural Factors in Sexuality and Family Life*. Lexington, Mass.: Lexington Books—D. C. Heath, 1974.

72. Straus, Murray A., "Sexual Inequality, Cultural Norms, and Wife-Beating," *Victimology* **1** 54–76 (Spring 1976), also reprinted in Emilio C. Viano (ed.), *Victims and Society*. Washington, D.C.: Visage Press, 1976, and in Jane Roberts Chapman and Margaret Gates (eds.), *Women Into Wives: The Legal and Economic Impact of Marriage*, *Sage Yearbooks in Women Policy Studies* **2.** Beverly Hills, Cal.: Sage Publications, 1977.

73. Surgeon General's Scientific Advisory Committee on Television and Social Behavior, Report of the Surgeon General's Scientific Advisory Committee on Television and Social Behavior. Washington, D.C.: U.S. Government Printing Office, 1972.
74. Zagaria, Pam, "Battered Women: The Hitten Problem!" A report of the Board of Directors of the Community Planning Organization, Inc., submitted by the Battered Woman Study Committee, Carol C. Ryan, Chairperson, St. Paul, Minn.: Community Planning Organization, Inc., 1976.

MEDIATION AND THE COMMUNITY DISPUTE CENTER

Fred Dellapa, Director of the American Bar Association's Special Committee on Resolution of Minor Disputes; Member of the Executive Board of the Dade County Task Force on Battered Women

Ms. X had taken the last beating she was going to from her husband. This time she was going to do something about the abuse; after all, there are police, prosecutors, and courts, and they are there to help people with problems like these. Still aching from the beating, she dials the police and reports the attack. A squad car is dispatched to the household. The police officers note that Ms. X has visible, recently administered contusions and abrasions; they listen passively to her accusations. She tells them that her husband has done this to her, as he has so many times before. "Where is your husband now?" the police ask, almost indifferently. Not really knowing, Ms. X states that he stormed out in a rage and could return at any moment. The police are not going to wait for a suspected misdemeanant to return home, and even if they did, there would be little they could do. In most states, the law of arrest is such that a police officer can not arrest, without warrant, a misdemeanant unless the crime was commited in the officer's presence. In smaller communities, a police officer or a private citizen may get a misdemeanor arrest warrant with relative ease, but in larger, urban areas, such a legal writ is an oddity. The bulk of the urban misdemeanors are handled by citation into court, and a misdemeanor arrest warrant is rarely, if ever, granted.

The police complete their report, ask if Ms. X feels like going to a hospital, and then advise her to report the incident to the Prosecuting Attorney, where an Assault and Battery case may be filed. The next day, Ms. X goes to the Prosecutor's office to attempt to file her charge. It is at this point that the hard realities of the Criminal Justice system begin to unfold. Contrary to widely held belief, a citizen does not have the right to have a criminal charge entertained in court. The prosecutorial right is vested solely in the State, and the bringing forward of the State's criminal charges is at the discretion of the State's Prosecuting Attorney. In the United States, most prosecutors will endeavor to decline the prosecution of domestic misdemeanors for a number of (what they consider) valid reasons. One such reason, generally the most valid, is that the majority of female assault and/or battery victims will voluntarily withdraw the charge somewhere between filing and trial or just not show up in court on the docket day. The prosecutors do not really look into the reasons for such dismissals and, again, even if they did, there would be little they could do about it. To prevail in a criminal prosecution, one must have evidence, and most evidence is solely in the appearance, demeanor, and testimony of the misdemeanant's victim; ergo—no chief complaining witness, no case. A pragmatic prosecutor knows that criminal court dockets are hopelessly jammed and backlogged, and that adding to the morass creates more delays and wastes more taxpayer dollars. In addition, criminal judges tend to dismiss domestic complaints, feeling that such difficulties do not belong in criminal court, but should be before a civil divorce court or a family counselor. This attitude is a good one, in that a criminal judge's duty is to adjudicate criminal innocence or guilt and punish if appropriate. The reader must remember that there is not very much latitude to the traditional criminal justice system, its sole purpose being to determine if a crime has been committed and, if so, then a punishment, in way of fine or imprisonment, is meted out. From Ms. X's perspective, there seems to be an illogic to frustrating her attempts to prosecute; after all, her husband beat her and now he is apparently getting away with it.

People are generally outraged at acts of violence, especially when they are the victims, and rightfully feel that a criminal act has been perpetrated. However, the issue really turns on the remedy and relief available and the criminal courts ability to effectively deliver same; much emphasis must be placed on the phrase "*effectively* deliver same." In the case of severe, grossly injurious, felonious assault, the criminal courts can, and generally will, levy a severe penalty on the offender; but most domestic, primary and neighborhood assaults, although wrongful, never attain the felony level. Rather, such assaults are in the misdemeanor crime category, and the truth is that traditional criminal justice system methodology can not effectively remedy these problems on a long-term basis. Consider: Ms. X and her husband, 90 days after the assault, finally arrive at trial. The prosecution proves the case and the defendant husband is found guilty of the wrongdoing. The court must do something in way of punishment, but what can it do that will not have an adverse affect; these parties have an ongoing relationship of mutual dependence— they live together. If the judge heavily fines or imposes a stiff jail sentence, he may very well be causing a hardship on the entire family unit. If he gives a soft sentence, the offender may feel he got away with it and can very well get away with it again. The suspended sentence with a period of time to prove good behavior is a rational alternative; but in some states, this form of misdemeanor probation is not allowed, as the staggering costs of parole and probation make it impossible to effectively administer. Hence, the judge finds himself between the proverbial rock and the hard place. Even if he does punish, there is no real surety that the remedy will be successful in preventing further violence. In fact, as likely as not, the parties will be there again, and probably on a more serious charge.

Criminal justice, as it is operating today, is punitive, not preventative, and a great grey area of ineffectiveness is slowly becoming apparent in the ways of handling "small crimes." The conclusion that misdemeanor crime, if not effectively dealt with, results eventually in felony crime is inescapable, and the criminal justice system must accept the responsibility. The criminal courts treat only the results of adverse behavior, and rarely, if ever, attempt to treat the causes of the behavior. The typical misdemeanor case goes to court and, if a finding of guilt is made, the offender is fined or jailed and the parties are then returned to exactly the same position they were in before. The two areas where this is just not the effective remedy are primary relationship and neighborhood altercations. The simple fact is that the complainant and defendant either live together or are in close proximity to each other, and the probability that the dispute will flare up again is virtually assured unless the real underlying causes of the conflict are dealt with on a rational, adult level.

Stepping into the breach, in an attempt to remedy such difficulties, is the concept of dispute settlement mediation; new by today's standards, but really as old as humanity itself. In such cities as Miami-

Dade County, Florida; Rochester and New York, New York; Columbus, Ohio; Kansas City; Philadelphia; and others, a new alternative to criminal prosecution is functioning—and with marked success. The alternative is the Citizen Dispute Settlement Center (as it is called in Miami), which offers a service that is unique in the world of Criminal Justice.

Under the auspices of the Chief Judge and the Administrative Office of the Eleventh Judicial Circuit of Florida, Metropolitan Dade County (Miami, Florida) began an ambitious criminal justice program that had five objectives:

1. To provide a forum where the citizens of Dade County could find a meaningful and longlasting solution to interpersonal conflicts, that would be short of formal judicial proceedings;
2. To provide a system that would effectively divert complaints of a minor nature evolving principally in the areas of primary relationship and neighborhood altercations;
3. To rapidly and fairly dispense justice to the citizens of Dade County who become involved in minor criminal conduct;
4. To ease the burden of the Eleventh Judicial Circuit's Criminal Division, by reducing the number of minor criminal cases causing a backlog in the system; and
5. To ease interpersonal and community tensions, by helping the parties involved arrive at an equitable, reasonable, and just solution to their problems, wihout resorting to a costly, time consuming, and usually counterproductive criminal remedy.

On May 1, 1975, a $55,000 federal Law Enforcement Assistance Administration (LEAA) grant was awarded to Metro-Dade County for a six month pilot project, and the Miami Citizen Dispute Settlement Center was born.* To date, the progress made toward accomplishing the goals of the Miami program have been astounding, far exceeding the court's expectations. In the first six months of operations, the Metro-Dade County Citizen Dispute Settlement Center (CDSC) handled 2,063 cases and successfully resolved 94.9% of them.

---

*This is not to infer that Miami gave birth to the concept, for it did not. The original CDS program was founded in Rochester, New York, under the auspices of the American Arbitration Association's National Center for Dispute Settlement, in late 1973. The Miami planners modified the concept, tied it to the judicial branch, and geared it to a major, multicultural, urban-metropolitan area.

Even more astonishing was the recidivist rate. Of 1,597 matters regarded as serious enough for formal prosecution, only 81 were not successfully deactivated by dispute settlement mediation, and therefore returned for the filing of criminal charges (54 matters) or reheard by the Center (27 matters). On top of that, CDSC cut the wait time, from date of complaint to hearing, from 94.3 days through the Criminal Court System to 7.2 days through the Citizen Dispute Settlement Center. Currently, the Miami CDSC absorbs an estimated 42% of the County Court Crimes Division's misdemeanor penal caseload, and CDS's cost per case is only $26.40 as compared to the Justice System's approximately $250.00 per case.* Simply stated, the Citizen Dispute Settlement Center provides a staff of professionally skilled and trained Mediators to listen to complaints, counter-complaints, and defenses in a totally informal, neutral setting. The mediator deals only with conflict between two parties who have some existing, ongoing relationship; the conflict which led to the filing of a minor criminal charge. The parties may be husband and wife, parent and child, employer and employee, homeowner and garbagecollector, neighbor and neighbor, lovers, roommates, partners, or just about any other combination of interpersonal relationships. The conflicts between the parties range from simple harassment to battery, but almost inevitably have their roots in some deep interpersonal conflict, dispute, or misunderstanding. It would appear that criminal punishment ought be adequate remedy for wrongdoing. However, how does one then explain the spiraling crime and recidivist rate. Even the most unsophisticated of minds can conceptualize that a small problem, unless promptly and effectively resolved, can escalate into a big problem with, perhaps, dire consequences. In the misdemeanor crime arena this is becoming more of a truism. As criminal justice becomes more sophisticated, the lesser crimes become more neglected. Perhaps the word "neglected" seems too harsh on an already staggering justice system, but it is fairly accurate. A visit to a small crime court is all that is necessary to prove the point. A harried and overworked judge presides over structured chaos in the misdemeanor courtroom. Every conceivable wrongdoing, dutifully codified into a criminal act, is before him: squabbling neighbors, fighting spouses, owners of indiscreet animals, revengeful complain-

---

Final Report, Project No. 74-AS-15-0036, Metro-Dade County, Citizen Dispute Settlement Program.

ants, and belligerent defendants. As a person, the judge might very well have some good solutions to some of the difficulties, but as a judge of the criminal bench, he is prohibited from using them. The constraints imposed by the rules of evidence and the requirements of due process may require dismissal of the specific charge. Criminal law mandates that only the incident at hand be dealt with and that indirect circumstances and causes may not be discussed at all. Further, the burden of proof in any criminal matter must be beyond a reasonable doubt in order to have a finding of guilty as charged. Yet the parties are still in front of the bench and clearly the dispute between them continues to simmer and remains unresolved. Forty-eight percent of the matters before the Dade County Court (Misdemeanor Court) were dismissed because of evidentiary or procedural flaws, but the Court's dismissal of the charge does not dismiss the problem. Even the Court's rendering of a penalty doesn't really prohibit a reoccurrence, if the basic difficulty is not in someway dealt with. All too often, the same parties are back again and again, as either complainants or defendants, until finally they settle the matter on their own terms, and that, oftentimes, necessitates a felony court.

To illustrate the workings of interpersonal conflict resolutions by mediation, let us follow the problem of Ms. X's Battery complaint through a jurisdiction that has a Citizen Dispute Settlement Center such as Dade County's. Upon arrival at the State Attorney's Office, Ms. X is preliminarily interviewed by a paralegal. Noting that the wrongful act is a misdemeanor that involves persons in a primary relationship, i.e., Male-Female relationship, regardless of legal status, the paralegal immediately refers the complainant to the Intake Counselors of the Center.* At the Center, Ms. X is talked to calmly and reassuredly by the Intake Counselor. She is not treated bureaucratically, as if she were a mere number, nor is she put through an embarrassing grilling. Rather, Ms. X is put at ease and gently supported to give the whole story. One female victim, quoted in the Miami Herald, said, "There were none of those terrible looks that say, 'What did you do to aggravate him?'"** Ms. X is informed of all her legal remedies, their benefits and shortcomings, and then told of the mediation process. Basically, she is advised that the hear-

---

*Over the last year, the Police Agencies of Dade County have begun to refer victims of such difficulties to the CDSC.
**Naunton, Eva, "Evelyn: A Battered Wife Tells Her Story," *Miami Herald, Living Today* section (February 20, 1976).

ing is a voluntary one, that although her husband will be sent a notice to appear, he is under no legal duress to appear, and that no legal sanctions will be levied. Ms. X is advised that no presumptions as to guilt are made and that her matter will be heard by a non-lawyer— a psychologist, sociologist, or other counseling specialist.

The sole objective of the mediation hearing is to resolve the conflict on a long lasting basis at a human, one to one, level. The mediator is there to do exactly the above and will remain absolutely neutral; the forum itself is non-adversary and neither party needs legal counsel, although there is no prohibition of counsel. If Ms. X accepts the Center's format, her potential criminal or civil legal remedies are in no way jeopardized nor are they enhanced, in case of failure of mediation.* She is further advised that every effort will be made to get her assailant to appear, and that in the overwhelming majority of instances, the assailants do appear. In short, Ms. X has absolutely nothing to lose and much to gain.

At this point, let it be made clear that such a forum is not to be looked upon as a therapeutic counseling session; the mediators do not have a goal of "kiss and make up, so everything will be better." The mediators will use a variety of techniques, but the only goal is to get the disputing parties to talk through their difficulty, to grasp reality, and to mutually understand and respect the other's feelings and position. Ms. X accepts the Center's process and her matter is docketed immediately, as she is still residing with her spouse. The matter of *Ms. X* v. *Mr. X* is set for an 8.15 P.M. hearing at the Courthouse, three calendar days from the date of complaint.

The appointed day arrives and the parties appear at the Courthouse for their hearing. After being ushered into a chamber, jury room, or courtroom (if a courtroom, the bench is not used), the parties are introduced to the mediator, who once again explains, in detail, what is to occur. If either party feels reluctant or insecure, the mediator patiently reassures and positively reinforces with a calming demeanor. It is here that the real work of dispute settlement mediation begins and ends. Three persons, two in conflict and one unknown to both, totally neutral and advised only as to the basics of the complaint, sit down and begin to talk things through. Procedurely, the offended party speaks first, giving her version of the incident or incidents and the truth as she sees it. The offender is told that interruption is not permitted and that he will get his chance to discuss the problem from

*All Dade CDSC hearings are privileged and confidential and not of record.

his perspective and also without interruptions. Unhampered by the constraints of time rules of procedure or evidence, the mediator can hear all the issues and pinpoint the real underlying causes of the dispute so as to better facilitate an agreement.

Dealing with people in this setting is a challenge that the legal system rarely, if ever, attempts. The whole objective of litigation is to narrow issues down to a manageable concept and resolve it under theories of law. Unfortunately, the representatives of the law fail to inform people that when they have an interpersonal conflict, they must be able to confine it to a single premise or causal motive. As humans, we know that this is just not possible. The human psyche is wide-ranging and complex; the simple act of striking another person has many roots, conscious, unconscious, sexist, ego-related, etc. This is not to say that a mediator can deal with all of them successfully, but such an individual is in a much better position to sort them out than the court is. A judge may very well have his own feelings about a situation before him, and eventually may even reach a verdict based on those feelings, but he is generally not permitted the luxury of exploring the underlying causes. Restricted to the rules, of which there are many, the judge can only deal with the question of: did you or did you not strike the person wrongfully?

The mediator, on the other hand, can listen and observe the individual and react accordingly. Suppose Mr. X is an insecure male who must constantly prove his superiority to females for his own conscious or unconscious reasons. How is a judge to elicit that type of information, unless he is particularly observant and astute? A judge, prosecutor, or defense attorney cannot ask "Do you feel some form of gratification when you strike a woman?" as it is in no way germain to the issue of *did he strike her*. The mediator, skilled in understanding people, could sense such feelings and then query about them. If Mr. X responded that he feels better after a violent argument with his spouse, especially when he prevails, the mediator could seize on this admission and lead the discussion to it. The parties can mutually discuss the problem and actively work towards a solution if they can easily get there. In the formal court proceeding, getting there is an obstacle in itself.

Surprisingly, most persons in mediation sessions are not at all reluctant to bare their souls, as it were, as long as they are reassured that nothing adverse is going to happen. It may be based on the individuals overwhelming compulsion to justify his or her action or the exhilaration of having someone's ear, but regardless, people can and will discuss their motivations if just given the opportunity. Once the discussion starts openly and frankly, a solution can generally be reached. The mediator, after hearing both versions of the incident then begins to search for the resolution. Turning to the offended, the query is posed: "How would you like to see this resolved?" and the same, in time, is posed to the offender. The number of times that both parties almost immediately become sensitized to the others viewpoint is astounding; many of their responses are made in consideration of the other's viewpoint. Of course, this does not occur in every situation, but it does with a gratifying frequency; enough so that it tends to rekindle one's belief in the rationality of human beings. However, if a solution is not forthcoming from the parties, the mediator is prepared to begin probing for a solution. Suggestions, formats, and ways of conducting oneself are all presented. The parties are urged to give a little to gain a little, they are shown that compromise is the child of understanding and mutual respect. In some instances, the mediator will lay out a detailed agreement and request that the parties sign it and try to live by it for a few weeks, reporting back to the Center on the effectiveness or ineffectiveness. Together, the parties develop their own, personal accord with the guidance, not dictates, of the mediator.

After the parties have voiced their positions and discussed them with each other and the mediator, it then remains to commit them to an agreement. Generally, the mediator writes down the agreed-upon points and has each party sign it in the hearing room. The next day, both parties are sent copies of the agreement and told that the original will remain in the Center's files. If a violation of the agreement occurs, the persons are instructed to notify the Center. Such violations do occur and depending upon the severity—a minor breach as opposed to a vicious physical assault—the Center has many options available. It can return the whole to the prosecutor, rehear it, or refer to another court or social agency. The Dade County experience has been that most violations are minor ones and a rehearing is the general remedy. Both parties seem willing to return for a rehearing, and generally a second mediation is quite effective. In some instances, however, sterner measures are mandated and the Center has no qualms about sending an unresolved matter to the proper authorities. Another unique service is the social referral aspect of the Center. As stated earlier, the mediation session is designed to solve an immediate problem, not be a therapeutic counseling session; hence some parties are referred to various mental health, drug and alcoholic addiction, vocational rehabilitation, and other helping agencies, both public and private. This facet of the operation places many persons in the hands of people who can help them over the long haul. The number of persons who get the assistance they need, but may never have received through the justice system, is a story in itself. Citizens Dispute Settlement as an alternative to criminal or civil justice proceedings is a growing concept. Why? Because it works! Perhaps the experience of a Dade County CDSC participant, a battered female, can reemphasize the potential of mediation as a problem-solver:

> . . . she is satisfied. Since last fall, although she has seen her ex-husband on the street—he lives in the neighborhood—he has not troubled her.
>
> "This has certainly proved to me my own sense of worth," she said. "I won't be intimidated. I can look anyone in the eye." As for her ex-husband, she said the mediation hearing "put him on his honor." Dispute Settlement Program representatives gently offered him help with his drinking problem but did not press the offer, which Evelyn does not think he will take.
>
> As for his written promise not to trouble her, she said, "They did not rob him of his dignity. They gave him the option to stand on his word. They left him his pride."
>
> She wept as she said it . . .*

This writing is not intended to be a treatise on techniques of mediation, nor is its purpose to proclaim mediation as the magic panacea for all that ails us. Rather, it is to show that there exist other ways to assist persons in conflict, ways that do not necessarily have to be punitive. It is submitted that a 94.9% successful resolution for the Dade County Citizen Dispute Settlement Center speaks for itself, especially when the recidivist rate is 4.1%. It remains to be seen whether the first full year of operation will reach the same level, but preliminary indicators are that it will. Florida was so enthralled by the results of the pilot CDSC project that the director was summoned to Talla-

---

*Naunton, "Evelyn: A Battered Wife Tells Her Story."

hassee to draft legislation to begin state-wide implementation. There are many ways to approach the problems of our society and legal system; dispute settlement mediation is only one—there are others. People of vision, compassion, and insight must continually work to reshape our society; it is the only way to progress and to preserve this living, independent freedom that we as a people have created.

YO YO CHILDREN: A STUDY OF 23 VIOLENT MATRIMONIAL CASES
NSPCC School of Social Work, London, England

Foreword

It is unfortunately the case that there are innumerable ways in which parents can and do abuse and neglect their children. One of the saddest and most dangerous situations in which this occurs is found in families in which there is serious matrimonial discord accompanied by quarrelling and physical fighting.

All too little is known about this tragic problem, but recently the Training Department of the NSPCC carried out a pilot study into 23 cases of families which are battle grounds of this kind and which are known to the Society's Inspectors. They gave their study the title of the "Yo-Yo Syndrome."

To highlight some of the tragic aspects of life for children involved in this syndrome, it is clear that they move about a great deal from place to place and are regarded by their parents as pawns in the matrimonial conflict. This attitude may well be largely unconscious since as the authors of the study say "The parents' own problems are shouted out so loudly that they were not able to hear or see their children's difficulties."

These children are often removed from their homes and usually sent to live with a maternal grandmother, who plays an ambivalent role in the situation, since whilst she provides a haven of refuge for the children, she also often plays a considerable part in causing the matrimonial conflict.

While the children are away from home the parents usually separate for a time and the unfortunate children yo-yo or shuttlecock between them and are occassionally taken into care. In one of the families in the study, three children all under the age of five, had moved house not fewer than 12 times in seven months. Our researchers point out, with stark realism, that children such as these can never be sure of going to bed in the house in which they awoke in the morning.

Without the intervention of a social worker the risks of major physical and emotional damage to the children are great. In nine of the cases in this study, children had either been physically injured or threatened with assault. Others showed unmistakeable signs of damaging emotional stress.

Without the intervention of a social worker the risk is also high that these tragedies will prove to be self-perpetuating, since when these children grow up and have families of their own, they will tend to repeat the behaviour patterns of their parents unless the vicious circle is broken.

This yo-yo syndrome with all its potentiality for tragedy is doubtless far commoner than is currently realised. It calls for a major effort of research into its incidence and methods of treatment.

ARTHUR MORTON, Director, NSPCC

I. The Study

This is a pilot study of 23 Society cases, where violent matrimonial conflict is the outstanding feature, carried out by the NSPCC Training Department from September to December, 1973.

II. Reasons for Study

The Training Department is responsible for training Inspectors in the Society and for a comprehensive staff development programme and, in carrying out these tasks, has long been aware that these tragic cases where children are suffering as a result of violent matrimonial conflict form an intrinsic part of an Inspector's caseload. Little has been written about the effect on the children of this kind of acted-out matrimonial problem and the study was, therefore, undertaken to shed more light upon the problem so that Society workers and others in the helping professions could be trained more effectively to help the families concerned and particularly to understand more fully the needs of children in these situations and how their needs could best be met.

It is known that the NSPCC attracts referrals of cases where there is violence—either directly towards children or between parents—and it is possible that this is because both clients and informants have a particular expectation of the Society's workers—an expectation that the Inspectors will not be destroyed by the clients' negative and often violently acted-out feelings*. This has enabled the Society to build up a great deal of experience in dealing with families where violence is a feature. The Training Department is thus in a unique position to be able to study a cross-section of cases where there is violence between the parents and where the children are suffering as a result.

III. The Sample

The number of cases studied, 23, is small and yet striking patterns emerged. This was intended to be a pilot study in order to highlight the areas in which more research would be fruitful.

1. The Families Studied. The cases studied came from the North-East of England and the London area and its environs and are thought by the Inspectors to be typical of the cases of violent matrimonial conflict which are referred to them in the particular areas where they are working. There were 67 children and 45 parents in these 23 cases, the mean average of children per family being 2.91. The ages of the children at the time of the study range from 1 month to 17.33 years and the average age of the children is 6.33 years. The parents' ages range from 20 years to 47 years, the mean average being 29.25 years. The average age of the fathers concerned is 30.41 years and of the mothers 26.75 years. Of the 67 children, 32 are male and 35 are female.

2. Size of Family. These facts highlight some interesting points. Firstly, these are not large families—the average number of children is 2.91. The average age of the children is 6.33 years, so the violent matrimonial conflict would seem to erupt after the marriage has become established. This sample is thus able to highlight the effect of these situations on the schoolchild. It could be that such situations have been smouldering for a number of years before they begin to erupt, but it could not be said that they are caused by frequent childbirths as the size of the family is not over-

---

*"Supportive Casework in an Authoritative Setting" by Beryl Day (Case Conference, March 1965).

large. Furthermore, the average age of the parents is 29.25 years, therefore, these are not teenage parents, although they may well have married as teenagers.

3. Father's Occupation. The study included families where the father was unemployed (or had frequent periods of unemployment), families where the father was in regular work and, in one case, a father who owned his own business. The problem would not appear to be related to any particular race or creed.

4. Physical and Mental Illness. Physical illness as such did not play a large part, although one mother was diabetic, one father was epileptic and another had a facial deformity. In 9 of the 23 cases one or other parent was having treatment for a psychiatric condition (as an out-patient) usually by way of drugs, or took an overdose of drugs. In one of these cases the mother was taking tranquillizers and the father took an overdose of these.

5. Reasons for Referral. The reasons given for referral are as follows:—

Violence to parent or child	7
Matrimonial problem	2
Parent left home	6
Parent turned out of home	2
Neglect of children	2
Children out in rain	1
Children left alone	1
Material aid required	2
	23

6. Persons Referring. The cases were referred by:—

Parents	6
Statutory social work agency	4
Health Service	7
D.H.S.S.	2
Work colleague	1
Neighbor	1
Anonymous	2
	23

IV. Patterns Emerging

The main points to emerge from the study are:—
(a) the number of times the children were moved from place to place and the feeling of restlessness about these families;
(b) the active role played by the maternal grandmother;
(c) the fact that the parents studied were so caught up in their own unmet needs that the children have little chance of becoming anything but pawns while the battle is raging, however much an individual parent may feel for a child;
(d) the role played by real or fantasied extra-marital relationships;
(e) although money was mentioned in some of the records, it would not appear to be a significant factor in the marital conflict. Sex, both inside and outside the marriage, was an important factor. Some of the conflict also centred around food or the freedom to go out.

1. Restlessness. The most striking feature to emerge is that the children in the families studied seemed to spend the greater part of their lives on the move. They may start off in the family home, then one parent may take some of the children to a grandparent's home, the parents then may separate and the children go back and forth from father to mother and vice versa. Occasionally, the children may go into care, but the whole picture is one of restlessness and rootlessness, with the children being used as pawns—or as shuttlecocks sallying back and forth.

Frequently it is the wife who runs away, complaining of the husband's violence towards her and taking some of the children with her, or the father turns the wife and children out. It is interesting to note that not always are all the children taken. Some may be left with the father—it might be thought that this is something to do with the 'sharing out' of possessions, but what seems far more likely is that it is indicative of the mixed feelings of the partner who is leaving the matrimonial home. Perhaps they are leaving part of themselves behind in the shape of one or two children and this gives an entree for the partner to return. And return they probably will, for another point to emerge from the study is that leaving the home and returning to it is a pattern which is repeated over and over again.

'*The Yo-Yo Syndrome.*' The situation might be described as the 'Yo-Yo Syndrome'—children and one or both parents go back and forth as the yo-yo travels up and down the string. When the impetus seems to have left the situation and the yo-yo is lying still at the bottom of the string it is reactivated, or re-wound, either by intervention from grandparents or by one of the parents themselves and the yo-yo starts to travel up and down the string again. In one of the cases studied the maternal grandmother actually referred to the situation being like a yo-yo. The case was referred because the wife, who was pregnant, and her two children had been put out of their house by the husband and had gone to live with the wife's mother. This has happened previously. The Inspector records, "from the maternal grandmother's point of view it would seem that the couple go back and forward, out and in just like yo-yo's. . . . . they seem to be very unsettled".

The Violence in the Pattern. The pattern would seem to start with a breakdown in ability to discuss problems. This may never have been at a very developed level to start with, and it is highly likely that many of the families studied would have what Bernstein* describes as a "restricted code" of communication. Then the husband accuses the wife of provoking him, either by her extra-marital sexual relationships, or by an excessive dependence on her mother. Next the husband beats the wife and she runs away to her mother, taking one or more children with her, but frequently, as indicated earlier, leaving some children behind with the husband.

Usually, the Inspector hears about the conflict soon after the event, either from one of the partners or from an eye-witness. In one of the cases studied a witness described how the husband "grabbed his wife by the hair and punched her in the face". The children were then got out of the immediate vicinity and into a corner. The husband was then "trying to kick his wife, who was by now on the floor and screaming from the pain of having her hair pulled". In another case the Health Visitor told the Inspector how the husband had assaulted the wife. "Apparently he had come in drunk and had taken his fist to her and broken her nose and dislocated her jaw and scratched her face and bruised her in several places". Another example was of a husband frequently threatening his wife with a

---

*Basil Bernstein, "Social Class, Speech Systems and Psychotherapy", paper delivered to the British Association for the Advancement of Science, 1963.

Basil Bernstein, "A Socio-linguistic Approach to Social Learning" in 'Social Science Survey', Pelican, 1965 quoted by Jean Mursten in "Social Work, Social Class & Speech Systems", in 'Social Work', October, 1965.

knife. On one occasion the wife ran to the police station and brought the police back with her, and her husband had answered the door with a knife and a dog.

In a number of cases the evidence of violence was very severe. One husband kicked his wife in the stomach and caused a miscarriage. Later, after another miscarriage, he sprang on her from an outside toilet, severely bruising her jaw and neck and cutting her quite deeply. She left home and he carved up the furniture and slashed all the clothing in the wardrobe.

The Yo-Yo Re-activated. To come back to the pattern—after a few hours or a few weeks the wife returns and the pattern begins again. It is almost as if not enough satisfaction was gained from the first cycle of the pattern and so another attempt to gain satisfaction is made and in this way the repeated pattern can be seen as part of the couple's sexual interaction. Alternatively, so much satisfaction may have been gained in the actual carrying out of the pattern that none can be gained after it is completed and, therefore, the cycle is re-activated.

Movement of Children. The children in these families can never be sure they will go to sleep at night in the same house in which they awoke in the morning. One of the factors which makes these cases complicated for the Inspectors is that he can never be sure where to find the family and has to spend a great deal of time looking.

One such case was referred because the children were left for a weekend in the care of a boy not old enough to exercise adequate responsibility for them. During a period of seven months the three children, all under five years, were moved at least twelve times. The mother left home with the children for an unknown destination and returned the next day; the family then went to the maternal grandmother and later were rehoused. Father then left home for ten days and was followed by the mother and children, going to the grandmother's again twice, and returning each time to the family home. Mother then disappeared with two of the children—the third remaining with the father. Some days later the mother then took these two children to her mother. The third child later left the father and went to the grandmother. The father then took all the children home and the grandmother took one child back. The father thereupon put the other two children in care.

2. *Active role played by Maternal Grandmother.* One of the significant points to emerge was the important role played by the maternal grandmother. In 11 of these cases the maternal grandmother was very actively involved. (In one other case a maternal aunt played a similar role.) Frequently she was used as a refuge, with mother and children returning to grandmother for shelter. Not only did she provide a haven but also other forms of help—food, clothing, money and a sympathetic ear. It is perhaps indicative of the level of maturity, as well as the strength of the primary family bonds, that the mother should place herself in a dependency role upon her own mother as when she was a child.

Maternal grandmothers had a very useful role to play—often their daughters acted as if they had no one else to turn to, and indeed, this may well have been the case. However, the grandmother also seems to have played an active part in the matrimonial conflict, and perhaps this links to the grandmother's (often unconscious) anxieties about how she mothered her daughter. She has a need to keep her daughter dependent and the daughter plays into this by running away from husband and taking the children to the maternal grandmother. In other cases the maternal grandmother can be seen to add fuel to the conflict, particularly when the conflagration is at its hottest. For instance, in one case the grandmother attempted to encourage the twelve-year-old boy to enlarge on his father's faults to the Inspector. It was significant that in only 4 cases were the father's relatives involved.

3. *Pawns, not People.* It became evident in the course of this study that the children are often used by the parents as pawns in the matrimonial conflict and not as people with their own individual needs and rights, although the parents may not be aware they are doing this. Indeed, the parents' own problems shouted out so loudly that they were not able to hear or see their children's difficulties. For instance, one mother, in one mood, complained that her two-year-old son was 'difficult' and that the five year old provoked her, and left them at the Social Services Department, but later, in a different mood, was very reluctant to use a day nursery placement. It is, of course, very easy to be so concerned about the bruised eye of a battered wife that the damage to the children is obscured. The dramatic presentation of the parents' problems must not blind us to the needs of the children. Section V will look more closely at the needs of the children in these cases and the effect which such conflict has on them.

4. Real or Fantasied Extra-Marital Relationships. Real or fantasied extra-marital relationships seem to play a significant part in the conflict. In 11 cases extra-marital relationships were actually a feature. Furthermore, in the violent outbursts between husband and wife, the problem was often expressed in terms of unfaithfulness or sexual difficulties. It must be remembered, however, that while the problem may be expressed in these terms, real or fantasied extra-marital relationships, while certainly a contributory factor, were not the whole cause of the violent outbursts.

5. Money, Sex, Food and Freedom. In one case the mother complained after she had been turned out of the house, that the father spent his money on drink and gambling, and that he had assaulted her after a court appearance for the non-payment of a fine. On the whole, though, money did not figure very significantly as a cause of the marital conflict.

The most frequent cause of conflict mentioned was sex. Sometimes it was the sexual performance within the marriage that was the problem. One husband beat his wife because she would not let him make love to her on one occasion, while another woman complained that her husband made excessive demands. In yet another case the problem seems to have been the husband's impotence.

Sometimes the conflict centered around the provision of food and drink. In one case the mother offered a cup of tea to a visiting relative and not to the father, who then went out to buy his own food. The mother was not eager to warm this for him on his return and threw it to the floor. The father retaliated by holding his wife by the hair and hitting her on the arms, whereupon the mother went out and returned with the police but was not allowed in. She stayed away all week, leaving the father with the children.

In a few cases the conflict was about going out or coming in late. One man hit his wife because she came in late, having visited her sister, while another complained that his wife was always at her mother's and never had meals ready for him.

On a number of occasions the incident which triggered off the violence or row seems to have become irrelevant and is not mentioned. It is as if the violence is so much an accepted part of the pattern that it does not have to be explained or justified.

V. Effect on the Children

The effect on children in these restless, rootless situations can vary. Some may be resilient enough to cope. However, the effect on others is much more serious. When one considers the known effects of separation from parents or parent substitutes, it is small wonder that in the cases studied, where the pattern of frequent moves was coupled with violent behavior between parents, the children were variously described as being extremely nervous and jumpy, frightened and withdrawn and, not unnaturally, their school work was suffering. To the casual observer other children may not seem much affected, but their sufferings are frequently hidden because they try to keep out of the limelight.

In one case the father went to school and was allowed to see his daughter in the presence of the headmistress. He then waited until the mother met the child from school and tried to snatch her to try to force the mother to return. A fight developed in which the grandparents also became involved.

In another case an Inspector records that '*B*', *a boy of 11*, showed obvious signs of the strain that the break-up of his parent's marriage had had upon him. "He has always tended towards appearing very extrovert and this takes the form of talking for ages non-stop." '*C*', *a girl aged 12,* was too tired to go to school after a particularly stormy row between the parents. Later she was kept off school by the father to help when her mother left the home. '*D*', *a boy aged 10*, was terrified when he was left for hours on end on his own at night by his father, mother having left. He was particularly frightened of the hot water pipes when they banged at night. The Inspector described him as "quite a little bundle of nerves" and it was stated by him that the boy was "acting-out at school". '*E*', *aged 4*, took the strain physically. The Inspector states that he is "terrified of his step-father and his eczema always comes out when his mother and her 'husband' row— sure enough, this little child's face was covered!" '*F*', *a boy aged 10*, "will not go to sleep until his father comes in. This is often at two or three in the morning" probably for fear of what is going to happen between the parents. Another child, '*G*', *a boy of 1 year*, is described by the Inspector as "rocking back and forth, sitting banging his head on the arm of the chair, when given anything, he throws it back at the giver".

In 9 cases children were either physically hurt or threatened with violence, sometimes getting hurt in the cross-fire of parental blows. The parents were so overwhelmed by their own needs that they were unable to fully appreciate the needs of their children. Indeed, were it not for the social worker's intervention it would be likely that such children could be irreparably damaged emotionally or physically, or both, and it would also be extremely likely that the pattern could repeat itself when these children became adults and had their own families.

These yo-yo children are very dependent on skilled social work intervention. Frequently the yo-yo does not only rotate in its vertical path, but spins horizontally off course. It is often only at this juncture that the Inspector is called in. Sometimes he is able to contain the situation so that yo-yo and string remain together, but in some cases he decides a new string is needed, e.g. substitute care.

VI. Further Comments

It may well be that some husbands and wives need violence in their marital relationship in order for that relationship to continue. One woman told the Inspector that she was attracted to violent men—her husband had been violent and so was her cohabitee. Be that as it may, in a significant number of the cases studied the children were being damaged, either physically or emotionally, or both. The social worker may then be faced with the decision that if the marriage can only work when surrounded by violence and the children are being damaged by this violence, the children may have to be removed and placed in a stable environment, which could well be the grandparents' home, perhaps supported by the security of a Care Order. In the cases studied two involved court proceedings.

Although it is often felt than an emphasis on the immediate family and the cutting off of close ties with grandparents, uncles, cousins and aunts is not a helpful thing for the children, this view may need to be modified. The indications in the cases studied suggested that even relatives who are very well-meaning may not always be intervening in the most helpful manner. Nor is finding new accomodation always the answer. It would seem that if the wife does set up home with her children away from her husband, then sooner or later she may return to him, or set up a relationship with another man following the same pattern. It is interesting to note that despite housing shortage in the country as a whole, these wives were able to find alternative accommodation, either with relatives or from the local authority or housing associations.

VII. Implications for Treatment

Though it was not possible to draw from the study of 23 cases the significant implications for treatment, from the general experience of handling such cases within the Society, we feel that the following points are of importance as to the casework management of such situations.

Work with the Parents

1. Because of the parents' insecurity, which is so dramatically demonstrated both in the violence and in the restlessness, it is important for the worker to use a casework approach, which combines the skillful use of authority and an understanding caring, which can best be described as the sort of love and control used by a good parent.* On many occasions he will need to contain and hold the warring partners, using the sort of approach which works with quarrelling children, i.e. holding and calming at the same time and then staying with the situation long enough to help the participants to take a positive forward step. This sort of treatment would enable them to experience that their very destructive feelings are not, in fact, destroying the worker and eventually they may become less destructive.

2. So much fantasy is involved in these families that the worker

---

*Worker-Client Authority: Relationships in Social Work, Elliot Studt Published in Social Work New York, Vol. IV, No. 1, Jan. 1959.

The Use of Authority in Casework—A Personal View, Fred. W. Hill Marriage Guidance, March, 1973.

Authority in Social Casework, Foren & Bailey, Pergamon Press.

Authority & The Casework Relationship, Hershel A. Prins, Social Work, April, 1962.

Authority & Social Work, E. Spelman, Case Conference, December, 1954 must remain firm in the midst of the drama and focus clearly on the harsh realities of the here-and-now situation, particularly as it affects the children.

3. Because of the "restricted code" of communication mentioned earlier, often the more interpretative methods may not be helpful. There have to be practical demonstrations of caring and firmness that will enable the parents to use the social worker as an ego strengthener.

Anthony Storr* writes that maturity is characterized by the assertion and affirmation of the personality *without hostility*. Some marital partners, locked in combat, will need a social worker to provide them with opportunities to assert and affirm in a more mature way.

Work with the Children

As indicated in this report, it does seem important that social workers concerned in these cases should focus attention upon giving help and support to the parent or the substitute parent, who can give some stability to the child. This may mean giving casework support to, say, the grandmother, who takes on the responsibility for caring for the children and perhaps providing financial support. In other instances it may be necessary for the Social Services Departments to offer residential care, either by way of a statutory order or by voluntary agreement. In these circumstances it is of immense importance that any placement in residential care must be most carefully thought about so as not to put the child into situations where there is likelihood of there being a quick changeover of staff or, through lack of advance work, with foster parents who cannot cope with the likely demands and intervention of the parents.

The children in these circumstances are often in great need of direct casework help.** Caseworkers undertaking such work should be

---

*The Integrity of the Personality, Anthony Storr—Pelican.

**Helping Children Directly, Juliet Berry. British Journal of Social Work, Autumn 1971, Vol. 1, No. 3.

The Child as a Client of the Social Services, Joan Vann. British Journal of Social Work, Summer, 1971, Vol. 1, No. 2.

Communicating with Children, Longman Papers on Social Work, Edited by Eileen Holgate.

Casework with Young Children, Joan Brown, Case Conference, March, 1965.

Children as Scapegoats, Pauline Shapiro, New Society, 30th September, 1965.

prepared to share and ventilate with children their deep feelings of anger, anxiety and depression. Such sharing may make the worker experience acute discomfort as repressed feelings and fantasies from their own childhood, thought long forgotten, are resurrected. Feelings of inadequacy may become overwhelming as the worker realises that children of tender years may have to be helped to face up to situations of momentous proportions, but only if such sensitive and on-going work is attempted directly with the child and real communication established can children caught in these problems be helped.

For children involved in these situations the social worker is often the only stable figure, and in order to be an anchor in the lives of these who are, perhaps, constantly on the move it will demand considerable commitment on behalf of the social worker concerned to keep the case and continue to work with the family, even though they may cross geographical boundaries.

Dr. A. J. Dalzell-Ward MRCS, LRCP, DPH, FFCM, Chief Medical Officer of The Health Education Council comments: Information thus obtained can be used for educational activities aimed at long-term reduction of this problem. Violence is a symptom of an immature personality and the marital situation, virtually isolated from legal and social sanctions (until a disaster occurs), contains stresses which are introduced to those whose personality is under-developed. Frequently, too, the marriage partners have in common an upbringing by immature, violent parents and this is the only model of behavior known to them.

Prevention must be through health education in human relations, handling anxiety effectively, and acquiring realistic expectations of marriage and, particularly, finding a "code of communication". This education should particularly start at puberty when sexual instincts and aspirations have reached consciousness after the usual period of latency. Such education should be reinforced during adult life and the new interest in parent education, concentrating on the psychodynamics of family life, offers a promise of facilities which as yet are limited to one or two areas in the U.K.

Active learning methods such as role-playing, group discussion and the use of thematic films or videotaped incidents are practised by health educators and are available for application to parent education. The findings of this pilot study suggest that grandmothers should also be included in parent education schemes.

Acknowledgments

The research and preparation for this report was undertaken by the whole of the NSPCC Training Department team and I would like to thank the following members of the Training Department:— Miss B. M. Day, E. P. Lee, Mrs. M. J. Ryan, B.A. (Hons.), Miss M. V. Waldron, B.A. (Hons.), R. Fenton, B.A. (Psychology), J. G. Farncombe, K. G. Gray, P. G. Wetherly, Miss S. E. Stevens, Miss S. Brown, B.A., Miss C. M. Palmer, Miss J. N. Boston, Miss D. C. Lavender.

I would also like to acknowledge the generosity of H. G. S. Harris, Miss B. Evans, Mrs. P. G. Wetherly and J. W. Hall & Co. (Ashford, Kent) Ltd., plus many other friends in contributing towards the cost of the publication of the report.

Jean G. Moore
Senior Tutor in Charge of Training

BATTERED WOMEN; BATTERED CHILDREN

Margaret Varma, Ph.D., Education Director, Cardinal Spellman Headstart and Graduate Programs Faculty of the Bank Street College of Education, New York.

Child abuse and wife abuse are serious social problems which have plagued man in one form or another since time immemorial. They prevail at all levels of society, running through all segments of the human race. Cases of severe abuse, as demonstrated by the study in the preceding article of this book, are found to be most rampant in families where there are serious marital problems resulting in quarrels, physical fights, and the battering of women and children. Fortunately, however, today there is a new and growing concern about child abuse and its correlation to wifebeating, and a greater interest in restoring to every child his rights as a child, and to every woman her rights as an adult.

Violence is not an isolated phenomenon; it feeds on itself. A climate of violence and physical abuse in a home permeates the relationships of all individuals involved. It is not possible to talk of child abuse without discovering a history of abuse in the families from which the abusing parents have come. A man who beats his child has been beaten as a child; a woman who beats her child has never learned to be a mother, and has, at the least, been neglected by her parents to the point that she takes out her frustration and anger on her defenseless progeny. And, of course, a man who beats or abuses his wife will do the same to his children. A wife who is abused will often turn to her child to express the rage that has been heaped upon her by a brutal spouse.

That it is a vicious circle, that violence begets violence, is supported by data. It has been found to be statistically true that most adults who abuse their children today had not only themselves been battered by their fathers, but had also witnessed their siblings and mothers being battered. From research material available, it seems clear that children who witness violence in their own families—children who are helpless spectators to physical and verbal violence between their parents—end up being abusive adults. Hence, statements made by researchers of child abuse and wife abuse, indicating that violence is a self-perpetuating phenomenon, seem to be true.

The disposition to use violence is considered to be a learned behavior, and therefore, the greater a child's exposure to violent experiences (such as witnessing the mother being beaten by the father) the greater will be his tendency to use violence as a means of social control later on in life.[20] Research on imitative and modeling behavior points out that children generally imitate the behavior of aggressive models,[2] and especially of the significant others in their lives.[23] This is another reason why observation of violence in the home during childhood is detrimental to healthy child growth and personality development. The structural theory of violence[26] gives a fuller explanation of the above with particular reference to social learning and role modeling behaviors. Hence, we have to accept the sad but realistic possibility that many of today's children will be tomorrow's abusing adults.

Stressful situations on neglect and abuse seem to have been rampant in the early childhood experiences of almost all criminals. Practically every researcher of child abuse has a list of names of criminals who were victims of child abuse and intrafamilial violence in their early childhoods (Lee Harvey Oswald, Jack Ruby, Arthur Bremmer, Sirhan Sirhan, and James Earl Ray, to name just a few). Thus we also have to accept the disturbing possibility that many of today's abused children brought up in violent homes will grow up to be the nation's hard core criminals.

The figures available of cases of child abuse, though not complete, are staggering. The Children's Division of the American Humane

Association estimates that 10,000 children are severely battered every year, at least 50,000 to 75,000 are sexually abused, 100,000 are emotionally neglected, and another 100,000 are physically, morally, and educationally neglected.[9] The Children's Bureau of the U.S. Department of Health, Education and Welfare informs us that 4,000 children are killed each year by their parents, 90,000 are beaten, injured, starved, or locked in rooms, and hundreds of thousands more are simply neglected, physically and mentally.[5] A report by the National Institute of Child Abuse and Neglect states that one million children risk bodily harm from their parents.[16] Though some hope arises when one reads what is being done to eradicate child abuse and wife abuse, this is just a drop in the ocean when contrasted with what remains to be done. Today it is estimated that nearly 3 million Americans grew up in violent home situations.

Child abuse reporting laws, which are by definition and intent case-finding devices, are perhaps a first step in insuring the child's protection. (Refer to Kutun, B., in this book for proposed legislation regarding reporting laws for wifebeating.) The legal area of child abuse has been radically changed, with several states revising or introducing new laws on how best to deal with the problem of child abuse. Today, all of our 50 states have laws requiring professional workers and others to report all suspected cases, often within 24 hours. But we still do not have laws that make child abuse or wife abuse a criminal offense, except in the case of death. It seems essential that similar systems for reporting wife abuse need to be designed and implemented as well.

Desperately needed are more workers and more money so we can attack this dual problem from every direction and stop perpetuation of this senseless cruelty and harm by giving both adults and children our continued specialized treatment, care, and help. The root cause has been identified as a deterioration of family life in the United States, the breaking up of close family ties, and a prevailing pattern of violence amongst family members. Several professionals of various disciplines, using a multi-disciplinary approach to analyze the situation, have suggested that more intense work needs to be done to unify our efforts, to strengthen our child-parent ties, and to discover ways and means of getting our families back into harmonious, loving relationships based on respect and not on sexism.

Characteristics common among abusing spouses and parents include a lack of nurturing in their own childhoods. (Refer to Roy, M., in Chapter 1 of this book.) Authors describe abusive spouses and parents as inadequate, self-centered, hypersensitive, incompetent, anxious, impulsive, diffident, lonely, and isolated. The child-rearing of these adults seems to have been identical with what they offer their own children.[24] The result is a life pattern of aggression and violence repeating itself from generation to generation. Abused children lacking the experience and opportunities which help develop inner controls for adult life, get into intense, senseless fits of temper, often unaware of their own brute actions. Their inadequate early childhoods and growing years make them selfish, immature adults. In fact, often these adults look to their children, or their spouses, to satisfy all their own needs—and they lash out with uncontrolled, savage strength when these expectations fall short. In these types of relationships neither the children's needs nor those of the spouses are met. The children, like the abused wives, do not lash out at the fathers/husbands, both because of physical limitations and because of feelings of guilt. For the children the anger is directed inward, but the frustrations linger and are likely to cause problems when these children are older and are in contact with other people.

We see almost daily in certain children with whom we work the devastating effects of parental strife and violence between mothers and fathers. We see a child who continually speaks in a loud, shrill voice, often merely babbling about fantasy persons in distorted activities or alternately making plaintive comments about "mommy and daddy" with tears in her eyes. Or a child whose needs for medical care for an orthopedic problem are ignored by a mother completely absorbed with fear of the man she lives with; the man refuses to leave her apartment and threatens to murder her and her child if she calls the police. Understandably preoccupied with this situation, the mother knows there is no way the police can really protect them from him, and she has little energy to devote to her child's medical needs.

Some other psychologically stressful characteristics mentioned as leading to child and wife abuse are unemployment of the husband;[19] an unwanted pregnancy;[3] a child conceived out of wedlock;[26] and marriage partners of different religious faiths.[3] It is therefore necessary that determined efforts be made to tackle the multiple social factors that influence child and wife abuse.[12] (Refer to Straus in this chapter.)

The National Symposium on Child Abuse enumerated eight conditions of poor child care:

- physical neglect
- moral neglect
- emotional neglect
- medical neglect
- educational neglect
- physical abuse
- sexual abuse
- community neglect[18]

All of these conditions, or various combinations of these, exist in households where child and wife abuse exist.

When children are deprived of their basic needs of proper food, clothing, and shelter, these deprivations automatically make them susceptible to all health hazards and stunt their normal healthy growth and development. In families where there are cases of child abuse and wife abuse, medical neglect also prevails. It is prevalent in homes which are characteristic of lack of control and defiance of authority, cruel punitive practices, excessive use of drugs and alcohol, and parental discord and violence, often resulting in the mothers being battered. Medical neglect occurs when a parent ignores the treatment needs of a child, resulting in a child who whines, is irritable, and is overly dependent. The parent responds by using physical abuse to discipline the child's aggravating needs. Physical child abuse ranges from mild to severe injuries, and the objects used by the parent may be a hand, brush, cord, belt, or some electrical appliance.

When young children continually live in an environment reeking of family disruption, their fathers constantly physically attacking their mothers, their mothers perpetually screaming and weeping, they do not know where to go, or to whom to turn. They are denied parental love and nurturing, important needs of young children. Parental interest, concern, and empathy give the young child his first feelings of his own familiar surroundings and the confidence in the world at large. If these are not available to children when very young, they are denied satisfaction of their basic emotional needs; they do not acquire the sense of trust in their surroundings that leads up gradually to the different senses of autonomy, initiative, accomplishment, identity, intimacy, generativity and integrity laid down by Erikson[8] as fundamental steps to healthy personality development. These children, therefore, suffer from emotional neglect as well.

A child is considered to be emotionally neglected when the parent does not provide the nurturing qualities so necessary for sound growth of personality. What this really means is that the chances that a child coming from a generally neglectful and violent home situation will receive parental support and acceptance are negligible or nil, because the parents themselves come from homes where they were not valued or gratified. For no fault of his own, a child whose basic emotional needs are inadequately met, or not met at all, grows up with feelings of fear, anxiety, hostility, and suspicion that follow him to adulthood.

There are several studies that suggest ways of helping the abused child: by changing his environment and separating him from the parent, if and when considered absolutely necessary; by making available "specially trained" people who could try to remedy the damage done by rehabilitating the abused child, knowing in advance, however, that the longer the child has been abused and has suffered in an unwholesome environment, caused by violence among his parents, the longer it is bound to take for him to get out of his abnormal, withdrawn, frightened behavior and be a natural, spontaneous child again. Most abusive parents do not seem to be wilful abusers; it is their social and/or economic situation that causes their violent behavior. The extended family, the community, and medical and social services must, therefore, be available to these abusing adults.

It is often said that seriously emotionally disturbed children are seldom found in simpler societies where extended family relationships prevail and where the very fabric of the society cannot allow a child to be abused or abandoned, physically or emotionally. It is only logical to conclude that wife abuse is also quite uncommon in such societies because in more extended-family arrangements, the wife's family would not allow it nor would the husband's family condone it. We must face the fact that intra-familial violence cannot be eradicated by good police work, good psychotherapy, or even good legal assistance in a complex society typified by competition, and alienation, and the nuclear family driven by the media to ever more conspicuous consumption. It is the patriarchal nature of the nuclear family which guarantees that violence, kindled by the frustrations of urban and suburban life, will be directed toward the more oppressed and less legally protected family members—women and children.

In what ways could abusive adults be helped to cope with the parent-child and parent-parent interactional roles in a positive, constructive, wholesome manner? Perhaps, by helping them to:

- shed feelings of inadequacy and gradually improve their self-images
- love and respect their marriage companions
- gain an understanding of children's normal developmental stages
- go through attitudinal changes of accepting their children and spouses as their genuine concern and not as their property
- control their tempers so as not to use their children and spouses as outlets for their frustrations
- accept and tackle their own problems without blaming their children and spouses for their multiple problems
- speak less of the duties of children and the role of the spouses and more of their needs and rights as human beings.

The Children's Division of the American Humane Association has put together a list of indicators of a child's need for protection and directed it towards teachers, school administrators, nurses, and counselors.[9] If there is reason to suspect that the child in question is being abused, it is recommended that signs of the presence of one or more of the following indicators be examined:

1. A child who is frequently absent or late. Whether his problem is at home, in school, or within himself, known to his parents or not, his habitual lateness or absence strongly suggests a maladjustment.

2. A child who arrives at school too early and hangs around after classes without apparent reason. He may not be welcome or cared for at home, he may hate his home, or be afraid of it.

3. A child who is unkempt and/or inadequately dressed. If he is

dressed inappropriately for the weather, if his clothing is dirty and torn, if he is habitually unwashed, if other children don't like to sit near him because they think he smells bad, he is clearly neglected.

4. A child who more than occasionally bears bruises, welts, and other injuries. Will he say how he got them? Does he complain of being beaten at home? Or is he always fighting?

5. A child who is hyperactive, aggressive, disruptive, destructive in behavior. He may be acting out his own hostility. He may be reflecting the atmosphere at home. He may be imitating his parents' behavior. He may be crying out for attention and help.

6. A child who is withdrawn, shy, passive, uncommunicative. He *is* communicating. Whether he is too compliant or too inattentive to comply at all, he has sunk into his own internal world, a safer one, he thinks, than the real world. His message is in his passivity and silence.

7. A child who needs, but is not getting, medical attention. He may have untreated sores. He may have an obvious need for dental work. He may need glasses to see the blackboard.

8. A child who is undernourished. What is the reason—poverty or uncaring parents?

9. A child who is always tired and tends to fall asleep in class. Either he is not well, his parents are neglecting to regulate his routines, or he is simply unable to get to bed and to sleep because of family quarrels.*

10. The parent who becomes aggressive or abusive when approached with a view to discussing the child's apparent problems.

11. The parent who doesn't bother to show up for appointments, or is so apathetic and unresponsive that he might as well have stayed at home.

12. The parent who is slovenly, dirty, and possibly redolent of alcohol.

13. The parent who shows little concern for the child or what he is doing or failing to do.

14. The parent who does not participate in any school activities or come to any school events.

15. The parent who will not permit the child to participate in special school activities or events.

---

*AWAIC, Inc. has found that many children dread going to sleep because of the constant fear of their fathers returning home drunk and violent at night to beat up their mothers.

16. The parent who is not known to any of the other parents or children.

17. The parent whose behavior as described by the child is bizarre and unusual.

18. The parent whose behavior is observed by school personnel to be strange, bizarre, irrational, or unusual in any way.

Helfer and Kempe were among the early pioneers to bring child abuse to the attention of the American public. Their book, *The Battered Child,* [14] deals with the theoretical and diagnostic aspects of child abuse. Its contents include: History of Child Abuse and Infanticide; Incidence of Child Abuse and Demographic Characteristics of Persons Involved; and Medical, Psychiatric, Social and Legal Aspects of Child Abuse.

Their second book, *Helping the Battered Child and His Family,* [15] is based on the premise that the home can be made safe, in most cases, by the early initiation of a practical and feasible community hospital-based treatment program. The primary concern of the editors is to quickly offer the best help to the child and his troubled family. What is even more encouraging and promising is their statement that they are "rapidly moving toward the point when, by early recognition of the potential to abuse small children, a treatment program can begin even before the child is born; and possibly even before the child is conceived."

Another very important book, *Somewhere a Child is Crying,* [9] is written by Vincent Fontana, who feels that it is a myth that in the United States of America we love our children . . . for each year at least 700 American children are killed by their parents or parent surrogates. Fontana's estimates include: 100,000 children severely battered every year; 50,000 to 75,000 sexually abused; 100,000 emotionally neglected; and another 100,000 physically, morally, and educationally neglected. Alarming, long-needed, and exhaustively researched, this unique, in-depth study of a growing national problem skillfully outlines a concrete program for eliminating its causes and preventing further tragedies.

A Child is Being Beaten, [4] by Naomi Chase, another book of much importance, reveals in shocking detail how, as a result of the failure of our families, our schools, our welfare systems, and our child-custodial system, a three-year-old child in New York City can be beaten to death by a brutal stepfather with the tacit acquiescence of her drug-addicted mother and thrown into the East River, although the parents in question were being helped by supposedly professional social workers. Chase goes on to say that there are many battles for child welfare we will have to undertake in the years ahead.

"We should start with the idea of restoring value and significance to the idea of nurturing, recognize that all our children need it, and create programs and institutions that will help us give it to them . . . If we're worried about the cost, we might look at it this way. The less care a child has in the early years, the more society will have to pay for it later on."

From the various research studies done so far and the ample statistics available, it is very clear that the problem of child abuse and wifebeating needs our immediate attention. In addition to the several constructive and reformative measures proposed by specialists studying the subject of child abuse, I would like to make some practical suggestions from the human development point of view. They are simple in essence and not difficult to implement, provided they are accepted with a genuine feeling of cooperation, enthusiasm, commitment, and dedication to the cause of solving the problem of battered children and battered wives.

Perhaps this could best be done by setting up special educational councils, both on federal and state levels, to examine ways of implementing the following suggestions:

Right from the nursery school years, we could ensure that young children have direct, real life experiences in the exploration of living things: observation and examination of plants, flowers, and animals; and involvement in their care and growth; having opportunities to watch birds, fish, or other small animals; having them as pets at home or in school, playing with them affectionately, holding them close, fondling them, helping wash the fish bowl or changing the water and sprinkling some fish food in; and taking walks in woods and parks. All of these are experiences which would help children develop feelings of tenderness, sensitivity, mutual concern, and dependence, and at the same time, give them much-needed information about the beauty of nature and the joy of living things.

Head Start pre-school centers, along with group day care centers, can act as conduits to bring about immediate action. Parent-oriented workshops, seminars, etc. can be expanded to include discussions on and for the abused adults. Head Start consulting psychologists can offer guidelines to its parents. Group day care centers lacking staff psychologists should make use of community resources for this purpose.

Another solution is for Day Care and Head Start, servicing 50,000 children in this city (New York), to lay the foundation for a curriculum free of sexist trappings. It is essential that boys and girls be taught that both sexes can do almost anything and that 'free to be you and me' experienced as a child will shape the liberated adult of the future. Books, outdoor play equipment, and toys should not be used if they reflect a rigid sexist society. Teachers, assistants, and other participants should be sensitized to reflect healthy non-sexist attitudes in the classroom.[21]

From the ages of 6 to about 12, youngsters could be encouraged to take care of children younger than themselves, their own brothers and sisters or other children in the neighborhood, church group, or after school program. Such experiences, if available with proper adult guidance, would be of immense mutual gain. For the older children, it would result in initiation and maintenance of social contacts, a feeling of service to others, an assertion of a sense of self, and the fulfillment of a sense of accomplishment. For the younger children, it would perhaps provide experience in several areas of learning and help them cope with new situations, with a renewed feeling of confidence and adequacy.

It is at this point that children are quite generally aware of physical differences between males and females and it becomes incumbent upon us to begin helping them to understand the psychological and transitory nature of sex roles and sex role stereotypes. The boy who is socialized to be an emotionally shallow or physically brutish male is most likely to be an abusive husband or father. The girl who is told that she must eventually accept the role of passive, quiescent chattel is most likely to be initially attracted to a man who will abuse her or have no regard for her development as a total person. As long as we accept the notion that "boys will be boys," we will continue to turn out demi-persons who objectivize and ultimately brutalize women and children.

In the high school years, young people could be given a first hand exposure to working with young children in classrooms, day care centers, day camps, after school programs, hospital wards, church groups, and recreation clubs. Compulsory enrollment of all high school students in child development and family living courses could be planned, acquainting them with essential elements of physical care of children and the basic principles underlying child development and the qualities necessary for establishing healthy, intimate, adult relationships. This could have preparation for spousehood and parenthood as focal points, stressing the immense obligations and total commitment spouses and parents have to make before getting married or parenting children.

It is the man who does not know *how* to be a husband and father who, in a fit of rage at his perception of his own inadequacy and inability to form emotionally satisfying relationships, strikes out at his wife and children. It is the woman who feels inadequately prepared for motherhood because she was treated coldly and/or brutally by her parents who thinks she can find love and even momentary security with such a pitiful man.

Practically all professions require a probationary period or some trial learning time. How much more binding is the role of parenthood, which can never be shirked or exchanged? It is time we took this role in family life with the seriousness it deserves. Direct exposure to and involvement with young children and viable life-styles should be made a compulsory laboratory course, an apprenticeship which all high school students, sometime during the high school years, should take to acquaint themselves with children's rights.

Young adults in colleges, vocational schools and other service centers could be given the opportunity of taking marriage and family courses, including marriage counseling, with emphasis on obligations and responsibilities, mutual respect for the marriage partner, and knowledge of birth control and family planning measures, stressing the gravity, personal and national, of giving birth to unwanted babies. Encouragement could also be given in the observation of and participation in everyday activities of young children, in schools or service centers, and young adults could be provided with opportunities for taking courses in human relations-based subjects like child development, sociology, psychology, cultural anthropology, and women's studies.

Prenatal and postnatal education courses, with special emphasis on maternal nutrition, maternal health, and other influencing factors would familiarize them with knowledge available regarding infant care and infant development and the importance of tactile stimulation, language acquisition, verbal interraction, social attachment, cognitive development, personality development, emotional development, and moral development in the early years. They could also be provided with pertinent information on the growth and development of a human being along with various critical periods of development during the entire life span, with examples of neighborliness, sensitivity toward others, concern for the young and helpless, respect for the aged and infirm, and love for all.

The role of good, humanistic sex education cannot be overemphasized in prescribing an overall educational program which will enhance the total development of the individual. It is much less likely that, a person, who is sexually satisfied in the context of a meaningful interpersonal relationship will turn to violence within that relationship. We also need more quality research into the development and practice of sado-masochism so that we might better understand the essential relationship between sexuality and physical aggression.

And finally, as a more involved community, we could determinedly strive to uphold the protection of children, to safeguard the rights of women, and to make available special counseling services to spouses and parents. The formation of neighborhood centers, equipped with good libraries of books and audio-visual material, recruiting volunteers from amongst older parents and grandparents and other adults interested in being of assistance to young parents needing help would be an immense support system.

That large numbers of women and children suffer immense abuse in silence to the outside world is testament to fact that oppressed persons are usually so used to oppression that they accept society's judgment that they are worth little and that no one *will* really care. Our educational systems and social service organizations must work to eradicate such thinking and teaching such acquiescence.

We could be a community full of caring, concerned individuals working together and re-educating ourselves in the laws of humanity, anxious to restore to children and women their rights, anxious to understand the genuine difficulties of abusing adults and to help them combat their problems—a community hopeful of putting a stop to the battering of children and wives and fulfilling every child's rights as a child and every woman's rights as a woman.

It is my sincere wish that the awareness and understanding gained from the research available on child abuse and wife abuse will lead to a deepening of concern, investigation of the extent of the problem in individual communities, a personal and a group commitment to action, including a genuine involvement and an active participation of every member of every community, so that together we may have a nation that is good for all and freed from the problem of battered women and battered children.

REFERENCES

1. AWAIC, Inc., Abused Women's Aid in Crisis, Inc., New York, N.Y.
2. Bandura, A. and Houston, A. C., "Identification as a Process of Incidental Learning," *Journal of Abnormal Psychology* 63:311–318 (1961).
3. Bennie, E. and Sclare, A., "The Battered Child Syndrome," *American Journal of Psychiatry* 125(*7*):975–979 (1969).
4. Chase, Fiegelson Naomi, *A Child is Being Beaten*. New York: Holt, Rinehart & Winston, 1975.
5. Children's Bureau of the U.S. Department of Health, Education and Welfare, 1974.
6. Children's Division of the American Humane Association, 1973.
7. DeFrancis, V. and Lucht, C., *Child Abuse Legislation in the 1970s*. Denver: American Humane Association, 1974.
8. Erikson, Erik, *Childhood and Society*. New York: Norton, 1963.
9. Fontana, V. J., *Somewhere a Child is Crying*. New York: Macmillan, 1973.
10. Galdston, R., "Observations of Children Who Have Been Physically Abused by Their Parents," *American Journal of Psychiatry* 122 (*4*):440–443 (1965).
11. Gelles, R. J., "Child Abuse as Psycho-Pathology; A Sociological Critique and Reformulation," *American Journal of Orthopsychiatry* 43 (*4*):611–621 (July 1973).
12. Gil, D., *Violence Against Children: Physical Child Abuse in the United States*. Cambridge, Massachusetts: Harvard University Press, 1970.
13. Goode, W., "Force and Violence in the Family," *Journal of Marriage and the Family* 33: 624–636 (November 1971).
14. Helfer, R. and Kempe, C. (eds.), *The Battered Child*. Chicago: University of Chicago Press, 1968.
15. Kempe, C. and Helfer, R. (eds.), *Helping the Battered Child and His Family*. Philadelphia: J. B. Lippincott, 1972.
16. National Institute of Child Abuse and Neglect, 1975.
17. National Society for the Prevention of Cruelty to Children, London.
18. National Symposium of Child Abuse, 1971.
19. O'Brien, J., "Violence in Divorce Prone Families," *Journal of Marriage and the Family* 33: 692–698 (November 1971).
20. Owens, D. J. and Straus, Murray A., "The Social Structure of Violence in Childhood and Approval of Violence as an Adult," *Aggressive Behavior* 1: 193–211 (1975).

21. Proceedings from the Conference entitled: "The Abused and Battered Woman in Crisis—A Multi-Faceted Approach," presented at the Cardinal Spellman Head Start Center, New York: January 1975.
22. Reiner, B. and Kaufman, I. *Character Disorders in Parents of Delinquents* New York: Family Service Association of America, 1959.
23. Singer, J. *The Control of Aggression and Violence.* New York: Academic Press, 1971.
24. Steele, B. and Pollack, C, "A Psychiatric Study of Parents Who Abuse Infants and Small Children," in *The Battered Child,* Helfer, R. and Kempe, C. (eds.). Chicago: University of Chilcago Press, 1968.
25. Straus, Murray A, "Some Social Antecedents of Physical Punishment: A Linkage Theory Interpretation," *Journal of Marriage and the Family* **70**: 658–663 (November 1971).
26. Straus, Murray, A, "A General Systems Theory Approach to the Development of a Theory of Violence Between Family Members," *Social Science Information,* **12**: 105–125 (1973).
27. Wasserman, S, "The Abused Parent of the Abused Child," *Children* **14**: 175–179 (September–October 1967).
28. Young, L, *Wednesday's Child: A Study of Child Neglect and Abuse.* New York: McGraw-Hill, 1967.
29. Zalba, S., *"Battered Children,"* *Transaction* **8**: 68–71 (July–August 1971).

LEGISLATIVE NEEDS AND SOLUTIONS

Barry Kutun, State Representative of the Florida House of Representatives
Assisted by **Michael E. Dunn**

My awareness of the problem of domestic violence became increasingly acute after meeting and discussing the crisis faced by the abused spouse with women representing the Dade County Task Force on Battered Women. While statutes that apply to the areas of domestic violence are presently in effect in Florida, the Task Force suggested that specific legislation be introduced to address the problem directly. Unfortunately, at the time it was difficult to document the scope and severity of the problem since there was insufficient statistical and factual information relating to the problem specifically.*

Acting in my capacity as Chairman of the Committee on Health and Rehabilitative Services, Florida House of Representatives, I instructed the Committee Staff to prepare a survey exploring the spouse abuse problem and distribute it to the Public Defender, State

---

*Editor's footnote: Legislation concerned with establishing emergency shelters and mandatory reporting of domestic violence are currently under consideration in thirteen states (Ak., Co., Md., Ca., Ma., Or., Ne., Ct., Fl., Pa., Va., Mn., and Wa.).

Attorney, and Chief Circuit Judge for each of the Judicial Circuits of Florida. The survey is set forth herein.

I. *Incidents*
  1. Does your office keep separate records of wifebeating? Incidents of wifebeating reported to your office
     1971   1972   1973   1974   1975
  2. Are there more incidents you suspect that are not reported to your office? to the police? If so, what, in your opinion, prevents or discourages reporting?

II. *Prosecution*
  3. Are charges filed? What charges?
  4. How many cases were prosecuted?
     1971   1972   1973   1974   1975
     By information:
     By indictment:
  5. What particular difficulties are encountered in prosecution?
  6. Are there particular problems with juries in wifebeating cases?
  7. If there are problems in prosecution, what causes them?
  8. What solutions, legislative or otherwise, would you suggest to any problems in prosecution?

III. *Recommendations/Comments*
  9. What solutions would you suggest to the problem of wife-beating? (Possibilities: legislative approaches? changes in rules of evidence? no state involvement?)

This survey was mailed in November of 1975 and most responses were received by January of 1976.

The survey demonstrated conclusively that no public office in Florida kept separate records of wifebeating or spouse abuse, and therefore, it was impossible to tell exactly how many cases occur on a yearly basis. Nearly all respondents to the questionnaire stated that the problem was far greater than had been reported to their offices. One State Attorney felt that as few as 10% of wife abuse cases are reported. Another said that about 70% of the assault and battery cases in his Judicial Circuit are family disputes and about 50% of those are wife abuse or spouse abuse cases. Nearly all respondents said that the problem of reporting and prosecuting incidents of spouse abuse was compounded by the woman's fear of further abuse, her economic dependence on the spouse, and her inability to provide financial support should the husband be incarcerated or heavily fined. In addition, several respondents noted that, in some cases, women were willing to "make up" for the good of the family or to prevent further dissension. Moreover, while many abused women become passive, the consensus indicates that it is clearly because the victim has no viable alternative; that is, nowhere else to turn.

Presently in Florida, criminal charges can be filed against a husband for beating his wife under normal criminal statutes. Assault (second degree misdemeanor), battery (first degree misdemeanor), aggravated assault (third degree felony), and aggravated battery (second degree felony) all could be filed against a husband for the physical abuse of his wife, just as those charges could be filed against anyone who committed these crimes. However, under present Florida statutes, a woman does not have the alternative of filing any other type of charge or action.

Unfortunately, public awareness of the problem is apparently still minimal. One State Attorney reported that he was not even aware of any occurrences or growing concern for this type of offense.

It is important to note that the survey responses indicated a definite reluctance of the wife to testify and the absence of interested witnesses in this type of case. Normally, the wife will enlist the aid of the police only when in real fear but not in *all* beating situations. Presently, according to Florida statute, the police can only arrest in misdemeanor cases when the crime is committed in their presence. Consequently, by the time the police respond to a complaint of domestic violence, they rarely can make an arrest, since the beating is usually over and the damage is done. In addition, after the disturbance has been quelled, the victim, in most cases, does not follow through by filing an affidavit on which information can be predicated. In the event the victim does file an affidavit and a charge is filed, in more than half the cases, the wife and husband reconcile and the wife then seeks to have the charge dismissed. If the State Attorney does withdraw the charge, the offender is released unpunished. However, if he or she does decide to prosecute, the State Attorney ends up in court with a victim who does not wish to cooperate, if, indeed, she appears for trial.

Based on the responses to the survey, it was apparent that three major areas had to be considered and addressed specifically in Florida by remedial legislation. These areas are as follows:

1. A statistical basis has to be established to determine the frequency and severity of the problem of spouse abuse in Florida.
2. A provision must be added to the present Florida arrest statutes in order to provide police officers with the legal authority to make arrests on probable cause for a misdemeanor criminal charge, with specific reference to domestic violence and disturbances.
3. Shelter, care, and counseling are necessary to provide a viable living alternative to those abused individuals who are subjected to severe, recurring violence.

These three proposals were incorporated in legislation drafted during the 1976 session of the Florida Legislature by myself and others. However, since the legislation was introduced immediately prior to the Legislative Session, research and appropriations estimates had to be formulated without sufficient statistical and factual information. Consequently, the legislation was never given due and proper consideration during the 1976 Legislative Session. However, the legislation has already been filed in substantially the same form for consideration during the 1977 Legislative Session.

Recognizing that spouse abuse is one of those crimes that occur with great frequency but is often unreported, I have proposed legislation which provides that incidents of spouse abuse shall be reported to the Department of Health and Rehabilitative Services, that failure to do so is a second degree misdemeanor, and that anyone reporting a case of spouse abuse while acting in good faith shall be immune from any liability. In addition, the Bill further provides that the Department shall investigate cases of spouse abuse and, when appropriate, shall transmit the information to the State Attorney for further action.*

---

*Editor's footnote: The notion of required reporting is controversial. Opponents regard it as a possible violation of the spouse's right to privacy; proponents justify it for purposes of statistics gathering. The idea is currently being explored in several states. Perhaps, the formation of a Central Registry for complaints could be established for the *voluntary reporting* of cases that need to be investigated. This would provide a data bank and insure data collection without invasion of privacy.

Basically outlined, the Bill contains nine key provisions. They are as follows:

1. Requires that any person who has reason to believe that an act of spouse abuse has occurred shall report to, or cause a report to be made by, the Department.
2. Delineates the conditions of evidence to be considered preliminary to the submission of a report.
3. Requires an oral report to be made to the Department immediately followed by a written report as soon as possible. Outlines the nature and content of the report.
4. Requires the Department to make an investigation immediately upon receipt of a report.
5. Provides that the Central Registry shall record and maintain reports of spouse abuse.
6. Provides that, when appropriate, the Department shall transmit reports of spouse abuse to the State Attorney where the incident has occurred.
7. Provides immunity for anyone making a report or participating in a judicial proceeding involving spouse abuse.
8. Removes all privileges except attorney/client privileges, in any civil or criminal litigation resulting from a report of spouse abuse.
9. Provides that anyone violating the provisions of this section is guilty of a second degree misdemeanor.

An accurate account of the number of spouse abuse cases that would be reported and require investigation by the Department is presently unavailable, primarily because those cases involving spouse abuse are now classified in the general categories of assault and battery. However, it would be possible to anticipate a program modeled after the Central Registry for child abuse, which maintains a computerized data bank and employs social workers to investigate complaints. Any personnel, of course, would require specific training in the proper methods of investigating and handling cases involving marital disputes.

The Legislation, in its full context, is as follows:

A bill to be entitled

An act relating to spouse abuse; creating s. 827.10, Florida Statutes; providing definitions; providing a purpose; requiring persons to report incidents of spouse

abuse to the Department of Health and Rehabilitative Services; providing certain conditions as evidence of maltreatment before a report is required; providing the nature and content of the report; requiring the department to notify the State Attorney upon receipt of a report when appropriate; requiring public agencies to cooperate with the department; providing for the creation and maintenance of a central registry in the department; providing for the transmittal of spouse abuse records by the department to the State Attorney when appropriate; providing that persons participating in making a report shall be immune from liability; exempting the application of certain privileges; providing a penalty; providing an effective date.

Be It Enacted by the Legislature of the State of Florida:

Section 1. Section 827.10, Florida Statutes, is created to read:

827.10 Abuse of spouse; reports; penalties.—

(1) DEFINITIONS—As used in this section:

(a) "Abuse" means physical injury inflicted other than by accidental means.

(b) "Abused person" means any person lawfully married to another who has been subjected to abuse or whose condition suggests that he or she has been abused.

(c) "Department" means the Department of Health and Rehabilitative Services.

(2) PURPOSE—The purpose of this section is to provide for the detection and correction of the abuse of persons whose health and welfare are adversely affected or further threatened by the abusive conduct of their spouses. It is intended that the mandatory reporting of such cases will cause the protective services of the state to be brought to bear in an effort to prevent further abuse and to protect and enhance the welfare of such persons.

(3) REPORTS OF ABUSE—Any person who has reason to believe that a person has been subjected to abuse by his or her spouse shall report, or cause reports to be made, to the department. When the attendance of any person with respect to an abused person is pursuant to the performance of services as a member of a staff of a hospital, training center, clinic, school, or similar facility, he shall also notify the person in charge of the facility or his designated delegate, who shall also report or cause reports to be made in accordance with the provisions of this section.

(4) CONDITIONS PRELIMINARY TO SUBMISSION OF THE REPORT—In consideration of physical injury, the following items shall be considered evidence of abuse before the report is required:

(a) Characteristic distribution of fractures.

(b) Disproportionate amount of soft tissue injury.

(c) Evidence that injuries occurred at different times or are in different stages of resolution.

(d) Cause of recent trauma in question.

(e) Family or facility history.

(f) History of previous episodes.

(g) No new lesions occurring during the abused person's hospitalization or removal from custody of the spouse.

(5) NATURE AND CONTENT OF REPORT—An oral report shall be made immediately by telephone or otherwise to the department, followed as soon thereafter as possible by a report in writing. Such reports shall contain, if known, the name and address of the abused person, the abused person's age, and the nature and extent of the injuries, and any other information that the reporter believes might be helpful in establishing the cause of the injuries or abuse, and the identity of the perpetrator.

(6) RESPONSIBILITIES OF PUBLIC AGENCIES—Upon receipt of a report of abuse of a person by his or her spouse, the department shall cause an immediate investigation to be made and shall in turn, when appropriate, notify the State Attorney. All state, county, and local agencies have a duty to cooperate fully with the department, transmit reports of abuse to the department, and protect and enhance the welfare of abused persons and persons potentially subject to abuse by their spouses detected by a report made pursuant to this section.

(7) CENTRAL REGISTRY—Reports of abuse shall be recorded in central registries established and maintained by the department as required by ss. 827.07 and 827.09 dealing with abuse of children and of developmentally disabled persons. Each registry shall contain information as to the name of the abused person and his or her spouse, the facts of the investigation, and the result of the investigation. The information contained in the registry shall not be open to inspection by the public. However, appropriate disclosure may be made for use in connection with the treatment of the abused person or the person perpetrating abuse, and to counsel representing either person in any criminal or civil proceeding. Appropriate disclosure may also be made for use in connection with the hiring or employment of persons to serve abused persons. In addition, information contained in the registry may be available for purposes of research relating to the abuse of persons by their spouses. The department shall make such information available upon application by a researcher or research agency of professional repute provided the need for the records has been demonstrated to the satisfaction of the department. Records shall not be opened under this provision unless adequate assurances are given that names and other information identifying abused persons will not be disclosed by the applicant.

(8) TRANSMITTAL OF RECORDS—With respect to any case of reported abuse of a person by his or her spouse, the department, when appropriate, shall transmit all reports received by it, which shall contain the results of the investigation, to the State Attorney of the county where the incident occurred.

(9) IMMUNITY—Anyone participating in the making of a report pursuant to this section or participating in a judicial proceeding resulting therefrom shall be presumed prima facie to be acting in good faith and in so doing shall be immune from any liability, civil or criminal, that otherwise might be incurred or imposed.

Recognizing that effective law enforcement and comprehensive reporting of incidents need to be carefully coordinated with effective counseling and shelter programs to provide an overall solution to the problem, I have proposed legislation which would establish therapeutic or rehabilitative programs aimed at reaching both the abused and the abuser. These programs would be staffed by case workers trained in the best available methods of dealing with spouse abuse.

Further recognizing the fact that since most abused women are economically dependent and have children that need to be cared for, they often must return to the same environment where the incident of abuse occurred. Obviously, this has created a need for establishing temporary receiving facilities where persons subjected to spouse abuse may receive appropriate treatment and care while the situation is properly investigated.

Reducing the Bill to its simplest terms, it would provide for the Department of Health and Rehabilitative Services to establish a program for the care, treatment, and rehabilitation of persons engaging in, or subject to, spouse abuse. Additionally, it would require that the Department establish temporary placement facilities for the purpose of providing treatment and care of the abused spouse. Key provisions of the Bill include:

1. That the duties of the Department shall be to provide services through existing programs and resources, make suitable arrangements for treatment facilities, initiate educational and informational programs, conduct research and serve as a clearing house for information relating to spouse abuse.
2. The Bill would also require that the Department establish temporary receiving facilities to accommodate and care for the abused spouse.
3. It would provide that the information received regarding the identity of individuals or facilities remain confidential.
4. It would require that law enforcement officers advise the abused spouse as to the availability of treatment facilities and programs.

The Bill appears in its full context as follows:

A bill to be entitled

An act relating to arrests; adding subsection (6) to s 901.15, Florida Statutes, authorizing a peace officer to arrest a person without a warrant if the officer has probable cause to believe that the person has committed a battery upon the person's spouse and the officer finds evidence of bodily harm or reasonably believes that there is danger of further violence; providing an effective date.

Be It Enacted by the Legislature of the State of Florida:
Section 1. Subsection (6) is added to section 901.15, Florida Statutes, to read:

901.15 When arrest by officer without warrant is lawful.—A peace officer may arrest a person without a warrant when:

(6) *The officer has probable cause to believe that the person has committed a battery upon the person's spouse, and the officer finds evidence of bodily harm or the officer reasonably believes that there is danger of violence unless the person alleged to have committed the battery is arrested without delay.*

Section 2. This act shall take effect upon becoming a law.

A bill to be entitled

An act relating to the Department of Health and Rehabilitative Services; providing intent; providing definitions; providing duties and functions of the department in the establishment of a program for the prevention, care, treatment and rehabilitation of persons engaged in or subject to spouse abuse; requiring the department to furnish certain assistance, conduct research, carry out programs and establish diagnostic-intervention centers; providing for the temporary receipt of persons subject to spouse abuse at the center until the conflict can be properly investigated; requiring the center to refer such persons and their spouses to appropriate treatment or rehabilitation agencies; providing confidentiality; requiring law enforcement officers to notify persons subject to spouse abuse of the availability of a center; providing an effective date.

Be It Enacted by the Legislature of the State of Florida:

Section 1. Intent—The Legislature recognizes that certain persons who assault, batter, or otherwise abuse their spouses and persons subject to such abuse are in need of treatment and rehabilitation which often cannot be effected if such behavior is treated on a criminal basis. In light of such recognition, it is the intent of the Legislature to provide for the medical and psychological rehabilitation of such persons and to provide a place where the parties may be separated until they can be properly assisted and rehabilitated in the avoidance of repetitions of incidents of spouse abuse.

Section 2. Definitions—As used in this act, unless the context otherwise requires:

(1) The term "spouse abuse" shall be construed to include any assault, battery or other physical abuse by a person upon his or her spouse.

(2) "Department" means the Department of Health and Rehabilitative Services.

(3) "Diagnostic-intervention center" means a facility established by the department to receive persons on a temporary basis who are subject to spouse abuse.

Section 3. Duties and functions of the department—

(1) It shall be the duty of the department to formulate and effect a plan for the prevention, care, treatment, and rehabilitation of persons engaging in or subject to spouse abuse.

(2) In formulating and effecting the plan defined in subsection (1), the department shall:

(a) Furnish such aid to persons engaging in or subject to spouse abuse in any manner which, in its judgment, will afford the greatest benefit to them, and shall have the power in this connection to make suitable arrangements with hospitals or clinics which, in its discretion, shall be deemed advisable to afford the proper treatment, care, or rehabilitation of such persons.

(b) Provide services through existing health centers, clinics, and other appropriate treatment resources.

(c) Carry on educational and informational programs on spouse abuse for the benefit of the general public, persons engaging in or subject to spouse abuse, professional persons, or others who care for or may be engaged in the care and treatment of persons engaging in or subject to spouse abuse.

(d) Formulate, undertake, and carry out a research and evaluation program on spouse abuse; participate in programs of, cooperate with, and assist, as in its discretion shall be deemed advisable, other properly qualified agencies, including any agency of the federal government, schools of medicine, and hospitals or clinics, in planning and conducting research on the prevention, care, treatment, and rehabilitation of persons engaged in or subject to spouse abuse.

(e) Serve as a clearing house for information relating to spouse abuse.

(f) Review, comment upon, and assist public agencies and local governments with applications to be submitted to the federal government for grants or other funds for services for persons engaged in or subject to spouse abuse.

(g) Enlist the assistance of public and voluntary health, education, welfare, and rehabilitation agencies in a concerted effort to prevent and to treat persons engaged in or subject to spouse abuse.

(3) The department shall promulgate such rules as are necessary to implement this act.

Section 4. Diagnostic-intervention centers—

(1) The department shall establish diagnostic-intervention centers to serve as temporary receiving facilities to which persons subject to spouse abuse may be admitted until the situation which resulted in the abuse can be properly investigated. The center shall refer such persons and their spouses to any public or private facility, service, or program providing treatment or rehabilitation services, including but not limited to, the prevention, care, treatment, and rehabilitation of persons engaged in or subject to spouse abuse.

(2) The department shall establish procedures whereby persons subject to spouse abuse may seek admission to these centers on a voluntary basis.

(3) The department shall have an authority to contract with other governmental or private agencies for additional facilities or programs.

Section 5. Information confidential—Information received by authorized persons employed by or volunteering services to a center through files, reports, inspection, or otherwise shall be deemed privileged and confidential information and shall not be disclosed publicly in such a manner as to identify individuals or facilities.

Section 6. Referral to centers required—Any law enforcement officer who investigates an alleged incident of spouse abuse shall advise the person subject to the abuse of the availability of a diagnostic-intervention center at which he or she may be admitted to facilitate a temporary separation until the incident may be properly investigated or until he or she is referred to an appropriate agency providing treatment or rehabilitation services.

Section 7. This act shall take effect October 1, 1977.

This Bill would specifically address itself to the void created by the lack of facilities or alternative living situations presently available to a victim. In addition, this Bill would deal with spouse abuse not only as a criminal problem but also as a social problem. Presently, no alternative environment or living situation is being offered or made available to those victims seeking help. In addition to providing counseling care, treatment, and rehabilitation, and temporary placement facilities where this treatment may be administered, the Bill would also provide that the Department make available services through existing treatment programs and resources, prior to the establishment and funding of separate programs.

A MODEL FOR SERVICES

Maria Roy, Founder and Executive Director of Abused Women's Aid in Crisis, Inc.

Prior to 1975, most Americans went about their lives oblivious to the all-pervasive problem of violence within the American home. Behind closed doors, husbands indulged in gratuitous violence, beating, maiming, and sometimes killing their wives while their disturbed children watched and learned in horror. Generation after generation, violence begat violence. Children grew up accepting, tolerating, and perpetuating this same violence in their own adult lives. The nation pulsed out an irregular beat—the family out of sync with the rest of national concerns. The people of the nation listened with indifference as women were heard screaming and whimpering in the night. Ambulances and police cars came and went, sirens fading in the distance. But no one reached out to help—if the women go hurt, killed, it was nobody's business; neighbors had no right to interfere.

Official national policy to provide assistance was also non-existent: State, City, public, and private agencies assumed this same posture of non-involvement. In short, before 1975, the horrendous problem of wifebeating in the United States was not identified as a major serious social problem.

In 1977, things are changing, partly through the initial efforts of the social service organization, *Abused Women's Aid in Crisis, Inc.* (AWAIC, INC. [pronounced a-w-a-k-e]). Since its inception in early 1975, AWAIC has offered assistance to thousands of women in the U.S. AWAIC is the first major attempt in the U.S. to focus on the problems of abused women and their children, and to inform the public of the gravity of the problem. Through its work, happily, other individuals, groups, agencies, and governmental officials have become interested in learning about all aspects of the problem. As a nation-wide clearinghouse for information and referrals, AWAIC has had inquiries from all parts of the country. Similarly, requests for training workshops are received from both traditional agencies and collective type women's groups eager to provide quality help.

Since AWAIC has developed and implemented services to battered women, and since the organization is recognized by the medical, legal, and social service professions as expert in the delivery of services for battered women, its structure and program could easily serve as a model for other like-minded incipient groups desiring to offer help. For this reason, the substance of the article will address itself to the following organizational questions:

1. How to start the organization and plan for future programming.
2. How to look for funds and keep them coming.
3. How to recruit and train volunteers.
4. How to use the media and not vice versa.

1. *How to start the organization and plan for future programming.*

Publicize the problem and inform your community about wife-beating with a conference. Charge admission to cover the cost of printing programs and conference proceedings, postage, and telephone bills.

AWAIC was established after the first statewide conference on wife-beating was held in New York. This event marked the beginning of TV and radio coverage of the problems concerning battered women. CBS local news in New York City was contacted and responded by sending a film crew to cover the Conference. Since then, the media has shown continued interest in the subject. The Cardinal Spellman Head Start Center, fully aware of the existence of wifebeating, organized the conference and invited attorneys, social workers, public health nurses, teachers, etc. to attend. Professionals were invited as panelists or to direct workshops. Your group should also plan for women to speak out and testify from the audience. (See Appendix for conference proceedings). Record names, addresses, and telephone numbers of guests in a guest book. Then follow up the conference with subsequent meetings to determine the structure of the organization—collective, membership, non-membership, dues-paying. AWAIC strongly advises that some fund raising be done to pay for any legal fees that may be incurred. Pro bono legal help may cost the group more money in the long run. Draw up by-laws; seek out a reputable lawyer to incorporate the group as a not-for-profit organization. In addition, have the lawyer, a CPA, or someone officially appointed by the organization prepare the necessary papers for submission to the IRS for the purpose of obtaining Tax-Exempt status. After the corporate seal is received, a bank resolution necessary for opening a corporate bank account should be prepared. Except to wait for six months to one year for all the papers to come through. This waiting time should not discourage the group from continuing to plan and implement a program on a small scale. AWAIC started by setting up a limited telephone counseling service. The program was strictly voluntary. Concomitantly, an intake questionnaire was devised for telephone interviewing and statistical purposes. Monthly evening meetings were set up and women phoning in for help, as well as professionals, were invited to come. Daytop Village in New York City offered us meeting room space free of charge for this purpose. Inquire of your city's Parks and Recreational Department for listings of free space available. In New York City, a publication entitled, "Spaces," is a directory of auditoriums and meeting rooms. It can be purchased for two dollars through The Department of Parks, Recreation and Cultural Affairs.

The contacts made through the Evening Outreach program will help build up resources to draw upon and likewise to establish the organization as a resource for various professionals attending the meetings. AWAIC, through its telephone service, was able to hasten police response to calls for help and to provide information regarding court procedures. Assistance from churches and relatives of victims was sought out and a carfare fund was set up for those women who needed to leave home in a hurry. AWAIC proceeded accordingly for about six months, at which time it was ready to apply for foundation grants.

2. *How to look for funds and keep them coming.*

There are several how-to-raise-money books on the market—a trip to your local book store or college library will be most helpful. Linkage with a community service organization, such as The Community Service Society of New York, could prove rewarding for information and technical assistance in fund raising.

In New York City, several days spent at the Foundation Library are a must. Note those foundations most likely to fund your particular project. Look under categories such as Women, Child Abuse, Alcoholism, and Mental Health, for starters. Find out the maximum grants given in the past and use the information as a gauge for requesting money.

When you have a clear idea about which foundations to approach, begin writing the proposal. AWAIC decided to start with the private foundations first, leaving application for State and Federal monies as subsequent projects. General support monies were requested from the private foundations in order to expand the telephone service, further develop the volunteer training program, augment on-site individual and group counseling, and develop the clearinghouse into a full-fledged clearinghouse for information and referrals. The ultimate and primary objective was to design and develop a shelter program for battered women and children. Enlargement of the information and counseling services were necessary before undertaking such a large scale project.

Budgeting included predicted expenses encompassing salaries for administrative and programmatic personnel, on the one hand, and operational costs, on the other. The more costly expenses will be telephone and paper and printing. Be sure to include rent costs when itemizing expenditures, since any free space secured along the way will inevitably be temporary. When selecting board members, be sure to include someone who is known to the philanthropic community or who has had considerable experience with fund raising.

The proposal should reflect the nature of the problem of wife-beating. Backing up information with data compiled from the telephone intake questionnaire will make for a more convincing statement of the problem. Part of the proposal should include a section on research, evaluation, and related problems such as alcoholism and child abuse. The bulk of the proposal should be a development of your organization's needs and priorities. Attach an appendix containing case histories, relevant legislation, proceedings from conferences, board members, and references. Private foundations will review the proposal for content and merit. Political endorsement does not count. Remember that the proposal, if considered meritorious and falling within foundations guidelines, will have to be scheduled for review and approval by the foundation's board membership at some future date. Do not expect an immediate decision and do not be discouraged when requested to wait three or four months for a response. Submit a cover letter with the proposal describing your organization's reasons for choosing each particular foundation.

If you have discovered ten possible foundations, submit ten proposals simultaneously. Wait one week after mailing them, and then follow up with a call: Have they received the proposal? Are they interested in meeting with your director or several members of the board? Be patient and, most of all, be courteous. When funds are received, be sure to note each foundation's requirements for record keeping and reporting.

State and Federal funding require a different approach. Be sure to know your state senators and assembly persons. Involve them by inviting them to conferences, to work jointly on needed legislation, and on securing state appropriations. In New York City, Council Resolution #491-A was introduced and passed largely through the efforts of City Councilperson Miriam Friedlander. (See Appendix for the Resolution.) On the Federal level, secure the help of your U.S. Senator's and Congressperson's legislative aid. Write to the League of Women Voters in your city for the booklet entitled: "They Represent You." It includes all the elected representatives in Washington, D.C., your state, and your city. Research possible sources of funding. (Refer to Norback, C. and Norback, P., in the Appendix of this chapter for a complete listing of governmental programs and services available).

When the organization can demonstrate that it has sufficient funds to cover its operational costs for a one year period, request government funds that would augment the existing program. Be sure to know the required guidelines inside and out. Seek official help and advice. Do not submit a proposal unless it is thoroughly scrutinized and edited by those contacts made who are experienced in writing governmental proposals.

Your groups may seriously consider linking up with an already existing organization like the Salvation Army or the Red Cross. Practically speaking, during these hard economic times, efforts should be made to secure support from many interested groups and organizations situated in one locale. Working cooperatively to help find solutions is most feasible. If all groups decide to establish shelters in the same city or town, talent and expertise will be dissipated. What might ensue are factions and unhealthy competition and possibly even exploitation of the very serious social problem of wifebeating. Incipient groups should lend a hand to that group which is farthest along in terms of organization and fund raising. Today's Women's Movement is blessed with the multi-talents of many bright and capable women. Remember that the women/victims must always be the priority and that with the combined support of individual woman activists and women's groups in the area, the women/victims can be assured help speedily and effectively. Once the group has achieved firm financial roots, it becomes easier, though not without great effort, to apply for more and more grants. Your program's efficacy will be a model on which other groups can plan similar projects.

3. *How to recruit and train volunteers.*

Very often, volunteers will come to you; nevertheless, find someone who will be responsible for recruiting and training volunteers. Your whole program during the formative years will depend heavily on the work of unpaid professionals. Consider these volunteers a national treasure. Cherish their good works.

Volunteers can be drawn from women's groups or work study or field placement programs in schools of social work, law, or psychology. Hiring a paid professional to supervise the volunteers will help tremendously. A municipal agency, such as The Mayor's Office of Volunteers in New York City, should be tapped. Your local chapter of NOW could post notices requesting volunteers. Send letters to nearby university department heads requesting students for field placement or work study programs. Public service spots on TV and radio are another great way to solicit volunteers.

Remember that not all who respond, though well-meaning, will be suited to the task. It is extremely important that the volunteers be well versed in the literature, know the issues very well, be skilled in interviewing techniques, and be monitored during the first few months on the telephone. Refer to Tables 1 and 2 for a listing of AWAIC's job descriptions for volunteers and summary of the AWAIC hot line functions.

4. *How to use the media and not vice versa.*

The media can be a crucial link to hundreds and thousands of women, listening and watching at home, who are too frightened to seek out help. The media, powerful as it is, can perform a tremendous public service by encouraging battered women to find help without feeling shameful or guilty.

AWAIC is usually beseiged by telephone calls after TV and radio coverage. After one highly visible TV show broadcast our telephone number last year, our organization received non-stop telephone calls for a three month period—not to mention all the mail written by desperate women.

Be on guard against media people who over-emphasize "visual impact." They may say something like, "Provide us with a victim or no show." This puts the organization in a very compromising position. After all, the organization's function is not be a talent agency for battered women. Do not let any media person exploit the many emotionally fragile women who come into your office for help. Occasionally, there will be some battered women who will not mind TV or radio coverage—they may have extricated themselves from their dangerous home life; their husbands are no longer a threat. These women will definitely be important success models for the other women tuning in. Be sure to take measures to insure their anonymity—change names, photograph with backs to camera, use disguises. The safety and emotional health of each client should be of paramount importance—not the media coverage.

Spokeswomen working for the organization can be just as effective on radio and television. Women need to know about your organization. There is comfort in knowing that help is a telephone call away. Very often, a woman will indicate that she saved a newspaper clipping

TABLE 1. JOB DESCRIPTIONS.

---

1. *Information and Referral Counselor:*

   Answer hot line telephone calls and letters from battered women throughout the nation.

2. *Initial Intake Interviewer:*

   On-site interviewing of clients to determine their specific needs.

3. *Client Advocate:*

   Accompany client to Family Court, Legal Aid, and Department of Social Services. Write follow up letters on clients behalf.

4. *Public Information Assistant:*

   Public relations work contacting media, disseminating information, and responding to special requests for information on AWAIC's services and activities.

TABLE 2.   AWAIC HOT LINE.

What Does It Do?

The AWAIC Hot Line offers immediate emotional support and practical information and referral services. It has handled nearly 2500 calls since its inception in February 1975. The Hot Line staff consists of a Hot Line Coordinator and Hot Line operators who have received training and supervision from the AWAIC staff.

How Does It Operate?

When a Hot Line call comes in, our primary concern is to respond to the immediate needs of the caller. She may have difficulty in talking about her problems. She may have tried unsuccessfully to find help or may never have spoken to anyone about it before. It is important to establish a rapport with the caller so that she will feel at ease to tell her story to you. We do not require the caller's name unless she wants to tell us. We do ask the name of the borough, county, or town in which she lives. After rapport has been established, we begin our initial intake procedure. As the caller and the operator discuss her problem, the operator writes detailed information on the Hot Line Intake form. This procedure is valuable in performing follow up work and also serves as documentation of the problems of the battered woman. Finally, the caller is asked what specific practical help she needs and is offered an appointment to see someone from the AWAIC staff. Our daytime group support programs, legal counseling, and evening Outreach Meetings are also available to the caller.

How to Become a Hot Line Volunteer

The Hot Line Coordinator offers a training program for Hot Line Volunteers. Anyone interested in participating can call the AWAIC office number to set up an appointment for an interview. Sources of volunteers are former AWAIC clients, Mayors Office of Volunteers, Legal Aid and Social Service University students, Volunteer Programs from Social Service Organizations, and women who have heard of or read about AWAIC and want to become involved in helping the battered woman.

Screening Volunteers

Our screening process attempts to determine the volunteer's suitability for this important and sensitive work. Initially, the volunteer fills out a questionnaire:
   1. Name—address—phone
   2. Referred by
   3. Education
   4. Volunteer experience
   5. Special skills
   6. Hours available for training and work
Some of the special qualities needed in a Hot Line Volunteer are high motivation and strong commitment, as well as reliability and punctuality. We look for emotional maturity and the ability to make clear and cool-headed decisions in a crisis situation.

Hot Line Volunteer Training

The Hot Line volunteer is required to participate in 10 classroom hours of training under the supervision of the AWAIC staff. The training is extensive and intense. AWAIC is represented by the high quality of the Hot Line volunteers. They are considered an integral part of AWAIC's services. There are five two-hour training sessions. These are followed by three months of closely supervised telephone counseling.

with AWAIC's number on it for a year before actually calling. It's the telephone number that they remember—the link to help.

Press conferences prepared in advance to publicize conferences, an open house, and proposed new legislation are a must. Know the producers of the various local and national news networks. Do not fail to invite them. Have someone follow up invitations with phone calls. The more press contacts, the more coverage.

The point is to use the media as a catalyst for helping battered women help themselves by contacting your organization.

An Example of Successful Solicitation of Governmental Support

AWAIC/Henry Street Settlement/Human Resources Administration; New York City

Approval for A Pilot Project

City Council Hearings on Battered Women in New York, held on October 14, 1976 and the subsequent adoption of Resolution #491-A introduced by Councilwoman, Miriam Friedlander in its original form in May 1975 and then subsequently in November 1976 (refer to Appendix B in this book) launched the beginning of a city-supported program for battered women and their families.

A Battered Women's Task Force chaired by Miriam Friedlander met regularly for several months and resulted in the adoption of an unprecedented pilot project with The Human Resources Administration, the Henry Street Settlement and AWAIC. Councilman Robert Steingut, an active and committed member of the Task Force, was also very constructive in the planning stage. His ultimate goal, for the city to adopt measures on a citywide basis, will become effective in September 1977.

Bertram Beck, Executive Director of the Henry Street Settlement, announced the plans for the city's first shelter to house battered women on February 17, 1977. The Henry Street/AWAIC shelter program currently provides shelter and basic services for approximately 60 women and 140 children over the course of a year. The program can accommodate 32 individuals in 18 apartments at a given time. Counseling, education, and recreation are also components of the program. While Henry Street provides the actual shelter for the women and children, AWAIC provides a system of intake and referral to the shelter, a telephone hotline, monthly workshops and semi-nars. In addition, a training grant to AWAIC, from The Human Resources Administration to implement a training program with the city agencies involved, and the Henry Street Settlement, enables the city to participate in the project in an ongoing way. AWAIC will also provide training to the municipal agencies involved in the city-wide program. Candice Butcher of HRA has been instrumental in devel-oping the project and drawing up the necessary contracts.

It is important for groups interested in helping battered women to make their government accountable to the needs of battered women and to work side-by-side with their Representatives in planning and implementing programs. It is equally important for these same groups to participate, in some way, in the program itself. Participation can be either directly through services, or indirectly through training programs for government personnel.

The above Pilot Project represents a mixing of the public and private sectors working together for a common goal—protection and advice to battered women and their families.*

SUGGESTED READINGS

1. AWAIC, INC., 1976, G.P.O. Box 1699, New York, N.Y. 10001
2. Erickson, Nancy, *A Woman's Guide to Marriage and Divorce in New York.* New York: Women's Law Center. 1414 Sixth Avenue, New York, 10019.
3. Sohmer, Muriel, Winston, Myrel, and Lifton, Sue, *Call for Action: A Survival Kit for New Yorkers.*
4. Catalogue of Federal Domestic Assistance: Information Center Office of Eco-nomic Opportunity.
5. 1977, Director of Social and Health Agencies of New York City. Published for the Community Council of Greater New York, Inc. New York and London: Columbia University Press.
6. Norback, Craig and Norback, Peter, 1975, *Everything You Can Get From the Government for Free . . . or Almost for Free.* New York: Van Nostrand Reinhold Co.
7. Weiner, F., 1969, *First National City Bank: How to Survive in New York With Children.* New York: Charles Scribner's Sons.
8. 1972, Fortune 500 Directory, Time, Inc., Time & Life Building, 541 North Fair-banks Court, Chicago, Illinois 60611.
9. "Foundation News," Council on Foundations, Inc. 888 Seventh Ave., New York, N.Y. 10019.

---

*Refer to Appendix A for AWAIC's Progress Report (1976–1977).

10. "Grantsmanship Newsletter." Grantsmanship Center, 1015 West Olympic Boulevard, Los Angeles, California 90015.
11. Allen, C. M., 1975, *How to Get a New York Divorce For Under $100*. New York: Allen Advertising Co.
12. 1976, "How to Secure Help for Those Who Need It" (pamphlet in Spanish and English). Information Bureau of the Community Council of Greater New York.
13. "Is There a Crisis in the Family Courts?" (pamphlet by the New York State Family Court Monitoring Project State Headquarters). The Fund for Modern Courts, Inc., 36 West 44th Street, New York, N.Y. 10036.
14. Weber, J., "Managing the Board of Directors," The Greater New York Fund, Inc., 99 Park Avenue, New York 10016.
15. Foster, Henry H. Jr, and Freed, Doris Jonas, *Matrimonial Law: An Overview*. New York: The Lawyers Co-operative Publishing Co., Rochester, New York, 14603.
16. "Standard and Poors," Standard and Poor's Corporation, 345 Hudson Street, New York 10014.
17. Alexander, Shana, "State by State Guide to Women's Legal Rights," Wollstonecraft Inc. 1975.
18. "Taft Information System: A Method for Keeping Current on Foundations": Taft Products, Inc. 1000 Vermont Avenue N.W. Washington, D.C. 20005.
19. "The Foundation Directory," 1977. Columbia University Press, 136 South Broadway, Irving on the Hudson, New York 10533.
20. "The New York Woman's Directory" Womanpower Project: Workman Publishing Co. New York City 1973.
21. Ross, Susan, *The Rights of Women*. New York: Avon Books.
22. Kanowitz, Leo, 1969, Women and the Law. Albuquerque, New Mexico: University of New Mexico Press.
23. "Women in Transition: A Feminist Handbook on Separation and Divorce" Charles Scribner's Sons, New York, 1975.
24. WNET/13 and N.Y.U. Law School (New York) OUTREACH: LIFEBOAT NEW YORK FACT SHEETS, Nov. 23, 1975.
25. Miller, Thomas F. and Orser, G. R., "You Don't Know What You Got Until You Lose It: An Introduction to Accounting, Budgeting and Tax Planning for small, non profit organizations and Community Groups." The Support Center/ The Community Management Center; 1424 16th Street, N. W., Suite 201; Washington, D.C. 20036.

Appendices

And suppose the wife not as the wife, but as a woman only. . . . Tell me likewise to what end should men attempt such violence? If a woman be perverse, she thereby amends not; if gentle, she deserves it not; if you seek praise thereby, you shall merit laughter: if reward you shall be sure of shame. Whereas therefore, you are guided by no virtue, nor directed into any end, who but stony hearts will lay their violent hands on a woman. . . ?

HEALE, WILLIAM, 1609

Appendix A

ABUSED WOMEN'S AID IN CRISIS, INC. (AWAIC): A PROGRESS REPORT, 1976–1977

WHAT IS A BATTERED WOMAN?

"My husband held a gun to my head all morning and dared me to breathe. When I finally went to the probation officer, she didn't believe me. It took three weeks to see the judge, and when I did, he told me to go home and try to work it out. Now my husband has left, and welfare has told me that I have to find him so they can make him pay child support."

"My husband has threatened to cripple the child and kill me. He has assaulted me. I had him arrested, and he got a two-month suspended sentence. Finally, I had to move out of my apartment, and he is in possession of all my worldly goods. I can't afford a lawyer, and Bronx Legal Aid is not accepting any divorce or legal separation cases. Where do I go from here?"

"When the police answer a call, you feel they are smirking, you feel put down. After a few calls they stop responding. Once when I called and asked them to make an arrest, they refused."

"My children scream because he shouts and hits me in front of them. He has thrown me out at night and told me to go, but I can't leave the children, and it's a job to get a room with children."

"Had there been someone years ago to listen to me, to advise me of my rights, of my alternatives, I might have avoided a tragedy in my life—my son wouldn't now need psychiatric care—and possibly, my husband would have sought help."

Background

Abused Women's Aid in Crisis (AWAIC) was founded in 1975 by Maria Roy, then a social worker at the Cardinal Spellman Head Start Center on the Lower East Side of Manhattan. Ms. Roy was concerned about the number of women she encountered who were brutalized by husbands who literally threatened their lives and the lives of their children.

Ms. Roy brought together a group of like-minded women, and together they established a hotline, which any battered woman might call for assistance. At the beginning, all assistance was rendered by part-time volunteers, including Ms. Roy. AWAIC attempted to help women being beaten by their husbands to secure legal services, housing, child care, public assistance, and, when necessary, psychological counseling.

In those early days, while operating on a part-time basis out of borrowed space, Ms. Roy sought the assistance of various organizations on the Lower East Side, including the Henry Street Settlement. As funds were secured from various foundations, AWAIC was able to stabilize itself as an organization, the only one now providing comprehensive services for abused women and their children. Today, AWAIC has an office centrally located in mid-Manhattan and a full-time staff, consisting of Ms. Roy as Executive Director and Carolyn Chrisman as Director of Training. In addition, over 20 volunteers donate their time regularly.

AWAIC, then, is the only specialized social service for battered women in the New York metropolitan area. It is now recognized by medical, legal, and social service professionals as expert in the delivery of these services for battered women. Requests are received daily for emergency intervention, counseling, general information, workshops, and training sessions. AWAIC has also received a fair amount of recognition nationally.

Until the emergence of AWAIC in 1975, other service agencies in New York City had generally denied the existence of "the battered woman problem." The problem of the battered women is certainly not a new one. What is new is the view that it is an important *social* problem—one for which society has failed to make satisfactory provision. In the past two or three years, recognition of the problem has been growing in the United States. There is at last an increasing awareness of the need to provide assistance to battered women and their children, in the form of a network of shelter, counseling, legal, health, housing, and vocational services. These services enable the abused woman to address her problems and those of her children humanely, speedily, and effectively; AWAIC therefore provides (1) telephone counseling and crisis intervention; (2) individual and peer group supportive counseling; (3) advocacy and escort service through the various city agencies; (4) a nationwide clearinghouse function for information and referrals; (5) referrals to protective shelters; (6) training and consulting services to other social service deliverers; and (7) various community outreach programs, including a speakers' bureau, family life dramatizations, and so on. AWAIC's services are offered free to anyone who needs them. All calls and letters are kept strictly confidential. A description of how AWAIC delivers these services follows.

1. Telephone Counseling and Crisis Intervention. AWAIC has installed two hotline telephone lines in addition to its regular office lines. To provide crisis intervention for battered women and their children, a core of well-trained volunteers answer calls from abused women and engage in telephone follow-up services for them between 10 a.m. and 4 p.m. The volunteers also make appointments for women to come in for counseling, and they arrange for escorts through the various city agencies, such as HRA's Income Maintenance Centers and the Family Court.

Data are collected on all callers, and recorded on a short form intake questionnaire. To date, approximately 2,000 women have phoned AWAIC for hotline assistance.

2. Individual and Peer Group Supportive Counseling. AWAIC's basic approach to counseling is through peer support, where the stigmas and taboos of wife beating can be removed and the woman comforted and reassured as much as possible. At the same time, AWAIC offers individual counseling to battered women.

The group sessions are held during the day at AWAIC's office, with each session lasting an hour and a half. (An evening group will soon convene.) The groups are limited to ten women, to insure a close, responsive setting, and each group runs in six-week renewable cycles. During the course of the year, over eighty women have participated in these intensive group counseling experiences. Thus, most of the counseling AWAIC has performed has been on a short-term basis—assisting the women through a crisis stage and helping them to proceed from there. There is, however, provision for longer-range treatment.

3. Soliciting Government Responsiveness. AWAIC has been instrumental in making New York City accountable for the problems of battered women in two major ways:

a. Through providing testimony and other information that led to the passage of the City Council's Resolution No. 419-A, which directs city agencies to provide assistance to abused women and their children.
b. AWAIC has also been an active participant in a series of meetings held by the Council's Task Force on Battered Women, chaired by Councilwoman Miriam Friedlander with Councilmen Robert Steingut and Leon Katz as members. Other Task Force participants include the staff from the Henry Street Settlement, and Candice Butcher of the Human Resources Administration. Thus far, these meetings have resulted in a pilot project involving the Henry Street Settlement and AWAIC in a cooperative shelter care and follow-up for battered women. The City's Department of Social Services has agreed to amend regulations governing income maintenance, so that women, whose resources are not readily available to them because of life-threatening situations, would qualify for emergency public assistance. In the past, victims of domestic violence were asked to return to their husbands and homes in order to locate documents and to tap resources. This often dangerous procedure will not be required under the pilot project.

The Henry Street Settlement provides shelter care for up to sixty women and children during a year's time. AWAIC is responsible for the intake, the screening of appropriate clients for the shelter, and the provision of follow-up counseling for the women residents. In addition, AWAIC has set up a training and evaluation program for the city agencies directly involved with the project, for the Henry Street staff, and for the volunteers with student interns needed to carry out this project.

4. Clearinghouse for Information. Newspaper and magazine articles, and radio and television coverage of AWAIC services have encouraged many battered women throughout the country to write in for personal advice. In addition, letters of inquiry about the nature of the specific services and the problems of battered women in general have come to AWAIC from service organizations and developing groups around the state and country. When the request for assistance comes from a battered woman not living in the metropolitan area, AWAIC responds, when possible, with the name and address of the nearest service in their geographical area, and by giving other suggestions, including information about the steps the women should take to protect themselves. To others, AWAIC sends relevant information, references to publications, and so on.

5. Outreach

A. Speakers' Bureau

AWAIC's executive director has been invited to speak at numerous workshops, conferences, and social gatherings. For example: the New York Urban Coalition's all-day Conference on the Family, the Law Enforcement Administration Association Conference, the New York Women's City Club, Queens College Women's Festival, American Friends Service Committee, and numerous other engagements at colleges, women's organizations, and service agencies.

B. Media Coverage

AWAIC's executive director has also appeared on numerous radio and television programs, many articles have been written in magazines and the newspapers about AWAIC. For example: the Today Show, WMCA Call for Action, Conference Call, A.M. New York, Midday Live, Straight Talk, the Jeanne Paar Show, CBS Morning News, major network (both local and national) news shows, and numerous other programs.

C. Brochures

A grant was made by the Eastman foundation so that 30,000 brochures on AWAIC could be produced. These brochures are being disseminated by mail and by hand to hospital emergency rooms, hospital departments of social service, the New York City Family Court, the emergency assistance unit of the city's Welfare Department, and to all agencies requesting information about AWAIC's services.

D. Community Outreach Projects

AWAIC holds periodic evening meetings in a secure central location. Members of the professional community and battered women convene for the purposes of exchanging information, learning about the problem, and increasing resources.

6. Volunteer Training Program. AWAIC's training program has two components: volunteer training and training for outside agencies.

a. AWAIC's core of volunteers are trained for telephone and on site counseling; answering mail from around the country; escorting clients through the various city agencies; compiling data for research purposes; representing AWAIC at speaking engagements; and providing office skills as clerk, receptionist, and typist.

b. AWAIC's training for outside agencies is primarily based on training workshops that come in from many organizations. AWAIC has provided training for the following agencies: Victims Information Bureau of Suffolk, New York Family Court, Department of Probation, the Henry Street School and Maternal and Infant Care Unit of the Department of Social Services.

AWAIC will soon begin a training program for city government workers that has recently been approved by the Human Resources Administration. AWAIC will train staff at the City's Emergency Assistance Unit, the Division of Protective Services for Adults, and Income Maintenance Centers throughout the city.

AWAIC'S PROGRAMS

- VOLUNTEER TRAINING PROGRAM
- TRAINING AND CONSULTING TO OUTSIDE AGENCIES
- RESOURCE MANUAL
- PROJECT INFORMATION
  Family life dramatization in workshop setting
  Speakers' bureau
  Community outreach
  Research

Since all of our services are offered free, we appreciate your *financial support*. Tax-exempt contributions should be sent to AWAIC, Inc., G.P.O. Box 1699, New York, N.Y. 10001.

AWAIC'S LISTING OF: EARLY WARNING SIGNALS

Statistics show that violence is a way of life. Learn to recognize the warning signals—seek help immediately. Do not expect your situation to improve with time.

1 Parental Violence in the Home
If your husband or companion witnessed or was the object of violence while growing up, he is likely to be a violent adult.

2 Alcoholism or Drug Use
Alcoholism or drug use often leads to violence in the home. Urge your husband or companion to seek help. Treatment for his problem may stop or prevent violence in your home. If he refuses to go for help, do not expect things to improve.

3 Criminal Record

If your husband or companion has committed a violent crime outside the home, he is likely to be violent in the home.

4 Unplanned or Unwanted Pregnancy

Take precautions to avoid unplanned or unwanted pregnancy. Pregnancy may cause a great strain on your relationship, which may lead to frustration and violence.

SERVICES FOR WOMEN

1 TELEPHONE COUNSELING AND CRISIS INTERVENTION

2 INDIVIDUAL COUNSELING AND SUPPORT GROUPS

3 ADVOCACY AND ESCORT SERVICE THROUGH THE VARIOUS CITY AGENCIES

4 NATIONWIDE CLEARING HOUSE FOR INFORMATION AND REFERRALS

5 REFERRALS TO PROTECTIVE SHELTER

All of our services are offered *free* to anyone who needs them. We urge you to call or write. All calls and letters will be kept strictly confidential.

SECURITY PROCEDURE EMPLOYED BY AWAIC'S STAFF AND COUNSELORS

1. Telephone Inquiries

When a male caller, not known to AWAIC, telephones and asks for the location of the AWAIC offices or the mailing address: *DO NOT GIVE THE INFORMATION* unless he justifies his reason for the request. Ask for his name, phone number, and organization affiliation and advise him that his call will be returned. Then advise an AWAIC staff member of the request. Location of AWAIC offices should not be given to anyone not known to the counselor.

2. On Site Visits

When a client is to make an on-site visit to the AWAIC offices, follow this procedure:

a. Give client the address but not the suite number. Ask client to phone from pay phone in lobby of our building. Tell client she will be met by a counselor and escorted to our offices.

   b. If client's husband or companion is known to be a *predicate felon* (police record as a felon) or *extremely dangerous*, *do not* arrange an on-site visit. In such cases, arrange to meet the client in a nearby coffee shop, library, or a public place where you can talk with some ease, and still be in the company of many people.

3. Never open the office door to anyone not known to you, unless you have been given the name of the expected visitor from an AWAIC counselor or staff member.

ABUSED WOMEN'S AID IN CRISIS, INC.

SHORT FORM INTAKE QUESTIONNAIRE

DATE _____ COUNSELOR _____

NAME _____ BOROUGH _____

ADDRESS _____

HOME TELEPHONE _____ TIMES TO CALL ____ OFFICE # ____

REFERRED BY _____ REASON FOR CALLING _____

HUSBAND ___ EX-HUSBAND ___ COMPANION ___ (HIS NAME) _____

SINGLE ___ MARRIED ___ DIVORCED ___ DURATION OF RELATIONSHIP ___

YOUR AGE _____ HIS AGE _____

LIVING TOGETHER NOW? ___ DATE YOU LEFT ____ DATE HE LEFT ____

NOW STAYING AT _____ PHONE _____

NO. CHILDREN _____ AGES _____ MALE _____ FEMALE _____

WHERE ARE CHILDREN LIVING? _____

IN WHAT WAYS HAVE YOU SOUGHT HELP? _____

IS THERE A PATTERN OF LEAVING AND RETURNING TO HUSBAND OR COMPANION _____

VIOLENCE

FIRST OCCURRENCE _____

FREQUENCY _____ DATE OF MOST RECENT OCCURRENCE _____

DESCRIBE VIOLENCE _____

DESCRIBE INJURIES _____

RECEIVE MEDICAL ATTENTION? _____ HOSPITAL EMERG. ROOM? _____

PRIVATE PHYSICIAN? _____

PRESENT PHYSICAL CONDITION _____

HAVE YOU HAD A PHOTO TAKEN OF YOUR INJURIES? _____

IS HE VIOLENT TOWARD THE CHILDREN? _____

HAVE YOU REPORTED THIS TO SPECIAL SERVICES FOR CHILDREN? _____

OR SPCC? _____ THEIR RESPONSE: _____

FINANCES

ARE YOU EMPLOYED? _____ TYPE OF WORK _____
IF NOT, DO YOU HAVE SKILLS? DESCRIBE: _____ EDUCATION _____
DO YOU HAVE A CHECKING OR SAVINGS ACCT? YES ___ NO ___ JOINT ___
IS HE EMPLOYED? _____ TYPE OF WORK _____
DOES HE SUPPORT YOU? _____
DO YOU HAVE PUBLIC ASSISTANCE? _____ WELFARE _____ SSI _____
DO YOU OWN PROPERTY TOGETHER? _____
IF RENTING, IS *YOUR* NAME ON THE LEASE? _____
OTHER FINANCIAL ASSETS OR RESOURCES? _____

PERSONAL HISTORY OF COUPLE

HAVE YOU DISCUSSED THE PROBLEM WITH HIM? _____
WHAT DO YOU THINK CAUSES HIS VIOLENCE? _____
_____
DRINKING PROBLEM? YOU _____ HE _____ A.A.? _____ ALANON? _____
DRUG USE? YOU _____ HE _____ FORMERLY _____
DRUG TREATMENT PROGRAM? YOU _____ HE _____
NAME OF PROGRAM _____
WHO IN FAMILY HAS RECEIVED COUNSELING? _____
PAST _____ CURRENT _____
TYPE, LOCATION, & FREQUENCY OF COUNSELING _____
_____
HAVE EITHER OF YOU HAD LONG-TERM TREATMENT FOR ANY PHYSICAL
OR MENTAL CONDITION? YOU _____ HE _____ DESCRIBE: _____
DO EITHER OF YOU HAVE A PHYSICAL DISABILITY? YOU _____ HE _____
DESCRIBE: _____
PRESENT EMOTIONAL STATE: _____
_____

POLICE

WERE POLICE CALLED? _____ BY WHOM? _____
HOW SOON DID THEY COME? _____ (DIDN'T COME) _____
POLICE RESPONSE:
   1. HELPFUL? YES _____ NO _____ DESCRIBE: _____
   2. DID YOU REQUEST THAT POLICE ARREST ASSAULTER? _____
   3. DID POLICE ARREST HIM? _____
   4. DID POLICE ADVISE YOU OF YOUR RIGHT TO MAKE A CITIZEN'S
      ARREST _____
   5. DID POLICE ESCORT YOU/HIM FROM PLACE OF ASSAULT? _____
   6. IF AN ARREST WAS MADE, DESCRIBE ACTION TAKEN BY POLICE: ___
      _____
   7. COMMENTS: _____

FAMILY COURT

HAVE YOU BEEN TO FAMILY COURT? _____ # OF TIMES _____
REASON: ORDER OF PROTECTION _____ SUPPORT _____ CUSTODY _____

RESULTS FROM COURT APPEARANCE:
  DID HE SHOW UP? _____
  TEMPORARY ORDER? _____ DATE OF HEARING _____
  PERMANENT ORDER? _____ DATE ISSUED _____ EXP. DATE _____
  WERE YOU AWARDED SUPPORT? _____ CUSTODY? _____ __
  DID NOT FOLLOW THROUGH: DIDN'T SHOW UP ___ DROPPED CHGS. ___
  OTHER: _____
HAS YOUR ORDER OF PROTECTION BEEN VIOLATED? _____
DID YOU REPORT VIOLATION TO POLICE? _____ FAMILY COURT? _____
DO YOU HAVE A HEARING DATE FOR VIOLATION OF O.P.? _____
DOES YOUR HUSBAND MAKE SUPPORT PAYMENTS? _____
JUDGE'S NAME _____

CRIMINAL COURT

HAVE YOU BEEN TO CRIMINAL COURT? _____
DESCRIBE CIRCUMSTANCES: _____
_____
DATE OF HEARING _____ NEXT HEARING? _____
CHARGES _____
DISPOSITION OF CASE: _____
DOES HUSBAND OR COMPANION HAVE A CRIMINAL RECORD? _____
COMMENTS:

RECOMMENDATIONS TO CLIENT:

FOLLOW-UP:

Appendix B

Work on the following Resolution began in the Spring of 1975 when City Council-woman, Miriam Friedlander introduced an unamended version of it to the City Council. Since it did not pass, Resolution (491) was referred to The Public Safety Committee which subsequently sponsored public hearings on October 14, 1976. These hearings inspired the amended Resolution (491-A) which was voted on by the Council and adopted on November 9, 1976.

THE COUNCIL

346

May 9, 1975.

Amended Res. No. 491-A

Resolution Calling Upon New York City Agencies to Inform Women Who Are the Victims of Violence in Domestic Relationships of the Services Available to Them, and to Provide Concrete Assistance to These Battered Women and Other Family Members, and Calling Upon the State Legislature to Amend the Present Laws Pertaining to Jurisdiction of Family Offenses.

By Ms. Friedlander, Messers. Katz, Silverman, Samuel, Weiss, Vallone, Kaufman, Povman, Gaeta, Olmedo, Steingut, Mrs. Greitzer, Messrs. Gerges, Katzman, Ms. Pinkett, Messrs. Berman, Burden, Mrs. Ryan, Mr. Wagner, Rev. Gigante, Messrs. Sadowsky, Manton, Ward, Spigner, Horwitz, Simon, Mastropieri, De-Marco, Wright, Mele, Muratori, Gangemi, Biondolillo, Stern, Crispino and Ms. Stringer—

Whereas, As stated by Betti S. Whaley, Commissioner of New York City's Agency for Child Development, "Three years ago, the battered child was written off as an accident case and little was done to treat the problem; now the problems related to battered women demand the same concerted attention and action"; and

Whereas, The physical abuse inflicted upon women by their spouses or com-panions can no longer be left in the realm of personal domestic relationships and must be recognized as a form of assault and violence; and

Whereas, Many women within a marriage or companionship relationship remain there in spite of this violence because of social and cultural conditioning and economic necessity; and

Whereas, It should be recognized that the existing law defining assault and battery as a crime applies to domestic as well as non-domestic situations; and

• **Whereas,** Under existing law, the family court has original jurisdiction over all "family offenses" so that any "family offense" prosecution beginning in a criminal court must be referred to the family court; and

• **Whereas,** Under such law, it is entirely within the discretion of the family court judge whether or not to treat any "family offense" as a criminal matter so that the battered wife can make no determination as to how she wants the offense committed against her to be treated; and

• **Whereas,** In order to give the battered wife an opportunity to determine how she would like any disorderly conduct, harassment, menacing, reckless endangerment, assault or attempted assault against her person, to be handled, it would require the amendment of the family court act by the State Legislature.

• **Whereas,** Many women are not aware or have not been informed of their own personal civil rights and the resources available to them to secure these rights, such as immediate protection, emergency shelter, counseling, and legal recourse; and

Whereas, Definitive steps should be taken immediately to remedy this deplorable pattern of violence by the abuser, to heighten the awareness of the victim, and to make known the help available to alleviate the hardships endured by the battered woman and other family members; now, therefore, be it

Resolved, That the Family Courts of the State of New York in the City of New York, the Police Department, the Department of Social Services, the Health Services Administration, the New York City Health and Hospitals Corporation, and other pertinent agencies prepare for public distribution special materials on the immediate and long-term services available from their agencies to aid the battered women and other family members; and be it further

Resolved, That these same agencies take immediate steps to train personnel and to set up special programs to assist the battered women and other family members; and be it further

• **Resolved,** That the State Legislature amend the present laws pertaining to jurisdiction of family offenses.

Adopted. (11/9/76)

TESTIMONY ON RESOLUTION '491*

June J. Christmas, M.D., Commissioner, Department of Mental Health and Mental Retardation Services, New York City

I am Dr. June J. Christmas, Commissioner of the New York City Department of Mental Health and Mental Retardation Services. I am pleased to have the opportunity to speak at these hearings on the extremely important subject of wifebeating. Thousands of women are beaten, injured and even killed every year by abusive husbands, paramours, or boyfriends in a syndrome which has been largely, officially ignored. I hope that this is the beginning not just of discussion of this problem by our City, but also of action to begin adequately to address the problem which is endemic to our society.

Symptomatic of the nature of this problem is that data on the incidence of wife beating are vague and can only be estimated. Figures are not available through the police agencies, although assault is a crime. The reason is, in part, because the

---

*Presented before the Committee on Public Safety, New York City Council, October 14, 1976, New York, N.Y.

original jurisdiction for battered wife petitions is Family Court, and even they lump wifebeating with all "family offenses." Not until a woman is severely injured— or killed—or the husband is found in violation of a Family Court order not to beat his wife, and frequently not even then, is this considered a police matter. (It is ironic indeed that a man is apparently free to assault his wife unless ordered specifically not to do so.)

One estimate suggests that in 1973 there were 14,000 cases of wifebeating brought to Family Court in New York State. A *New York Times* article of June 14, 1976 on wife battering indicates that 80% of all "family offense" petitions are filed by women against their husbands. Based on the same formula, an estimated 18,500 women filed petitions in Family Court last year in the state as a whole (an increase of 32% over 1973) and 5800 women in the City filed petitions for protection from their husbands. Since the Family Court is largely ineffectual in preventing further assaults, and is often thought to provoke the husband to further violence, it is well known that the actual incidence is considerably greater.

Wifeneating has long been viewed as a "family matter" rather than one for public concern. The law supports this hands-off attitude and the women are left to the mercy of their husbands' violent rages. The same behavior on the part of a stranger would immediately be viewed as a crime. So we must address the problem for what it is: a crime committed against women which has the tacit approval of society. This crime will continue to be committed as long as women are seen as possessions, devalued, to be kept in line by the physically stronger male.

But it would be shortsighted to see this as "just a feminist issue." The ramifications of the problem are far-reaching—in other forms of family violence such as child abuse, in continuing violence within the family passed on from generation to generation, and in violence moving beyond the confines of the family into society at large. It is crucial to understand that in permitting—or even not taking strong action against—the physical intimidation and abuse of more than half this City's population, we are condoning a policy of brute force.

We must take action. We must insure that the laws as they are written are enforced so that wives get *equal* protection under the law as they would if they were beaten or abused by a stranger. We must coordinate existing City, voluntary, and private resources to provide for shelters and halfway houses so that women who are beaten can find a place of refuge. We must insure that they can get the help needed to solve the medical, social, economic, and psychological problems which surround their predicament. We must develop a public information campaign which would be used to educate and sensitize those who come in contact with the beaten women to the nature of the problem.

As Commissioner of the agency responsible for the mental hygiene system in the City, I will direct staff to examine, as part of the program evaluation process, the types of services mental health programs provide for battered women and their families to insure that the services are sensitive and appropriate.

We will expand our knowledge as to the most effective treatment and look for new approaches to the treatment of husbands, wives and families in which violence occurs. We will consider, for example, the approach used by Jewish Family Service of New York in which both husband and wife are treated together.

We will continue to focus attention on the problem and treatment of child abuse with the knowledge that the abused child frequently becomes the abusive parent and spouse.

Recognizing that a great deal of family violence and wifebeating is associated with the abuse of alcohol, I will see to it that the alcoholism treatment programs, in which the majority of clients are men, deal with the problem of wifebeating in the counseling process.

We will work in cooperation with other City and voluntary agencies, women's and community groups to establish linkages and facilitate obtaining mental health care for those who want treatment.

We will participate in a public information campaign through the Department's Borough Federations which are comprised of providers and consumers of mental hygiene services in each of the five boroughs.

These hearings can be the beginning of a major effort to bring the problem of the physical abuse of women to public attention and to work toward solutions for battered women, the families that suffer, the children who grow up observers and often also subjects of such horrible violence. We must insist upon and work toward a society which provides for and protects the rights of all citizens, no matter how weak, young or old—a society which condemns the imposition of second class status on any of its members. The City must officially recognize the seriousness and extent of the problem and begin to take action to remedy it.

PREFACE TO NEW YORK STATE LEGISLATION

Assembly Speaker Stanley Steingut announced on February 16, 1977 the introduction of the first bills in a series of proposals aimed at the physical and legal protection of women in New York State. Two of these bills appear below. In addition, plans for the creation of an Assembly Majority panel of six members—three men and three women—to consider and coordinate all legislative issues affecting women were noted. Assemblyman Steingut said, "The problem of domestic violence knows no economic or social boundaries. Instances of women—and men— terrorized by domestic assault are on the increase. This alarming situation is often referred to as the 'battered wives' issue but actually covers a much broader scope. For example, statistics show a dramatic rise in assaults on females in every possible domestic relationship—sister, mothers, relatives, common-law wives, and cohabitants."

Cosponsor of the lead bill in the Assembly, is Assemblywoman Estella B. Diggs (D-Bronx). This bill would give victims of domestic assault recourse to the criminal courts. At present, the Family Court of New York has total jurisdiction in domestic offenses. The law will give the victim the option of either the Criminal Court or the Family Court.

The second bill would amend the Domestic Relations Law by stipulating that abandonment by a "battered wife" would no longer constitute grounds for a divorce. A victim leaving a violent home situation would not, then, be penalized by having to face the possible loss of custody, support and property rights.

The panel will be concerned with four problem areas—personal safety, health, work-related issues, and public as well as private sector affirmative action.

These introductory bills resulted in the passage of the bill on pp. 317–321, signed into law by Governor Hugh Carey, and effective on September 1, 1977.

STATE OF NEW YORK

S. 3155   **A. 4304**

1977–1978 Regular Sessions

SENATE-ASSEMBLY

February 23, 1977

IN SENATE—Introduced by Sens. BELLAMY, BURSTEIN, OHRENSTEIN, PERRY, WINIKOW, McCALL—read twice and ordered printed, and when printed to be committed to the Committee on Judiciary

IN ASSEMBLY—Introduced by M. of A. STEINGUT—Multi-Sponsored by—M. of A. DIGGS, HARENBERG, SIEGEL, M. H. MILLER, LIPSCHUTZ, GOODHUE, GRANNIS—read once and referred to the Committee on Judiciary

AN ACT to amend the family court act, in relation to family offenses

The People of the State of New York, represented in Senate and Assembly, do enact as follows:

1   Section 1. Section eight hundred twelve of the family court
2 act, as amended by chapter seven hundred thirty-six of the laws
3 of nineteen hundred sixty-nine, is hereby amended to read as
4 follows:
5   § 812. Jurisdiction. The family court has exclusive original
6 jurisdiction, subject to the provisions of section eight hundred
7 thirteen, over any proceeding concerning acts which would
8 constitute disorderly conduct, harassment, menacing, reckless
9 endangerment, an assault or an attempt assault between spouses
10 or between parent and child or between *any* members of the
11 same family or *between any unrelated members of the same*
12 household. For purposes of this article, "disorderly conduct"
13 includes disorderly conduct not in a public place.
14   § Paragraph (iii) of subdivision (a) of section eight hundred

EXPLANATION—Matter in *italics* is new; matter in brackets [ ] is old law to be omitted.

15 thirteen of such act is hereby relettered to be paragraph (iv) and
16 a new paragraph, to be paragraph (iii), is hereby inserted therein,
17 to read as follows:
18 *(iii) the complainant objects to the transfer of the complaint*
19 *from criminal court to family court; or*
20 § 3. Section eight hundred fourteen of such act is hereby
21 amended by adding thereto a new subdivision, to be subdivision
22 (c), to read as follows:
23 *(c) Upon retaining jurisdiction upon complainant's objection*
24 *to transfer of the complaint to family court, proceed in accor-*
25 *dance with the applicable provisions of the criminal procedure*
26 *law and the penal law.*

1   § 4. Subdivision (a) of section eight hundred sixteen of such
2   act, as amended by chapter ten hundred ninety-seven of the laws
3   of nineteen hundred seventy-one, is hereby amended to read as
4   follows:
5   (a) The family court [may] *shall* transfer any proceeding
6   originated under this article, including one transferred to it by
7   criminal court, to an appropriate criminal court, if it concludes
8   that the processes of the family court are inappropriate, *or the*
9   *petitioner requests that the proceeding be transferred to criminal*
10 *court.* After the transfer, the applicable provision of the criminal
11 procedure law and the penal law govern.
12 § 5. This act shall take effect immediately.

STATE OF NEW YORK

S. 3154   **A. 4305**

1977–1978 Regular Sessions

SENATE-ASSEMBLY

February 23, 1977

IN SENATE—Introduced by Sens. BURSTEIN, WINIKOW,
GOLD, OHRENSTEIN, BELLAMY, PERRY, McCALL

EXPLANATION—Matter in *italics* is new; matter in brackets [ ] is old law to
be omitted.

—read twice and ordered printed, and when printed to be committed to the Committee on Judiciary

IN ASSEMBLY—Introduced by M. of A. SIEGEL—Multi-Sponsored by—M. of A. McGEE, LIPSCHUTZ, DIGGS, CONNELLY, M. H. MILLER, HARENBERG, GOOD-HUE, GRANNIS—read once and referred to the Committee on Judiciary

AN ACT to amend the domestic relations law, in relation to a defense in an action for abandonment

The people of the State of New York, represented in Senate and Assembly, do enact as follows:

1   Section 1. Subdivision two of section one hundred seventy of
2   the domestic relations law, as amended by chapter eight hundred
3   thirty-five of the laws of nineteen hundred seventy, is hereby
4   amended to read as follows:
5   (2) The abandonment of the plaintiff by the defendant for a
6   period of one or more years, *except that one or more beatings*
7   *inflicted by the plaintiff on the defendant, or cruel and inhuman*
8   *treatment of the defendant by the plaintiff shall be an affirmative*
9   *defense to any action for abandonment.*
10   § 2. This act shall take effect on the first day of September
11   next succeeding the date on which it shall have become a law.

STATE OF NEW YORK

◆

S. 6617

A. 8842

1977-1978 Regular Sessions

SENATE-ASSEMBLY

June 15, 1977

———

IN SENATE—Introduced by Sens. ANDERSON, OHRENSTEIN, BAB-
BUSH, BARTOSIEWICZ, BELLAMY, BRUNO, BURSTEIN,
CAEMMERER, CONKLIN, DUNNE, ECKERT, FARBER, FARLEY,
FLYNN, GAZZARA, GOLD, GRIFFIN, HALPERIN, LaVALLE,
LEWIS, LOMBARDI, MARCHI, MARINO, MASON, McCALL,
PADAVAN, PATERSON, PERRY, PISANI, PRESENT, B. C. SMITH,
TRUNZO, WINIKOW—read twice and ordered printed, and when printed
to be committed to the Committee on Judiciary

IN ASSEMBLY—Introduced by COMMITTEE ON RULES—(at request of M. of
A. Steingut, Duryea, Amatucci, Barbaro, Bersani, Betros, Burns, Burrows,
Bush, Calogero, Cochrane, Connelly, Connor, Cook, Culhane, Daly, D'Amato,
D'Andrea, Dearie, DelliBovi, DelToro, DeSalvio, Diggs, Dokuchitz,
Dwyer, Emery, Engel, Esposito, Eve, Farrell, Fink, Finneran, Flanagan,
Fortune, Frey, Friedman, Goldstein, Goodhue, Gottfried, Grannis,
Greenberg, Gulotta, Hanna, Hannon, Harenberg, Hawley, Healey, Hender-
son, Herbst, Hevesi, Hinchey, Hoyt, Hurley, Kelleher, Koppell, Kremer,
Landes, Lane, Lehner, Levy, Lipschutz, Marchiselli, Marshall, Martin,
McGee, McGrath, Mega, G. W. Miller, H. M. Miller, M. H. Miller, G. A.
Murphy, Nadler, Nagle, Nine, Nortz, Passannante, Pesce, Rappleyea,
Reilly, Riford, Ross, A. W. Ryan, Schumer, Serrano, Siegel, Silver,
Solomon, Stephens, E. C. Sullivan, P. M. Sullivan, Tills, Vann, Velella,
Walsh, Weprin, Wertz, Wilson, Zagame)—read once and referred to the
Committee on Judiciary

**AN ACT to amend the family court act, the domestic relations law, the
criminal procedure law and the judiciary law, in relation to family offenses
and repealing sections eight hundred thirteen, eight hundred fourteen, eight
hundred fifteen, eight hundred sixteen and eight hundred twenty-one of the
family court act relating thereto**

*The People of the State of New York, represented in Senate and Assembly, do
enact as follows:*

1   Section 1. Section eight hundred twelve of the family court act, as amended
2   by chapter seven hundred thirty-six of the laws of nineteen hundred sixty-nine,
3   is hereby amended to read as follows:

EXPLANATION—Matter in *italics* is new; matter in brackets [ ] is old law to be omitted.

1 § 812. Jurisdiction. *1.* The family court [has exclusive original] *and the*
2 *criminal courts shall have concurrent* jurisdiction, [subject to the provisions of
3 section eight hundred thirteen,] over any proceeding concerning acts which
4 would constitute disorderly conduct, harassment, menacing, reckless
5 endangerment, an assault or an [attempt] *attempted* assault between spouses or
6 between parent and child or between members of the same family or household,
7 *except that if such an act involves a child who is below the age of eighteen, the family*
8 *court shall have exclusive original jurisdiction.* For purposes of this article,
9 "disorderly conduct" includes disorderly conduct not in a public place. *For*
10 *purposes of this article, "members of the same family or household" shall mean the*
11 *following:*
12 *(a) persons related by consanguinity or affinity to the second degree;*
13 *and*
14 *(b) persons legally married to one another.*
15 *2. The presiding justice of each judicial department shall designate by rules of*
16 *court the appropriate law enforcement official, who may be a probation officer,*
17 *warrant officer, sheriff, police officer or any other law enforcement official, to advise*
18 *any petitioner or complainant bringing a proceeding under this section, before such*
19 *proceeding is commenced, of the procedures available for the institution of family*
20 *offense proceedings, including but not limited to the following:*
21 *(a) That there is concurrent jurisdiction with respect to family offenses in both*
22 *family court and the criminal courts;*
23 *(b) That a choice of forum by a complainant or petitioner bars any subsequent*
24 *proceeding in an alternative court for the same offense;*
25 *(c) The legal, social and practical consequence of an adjudication by the family*
26 *court and that an adjudication in family court is for the purpose of attempting to*
27 *keep the family unit intact. Referrals for counseling, or counseling services, are*
28 *available through probation for this purpose;*
29 *(d) The legal, social and practical consequences of an adjudication by the*
30 *criminal courts and that an adjudication in the criminal courts is for the purpose of*
31 *punitive action against the offender.*
32 *3. No official designated pursuant to subdivision two of this section shall*
33 *discourage or prevent any person who wishes to file a petition or sign a complaint*
34 *under this article from having access to any court for the purposes provided for in*
35 *subdivision one of this section.*
36 *4. The state administrator shall prescribe such forms as are appropriate to*
37 *effectuate the purposes of subdivision two of this section.*
38 § 2. Sections eight hundred thirteen, eight hundred fourteen, eight hundred
39 fifteen and eight hundred sixteen of such act are hereby **repealed.**
40 § 3. Section eight hundred twenty-one of such act is hereby **repealed** and a
41 new section, to be section eight hundred twenty-one, is hereby inserted therein,
42 in lieu thereof, to read as follows:
43 § *821. Originating proceedings. 1. A proceeding under this article is originated*
44 *by the filing of a petition containing the following:*
45 *(a) An allegation that the respondent assaulted or attempted to assault his or her*
46 *spouse, parent, child or other member of the same family or household or engaged in*
47 *disorderly conduct, harassment, menacing or reckless endangerment toward any such*
48 *person; and*
49 *(b) The relationship of the alleged offender to the petitioner;*
50 *(c) A request for an order of protection or the use of the court's conciliation*
51 *procedures; and*
52 *(d) An allegation that no proceeding specified in paragraph (a) of this*
53 *subdivision is pending in a criminal court with respect to the same act alleged in the*
54 *petition.*
55

1   *2. No proceeding under this article shall be originated, based upon the same act*
2   *which is or was the subject of an action commenced in a criminal court.*
3   *3. No application may be made to the criminal courts while a matter is pending in*
4   *family court with respect to the same acts.*
5   § 4. Section eight hundred twenty-three of such act is hereby amended by
6   adding thereto a new subdivision, to be subdivision (e), to read as follows:
7   *(e) If agreement to cease offensive conduct is reached, it must be reduced to writing*
8   *and submitted to the family court for approval. If the court approves it, the court*
9   *without further hearing may thereupon enter an order of protection in accordance*
10 *with the agreement, which shall be binding upon the respondent and shall in all*
11 *respects be a valid order. The court record shall show that such order was made upon*
12 *agreement.*
13 § 5. Section eight hundred twenty-eight of such act, as added by chapter one
14 hundred fifty-six of the laws of nineteen hundred sixty-four, is hereby amended
15 to read as follows:
16 § 828. Preliminary order of protection. Upon the filing of a petition under
17 this article, the court for good cause shown may issue a temporary order of
18 protection, which may contain any of the provisions authorized on the making
19 of an order of protection under section eight hundred forty-two. *A temporary*
20 *order of protection is not a finding of wrongdoing.*
21 § 6. Such act is hereby amended by adding thereto a new section, to be
22 section eight hundred thirty-eight, to read as follows:
23 *§ 838. Petitioner and respondent may have friend or relative present. Unless the*
24 *court shall find it undesirable, the petitioner shall be entitled to a non-witness friend,*
25 *relative, counselor or social worker present in the court room. This section does not*
26 *authorize any such person to take part in the proceedings. However, at any time*
27 *during the proceeding, the court may call such person as a witness and take his or her*
28 *testimony. Unless the court shall find it undesirable, the respondent shall be entitled*
29 *to a non-witness friend, relative, counselor or social worker present in the court room*
30 *in the event such respondent is not represented by legal counsel. This section does not*
31 *authorize any such person to take part in the proceedings. However, at any time*
32 *during the proceeding, the court may call such person as a witness and take his or her*
33 *testimony.*
34 § 7. Section eight hundred forty-one of such act is hereby amended to read as
35 follows:
36 § 841. Orders of disposition. At the conclusion of a dispositional hearing on a
37 petition under this article, the court may enter an order
38 (a) dismissing the petition, if the allegations of the petition are not
39 established [or if the court concludes that the court's aid is not required]; or
40 (b) suspending judgment for a period not in excess of six months; or
41 (c) placing the respondent on probation for a period not exceeding one year;
42 or
43 (d) making an order of protection in accord with section eight hundred forty-
44 two.
45 § 8. Such act is hereby amended by adding thereto a new section, to be
46 section eight hundred forty-two-a, to read as follows:
47 *§ 842-a. Notice of order of protection. A copy of an order of protection shall be*
48 *filed by the court with the appropriate police agency having jurisdiction. In the event*
49 *the court does not so file such order, a copy of the order may be filed by the petitioner*
50 *at the appropriate police agency having jurisdiction. Any subsequent amendment or*
51 *revocation of such order shall be filed in the same manner as herein provided.*
52 § 9. The domestic relations law is hereby amended by adding thereto a new
53 section, to be section two hundred fifty-two, to read as follows:
54
55

§ 252. *Effect of pendency of action for divorce, separation or annulment on petition for order of protection. In an action for divorce, separation or annulment or in an action to declare the nullity of a void marriage in the supreme court, the supreme court or the family court shall entertain an application for an order of protection or temporary order of protection by either party. The supreme court may provide in an order made pursuant to this section that the order may be enforced or modified only in the supreme court. If the supreme court so provides, the family court may not entertain an application to enforce or modify such an order of the supreme court.*

§ 10. The criminal procedure law is hereby amended by adding thereto a new section, to be section 100.07, to read as follows:

§ 100.07 *Commencement of action; effect of family court proceeding.*

No criminal action may be commenced based upon the same criminal transaction which is or was the subject of a proceeding commenced under article eight of the family court act.

§ 11. Such law is hereby amended by adding thereto a new section, to be section 530.11, to read as follows:

§ 530.11 *Protection for victims of family offenses.*

1. When a criminal action is pending involving a complaint charging disorderly conduct, harassment, menacing, reckless endangerment, assault, attempted assault or attempted murder between spouses, parent and child, or between members of the same family or household, as defined in section eight hundred twelve of the family court act, the court, in addition to any other powers conferred upon it by this chapter may issue a temporary order of protection as a condition of a pre-trial release. In addition to any other conditions, such an order may require the defendant:

(a) to stay away from the home, school, business or place of employment of the family or household member;

(b) to permit a parent to visit the child at stated periods;

(c) to abstain from offensive conduct against the child or against the family or household member or against any person to whom custody of the child is awarded;

(d) to refrain from acts of commission or omission that tend to make the home not a proper place for the family or household member.

2. Upon conviction of any of the following offenses: disorderly conduct, harassment, menacing, reckless endangerment, assault, attempted assault or attempted murder between spouses, parent and child, or between members of the same family or household, the court may in addition to any other disposition enter an order of protection. In addition to any other conditions, such an order may require the defendant:

(a) to stay away from the home, school, business or place of employment of the family or household member, the other spouse or the child;

(b) to permit a parent to visit the child at stated periods;

(c) to abstain from offensive conduct against the child or against the family or household member or against any person to whom custody of the child is awarded; or

(d) to refrain from acts of commission or omission that tend to make the home not a proper place for the family or household member.

3. A copy of any order issued pursuant to subdivision one, two or three of this section shall be filed by the court with the appropriate police agency having jurisdiction. In the event the court does not so file such order, a copy of the order may be filed by the complainant at the appropriate police agency having jurisdiction. Any subsequent amendment or revocation of such order shall be filed in the same manner as herein provided.

§ 12. Section two hundred eleven of the judiciary law is hereby amended by adding thereto a new subdivision, to be subdivision three, to read as follows:

3. *The office of court administration shall prepare forms for distribution to the official designated by the presiding justice of the appellate division of each judicial department for the compilation of data on family offenses, proceedings or actions, including but not limited to the following information:*

(a) the offense alleged;

(b) the relationship of the alleged offender to the petitioner or complainant;

(c) the court where the action or petition was instituted;

(d) the disposition; and

(e) in the case of dismissal, the reasons therefore.

§ 13. This act shall take effect on the first day of September next succeeding the date on which it shall have become a law.

Appendix C

PHYSICALLY ABUSED WOMEN ARE SUBJECT OF CONFERENCE*

J. C. Barden

The problems of thousands of women in the city who are physically beaten by their husbands are gaining official recognition. But official recognition is not the same thing as immediate solutions. And therein lies the problem.

At a recent day-long conference on the abused wife, a panel of social workers, police officers, lawyers, politicians and a Family Court judge expressed the need to define the scope of the problems and discussed possible steps to alleviate them.

Meanwhile, abused wives in the audience repeatedly pleaded for answers to such questions as how to assure themselves of firm police and judicial action against their husbands and how to sever ties with their husbands legally when they didn't have funds for a lawyer.

Most of the vocal victims of wife abuse among the more than 180 people at the conference, at the Cardinal Spellman Head Start Center, 137 East Second Street, had left in frustration by the time the conference ended in the late afternoon. But there were indications that their pleas for help had made an impression on some of the panelists.

"We need definitions of just what an abused spouse is," said one panelist, Dr. Joseph Zacker, who left his job as an assistant professor of psychology at City College to join the Rockland County Community Mental Health Center.

Physical Evidence

Another panelist, Marjorie Fields, a lawyer for the South Brooklyn Legal Service Corporation, responded: "We're talking about repeated blows. We're talking about women who are trying to escape serious injuries from their husbands. We're talking about women with black eyes, missing teeth and broken arms, because we see them every day."

In three years with the corporation, Miss Fields said she had handled about 2,500 divorce cases, some 800 of which involved violence. The Federally funded corporation provides legal help for those who cannot afford a lawyer, but there are long waiting periods for those seeking divorces, Miss Fields said.

The inability to free themselves legally from violence-prone husbands was one of the chief laments of the abused wives in the audience.

A mother of three, married for 26 years, said she had been attemping for two years to get legal help for a divorce, but that all the agencies she tried refused even to put her on a waiting list to see an attorney.

"I've gotten three Family Court orders of protection (from her husband) in 10 years, and every time he beat me up the court slapped him on the wrist and said,

'Don't do that again.' The court wouldn't remove him from the home, even after he tried to cripple the children and maim or kill me.

Fears Returning

"He told me—and the judge—that the piece of paper (the order of protection) didn't mean a damn thing and I finally believed him. I moved out of my five-room apartment and moved in with my parents with my youngest son, and he [the husban] is sitting there with all my possessions. I'm afraid to go back."

"All the havoc that can be created by the absence of the father from the home can be tremendous and Family Court judges are most reluctant to order spouses from the house," said Justice Yorka C. Linakis of Queens Family Court.

"There is nothing more pathetic than to see a husband going to his home—usually in the company of a policeman—to collect his meager belongings."

The reply brought hoots of derision from a number of women in the audience.

"It seems," said Maria Roy, the panel moderator and a consulting psychologist at the Head Start Center, who had arranged the conference, "that you've made a good case for the abused husband."

The comment drew loud applause from the audience and a disclaimer from Judge Linakis, who said that she understood the problems of the abused wife were many, but that she had seen wives misuse the Family Court, specifically orders of protection, which "they hang over the husband's head like a sword of Damocles."

Few Hours Peace

A woman police officer on the panel, Sandra Gonzales, who works in the Lower East Side precinct in which the conference was held, said it was her experience that abused wives most often wanted to get their husbands out of the apartment for a few hours rather than have them arrested.

Another panelist, Lieut. Mary L. Keefe, commander of the Police Department's Sex Crime Analysis Unit, said it was the primary aim of the police to try to resolve family disputes in the home, because of the ambivalent feelings of the women in most cases, which often results in the withdrawal of assault charges by the wife against a husband.

Family courts throughout the state handled 17,277 family offense cases—those in which violence occurred—in the 1972–73 judicial year, an increase of 10,000 in 10 years.

Mrs. Fields suggested shelters for abused wives, where they could go with their children to escape their husbands' rages, and where they could stay during temporary separations, until permanent residences could be found, if they decided on divorce.

State Senator Carol Bellamy, in an effort to bring the problem before the public, said she was "going back to the legislature and ring a couple of bells" to get a legislative committee to hold public hearings in the city on the problem.

"I feel that we've just begun to look at the tip of the iceberg today," she said.

New York Times, February 2, 1975.

PROCEEDINGS FROM THE CONFERENCE ENTITLED: "THE ABUSED AND BATTERED WOMAN IN CRISIS— A MULTI-FACETED APPROACH."*
Maria Roy

The conference, a first for New York City, was attended by people from all walks of life: attorneys, social workers, public health nurses, teachers, women's rights advocates, representatives from social agencies, victims of abuse, members of the press, parents, and interested and concerned residents of the Lower East Side community. An informal question and answer format was decided upon for the morning segment, so as to afford the audience the best possible opportunity to question, challenge and offer suggestions to the panel members. The afternoon session was conducted symposium-like—the panel members relating their expertise to the morning's findings, summarizing their thoughts and offering practical approaches to solutions. These approaches, suggested by a multi-professional panel, turned out to be multi-faceted. In order to maintain clarity and order, the following report of the proceedings will be divided into the various professions of the panel members, i.e., legislative, enforcement, legal, psychological, educational. Finally, enumerated follow-up recommendations accompanied by some of my own observations will appear.

Legislative

First and foremost the enormous task of educating the legislators must be given high priority. We must make people recognize the problem of wifebeating as a problem before we can proceed further. As far as laws are concerned, proposing legislation to change the law is not so important as making our existing laws more effective. Funding for reception centers can come in spite of our economic recession, provided that our legislators reorder their priorities. The public needs to pressure and educate. Senate public hearings are necessary. Future planning of mini-community mental health centers proposed by Governor Carey might be designed to include comprehensive shelters for women and children of abuse. Introduction of a resolution similar to that concerning rape crisis, should be undertaken by the City Council. City Council persons should go out into the community and participate in community organization to discuss with mixed cultural groups and men's clubs, the problems, thereby mitigating the cultural acceptance of the problem.

Enforcement

The Sex Crimes Analysis Unit is now training officers in crisis intervention techniques—universal concepts to be applied to victims of rape as well as to victims of assault. The unit hopes to bring its ideas down to the uniformed members of the force.

Women need to be informed of their rights by the police. Better interviewing

---

*Presented: January 23, 1975 at the Cardinal Spellman Head Start Center, New York City.

techniques may put her in a better position to make a decision that will be in her best interest. The Family Court has made available to police departments throughout the city, rules and procedures for handling family disputes when there is an indication of violence (overturned furniture, an injured party).

The Institute for Mediation and Conflict Resolution will be setting up in March a community dispute center—a pilot study of mediation-arbitration built into the precinct.

Legal

Definition of *to beat:* "to strike or hit repeatedly with hard fist, or other weapons—to inflict pain (often cruelly or oppressively). To assault and batter with intent to harm." The Family Offense Statute incorporated into the Family Court Act deals with assault. It is designed to protect petitioners from serious injury. There is an emergency proceeding in the Family Court Act. If the petitioner goes within 48 hours after the assault with visible marks, an emergency hearing can be gotten. But the petitioner must demand a hearing for that day and must testify under oath. The judge can issue a warrant for arrest and the respondent will be picked up that same day by police. He will then be brought before the Court the following day. If the judge believes that the assault is not so serious, he will issue a summons for the voluntary appearance of the spouse. The hearing will be sometime in the near future. The petitioner should always require that the judge write down on the record the bruises and injuries noted.

Assault and battery is a criminal offense—it is against the law. The Family Court acts as a screening device to determine what cases stay in court; what will be tried in Supreme Court (spouse murders and attempted murders are felonies).

In New York State, one cannot charge one's husband with rape. If the couple is legally separated, there may still be a problem. If not separated, for a specified amount of time, one can charge the spouse with assault accompanying rape, but not with rape. The sexual act is not a crime; the broken arm is. It is then necessary to introduce legislation in Albany to include the wife in rape cases. It was suggested that the Supreme Court be used in obtaining orders of protection in the course of a divorce action or grounds for separation. The orders could then protect during the pending of the divorce action until the judgment is entered and when the offense is regarded as a criminal one.

It was also noted that the wife make sure that *her* name appear on the lease to their apartment. Family Court cannot throw a husband out of his apartment unless the wife's name also appears on the lease.

Legal Aid has an obligation to help by asking the right questions of clients when litigating for divorce. Frequently, allusions to violence are left out.

Psychological

Little research has been done. Child abuse has not been conclusively correlated with wife abuse. Before the wife will admit that a problem exists and openly seeks out services, and presses charges against her spouse, she must become less confused about her role as a woman and wife. A bad self image will lead the wife to feelings of guilt about not being a dutiful wife. Economic dependence forces her to stay. It has been estimated that an average marriage lasts about eight years with a beating problem. This indicates that it takes a long time before a woman is willing to face up to the problem. Consciousness-raising is therefore a basic prerequisite to action.

Social Services

The Department of Welfare through its Emergency Assistance Unit, can offer temporary housing for women and children on evenings and weekends. During the day time, the unit's social service staff follows up cases with referrals to welfare centers where permanent housing should be taken care of. The temporary housing involves placement of women with children in hotels for one or two nights. If they arrive before midnight, they will find hotel placement; if, however, the crime occurs *after* midnight, they can sit on the center benches and "sleep" overnight.

Single girls, assaulted by their companions, have yet another problem. They don't rate with the Emergency Unit, and are therefore not directed to emergency hotel quarters. If they are "lucky" they may be permitted to stay in the women's shelter—the only 47 bed shelter for women in the entire city! Why not expand this shelter? Campaign for more beds—employ a team of professional experts as permanent staff.

Educational

Head Start pre-school centers along with group day care centers can act as conduits to bring about immediate remedies. Parent-oriented workshops, seminars, etc., can be expanded to discussions on and for the abused woman. The centers are responsible for assuming a leadership role. Head Start consulting psychologists can offer guidelines to its parents. Group Day Care centers lacking staff psychologists, should make use of community resources for this purpose.

Another solution is for Day Care and Head Start, servicing 50,000 children in this city, to lay the foundation for a curriculum free of sexist trappings. It is essential that boys and girls be taught that both sexes can do almost anything and that "free to be you and me" experienced as a child will shape the liberated adult of the future. Books, outdoor play equipment, and toys, should not be used if they reflect a rigid sexist society. Teachers and aides should be sensitized to reflect healthy non-sexist attitudes in the classroom.

Comments Concerning Follow-up

1. Arouse public interest—shake up awareness. Educate the public and become advocates of the cause.
2. Utilize the media to inform the public.

3. Attend precinct-council meetings in your precinct and educate the police— set up a liaison between the precinct and your organization.
4. Psychologists, social workers, doctors, nurses, lawyers, must become good listeners when confronting a possible abuse case—become experts on community resources and make proper referrals.
5. A pamphlet of women's rights (legal, welfare, etc.) must be compiled by joint effort and disseminated throughout hospitals, churches, social agencies, legal aid services, and police precincts.
6. A digest of referral agencies must be compiled and disseminated throughout hospitals, etc.
7. A Hot Line ultimately should be set up to handle the women in crisis. Maybe the already existing Emergency Assistance Unit can be modified to answer crisis calls 'round the clock, seven days a week. One could also be hooked into a separate comprehensive shelter when that becomes a reality.
8. New definitions of male-female sex roles are needed to instill self esteem— bring up children with less sexism—help insure better adjusted, more responsible adults.
9. Legislative hearings will serve to publicize the enormous scope of the problem.
10. Future planning of community health centers could be designed to include comprehensive shelters.
11. Police precincts could employ a social service unit within the precinct. It could offer on-the-spot counseling and follow-up services. Funding might possibly come from nearby hospitals, social service agencies, etc.
12. Introduce a resolution into the city council for an immediate emergency battered woman crisis program.
13. Investigate the current pilot study set up by the Institute for Mediation and Conflict Resolution.
14. Police should experiment by responding to family disputes in mixed pairs of men and women. A standard question all police should ask the wife is: "Do you want to arrest your husband?"
15. Wives should try to get on welfare as fast as possible. Welfare cannot require a court order or divorce before they put you on the rolls. Once on, you are obliged to cooperate.
   Vista volunteers, welfare rights groups can help. Welfare workers need to be informed of the rights of women—all too many of them make demands on women that are contrary to due process. Some welfare personnel have turned away women because they lacked a court order of protection. Welfare centers from the supervisors on down, need to be re-educated. Booklets enumerating the rights of women as victims of abuse should be compiled and disseminated.
16. The Family Court all too often is too lenient with the respondent. Orders of protection won't save the woman when her husband is killing her. Why not send the husband to jail—let him know that the law doesn't condone his violence through its failure to inflict penalty on him.
17. Since alcoholism is intrinsically related to incidence of violence in family disputes, see to it that chapters of Al-Anon receive information on this subject.
18. Contact the administrative Family Court judge to request the nature and

outcome of conferences dealing with family disputes scheduled with the Police Commissioner.

19. Cardinal Spellman Head Start shall act as a temporary clearing house for information and plan follow-up strategy.

20. Training sessions for staff of Day Care and Head Start should be set up in the near future. Possible topics for examination are the following:
   - Definition and scope of the problem—incidence reported in center populations.
   - Use of community resources to help.
   - The abused woman's rights.
   - How to identify and erradicate sexism in the pre-school curriculum—sexist sensitivity.
   - Methods for educating center parents—consciousness-raising, self help, etc.

THE BATTERED AND ABUSED WOMAN IN NEW YORK CITY: Background for a Conference
Maria Roy

This past year I confronted the Lower East Side of Manhattan and learned that life in that area is a constant struggle. People survive from day to day—the scars of battle branded as furrows in their foreheads. Here women, men, children, have no solace—no one is spared—no one is protected—no one is young.

Emerging from the grubby hollow of the IND Subway one morning in the spring of 1973, I headed for work—my first day as a consultant Social Worker for a pre-school program. I could see then the junkies hunched in darkened doorways, buildings badly in need of repair, children playing in streets and on fire escapes. The sound of a man and a woman screaming at each other brought me to a halt. I looked up in the direction of the conflict and saw a man, bare-chested, standing by an open window repeatedly smashing a woman in the face with his fist, as he screamed profanities at her. She was crying—the sounds of a baby crying also emerged from within. Not knowing what to do—also struck with the complacency of the people passing by—I phoned for the police from a corner booth. Relieved that justice somehow would prevail, I continued to walk to work.

A year has gone by. I have weathered many storms with the families of children enrolled in our program—have hassled with the welfare department and the Family Court. Concomitantly, I have learned a few harsh facts. Most importantly, I am now aware of the lack of effective legal recourse for a woman who is beaten by her husband or companion. My naive impulse to call the police that long ago day in June had been squelched. Futile attempts to rescue women and children in our program from the real possibility of death at the hands of a raging man are cruel testimony to this fact.

One case in particular stands out in my mind; it will confirm the shocking lack of responsiveness of the law to family disputes. Ms. L., the mother of four children ranging in age from 10 years to 6 months, has a history of battered syndrome; i.e., she and the children, especially the 4 year old boy, Louis, youngest of 2 brothers enrolled in the program, have frequently been physically abused by the man who was living with them for over a 10 year period. Ms. L. moved 3 times in one year in an attempt to secure protection from "her lover." Although a legal guardian of their children, he fails to contribute to their support; he is unemployed.

Approximately four months ago, the two boys were absent from school for one whole week. In light of past episodes of violence and a pattern of absence accompanying them, our Social Service Team made a home visit the following Monday. When no one answered the door, inquiries were made of neighbors. We learned that Joe, the abuser, had beaten up Ms. L. badly and that she was living in fear of a subsequent attack. We then hastened to her friend's place. There we found Ms. L. and her four children squeezed into three small rooms (no furniture, except for two double beds). In addition, her friend was there with her own four small children. The kids were clad in dirty underwear, had not been outside the apartment in one week—Ms. L. was too frightened to go back to her apartment for clothes. After advising Ms. L., we left. Within a day or two, the children returned to school. A few days later, Ms. L. came to the center to pick up the boys. She looked anxious and upset—on the verge of tears—her lower lip cut and bleeding. When questioned, she did not reply, but handed me a note stating that Joe was waiting outside our office. He had just thrashed her in the street and was obviously quite drunk. Ms. L. was frightened as he had threatened to beat her and the kids when they got home. Quickly, two staff members whisked Ms. L. off to one of the empty classrooms; another went running after the school handyman, another called the local precinct.

Concurrently, and with great dispatch, Joe followed us into the classroom. Our handyman exhorted him to leave the premises. He did so reluctantly, turning to Ms. L. and shaking his fist: "I'll get you outside". Ms. L. shook visibly. All of us returned to the office. Everyone on staff manned the phones and began calling all the possible city social agencies which might have helped. We started at 3:30 P.M. and by 5:30 had made no headway! Despite several phone calls to the neighborhood police precinct, the police never voluntarily showed up. It was only after our family assistant approached a patrol car stopped for a light that the police came up to the office commenting: "She'll be OK," whereupon they left. In the interim, exhausted and disillusioned with failure to secure any refuge for Ms. L. and her children, we asked our handyman to escort them home.

In N.Y.C. there is not one shelter designed to protect mothers with children from violent and abusive husbands or lovers. Children can be accommodated in emergency shelters, but their mother cannot accompany them—unbelievable!!

When I recount this day to groups throughout the city, the response is concern and disbelief followed by: "What can be done?" For one thing, I am now planning a conference on the Battered Woman.* I have already received confirmation from state senators and city council persons that they will appear as guest panelists. Other invited guests are representatives of social agencies and religious organizations. My aim is to publicize the plight of the battered woman in N.Y.C. and thus bring about changes that will benefit her. Reform to expedite court proceedings must be dealt with as well as the formation of a comprehensive habilitative shelter program for battered women and children—one which will provide legal, social service, and psychological counseling. It is only a beginning—I am hopeful.

The Conference was held on January 23, 1975.

Index

Psycho-pathic